CROCKETT 1837

FT SEDGWICK 1864-71

-44
861-4 *

FT ROBIDOUX 1837-8 *
1861

CP COLLINS 1863-4 *

PT VALLEY STN 1864-5   CP LIVINGSTON 1835

* FT COLLINS 1864-7

CP WHITE RIVER 1879-83

CP SANBORN 1864-5

FT ST VRAIN 1837-45 *   FT LATHAM 1864

FT MORGAN 1864-8

FT CHAMBERS 1864 *   FT VASQUEZ 1860
CP GILPIN 1861 *   FT LUPTON 1864
FT LOGAN 1889-1946 *   DENVER DEPOT 1859-65
CP FIELD 1861-5
CP EVANS 1864
CP WHEELER 1864   FT CEDAR PT 1867-8

* FT LINCOLN 1864

CP MONUMENT DELL 1869-70
OLD STONE FORT 1865-P

FT STEVENS 1866   * STN PIKE'S PEAK 1873
CP SODA SP 1838

* PT REED'S SPRINGS 1867

CT UNCOMPAHGRE 1880-90

PIKE'S STOCKADE 1807

FT PUEBLO 1807
CP PUEBLO 1860-?
FT EL PUEBLO 1842-54   FT REYNOLDS 1867-72   FT WISE 1860-7
CP LAS PINOS 1880   CP FILLMORE 1864-5
NEW FT LYON 1867-89
BENT'S OLD FT 1832-52

FT NARRAGUINNEP 1885   FT MASSACHUSETTS 1852-58 *   * FT FRANCISCO 1861

FT FLAGLER 1879 *
FT LEWIS #2 1880-91   CT RIO MANCOS 1880   FT GARLAND 1858-83
FT LEWIS #1 1878-80 *

* CP GRAY'S RANCH STN 1864

* PT TRINIDAD 1868

FT LOWELL 1866-9 *
* CP NAVAJO SP 1864   * CP LORING 1858

* CP TUHI-CHA 1856   CP RABBIT EAR CREEK 1864

*STN ABIQUIU 1849-51
PT TAOS 1847-65
CP CHUSCO VALLEY 1860   CT BURGWIN 1852-60   * PT RAYADO 1850-4
STN OCATE CREEK 1851-4   CP LINCOLN 1865-6
* FT WINGATE #2 1868-1914 *   FT MARCY 1846-94   * FT UNION 1851-91
PT GALISTEO 1851-8   PT LAS VEGAS 1840-51
CP CUBERO 1862 *   CP TECOLATE 1870   BARCLAY'S FORT 1850
PT LAGUNA 1851-2   CP HATCH'S RANCH 1859-64
PT CEBOLETTA 1850-1 *   CP CANON LARGO 1860
FT WINGATE #1 1862-68 *   CP BAIRD'S RANCH 1866   CP ANTON CHICO 1863-4
PT SAGUNA 1851   FT ALBUQUERQUE 1847-67   FT BUTLER
CP VIGILANCE 1852-3
STN LOS PINOS 1862-6   FT BASCOM 1863-70
* PT LAS LUNAS 1852-62
* STN BECK'S RANCHO 1859-60
* CP CASA COLORADO 1855

CP BEAR SPRING 1858 *   CP LA JOYA 1862-4 *
CP DATIL 1885 *

CP CONNELLY 1862 *   * FT SUMNER 1862-9
TULEROSA 1863-74   PT SOCORRO 1849-61   * STN ABO PASS 1861
PT OJO CALIENTE 1859-82 *
CP SAN PEDRO 1863-4   CP WINFIELD SCOTT 1860
* CP GALLINA 1858
CP CARISO 1858 *
FT CONRAD 1-51-4 *   CP COGSWELL 1860
CP VALVERDE 1864   * FT VALVERDE 1851
FT CRAIG 1854-84 *   CP CARSON 1862   * FT STANTON 1855-96
CP WISCHLER 1862-3   CP EIGHTY-THREE 1860
CP PINOS ALTOS 1863   CP DAGOFFIN 1864
ST 1863-4 *   CP HANGUES RANCH 1863
* CP UNION 1857   * FT WEBSTER #2 1852-60
FT BAYARD 1866-1900
1855-63   * FT WEBSTER #1 1852
URRO MTS 1853-9 *
LANE 1860-3 *   FT BLAKE 1856
MBRES 1863-6 *   FT THORN 1853-63
FT CUMMINGS 1862-85   CP ROBBERO 1857
E SADZ 1862   FT SELDEN 1865-82
CP ROBLEDO 1853-63
STN LAS CRUCES 1863-5   CP DONA ANA 1850-62
PT LA MESILLA 1862-5   CP LAS ANIMAS 1854
8-80   FT FILLMORE 1851-62
CP JOHNSON 1862-5   CP COTTONWOOD 1854-63   * CP GUADALUPE MTS 1855

* CP CARIZALLILLO SP 1885

8-3

78
P 1863

OLD FORTS
of the Far West

OLD FORTS of the FAR WEST

by
Herbert M. Hart

Drawings by Paul J. Hartle

FORT CHURCHILL, Nevada (opposite)

SUPERIOR PUBLISHING COMPANY-SEATTLE

LIBRARY OF CONGRESS CARD CATALOGUE NUMBER 65-23448

FIRST EDITION

DEDICATED

to the troopers and their
families who called these
forts home

and to Tracy Hart,
born March 14, 1965,
who has never been to an
old western fort—yet.

FOREWORD

"Stockades and forts built and garrisoned by the Army . . . became foot-holds of civilization on the wild frontier. Here could be found gristmills, sawmills, and blacksmith shops, all erected by the troops. On the site of many of these frontier forts flourishing cities were to grow, their founda-tions laid by the brave men in Army blue who first blazed the westward trail. Security and law and order largely depended upon the continued presence of these gallant soldiers in the West."

—From Department of the Army Pamphlet 360-217.

At a thousand and some places across the West in the nineteenth century, con-tingents of men in dusty blue uniforms picketed their mounts or mules and started to fashion logs or adobe bricks or hillside dugouts or tent cities. If the means were at hand, a flagpole was cut, trimmed, and planted next to an area facetiously called the "parade ground."

The Stars and Stripes were raised to the top and the senior man present pro-claimed the establishment of a new fort or camp of the United States Army. His next hand-written report to higher headquarters would include this fact and an explanation of the name he had selected. Assuming, that is, that his fort or camp lasted long enough for the next report.

The primary rule of western fort building would determine whether the in-stallation would continue. That rule: establish the Army post when and where it is needed and move it as soon as the need has ceased.

Perhaps it is because of this that the aura of glamour surrounds the memories of old Western forts. They often arrived before anything or anyone else. They were there during the peak days of activity. When these days came to a close, so did the need for the forts. But during their careers, they had been both observers and participants in those events that molded the image of the West.

These are some of the places visited in this book. No claim is made that his-tories are presented on the 60-some forts that are included; the complete story of any single one would fill a volume this size. The objective has been to recount a few of the stories of each fort that distinguish it from its contemporaries and to show how it once looked and looks today.

The selection of forts to be included involved considering what happened at it when it was active, and what the site looks like today. Every site was personally visited and photographed by the author during trips in the summers of 1962, 1963, and 1964 when more than 300 sites were inspected during 40,000 miles of driving.

The area emphasized in this volume is that of the so-called "Mexican Cessa-tion," these states received after the War with Mexico and whose traditions have common Hispanic origin. Although this should include New Mexico and Colorado and those states westward to the Pacific, some Texas forts also are included because they seemed to share the same traditions or were part of the events of those states.

The bulk of the coverage of forts in Texas and the remainder of the Southwest was in volume II of the *Old Forts of the West* series. Forts of the Northwest were in volume I. The final two volumes of the series can be expected to include some new forts of every western state. If this organization is inconvenient, an apology is submitted. It was caused partly by the desire to group the forts in order to tell their stories together, and partly by the simple matter of when it was possible to visit certain sites.

In several instances, the author did not learn of the existence of a fort until after he had been through an area. A return trip a year later was necessary if the fort was to be included. It is believed that other fort hunters will be spared such inconveniences if they are interested enough to follow the directions noted.

Sometimes these directions will conflict with data presented on oil company road maps—which notoriously delight in putting sites on the wrong banks of rivers and slopes of mountains or at the end of roads that no longer exist. Every one of these directions has been found true, sometimes after several false starts. If the author were going to return to a site, he would use the directions provided and it is in this spirit that the information is given.

Readers contemplating visiting sites are cautioned about respecting private property rights, closing all gates after them, and leaving all sites just as they find them. First aid and snake bite kits are suggested for the out-of-the-way places, plus the appropriate camping gear.

Visits to desert forts should be made only after preparing for the potential dangers. This is especially true of the isolated sites in the Mojave desert. Local inquiries always should be made. An estimated return time should be left with someone staying behind so that a search can be started if the party becomes overdue. Never venture alone into the desert.

Supplies should include extra water for both self and vehicle; food; tire chains to help get out of sand; some loose boards; some empty gunny sacks; extra motor oil and perhaps a gas can. Even some flares for signalling passing aircraft would be helpful in an emergency.

Maps should be obtained from the U. S. Geological Survey, Federal Center, Denver. The 15-minute, 1:62,500 maps for the Mojave desert were used in crossing the Mojave's "Old Government Road" by foot and jeep. A complete set would be these sheets: Newberry, Cady Mountains, Cave Mountain, Soda Lake, Old Dad Mountain, Kelso, Mid Hills, Lanfair Valley, Homer Mountains, and Davis Dam. They are 30 cents apiece.

The Mojave road is badly eroded and has disappeared in many places. Because of this, no attempt should be made to drive directly across the desert on the trace of the old road. Instead, follow the recommended route for each fort, even though this involves detouring back to trafficable surfaces. Use of a heavy duty vehicle of the 4-wheel drive or sand-buggy variety is recommended.

The directions given are designed for the reader who will leave his fireside and attempt a personal excursion to these fragments of the old Army of the Far West. In addition, it is hoped that this treatment will afford the less-active reader with equal pleasure and increase his appreciation of the tasks faced by the troopers of a century ago and how they faced them.

H.M.H.

Saint Thomas
Virgin Islands
Saint Patrick's Day, 1965

CONTENTS

WAR IN THE FAR WEST

> " 'Wanted, an Indian policy,' was the great and crying want of the government on the plains and the Pacific coast when I was there. . . . Three things, it seems to me, should be accepted about this Indian question as axiomatic, after which much becomes clear. First, that the white man is bound to go where he pleases across the American continent, no matter what opposes. . . . Second, that contact between the two races under existing arrangements, while never free of danger to the white man, is ruinous and destructive to the Indian; and, third, that a humane and Christian nation like ours, as a whole, will not consent to the wholesale extermination of the red man, like the panther and the grizzly."
>
> —Brevet Brigadier General Rusling to the 40th Congress, 1867.

THESE WORDS of a hundred years ago summed up the problem that faced an Army of regulars and militia, volunteers and draftees, foreigners and native born, soldiers and shirkers for half of the nineteenth century.

In the so-called area of Mexican Cessation—the "Far West" of some historians—the problem did not belong to the United States in the beginning. Spain, Mexico, and a short-lived Texas Republic faced or ignored it with varying degrees of finesse. The soldiers with the padres went into Spanish America; soldiers without padres occupied Mexican America; rangers with neither soldiers nor padres were the law in a Texas Republic.

When the area was joined to the United States in mid-century, it was logical that the Army be

RUSTED STAIRCASE serves only ghosts, Fort Point California (*opposite page*).

OFFICERS WHO figured prominently in the Wars of the Southwest include these who are pictured on these pages, although this "gallery" is far from being all inclusive. Edwin V. Sumner (1797-1863), known as "Old Bull Head" because of legend that musket ball once bounced off his head, was in command in Southwest in early days when his first action was to remove from town "sinks of vice" into relatively isolated forts; in Civil War he was oldest Corps Commander, but insisted on being at head of his troops rather than in rear planning operations. Philip St. George Cooke (1809-1895) commanded Mormon Battalion in early days, was in Utah War, but his Civil War service was limited, probably because he had close relatives on Southern side. Erasmus D. Keyes (1810-1895) was thrice aide to General Scott before Civil War, saw service in early California between these assignments, was commander in Civil War but seemed to be victim of circumstances and resigned to become wealthy West Coast businessman. Two officers who gained Confederate general stars were Richard S. Ewell (1817-1872), commander of early Arizona forts, and Albert S. Johnston (1803-1862), officer both in Texas and U.S. commands in 1850-era Southwest, commander of 2d Cavalry, leader of Utah Campaign, and head of Department of Pacific when Civil War broke out. He is honored as officer who kept his oath as U.S. officer until actually relieved by General Sumner, then went to Confederacy where he died in Battle of Shiloh. (Photograph of Ewell, Confederate Museum; others, National Archives.)

involved. It had lead the way of the explorers and surveyors. Many of the settlers were veterans of the 4,000 regulars who crossed Texas for the Mexican war. In an unfriendly land, the Army and its fort provided security, served as a beacon of civilization, stocked essential supplies, and even contributed economic support to the purveyors of both the legal and illegal.

The gold lure drew seekers of the rainbow by the uncounted thousands. Traditional occupant of the land, the Indian reacted with considerably less than hospitality to this invasion. As far as the Indian was concerned, the white man was the covetor of all worldly goods and the skies and the plains; he was the despoiler of the Gods and the young squaws; he was the killer of the buffalo and robber of the child's food. To many whites, the Indian was a savage who respected no right, possessed no soul, and deserved no pity.

The peacekeeper and disciplinarian was the undermanned and lightly-trained Army of the 1850's, hardly a couple of thousand men from a total military establishment of 15,000. With loyalty and fidelity in sharp contrast to their desolate and primitive posts, the officers and men walked tall in the shadow of the flagpole. They were the representatives of a power far to the misty East, of Congress and of the President.

In California, at first the soldiers moved into the shabby presidios lately abandoned by Mexicans and Spanish. Desertions to the gold fields decimated entire garrisons and the military was hard pressed to manage even the pretense of protection. Fortunately the opposition consisted of scattered bands of primitive savages who presented threats mainly to unguarded settlers, untended herds, and unaccompanied emigrants.

Both in California and Nevada these tribes accomplished their quota of raids and rape. The combination of an environment equally hostile to both sides, and of a pioneer settler who was hardy, unafraid, and a good shot provided a measure of security external to the stockade and brass

THE SOUTHWEST occupied many years in careers of these officers, some of whom won fame elsewhere. George C. Wright (1801-1865) had distinguished career when he took command of 9th Infantry in 1855, then Department of Pacific in 1861. He was drowned while enroute to Command of Division of the Columbia. James H. Carleton (1814-1873) began his military career in 1839, lead California Column in 1862, was in command of New Mexico Department during most of Civil War. William T. Sherman (1820-1891) is best known for his March Through Georgia, but he left lasting impression on West while head of Department of the Missouri after Civil War, then commander of Army for 15 years where he divided his time between fighting Indians and politicians; he was junior officer in pre-Civil War West. Irvin McDowell (1818-1885) won brevet in Mexican War but had no command until he took over Army of Potomac for Bull Run campaign of 1862; after that debacle, he was sent west where he headed Department of Pacific during last days of Civil War, then again 1876-82, important days of Indian campaigns. Adna R. Chaffee (1840-1906) was lieutenant at Gettysburg, won brevets there and in later campaigns in Texas and Arizona, retired after turn-of-century as lieutenant general. (Chaffee photograph from *Reminiscenses of an Army Wife;* Carleton from Library of Congress; others from National Archives.)

buttons. True, the pioneer expected the Army to protect him. But he was not afraid to provide his share in a paraphrase of the adage about help going to those who help themselves.

In Texas, the Comanche was feared by all. A line of forts was established to mark the frontier, but twice had to be shifted so that it would be in front of rather than behind the frontier.

The Navajo and Apache obstructed the trails of New Mexico and Arizona: the north-south highway paralleling the Rio Grande, the east-west routes that connected the Mississippi with the Pacific. Army protection made it possible to keep open these pipelines of trade and emigration.

When the Civil War pulled almost all regular forces from the Far West, volunteers were called to maintain order with a red man who considered this split in the white ranks an ideal matter to exploit. After the war, the government committed itself to a policy of westward expansion but sent only 5,000 of its 34,000-man Army to do the job. The total dropped to 28,000 in 1874 and remained in that vicinity for the next 20 years.

This was hardly enough to answer the summons from all parts of the West. In the Far West, the campaigns were vigorous and protracted. The Apaches, Piutes, Modocs, Navajos, and Utes occupied the soldiers until late in the 1880's, as is described in the stories of the forts involved. (The one exception is the Modoc War which will be in volume V of the *Old Forts* series.)

Gradually an Indian policy of centralized reservations took shape. With it came a new look in Army posts. Gone were the rude and rotted ramshackle shanties which sheltered handfuls of troops here and there about the territories. Large, permanent establishments were built next to telegraph lines—which could provide information—and railroad tracks—which could provide transportation. When help was needed, it could be rushed to the scene without delay, arriving rested, equipped, and ready.

This living room-type of campaigning did not last long. Now that the Army had brought a permanent peace across the deserts and over the mountains, the wars in the Far West were over.

INSTRUMENTAL IN taming of Apaches was this quintet, ranging in rank from general to lieutenant. Nelson A. Miles (1839-1925) entered campaign in last days after Crook was relieved, made final treaty with Geronimo. Oliver O. Howard (1830-1909), fought at Gettysburg and in Northwest, was spokesman for Grant "Peace policy" in days of Crook's Apache Campaign, effected peace pact with Cochise. George C. Crook (1828-1890), termed by many as greatest Indian fighter of all, conducted two campaigns against Apaches, was relieved in last days of second one; his use of pack mules for supply support and of Indians as scouts have applications in modern day Army operations. Emmett Crawford (1842-1886) was breveted major in Civil War, but was captain when he campaigned against Apaches, finally ending career during attack in Mexico when he was mortally wounded. Charles B. Gatewood (1852-1896) was unsung hero of Apache campaigns despite fact that he negotiated final peace with Geronimo because Chief would trust no one else. (Crawford and Gatewood photos from *The Truth About Geronimo;* others, National Archives.)

THE FORTS

As far as the Army in the Far West was concerned, a "fort" was anything that provided a base from which to operate. The degree of permanency and the extent of construction depended on the mission of the Army in the area. The results ranged from the mass of brickwood that made up Fort Point, California, to the dugouts of the redoubts across the Mojave Desert.

In construction and design, the only generalization possible is that they were utilitarian. Soldiers did much of the building in the majority of the cases. The architecture was basic and unadorned, although the permanent forts included buildings that resembled their civilian neighbors. The material was as simple as possible, usually drawn from the local resources. Adobe predominated in the dry, desert areas; log and lumber in the timbered regions.

Despite the common conception of a western fort, few were surrounded by log stockades. At first the Army and the settlers thought that a palisade provided protection from Indian raids. Then the psychology changed. The stockade seemed to provide protection only within its borders. By eliminating the wall, the soldiers took the hobbles off their thinking. They assumed a new psychology of moving into the surrounding area offensively and put the Indian on the alert.

The unstockaded or "open forts" appear in the majority of cases in this book. All of the ground plans are based on the most reliable sources available, usually the official plats on file in the National Archives or State historical societies. They have been redrawn to provide a uniform means of presentation and to eliminate the unmanageable clutter of engineer's specifications, utility and sewage incidentals, and other matters that make the blueprints hard to decipher and even harder to reproduce.

When no original plat has been located, and no local source has been able to provide an approximation of one, reliance has been placed on the author's personal inspection of the site. These sketches are studied guesses of the fort's layout, based on the remains that were on the site when it was visited.

No scale has been put on the plans because in most cases it was impossible to provide one that was meaningful. In most cases, however, the dimensions of the parade ground or some buildings are given in order to provide some idea of scale. Ground plans claim to represent the site only for the date indicated; buildings went up and came down with such regularity that a plat appropriate for one period may bear little resemblence to the years previous or following.

An old photograph of the fort is provided when one could be found. All possible sources were canvassed for these photographs or artist's representations and only when none could be found is this omitted from a fort's coverage.

For ease in identification, here are the abbreviations used on the ground plans:

HQ, OFF, or ADJ—Headquarters of Adjutant's office
S or ST—Stables
B or EM—Barracks
BK—Bakery
SH p—Storehouse or warehouse
H—Hospital
GH—Guardhouse
C or Chapel—Chapel
EM or NCO—Married enlisted quarters
T—Tower or Blockhouse
MESS or MH—Messhall
PO—Post Office
SURG—Surgeon
GRAN—Granary

LAUN—Laundry or laundress quarters
OQ—Officers' quarters
CO or COQ—Commanding officer's quarters
BLK—Blacksmith
TR, SUT, or TRAD—Sutler or post trader
M or MAG—Magazine
K or KIT—Kitchen
CEM—Cemetery
COM or COMM—Commissary
CARP—Carpenter
CAV—Cavalry
INF—Infantry
ART—Artillery
SHOP or WORK—Workshops
LIB—Library

THE TEXAS LINE

"We travelled from Corpus Christi to the western frontier through a dreary, desolate country, where nothing lived but Indians, snakes, and other venomous reptiles, and I expected to see some dreadful thing whichever way I turned. I never went to bed without making a thorough search for a snake, tarantula, or centipede . . ."
— Lydia Spencer Lane on the the Texas defense line, 1853.

HARDLY had the Army determined its line of defenses after the Mexican War than the line had to be moved. Then, again, the line had to be moved further to the west. A few more years, and another line of forts had to be established.

But at first the United States Army set itself up in a series of forts that supposedly provided protection along the Rio Grande from marauding Mexicans, and a connecting line that gave the same defense from marauding Indians. The first line cut through the center of Texas, from a supply post near the modern Oklahoma line, down the Rio Grande.

The fact that this line followed the track of the wartime Army for the Mexican War was not coincidental. At the time, this seemed the most logical. Then it appeared essential to provide a connecting line between the major port of Corpus Christi and the depots of San Antonio and Austin.

Small detachments of troops were sent out, given the usual orders to build forts at their own labors and at no expense to the government, and a line of forts resulted across the heartland of Texas.

From 1849 to about 1853 these primitive encampments—it would be presumptuous to call them "forts" in other than the figurative sense—provided a degree of protection for the traveler. By 1853 it was obvious that this line was too far to the rear. When settlements all but surrounded the garrisons and other settlements appeared even deeper in hostile territory than the military line, obviously the Army was being left behind.

Little if anything, had been expended from the Congressional budget on these hasty fortifications. With hardly a moment of hesitation, the Army abandoned the sites and moved westward.

Behind, it left its mark of progress: the frontier that was no longer a frontier.

13

FORT WORTH, TEXAS

Probably no one thought so at the time, but Fort Worth's one and only try at Indian defense was so effective that it was almost ridiculous.

It was in 1851 that Indians threatened the peace of East Texas settlements. The post at Fort Worth had been established in 1849 and all had been quiet after that. But two years later, a band of Tao-vaya Indians went on the warpath.

In the first meeting with the Indians while on patrol, the Army was credited with killing 52 hostiles. The army pursued the Indians and inflicted more casualties near what is now known as Lovers Retreat in Palo Pinto County, Texas.

That was when the fort came into play. Only revenge would change the bad medicine of the Redmen, so they decided to attack the post. Along the bluff where Summit Avenue in Fort Worth now runs, the tribe assembled and prepared to assault the fort.

Before the leaders had a chance to wave lances or sound their final incantations, it was all over. The Army had wheeled out its one howitzer. A single blast from the primitive artillery was all that was needed to disperse the Indian opponent.

Had the Indians attacked, they would have found a post with little in the line of defenses. It had been established on a wind-swept bluff overlooking the mudflats of the Trinity River, and little more than wind breaks had been constructed. Officers' quarters were of hewn logs and clapboards or of rough logs and mud chimneys. The barracks were of logs and puncheons. There were no floors. Mud and sticks were sufficient for chimneys.

Only the hospital was better; both the enlisted men and officers had frame medical buildings, that for the latter being somewhat smaller than for the men.

The river location was not too desirable. In the rainy season the valley was converted to a sea of mud, in the other months the fort—on a level 150-feet above the river—was exposed to relentless summer sun and bone-chilling winter northers.

The summer heat revealed another problem to the fort. In order to keep the horses near to the soldiers and unavailable to Indian looters, the stables were close to the quarters. Too close, as far as the sense of smell was concerned. Even though carefully cleaned, the stables provided an odor that was offensive and a source of flies that was downright unhealthful.

Despite the discomforts, the fort was successful in its mission. Other than the abortive Indian attempt to facedown the artillery, there were no other Indian incidents against the post. In 1853 the Army moved on and the settlers moved in.

The ready-made town provided stores, residences, and churches for the Texas citizens. With its own city in the making and, courtesy of the Army quartermaster, with such solid foundations, the citizens decided that now was the time to become the county seat. Civilian construction at the place dated to 1849, with a school and hotel dating to 1853 and 1856, respectively. By 1860, the citizens were ready to give nearby Birdville a run for the county seat election.

As the story goes, Birdville was a tad worried about the outcome so a barrel of whiskey was im-

FORT WORTH
TEXAS - 1853

"LEAKY" was a term used by inspector to describe almost all of these buildings. Only hospital, commissary storerooms, guardhouse, sutler's, and unfinished quartermaster's stables escaped this comment. Most of them had dirt floors. Commanding officer's quarters included two 18- by 18-foot rooms, Dragoon barracks had four 17- by 17-foot rooms under each roof. Malodorous stables at northeastern edge of parade ground was 150 feet long, 30 feet wide, had clapboard roof atop palisade walls. It, too, was leaky. (Redrawn from plat in National Archives.)

FORT WORTH site now is in center of city. When Army inspector visited it in 1853, he noted that one of nearest villages was Dallas, "with 350 inhabitants 38 miles east." He found, "The horses (60) were all serviceable, and in finer condition than those of any mounted troops in Texas. Their equipments were also neat and well preserved." He was pleased to find—"it was the solitary exception throughout my tour—the guardhouse, that saddest of all places in a garrison, without a single prisoner." The post commander credited this to the fact "most of his men belong to the temperance society."

ported to keep the voters happy. The Fort Worth faction not only siphoned off the Birdville booze, but took it to their own town where it spread joy and votes among their constituents.

Fort Worth won the election by a narrow margin. Tradition has it that a wagon was sent to Birdville and the county records were carried in style to the new county seat, three fiddlers atop the pile serenading the event.

TO GET THERE: "Where the West begins," according to the city's promotional literature, Fort Worth is a far cry from its namesake, although the site of the original Army post is downtown at the northwest corner of Houston and Belknap streets.

CLOSEUP of plaque shows early Fort Worth. Drawing does not match plat too well, but as sculptor's impression probably is acceptable. It credits post with protecting "the frontier against Indians and was the beginning of the city of Fort Worth." Camp was at site of earlier trading post where settler once was captured by Indians. He baked them biscuits until he ran out of flour. At his promise to obtain more flour and continue feast, Indians let him go. He did not stop hunting for flour until he reached Arkansas border, 300 miles away! Even after fort was set up, begging Indians frequently hovered about it.

FORT GATES, TEXAS

Call it imagination or improvisation, but the proverbial "mother of invention" was an active element in the early days around Fort Gates, Texas. It seems that if there was a unique way to solve a problem, these pioneers gave it a try.

An example was rancher Frank Miller and his half-blind horse. He noticed that the mare seemed to hover around the outer edge of his herd. By putting a fully clothed and rifle-bearing dummy on the animal's back, Miller set up an effective anti-Indian protection. He figured, and tradition says he was shown right, no Indian was going to bother a herd under such close scrutiny of a mounted rifleman.

Another settler was equally alert. When he learned that an Indian he had killed was worth a $25 bounty, the pioneer took no chances on anyone doubting the authenticity of the scalp. He left the scalp on the body and bundled up the whole corpse in a blanket, turning all of it in to claim his cash.

The pioneers didn't always have as much success against the Indians and in 1850 one Texan figured he was a goner. Not to be panicked when his horse bogged down in a creek bed and he was deposited in a thicket with pursuing Redmen hot on his tail, the settler decided there was only one thing left to do. He took out a notebook and pencil and wrote out a last will and testament. Fortunately for him, he wrote quietly and the Indians did not find him.

All of these incidents took place around one of the shortest lived of the early Texas posts, Fort Gates. It was on terrain that is part of a modern Army post, Fort Hood, a major camp that dates to World War II.

When Gates was begun in 1849, it was a slight shadow of the immense Fort Hood. Its 17 or 18 buildings were mainly of poles driven into the ground. Only the four officers' quarters were of frame and clapboard construction. The barracks was an uncommon design: a single-story octagon with a fireplace in each of its eight sides. Although only one drafty and sooty room, there were so many poles inside to support the shingle roof that a partition-like effect was achieved.

The fort was of the old-fashioned stockade variety. The octagon barracks was in its center inside the stockade, but the stables were outside and near a spring, the fort's water supply.

Gates was on the north bank of the Leon River, a spot the surgeon said exposed it to malaria-carrying winds from the marshy lands during the summer and freezing 'northers in the winter.

During most of the post's 1849-52 life, the garrison averaged around 100 men, representing two companies of the Eighth Infantry. The amount of Indian fighting involved is hinted by the 10 unmarked graves remaining in the post cemetery. Apparently the soldiers were still building the fort when they were attacked by Comanches. Carpentry had not impaired their fighting abilities and they severely trounced the raiders. No soldier death is recorded in the first five months of the post. There were four in April 1851.

Gates was the first of the early posts to be abandoned. When the troops were moved to Fort Phantom Hill, near modern Abilene, their commander was a Lieutenant Horace Halderman. Local tradition has it that at the start of the Civil War Halderman was offered a Union commission as a colonel, but rejected it in favor of a Confederate majority.

During the Civil War Gates was the headquarters for a Confederate militia regiment, but they camped nearer to Gatesville, six miles away. Confederate feeling ran high in the mid-Texan town. As late as 1916, in fact, the local school's attempt to place a bust of Lincoln was defeated by the midnight disappearance of the statue. For years the empty pedestal stood as silent testimony of old prejudices.

When the Army left, the post buildings were put in charge of a caretaker, Sergeant Hugh Sheridan. He permitted settlers to occupy the area, and the lucky ones moved into the buildings. Materials

DOUBLE STORY officers' quarters were last remnant of Fort Gates, but these collapsed early in twentieth century. Now only a plowed field and this marker are at site. For a long time at every harvest a lone row of corn stalks showed the track followed by grain wagons shifting the gear from Gates to Fort Phantom Hill when former was abandoned. Or so the story goes.

were in short supply and there were few other houses or the lumber with which to build them. The old buildings became headquarters and a refuge for the countryside. Frequently entire families were left here while the men went chasing horses or Indians.

The Indian depredations increased after the fort was closed. One rancher was found dead with 17 arrows pin-cushioning him. Horse stealing was a common Indian sin. This was usually accompanied by firing the prairie and spooking a herd under cover of the smoke and flame.

On at least one occasion a four-man Texas Ranger patrol bested a large group of Indians and recaptured 36 stolen horses. When the Rangers were in sight of the Redmen, they continued to signal to a main body following behind them and hidden on the other side of a hill. The Indians apparently figured they were no match for this larger force and abandoned their loot. They did not know that the Ranger detachment consisted of only the four-man "advance guard."

On another occasion, the settlers rushed to the fort and organized a defense in the wake of reports of an impending attack. The story was that the Indians had already kidnapped a rancher's wife and children, and would hit the fort next. After an all-night armed vigil, the settlers decided to recheck the report. They found the kidnapped family hidden in brush near their ranch-house where they had secreted themselves the day before when Indians appeared.

Despite the constant threat of attack, the soldiers and settlers at Gates appear to have enjoyed themselves. One civilian operated a sutler store near the fort and had a still as a lucrative sideline. In later days at the turn of the century, Gatesville had a section of Main Street known as "Rat's Row." This is described by Mrs. Tom Mears in her *Coryell County Scrapbook:*

"It consisted of a series of wooden buildings with a high wooden sidewalk in front of it," Mrs. Mears records. As late as 1905 she was warned by her mother "to hurry past these buildings and not look

17

POST CEMETERY still is tended by descendents of Sergeant Hugh Sheridan. A transplant from Ireland, Sheridan painted such romantic picture in correspondence to his old sweetheart that she packed up and came to States. His fellow soldiers presented Sheridan with log cabin after their honeymoon. They remained in area, tending fort buildings after Army left. Cemetery includes a mixture of new markers and many broken and obliterated sentinels of pioneer days.

in; that they were usually called 'dives.'"

In 1909 the shooting of a chief trouble maker was the undoing of Rat Row. Soon after the buildings came down. About the same time Mrs. Mears' husband, Tom, became mayor and was cornered by an inhabitant of the Row.

With his whiskey courage up, the drifter informed the mayor that he was going to be killed "for the benefit of the town."

Mrs. Mears records that her lawyer-husband fast-talked the gun-slinger into the uselessness of performing this good deed in private. The man agreed to wait a day until a crowd could be gathered as appreciative witnesses. And, besides that, the mayor figured correctly, the alcoholic audacity would have oozed out and all would be forgotten.

TO GET THERE: From Gatesville, Texas, take state 36 southeast three miles to the tiny settlement of Nothinsville. The name is prominently displayed on the grocery, left side of highway. Turn left, continue 1.5 miles to railroad tracks. Post cemetery is down tracks 200 yards to right; post site is behind farmhouse, 100 yards to left.

FORT CROGHAN, TEXAS

Picking up stray horses was one thing, but West Texas Indians soon learned that it was foolhardy to try it at Fort Croghan as long as Brevet Major Henry Hopkins Sibley was in command.

This was the same Sibley who invented the tent long used by both Federal and Confederate armies, and who wore the stars of a brigadier general as he lead Confederates into New Mexico nine years later.

But at the time in question, Sibley was in command of a log and clapboard Fort Croghan, founded in 1849 on a protected valley site that cost the government $50 a month in rent. With the instructions to "forage at least expense," the 130 troopers built the fort themselves, settlers sometimes offering a hand and occasionally keeping guard for the laboring soldiers against Indian attacks.

Sibley had not been in command at first. Captain Arthur T. Lee was one of the early commanders and from this has sprung the apocryphal tradition that Robert E. Lee was stationed at Croghan. It was another Lee, one who was a hero at Gettysburg on the Union side.

Actually Fort Croghan was in its last days when Sibley took over. Indian harrassments had been frequent, and the fiery officer decided firm action was the only course. When nine of his best mounts disappeared after a dark rainy night and Sibley found that a stable panel had been opened to take them out, he knew his next course.

He took 17 men and headed for the most logical point, 175 miles northwest to Fort Phantom Hill and, beyond it, the Indian Agency. He was sure he would find the missing horses in the Indian herd.

Sibley did find two Croghan animals in the herd, but was shocked to learn that they were not of the nine just stolen! He was told by the Indian agent that the herd had been brought in by a friendly chief, Koweaka, whose enthusiasm to restore stolen property had caused him to raid another tribe and make off with their stolen horses.

The Croghan commander was furious. He and the agent agreed that the chief and his braves would be held hostage until the other mounts were returned. But this plan failed in a tragic turn.

The Indians were placed under guard with the chief and his family in a tent. Around midnight, an Indian killed the sentry. As the shot roused the camp, the other braves rushed into the darkness. Koweaka threw himself from his tent onto the sentinel, stabbing him to death before dying himself.

Afterward, the soldiers found that inside the tent Koweaka's wife and their son were dead, stabbed in the heart. As Sibley wrote grimly to his wife:

"Both were carefully covered up to the breast, the child lying upon its mother's arms. The chief's moccasins were found near their heads. Nothing in romance or history that I have ever read approximated to this act of devotion and self-sacrifice . . . The bright moonlight upon the beautiful countenance of the mother—for she was beautiful and young—with her innocent boy by her side . . . the husband, father, and warrior still stretched upon the sod . . . the sentinel not five feet away from him, his cold blue eyes looking to heaven."

It was not long after this incident that Croghan was abandoned. When the Army Inspector visited it in 1853, he found that Sibley and most of his Dragoons had moved to Fort Phantom Hill "with a large train of wagons carrying off most of the property and leaving a small detachment . . . as a guard until the few stores remaining could be removed."

Along with the detail, he found that the surgeon and some sick men still were at the post, awaiting

"OLD AND LEAKY" is how Army inspector described officers' quarters when he visited in 1853. All buildings were of logs, hewn logs being used only in officers' quarters and hospital. Commissary storehouse and barracks had rough log walls, clapboard roofs and no floors. Inspector decried habitability of post but decided that since it was being abandoned it was "generally in as good a condition as could have been expected under the circumstances."

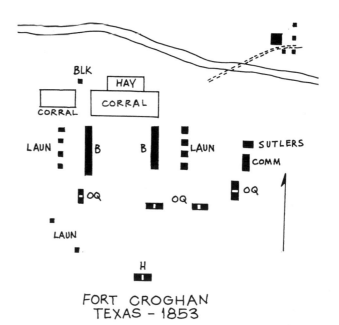

FORT CROGHAN
TEXAS - 1853

OFFICERS' QUARTERS—as hinted by hewn log exterior—included two rooms with a passage in between. Timber came from cedar trees along creeks in the area, as part of the lease with property owner. Limestone also was plentiful and easily worked, but official report did not indicate that it had been used in any buildings.

FORT CROGHAN was considered healthy at all seasons, despite malaria at earlier Texas Ranger station four miles away. "The local causes of disease are the stagnant water pools which occur on all the water courses during the summer months," stated an 1853 report, "giving rise to intermittent fevers of mild character and easily manageable."

transportation to take them and 100 boxes of medicines to the new assignment. He found them in the post hospital, the one building at Fort Croghan that he found acceptable. The other quarters he termed "very indifferent" and the barracks "wretched hovels not fit for occupancy."

TO GET THERE: From the signal light in Burnet, Texas, at the intersection of U.S. 281 and State 29, turn west on State 29. Marker can be seen on left side of highway in about five blocks. Drive down road which ends in 100 yards at fort site.

PARADE GROUND of Fort Croghan now is town park. After post finally was abandoned by caretaker detail in 1855, local citizens organized "minute men," forting up in old buildings where they stored arms and ammunition whenever Indian attacks were threatened. By the 1870's this fear had passed, but buildings were used as wagon rest for travelers, providing a camping spot until they moved on or built their own homes in area. Reconstructed buildings of fort are in background.

RECONSTRUCTED quarters buildings recall early days when fort was main defense against Indian attacks. Even before Army arrived at site, Texas Rangers under Federal contract operated from vicinity. Original location for fort was four miles from final choice. The move was prompted by a disagreement with the first property owner.

THESE THREE buildings show approximate appearance of original fort; stone building suggests use as guardhouse or magazine although different uses over the years have left their changes in it. Prior to reconstruction it was used as a goat shed.

FORT GRAHAM, TEXAS

A woman seems to have accomplished at Fort Graham what the Indians could not. As it was discussed in 1853 by Army Inspector Brevet Lieutenant Colonel W. G. Freeman, three days before the inspection the commanding officer "was killed by the assistant surgeon of the post and I found the command exercised by the next in rank."

He did not delve any further into the details, but added, "Orders had been received to abandon the post and the movement was only delayed by the want of transportation. Much of the company property was boxed up in readiness for the march."

Whatever the story, tradition in the area today says that the fight was over a woman. On one hand, the deceased officer was buried at Fort Graham and post records show that the supply officer paid $5.17 for lining his coffin. A year later the remains were moved to Fort Worth where they are buried today.

The doctor was faced with court-martial, at the time of the Freeman visit "having been taken into the custody of the civil authority the day of my arrival to undergo an examination on the charge . . . The hospital steward was also carried off as a witness."

Records show the surgeon was dropped from the Army three years later. Hillsboro, Texas, records add that he was the contributor of the land on which this town now stands.

Regardless of the disciplinary problems, Fort Graham was credited with having the most beautiful and appropriate location of all posts on the early Texas line. Fertile fields surrounded it and a clear creek passed near by. There was plenty of building stone available. Although not adaptable to building needs, small timber growths prevented the countryside from taking on the drab, plains appearance.

The Second Dragoons built the post with the help of hired civilian laborers. Most of the buildings were of logs, covered by shingles or clapboards. The site was originally a Waco Indian Village. The Indians were not pleased with their displacement by the Army, but fell back and nursed their resentment for future correction. In 1852 a meeting was held at Graham between the Indians and the Indian agent, but to no avail. Other meetings took place later but at different locations; by 1852, as an observer noted, Fort Graham "was in the midst of a settlement."

The same Indian agent took issue with the Army policy on the Texas line. "They have garrisoned these posts with infantry—which are of no service in carrying out this policy," he wrote from Fort Graham. He said it took the Indians only two days to get "where they are safe from the pursuit of infantry." Lessons were learned and by 1854 the infantry had been replaced by mounted troops at the posts.

In 1853 Graham had 85 men from two companies of the Second Dragoons. To compound the problem of a dead commanding officer and an arrested surgeon, one second lieutenant was sick in bed, another second lieutenant was under arrest—per orders of the late commander—, a third second lieutenant was on leave, and a captain was on duty in Florida. Two first lieutenants were running the post when it was inspected.

After Graham was abandoned, its buildings were taken over by cattle drivers. By 1860 a settlement had grown up at the site, with families living in the buildings until permanent homes could be built.

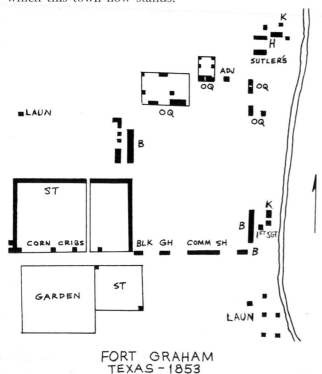

FORT GRAHAM
TEXAS – 1853

"THE BUILDINGS which are very inferior were put up by the troops," is how the 1853 Army Inspector described Fort Graham. Most were of logs, with shingled sidings, although upper officers' quarters was of stone. It had two rooms 15 by 16 in size with ten foot passage in between. Inspector found that storehouses were "affording inadequate protection against the elements, but the supplies on hand had sustained no damage and were of superior quality." Although he was unable to talk to anyone assigned to the medical department, he noted that the two wards seemed comfortable. (Redrawn from plat in National Archives.)

PREVIOUS USE of these posts is not apparent, but they could have been part of walls of quarters. Lake Whitney now laps at their base in front of former quarters, now hunt club. Brazos river at this point was crossed by a ferry; dammed up Brazos provides water for Lake Whitney.

TO GET THERE: From Whitney, Texas, take farm road 933 north in the direction of Blum. Turn left on second paved road. At next road, turn right, then left, then back right again. Follow signs to Fort Graham Hunting and Fishing Club on northeastern bank of Lake Whitney.

STONE FROM original fort was used in this partial reconstruction of barracks, although ground plan does not indicate actual barracks were made of anything but log pickets. It is likely that reconstruction in 1930's had recreational purposes in mind, rather than history.

FRONT OF remaining building shows that modern club use can do little to preserve old fort. Marker in front commemorates "George W. Littlefield 1842-1920—Pioneer, Plainsman, Soldier," obviously an early settler but not of the 1849-53 era of Fort Graham.

FORT MERRILL, TEXAS

When the Army inspector came to call at Fort Merrill in 1853, he found hardly enough men for a guard, let alone a fort. It was only three years old at the time, but even by then was being left behind by the frontier.

Brevet Lieutenant Colonel William G. Freeman found only one officer, two noncommissioned officers, and 13 privates at the post. He was informed that the post was in the process of abandonment. Two months before, two companies of the Mounted Rifle Regiment had packed up and moved to Fort Ewell. Left behind were so few men that "little was attempted beyond posting a sentinel nightly for the protection of the public property," he reported.

The post had been built about 50 miles northwest of Corpus Christi in 1850. Lumber was brought by boat from New Orleans to supplement what could cut locally. The result, of course, was that only $3,000 was spent on finished wood. The rest, as constructed by the troops, consisted of logs—the lumber merely serving as weatherboarding to finish off the log construction that predominated.

When the Army moved in, it found the area desolated from the ravages of the Mexican war. The town of San Patricio, only a few miles to the south, had 300 families in 1832, all of them emigrants from Ireland. An 1840 guidebook noted that the area was so healthy "not a death occurred amongst them." Another guidebook added that the town did not even boast a cemetery.

U. S. Grant, in his *Memoirs*, noted that in 1845, "There was not at the time an individual living between Corpus Christi and San Antonio . . . The country abounded in game, such as deer and antelope, with abundance of wild turkeys along the streams and where there were nut-bearing woods."

He found San Patricio "a few log cabins . . . but the inhabitants had all been massacred by the Indians or driven away."

This observation was in December, 1845. A month later, he passed through the area again and found, "A new settlement had been started there in our absence of three weeks, induced possibly by the fact that there were houses already built, while the proximity of troops gave protection against the Indians."

The area of Fort Merrill, as described by early travelers, "is a deep, black, rich soil and unsurpassed by any land in the world for the cultivation of cotton and sugar . . . It is the best stock raising country in Texas, on account of its being entirely destitute of flies, and the extensive Musquit (sic) prairies afford the best pasture in the world."

The presence was noted of wild herds of horses between 1,500 and 2,000 in a drove, "some of them animals of extraordinary beauty and great speed," and extensive herds of wild cattle.

Grant had three of these wild horses while he was in the area, waiting at Corpus Christi to march to Mexico. His servant let all three get away one day, but Grant never suspected him of malicious intent. "If they had not escaped," he explained, "he could have had one of them to ride on the long march then in prospect."

Fort Merrill was on high ground, as the 1853 inspector reported, "commanding a fine view of the surrounding country." This kept it away from the overflows of the nearby Nueces River and meant a healthy post, although he found "a few men were sick, though fortunately not serious cases . . . the

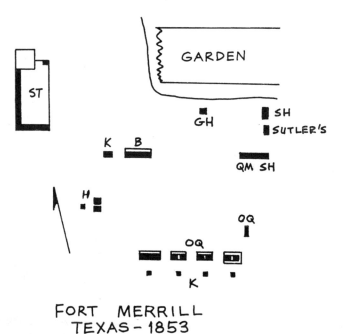

FORT MERRILL
TEXAS — 1853

ABOUT A DOZEN buildings made up Fort Merrill, most of them dressed logs with weatherboarding. Officers' quarters had two rooms, 16 by 18 feet, separated by 10-foot hallways, with porticos across front. Kitchens were 15 by 20 feet. Inspector termed barracks "insufficient for two companies," said they were of dressed logs and measured 40 by 18 feet. Both company kitchens were 16 feet square. Buildings made only of weatherboarding included headquarters, sutler's, storerooms, and company kitchens. Guardhouse had two rooms for a total of 16 by 14 feet with walls of "round logs." (Redrawn from plat in National Archives.)

NOTHING REMAINS of Fort Merrill although this is general site. Post was 500 yards from Nueces River and was along road between San Antonio and Corpus Christi.

most common diseases are malarious fever, dysentery, diarrhea, and scurvy." In 1854 this record was to be reversed when every single soldier, officer, and laundress was on the malaria list in a two month period.

The Army stayed periodically at Fort Merrill but on December 1, 1855, the post was abandoned permanently. By this time, Corpus Christi's influence was too strong and the dangers of the frontier had left the post in the backwash.

TO GET THERE: From George West, Texas, take U.S. 59 east and turn right on the blacktop after crossing three bridges. Take this south a mile to a right turn and a dirt road which shortly crosses Nueces River. Cross railroad tracks in a third of a mile. A hundred yards after passing through deserted Mikeska community, take left fork of the road just below crest of rise. This dirt, sand-drifted road crosses Fort Merrill creek in about 1½ miles. When road then reaches top of hill, site of Fort Merrill can be seen to left front (north); it is a 400 yard walk through private rangeland but there are no remains. Fair weather driving only.

FORT MERRILL CREEK is only formal trace remaining of post. Name still is carried on local maps. Its water content is limited to rainy season when it flows past fort site and into Nueces River.

FORT EWELL, TEXAS

Slowly rolled the wheels of justice and in at least one case at Fort Ewell, the accused had been under arrest for almost a year and died before he could stand trial.

The unlucky soldier was a captain who was interviewed by Brevet Lieutenant Colonel W. G. Freeman during the 1853 inspection of forts. "The officer was arrested on August 13, 1852, and he informed me that up to the period of my visit—ten months afterwards—he was ignorant of the charges against him, or the steps, if any, taken to bring him to trial," recorded Freeman. He suggested that the delay was caused by the illness of the departmental commander.

Although the accused died on August 30, 1853—two months later—Freeman explained, "as his case came under my observation officially, I have not felt at liberty to pass it over in silence."

Freeman was not enchanted by other things at Fort Ewell, especially its location. "A less inviting spot for occupation by troops cannot well be conceived," he said. "I had an opportunity of judging personaly of its discomforts, for a rain storm of a few hours happened to come on at the time of my inspection detained me nearly five days, and even then I was compelled to swim my animals to get away . . .

"The site was no doubt originally chosen because of its being on the old Indian thoroughfare to the Rio Grande, and without a knowledge of the serious objections to it."

At the time, Fort Ewell consisted of five buildings, plus tents to house the officers and troops of three companies of the Mounted Rifle Regiment. As usual, the buildings were soldier constructed, as described by one man in a letter in 1852.

"At present we are engaged in erecting the post," he wrote in a letter home, "and the buildings in general are to be made of burnt brick (called doby)

and you see by that, that we have laid down the sabre and the bow and taken up the shovel and the hoe, and got to work in the mud, making dobys."

The adobe effort was not marked by singular success. Freeman commented, "The adobes used for the walls of these houses are too soft to bear a roof without bracing."

Only one building, used as a quartermaster storehouse but planned for a barracks, had shingles and this too, drew its share of criticism. "The shingled building," he wrote "is sustained by props, and would tumble down without them."

"If the post is to be maintained," he suggested, "it is important that suitable buildings should be provided as soon as possible."

He noted that although the garrison seemed healthy, the surgeon was convinced, "from the cases operating, that it cannot fail to prove a sickly station. That the health of the troops has not been more unfavorably influenced by the locality—he attributes to the nature of the service which has kept the men actively employed upon scouting duty."

There were 150 men at the post at the time and "from the want of vegetable diet the command has suffered from scurvy, of which thus far there have been 35 cases . . . and there is at all times such a tendency to this disease as to make a constant supply of potatoes extremely desirable, as it is impossible to cultivate a garden, on account of the excessive heat, and the want of rain, dew, and even moist winds."

Despite his disapproval of everything else, Freeman was pleased with the troopers at Fort Ewell. "The men are mostly young and active," he wrote. "Their officers represent them to be generally temperate and subordinate, and judging by appearance I do not think I have ever met with finer material in the ranks of the Army."

He said that although the regiment had many desertions in Texas, this was because the soldiers were put to "mechanical labor, constructing adobe houses, etc." He believed the men resented this— "regarding it a violation of their contract of enlistment"—but "when ordered on scouts or escorts they obeyed with alacrity, considering this kind of service legitimately a part of their duties."

GRAVEYARD of Fort Ewell supposedly was at this spot. Only 50 yards from marker, it shows evidences of excavations and occasional rock mounds. Fort Ewell had no hospital, but sick soldiers were tended in tents where they were treated to luxury of "good hospital tents, iron bedsteads and excellent bedding," two surgeons, and a supply of medicines that "was abundant and of excellent quality."

TO GET THERE: The site of Fort Ewell, privately owned in the middle of the vast Coquat cattle ranch, is impossible to find without obtaining permission and directions in Cotulla, Texas. Although 1853 report said "good grazing for animals cannot be found in the vicinity," site now has purebred cattle which are shipped to markets all over the world.

THIS is only evidence of former Army use, a marker showing Fort Ewell's existence here from 1852 to 1854. Government never owned land and 1853 report said it was "claimed by a resident of San Antonio, who has notified the post quartermaster that he intends to present a bill for timber destroyed and for occupancy." Post had a commissary storehouse, blacksmith's shop, and three sets of adobe company quarters, all but one covered by canvas roofs. Sutler had a store "which appeared to be tolerably supplied with the articles most in demand by the soldiers." Because of the high cost of transportation, prices reportedly were 80 per cent higher than in the East.

DATING FROM Civil War, these posts were bridge pilings across the Nueces River (in background) at Fort Ewell crossing, only hard bottom suitable for fording in area. Bridge washed away in 1950 flood. Ewell was on other side of river. In 1852, soldier wrote, "Fort Ewell is situated on the Nueces River at the crossing where Gen. Wool's division crossed going from sanantonio (sic), into Mexico, it is some 90 miles from sanantonio." When it flooded in 1853, inspector noted that herders "who were out with the troop horses saved themselves and their animals with some difficulty, and one or two horses were drowned . . . The river being narrow with high banks at this point, can be easily bridged . . ."

THE POSTS AT AUSTIN, TEXAS

Austin, Texas, may have started in 1839 with armed guards protecting the workmen and a stockade hiding the finished construction from Indian eyes and arrows, but its military career was more involved with paperwork than patrols.

The Army character of Austin ranged almost the entire gamut: camp, depot, arsenal, post, district headquarters, but never fort. And despite an occupancy that ran off and on almost the entire last half of the 19th century, the Army never achieved much more than a transient status in the capital city of Texas.

Military protection—as provided by the Republic of Texas—was present when work began at the site in 1839. The town was laid out near a four-family village and within two years had more than 1,200 people. Of course, the Indians did not take kindly to this invasion.

Workmen erecting a drafty single-story capitol kept one hand for the job, the other for their rifle. Sentries were on continual alert. When the capitol was finished, it was surrounded by an eight-foot stockade, loopholed for rifles.

Straying from the center of town was discouraged. In 1840 a Comanche raiding party came almost in to town, making off with horses after killing two workmen.

"The Indians are stalking through the streets at night with impunity," a settler wrote at the time. "They are as thick as hops about the mountains in this vicinity, and occasionally they knock over a poor fellow and take his hair."

This was too much for at least the politicians. "You were sure to find a congressman in his boarding house after sundown," was a statement of 1840 affairs in Austin.

As an 1841 British emigration guide pointed out, "Austin, should it continue the capital, will doubtless one day be a very beautiful city. At present, however, having no settlements beyond, it is sometimes exposed to petty Indian depredations."

By 1845, when Texas joined the Union, the question of Indian attacks seemed settled, and the stockade was pulled down.

The U.S. Army established its first official post at Austin in 1848. The two-company garrison on the left bank of the Colorado river was named, appropriately enough, Camp Austin. It included temporary shanties of cedar posts sunk into the ground, weatherboarded and shingled, and was surrounded by a wooden fence. A storehouse outside the enclosure was 216 feet long, 18 wide.

Colonel William S. Harney reportedly planned to make Austin the military center of Texas, but it soon became only quartermaster and subsistence depots. Ninety civilians were employed in 1853, most of them teamsters for the 78 wagons used to move stores to the forts on the Texas line.

These activities took place across town from Camp Austin, at the Arsenal, where the district paymaster also had his headquarters. In 1853 this was Paymaster Albert Sidney Johnston, later to become the celebrated Confederate general. An 1853 report stated, "His accounts were correct and had been duly rendered," and that he kept the "public funds in his own safe."

It does not include mention that when Johnston made his 695-mile round of posts, he carried the funds in gold and silver coin in "a small iron chest, and always placed between the feet of its guardians," according to his son who spent a vacation traveling with him. Johnston made this trip every

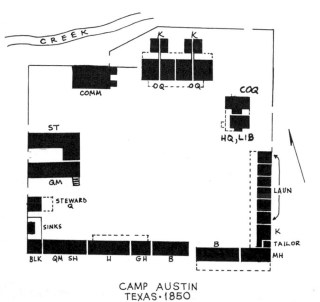

CAMP AUSTIN
TEXAS·1850

SECOND DRAGOONS and Mounted Rangers apparently occupied this camp that was half-mile north of capital. Wooden fence surrounded camp, measuring 339 feet across southern side, 329 along eastern, and 282 along western. Actually it consisted of only seven buildings because many activities were connected by porches. Building which included hospital was 206 feet long, 20 wide; row of laundress quarters with kitchen and mess hall at end was 137 feet long with porch across front. Original plat indicates proposal to build new eight-room hospital in northwest corner. (Redrawn from plat in National Archives.)

CUSTER AND COMPANY rest on steps of their headquarters in Austin in 1865. General Custer, Mrs. Custer and Tom Custer are in center of group on steps. During Texas tour, Custer took stringent steps to prevent his troops from contributing to reconstruction disorder. A much-criticized order of his announced: "Every enlisted man committing depredations on the persons or property of citizens will have his head shaved, and in addition, will receive 25 lashes on his back, well laid on." Mrs. Custer records one element of calm to Army visitors was family of mother and daughter who had retained Union loyalty throughout war. "In the early part of the war the girl had known of a Union flag in the State House, held in derision and scornfully treated by the extremists. She and her younger brother climbed upon the roof of a wing of the building, after dark, entered a window of the Capital, found the flag, concealed it in the girl's clothing, and made their perilous descent safely." Another incident with capital was in 1869 when state constitutional convention found it did not have a quorum in order to adjourn, finally appealed to current district commander, General E. R. S. Canby. Though he was "averse to taking any action which might savor of military interference or dictation," Canby finally agreed to take possession of the papers so that the Constitution Convention of Texas could close shop and go home . . . without formal adjournment.

two months and totaled more than 4,000 miles a year on his pay runs.

He was accompanied by a small escort from Austin, but found that his main danger was not from Indians but from his own servant. His son recorded that his father finally traced frequent shortages in his funds to their driver who had been following a "one for you, one for me" philosophy in guarding his master's money. As the son noted, this helped explain the driver's unusual popularity with the ladies of Austin and his high spending habits.

Army occupation of Austin seems to have ceased in the late 1850's, but was replaced by Confederate use in the Civil War. The arsenal was speedily put into operation turning out cannon which saw effective service. A cartridge and percussion cap factory was set up in the Supreme Court building using homemade machinery.

The Austin City Light Infantry was formed, followed by a regiment of cavalry. Then when the Civil War ended, unpaid and destitute veterans descended on the capital to demand relief. The situation was desperate as renegades roamed the city. One group broke into the state treasury and took what little they could find.

Twenty-six regiments of infantry and cavalry were used by the U.S. Army to restore order to the Texas area. These were headquartered in Austin where Brevet Major General George Armstrong Custer served his final tour wearing the two stars of that rank.

Elizabeth Custer wrote in *Tenting on the Plains*

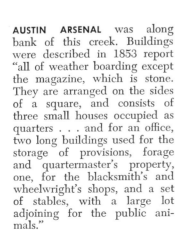

AUSTIN ARSENAL was along bank of this creek. Buildings were described in 1853 report "all of weather boarding except the magazine, which is stone. They are arranged on the sides of a square, and consists of three small houses occupied as quarters . . . and for an office, two long buildings used for the storage of provisions, forage and quartermaster's property, one, for the blacksmith's and wheelwright's shops, and a set of stables, with a large lot adjoining for the public animals."

POST OF AUSTIN was at this site, though no traces remain today. Post was mainly of tents. "Each set of officers' quarters consists of one hospital tent as parlor and sitting-room, two wall tents, one as dining room, the other as bedroom, and one common tent as kitchen," 1869 report recorded. "The sets are so arranged that they are about 10 feet apart and in a line on the east side of the encampment facing the guardhouse. They are heated by fireplaces and stoves and lighted by kerosene oil lamps and candles. The enlisted men are sheltered by common tents, two of them placed end to end, boarded up and floored, and arranged in a line on each side of the encampment. Four men occupy a set of quarters, each man having his own bunk, bedsack filled with hay, and blanket . . . In the rear of each company is a mess-room, kitchen, and bake-oven. Each married soldier has a wall tent for quarters and common tent for kitchen. The laundresses, who are not soldiers' wives, are similarly quartered."

Headquarters was a mile northwest of the city and the troops scattered at various points in the town. Regimental headquarters was behind the capitol building. When the volunteers were mustered out in 1866, three companies of the Sixth Cavalry shifted the post to a spot a mile west of town. Here they lived in tents. Buildings were put up for the guardhouse, library, kitchens and messrooms.

The guardhouse was an oak plank two-room affair surrounded by a piazza, condemned by the post surgeon in 1869 as "entirely too small and is badly ventilated." He criticized the practice of using it for both soldier and citizen prisoners, partly because "the citizen prisoners rarely, if ever, wash themselves or have change of clothing, and the exhalation from their bodies is very offensive."

His main argument was, "Soldiers who are confined for minor offenses, such as absence without leave, drunkenness, etc., are made to associate with murderers and thieves, which is certainly not well calculated either to improve their morals or to elevate the status of the enlisted men of the army."

By 1872, official reports hint that a better day was coming. The small frame buildings used for shops were noted as "being taken down and transferred to depot quartermaster's corral in the city of Austin, for the purpose of building quarters for one company."

By August, 1875, better days did come to the temporary Army installations at Austin. That was the date the garrison at Austin was officially closed in favor of locations closer to the Indian frontier.

that the arrival of the Federals was welcomed as "a great relief to the reputable on both sides. They said so frankly—the returned Confederate officers and the 'stay-at-home rangers,' as well as the newly appointed Union governor."

She described Texas as "a 'go-as-you-please' state, and the lawlessness was terrible. The returned Confederate soldiers were poor, and did not know how to set themselves to work, and in many instances preferred the life of a freebooter. It was as easy, if a crime was committed, to slip into Mexico . . ."

The Custers lived in the Blind Asylum. After her camp life expedition from the East, Mrs. Custer found even the high-ceiled rooms suffocating, but, "There was one joy—reveille could ring out on the dawning day and there was no longer imperative necessity to spring from a warm bed and make ablutions in ice-water."

The Post of Austin was established in 1865.

TO GET THERE: Of the many sites in Austin, two are the Post of Austin and Austin Arsenal. The post is at 1214 West 6th street, an area which includes an automobile agency and a vacant field. The Arsenal was near the Palm Elementary School at 700 East First street.

ARMY LIFE in Civil war was informal if this contemporary sketch is an indication.

CIVIL WAR WESTERN STYLE

"The time has arrived when individual rights must give way, and I shall not hesitate to adopt the most stringent measures to crush any attempt at rebellion within this department."

—Brigadier General Wright from San Francisco to the War Department, December 10, 1861.

THE WAR in the West was fought undercover. Aside from a single engagement in Arizona and several in New Mexico, uniformed troops of the Blue and the Gray did not meet on the battlefield. But there was a war all the same, a war of rumor and rallies, politics and pettiness.

Quickly the regular Army was called to Eastern battlefields. Volunteer regiments were raised in the West and most of them stayed in the West. To them fell the job of preventing a Confederate takeover and of continuing the unceasing battle against hostile Indians. The latter took the division among the white man as good excuse to increase their depredations.

California is credited with providing 15,725 volunteers for her own units, plus five companies for the Massachusetts Cavalry and eight for the Washington Territory Infantry. Nevada provided 159 men for the California total and 1,158 for her own volunteer units. New Mexico sent an estimated 3,500 men to the war. Arizona Guards were formed under the Confederate occupation and were replaced by Arizona Rangers when the Union reestablished itself in the territory.

Utah remained loyal and militia units guarded the Overland Mail line. Suspecting the motives of the Mormons, however, the government sent a regiment of California Volunteers to guard the route, too—and to keep an eye on Brigham Young.

Colorado recruited two regiments of volunteers, paid them with hastily improvised drafts on the Federal government, and sent one of them off to New Mexico. Here they provided the main force that defeated the Confederates at Glorieta and stemmed the rebel advance into the West. A Federal government on one hand procrastinated in recognizing the financial matter, but on the other hand expressed quick appreciation of the "Pike's Peakers'" strategic victory.

After the Confederates returned to Texas with two-thirds of their forces and equipment left behind, the Western war became one of rumor. But the danger continued to be present. It fell to the Volunteers to see that the peace and the Union were preserved.

THE POST AT ALBUQUERQUE, N.M.

When Confederate General Sibley pulled his forces into Albuquerque to withstand a siege by surrounding Federals, the besieging troops had both cannon and rumor to face.

The artillery was a real thing, dueling frequently with Union cannon emplaced near what later became the Albuquerque water works. With heads down and ditches dug, this could be faced. What was harder to combat were the rumors.

One story was that Sibley's Texas were headquartered in twelve buildings that were owned by California Volunteer General James H. Carleton, a regular Army major who was leading reinforcements across the California desert. The second story was that their commander, Brigadier General Edward R. S. Canby, was a brother-in-law of General Sibley.

One Colorado volunteer recorded in his diary, "Canby and Sibley are comrades of old . . . This was the first speciman of Canby we had seen, and it is idle to deny that we were disappointed . . . That he was loth to shell the town on account of the harmless inhabitants is no defense. That was a last resort, never rendered necessary until many other palable means of destroying the enemy had been exhausted. These were never even attempted."

The volunteer referred to the fact that after Canby had surrounded the city and demanded its surrender, he suspended artillery fire when Sibley refused to evacuate it to save innocent women and children.

There was hardly a basis for either rumor, however. True, Carleton did own the buildings rented by the U.S. Army for the Post of Albuquerque, but

these had been burned in March, 1862, to prevent the stores from being captured by the rebels. It was not until 1890 that Carleton heirs were reimbursed by Congress for the loss of the buildings and the $105 a month rent the Army once paid them.

The Carleton property was described by him when he arrived in Albuquerque, "a blackened mass of unproductive ruins." The twelve buildings had been bought by him in 1854 and were used by the Army for shops, stables, warehouses and a hospital.

The quartermaster later reported that he had sent as many stores and ammunition out of the town that he could, but when the rebels were within 35 miles of Albuquerque, "I ordered that every preparation be made for destroying the public stores, both quartermaster's and subsistence, which could not be carried off."

At 6:30 the morning of March 2, 1862, he continued, "I gave the order to fire the property . . . The destruction of the stores involved the destruction of the buildings containing them, as it would have been impossible with the force and the short time at my disposal to have removed the property from the buildings in order that it might then be burned." He also felt that "the native population would have overpowered me and saved the property for the enemy."

As to the matter of the opposing commanders being relatives, exhaustive researches by reliable historians have failed to find any link between the two families. Canby explained that he merely in-

(FROM W. W. H. DAVIS, EL GRINGO, 1857.)

PLAZA OF ALBUQUERQUE

"QUARTERS for the soldiers and the public stores were quite indifferent and insufficient for the post," Army inspector reported in 1853. He noted that buildings were rented at "over 2,000 dollars per annum" and felt "an effort should be made to lease land at a nominal rent and erect buildings in this vicinity that would remove the troops from the close contact with the citizen and afford a better state of discipline." Post was scattered in rented buildings around Albuquerque Plaza, described in 1851 by a soldier, "A very lively place. At night four fandangos furnished the same easy kind of acquaintance as elsewhere." Three months before he left Union Army in 1861, Captain R. S. Ewell—later a Confederate general—found Albuquerque, "Of all miserable places this is the worst. Whiskey is abundant everywhere and scarely anything else." Army moved to Albuquerque in 1847 and it became military headquarters when Colonel Edwin V. Sumner announced, "I find it indispensably necessary to move my headquarters from this post (Fort Union) to Albuquerque on the Rio Grande, in order to be nearer to the new posts in the Indian country. Circumstances might arise that would make it very important that I should be within striking distance of these posts."

CHURCH OF San Felipe de Neri was started in 1706 and is second oldest living church in United States. When Kearney's expedition marched into Albuquerque Plaza, "On our approach a salute of 20 guns was fired from the Balustrade top of the Catholic Church, old San Felipe de Neri." Its adobe walls are five feet thick and large windows 12 feet from floor, affording protection to settlers who frequently huddled inside during Indian scares. Towers were used for defense and served for sharpshooters.

tended to "continue the demonstration before Albuquerque in order that the Confederate forces might be withdrawn out from Santa Fe, and then by a night march place my command in a position from which the junction could be effected without danger of opposition to either column."

Apparently his plan worked as intended. He was able to join with the forces from Fort Union and the rebels did evacuate both Albuquerque and Santa Fe. Other than small actions in the area, Canby did not have to face Sibley's forces directly. But it was annoying to the volunteers.

"Sixty miles per day to catch the traitors," wrote one sarcastically, "and ten to let them go . . . We do not want to take any unfair advantage of them. We would be chivalrous, like them. God grant they may never get the same advantage of us."

TO GET THERE: From downtown Albuquerque, take U.S. 66 west to Romero Street. Turn right (north). In a block, Romero Street opens onto the Old Town Plaza, site of Post of Albuquerque.

CANNON buried by retreating Confederates were dug up 1892, four donated to State of Colorado and four to site of Old Albuquerque. All 12-pounders, they were part of artillery surrendered in Texas at start of Civil War. When they were being cleaned after 30 years underground, rusted remains of canister charges was found in one. Supposedly Union forces buried some cannon when they left Albuquerque before Confederates, but these have not been found.

CAMP WELD, COLORADO

Back in 1862 Denver, the question was which to fear most: Indian troubles and the threat of Confederate invasion, or the activities of the Colorado Volunteers at nearby Camp Weld?

Here was the situation as reported by Private Ovando J. Hollister in his *History of the First Regiment of Colorado Volunteers:*

"As the holidays approached, the boys began to 'scout the country round' to get forage for a big time," he wrote. "One party worked anxiously and assiduously a long time to pick the lock of a hen-roost door that was hung on leather hinges. Another, with great labor and no little risk of detection,

CAMP WELD looked like this in 1862. According to *Rocky Mountain News* contemporary account, "The buildings, which consist of officers' headquarters, quarters for soldiers, mess rooms, guard-house, hospital, etc., occupy four sides of what is nearly a square, and are built in the most substantial and comfortable manner. The building space occupied by each company is 180 feet, divided into mess rooms which are 30 by 18 feet, with high fireplaces at either end, and sleeping apartments of the same size, capable each of accommodating 25 men . . . The main entrance to the camp enclosure is on the eastern side. Immediately in front, after passing in, is the guard house, a commodious building, standing isolated from the main range of buildings." A porch ran around most of post, "affording a pleasant place for a covered promenade." Although the hospital 24 by 40 feet and double-storied had "ample accommodations for from 15 to 20 patients," an officer's wife noted in her diary, "The hospital accommodations at Camp Weld are rather limited." She said that 21 soldiers who had been snow-blinded on a scouting trip were kept in a darkened room because there were no eye shades available. "I had a dark green satin parasol, almost new, cut it up to make all of the shades possible for the afflicted soldiers," she added.

(COLORADO STATE HISTORICAL SOCIETY.)

carried a forty-gallon barrel of vinegar to the quarters, supposing it to be 'rot.'"

With the influx of miners, farmers, and other men who answered the call to arms and an enlistment bonus, Denver found that it could not contain the exhuberant spirits of the almost-soldiers. At the moment, the troopers' only claim to military status was a uniform—their legal status even was in doubt. The question of pay was settled for many months by just not paying them.

All of this, as far as Denver was concerned, meant trouble and a police force was organized to settle it.

Well and good, as the Volunteers' historian remembered, "Henceforth it became the object of many to create and foment variance with these minions of the city."

Christmas '62 found the police under cover. "The citizens gave it up and kindly allowed us to manage our own affairs," wrote Hollister. "The city was lawful 'loot,' the rest of the week. Everything was gobbled. Beef, mutton, vegetables, wine, cheese and clothing. Loads of hay were sold while the owner was 'smiling' with a confederate. The city complained, and no wonder!"

Basically, the problem at early Camp Weld was that the soldiers had nothing to do . . . and nothing to do it with. No one had been paid, the supply sergeant had sold most of the company property—"He averred he had lost it at 'monte,'" Hollister explained—, and mismanagement had exhausted the supply of food.

The camp in question had been founded in 1861 by the first governor of Colorado, ex-Army Major William Gilpin. Lacking official directives from Washington, the energetic governor issued his own drafts on the Treasury of the United States to the ultimate tune of about $375,000. Forty thousand of this was used to build "comfortable and sufficient barracks" at a site two miles west of the center of Denver.

First called Camp Elbert, then officially Weld—after the first secretary of Colorado—the post occupied thirty acres on the banks of the Platte River. Including a top-rail fence surrounding the post, a statistics-minded reporter of the *Rocky Mountain News*, said there were more than 800,000 feet of lumber, 30,000 bricks, "one hundred chimneys and nearly 200 fire places . . . all of which will have to be supplied with fuel for the coming four or five months."

Omnibusses shuttled visitors back and forth from town to watch the drilling. "Camp Weld is getting to be quite a resort of our citizens to witness the evening drill," reported the *News* in September 1861. "The barrack buildings are progressing quite rapidly and the soldiers will soon be comfortably quartered . . . The members of the House attended by some private citizens paid a visit to Camp Weld yesterday afternoon and remained until after the parade was over."

Hollister agreed on this score. "Drill was punctually attended to," he wrote, "and there was no better appearing set of men in the service than pa-

WHEN CIVIL war neared end in 1865, Elisha Millison, soldier stationed at Camp Weld, checked records in Denver Land Office and saw camp site was subect to homestead entry. No contest to his claim was made and he received entire site in December, 1865, including this building which he was occupying at time. This was part of officers' quarters and stood at south end of officers' row. When picture was taken at 1934 marker dedication, building was sole remnant of Camp Weld. Even by 1865, it was one of few original buildings remaining because two 1864 fires had destroyed almost entire fort.

raded every evening at Camp Weld."

This military façade covered a multitude of sins, however. The most serious was when a mounted company was shifted to the infantry and most of the men deserted. The company commander sided with them and was put in the Denver jail. A few days later most of the men had returned and were quietly mustered in, but two of the captains were cashiered.

"Ennui was becoming intolerable," Hollister wrote of Camp Weld. Then in February, 1862, a message arrived from Fort Leavenworth, Kansas:

"Send all available forces you can possibly spare to reinforce Colonel Canby, commanding Department of New Mexico," it directed. "Act promptly and with all the discretion of your latest information as to what may be necessary and where the troops of Colorado can do most service."

The troops "received the order to move south with unspeakable delight," Hollister recorded. The future was uncertain. As it turned out, the Battle of Glorieta was to be part of it.

Uncertain future or not, the Volunteers could care less. As Hollister added, "Any place but Denver."

ONLY MARKER remains at Camp Weld site. Officers' quarters present at 1934 dedication had been replaced in 1964 by steel industrial storehouse. Routine at post was described by newspaper article: "Reveille at daylight, and breakfast call at 7 o'clock. Guard mount at 8, and company drill at 9 a.m. Battalion drill at 2½ p.m., and Dress Parade a half hour before sundown. Tattoo at 8½ p.m., and at 9, lights are extinguished and all visitors withdraw from camp." Matter of financing Camp Weld, built with drafts issued by Governor Gilpin, finally forced removal of governor only a few weeks after his Colorado Volunteers had stopped Confederate invasion at Battle of Glorieta. Federal government ultimately redeemed most of Gilpin's drafts, and Coloradans recognized the importance played in Union victory by his zealous, if unorthodox, financing of state's mobilization.

TO GET THERE: From the State Capitol in Denver, head directly south six blocks to West 8th Avenue. Turn right (west) and continue on West 8th about two miles. Upon going on the 8th Avenue overpass, which begins at Mariposa Street, look to the right. This is the area of Camp Weld. Camp marker is on the right at the immediate western end of overpass where Vallejo Street deadends into West 8th.

FORT BUCHANAN, ARIZONA

Captain Richard S. Ewell's word was the law at Fort Buchanan. When he told a recruit to take the best horse and desert to Mexico, that is exactly what happened.

The story is told in the memoirs of Captain James H. Tevis, *Arizona in the '50's*. Tevis was staying with Ewell, Buchanan's commander, in 1857 when Ewell was superintending mounted drill. "The captain used to attend to the drill in person," Tevis wrote, "and when vexed he was not very particular about his language and would 'cuss' the soldiers very lustily . . ."

"When this recruit had tried repeatedly to mount his horse while in a trot, and had failed each time, the captain got out of humor and cursed him, saying, 'Clear out of here! Go to Sonora! Get out of my sight. Go to the stables and take the best horse and skip! Take your horse off the drill ground this instant!'"

Tevis records that the recruit did exactly that. He "left the drill ground . . . told the guard he wanted the captain's race horse . . . and was off for Sonora in a moment."

Two years later Ewell wrote a niece that absconding with his horses still was fashionable. "Every now and then the soldiers seem to be taken with a fit of deserting, and last Friday week a corporal and private of Dragoons took it into their heads to leave with two of my best horses."

Ewell chased the deserters across the Mexican line and was 128 miles from Buchanan when he ran them down. He found only the corporal alive; the private had been killed when their Mexican guides tried to rob them. Newspaper account of 1859, quoted by Nell Murbarger, tells of punishment for desertion and horse stealing at Buchanan being 50 lashes on the bare back, six months hard labor in irons, head shaving, and to be drummed out of service with dishonorable discharge and letter "D" branded on forehead.

Dealing with poor horsemen and deserters was not the worst of Ewell's worries at this primitive post. It was founded in 1856 as one of a chain of posts between the Colorado and Rio Grande proposed in 1853 by Army Inspector Mansfield. "Such a line would more effectually control the wild Indians, as well as afford protection to the emigrant and trader in live stock, and finally end in the establishment of mail across the country," he predicted.

Buchanan's appearance belied its strategic role. Although stables, huts, pens, and corrals were spread over a half mile, they were merely temporary jackals built of decaying timber coated with mud. The rooms were low, unventilated, narrow, dirt-floored, and could boast neither comfort nor neatness.

The soldiers did all of the work, but military duties kept them on continual alert. Ewell led a two-company patrol in 1857 that killed 40 Apaches who had ambushed a wagon train. Soon after, a sergeant and his 20-man detail attacked 50 Apaches near Buchanan.

The Indians took their harassments right into the fort and in 1859 made off with three horses. The next day they returned, and left this time with a dozen Army cattle, forcing Ewell to build an adobe corral to contain the post animals. Indians prowling around the fort buildings resulted in the troopers wearing pistols at all times.

Cochise was the leading agitator against the fort, although until 1859 he had been uniformly friendly to the whites.

What reportedly turned him against the whiteman started when a rancher was robbed and the man's son kidnapped. At the request of the sutler, "The commandant at Fort Buchanan dispatched a force of 75 men to the nearest Apache tribe," recounted a contemporary version. "The only interpreter to the expedition was the American who was directly interested in the result.

"Arriving at Apache Pass, the home of the tribe, the lieutenant in command raised a white flag over his tent. The principal chiefs and Cochise, one of the leaders of the Apache nation, came to the camp and were invited into the tent." The lieutenant was George N. Bascom and this event was to be known as the "Bascom Incident."

Although the Apaches insisted their tribe was innocent, the lieutenant ordered them to be seized. "One of the number in trying to escape was knocked down and pinned to the ground by a bayonet. Four others were bound, but Cochise, seizing a knife from the ground, cut his way through the canvas, and escaped, but not without receiving, as he afterward told, three bullets fired by the outside guard."

The account may be slightly exaggerated—other versions place Cochise's wounds as a bayonet stab in the knee, for instance—but there is little doubt that the result was a policy of wholesale extermination by the Apaches of the whites.

Ewell was involved in another affair with the Apaches while exchanging prisoners. Neither he nor the Indians trusted the other to return captives once they had given up their own hostages. So when the Indians had a kidnapped child, they would not give her up until Ewell agreed to let them see the Indians he would return in exchange. Each kept his own captives until, as if by signal, they were turned loose to run to freedom on their respective sides.

Returning captives sometimes posed problems because they had been hostages so long that they were more Indian than American. Tevis remembered that on at least one occasion, "The American captives were kept at Fort Buchanan until a wagontrain could take them to their homes in the fall, but before the train left they had all gone back to the Indians."

As the Indian situation worsened, it could not have happened at a poorer time. The incident of the over-eager lieutenant had resulted in five of Cochise's chiefs being hanged. "Our troops, after being badly beaten, were obliged to return to the fort," says a contemporary report.

"In the meantime, orders came for the abandonment of the territory by the soldiers. The country was thrown into consternation. The Apaches began to ride through it roughshod, succeeding in all their attacks. The settlers, mostly farmers, abandoned their crops, and with their families concentrated for mutual protection . . ."

Cochise led a 100-man attack on the horse herd at the fort, killing three troopers, wounding two more, and routing the herd. When a detail pursued him, they ran into an Apache ambush.

Troops were gathered at Fort Buchanan when orders were received by the commander to "abandon and destroy your post, burn your commissary and quartermasters stores, and everything between the Colorado and Rio Grande that will feed an enemy. March out with your guns loaded, and do not permit any citizen within three miles of your lines."

Ewell had resigned by the time and was on the way to the Confederacy and the stars of a lieutenant general. In answer to rumors that General Albert S. Johnson, recently resigned as departmental commander was reportedly en route to the south, Ewell's successor boasted, "He would take General Johnson's scalp, if he could catch him."

Johnson, according to his memoirs as written by his son, passed nearby and "a vast column of smoke from Fort Buchanan had previously warned them that the enemy had burned his depot."

In a letter to his wife, Johnson noted that he had taken command of Texan troops in New Mexico "to capture the United States troops from Fort Buchanan who were coming on." He noted "the disorderly character of their march" and complained that a messenger from Fort Craig had warned them of the nearness of the Texans. "They immediately destroyed their cannon, burned their train, all but eight wagons, mounted their infantry on mules, and marched or rather took to flight . . . a forlorn band . . . and saved themselves from the terrible Texans by an ignominious flight."

TO GET THERE: From Sonoita, Arizona, go west on State 82 about one mile. Approximate area of post is on low ground several hundred yards west of road, on privately owned Crown C Ranch.

"WE ARE TO have a large post and grand military etiquette," Captain Ewell wrote to his niece in 1860. He said he had a "great horror of these details," but "I suppose coats will have to be buttoned and minutiae of equal importance as if the safety of the world depended upon the amount of useless annoyance they can give." But this wasn't to be the future of Buchanan. Union troops reoccupied it temporarily in 1862 until General Carleton reported: "Owing to the fact that all of the buildings at Fort Buchanan had been destroyed, and to the fact that the site of that post being one of no military importance, in the present condition of this territory, I ordered its garrison to be withdrawn . . . The colors were put up there, thus consecrating the ground anew to the country." The site was outposted periodically and in February, 1865, 100 Indians attacked it. "They shot one soldier through the leg," noted the official report. "The soldiers, after the Indians fired the roof, made their escape. The Indians got about 200 rations, suits of clothing of six men, 250 cartridges, six cavalry horses and equipments, and some arms from the cavalry detachment near the post." The outpost was abandoned. A later official inspection of the site announced, "There is no public property at the post. A large number of adobes have been made, and are now large piles of mud, the last winter's rains have almost completely destroyed them." Today, nothing is left to mark the site, although scattered rocks and mounds suggest approximate locations of some buildings.

FORT CRAIG, NEW MEXICO

Everything else apparently having failed, Volunteer Captain Paddy Graydon felt he knew how to stop the Confederate advance on Fort Craig. His plan ended in laughter for everyone but Graydon; he was too busy running away from a pair of dynamite-laden mules!

In *Battles and Leaders of the Civil War*, the incident is described. Graydon headed an independent spy company that was assigned to harass the Confederates encamped across the Rio Grande from Craig in 1862. "Without explaining the details of his plan," the account described, "he had prepared a couple of wooden boxes, in each of which half a dozen 24-pounder howitzer shells were placed, with the fuses cut.

"These boxes were securely lashed on the backs of two old mules, and the captain, with three or four of his men, crossed the river just below the fort and proceeded in the darkness toward the Confederate camp. Graydon's project was to get the torpedo mules within sight of the enemy's picket line without being discovered, when he was to light the fuses, and the mules, being directed toward the picket line, would move in the direction of the animals there."

Graydon did not reckon with the disconcerting noise of the lighted fuses, however. Within 150 yards of the enemy camp, "the fuses of the boxes were fired and his party commenced their retreat, when to their consternation they found that the mules, instead of going toward the enemy, were following themselves."

Unaccustomed to the fuse noises, the mules had headed after the security of their master. "The shells soon began to explode, the Confederate camp was quickly under arms, and Graydon's party made its way back to Fort Craig without the mules." The tail of how he sacrificed two mules for the Union was to bedevil Graydon for the rest of his life.

When Graydon tried his mule experiment, times were desperate at Fort Craig. Founded in 1853 on the west bank of the Rio Grande as protection for the wagon road through the desolate Jornada del Muerto, Craig was described in 1855 by a Dragoon: "This is the best and prettiest fort in New Mexico . . . on a table land beside the Rio Grande . . . set in a grove of cottonwood trees."

Seven years later, a Colorado Volunteer put this description in his diary:

"It is a good post but a poor Ft. Situated on a high bluff overlooking the Riv. bottom. The walls are of adobes . . . the side walls are 900 feet long 10 feet high and 4 thick at bottom . . . the end walls 600 long . . . the same height and thickness as at the sides. No ditches around the post. There is a strong rampart on the S.E. corner supporting 4 guns two of them raking the wall on the E. & S. also one on the N.W. corner of 4 guns, two of the guns ranging along the N. & W. walls. Within these walls are quarters for officers of the Ft. two Co of soldiers, one Sutler store, commissary store rooms, 'Guard House' and stabling and corrells."

He noted that small pox "is very bad at this Ft." When a friend was afflicted with it, he was placed in "a small pox hospital on the bluff and it is full."

By this time, remnants of garrisons had converged from abandoned posts through Arizona and New Mexico. General Canby had upwards of 3,810 troops at Craig, regular and volunteer. Now ap-

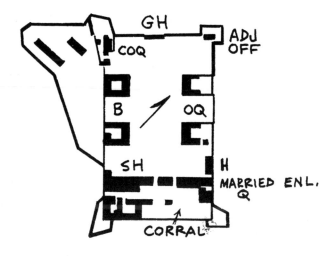

FORT CRAIG
N. MEX. – 1869

FORTRESS IN the European tradition governed design of Fort Craig, but adobe of local origin provided its materials. With few exceptions, it was used in post's buildings. Main area of fort was 1,050 by 600 feet. Designed for two companies, it included two 51 by 20 foot barracks with ceilings almost 13 feet high. In 1869 surgeon condemned them as "badly designed; the ventilation is defective; they cannot be heated; and should they happen to be crowded during an epidemic, the consequences would be serious." Each barrack unit was completed with dormitory, mess room, kitchen, and rooms for laundresses and noncommissioned officers. Unlike many crowded Western forts, iron bedsteads were used in dormitories. During the day, these served as chairs and benches, "the men rolling up their bedding each morning to the head of the bunk, employing the foot of it as a seat." Porches ran across front of both barracks and officers' quarters duplexes. Sally port, main entrance to fort, ran through center of guardhouse. (Redrawn from Surgeon-General Circular No. 4, 1870)

FLAT ROOFS of Fort Craig meant discomfort for occupants during rainy season. After a pre-Civil War rain of 57 consecutive hours, an officer's wife complained, "The dirt roofs of the adobe quarters were leaking all over! Mrs. Porter was quite ill, and the water was pouring into the room where she was in bed under a tent-fly, with an umbrella over her head! Colonel Crittenden's quarters were in the same building, and the rain steamed through like a shower-bath. . . . The rain ceased towards night and large fires were built; but the water still ran in front the roof." This 1870-era view is toward southwest across area of casemates. Sally port can be seen at left corner of picture. Officers' quarters are at left of flagpole, barracks at right. By 1872, fort included eight warehouses and a grainhouse, with capacity for supplying 3,000 men for six months if required.

peared to be the logical time to cut the Confederate advance.

Despite the supremacy of numbers, 3,810 to an estimated 2,600 Confederates, the totals were deceiving. Only 1,200 of Canby's troops were regulars. The rest were militia who had never heard a cannon fired in anger. The southern Army, under General H. H. Sibley, was tired and ragged, but it was tested.

It was the morning after the Graydon mule experiment that the critical test for Fort Craig took place, the Battle of Valverde. Confederates moving to the Rio Grande to water their animals surprised and routed a New Mexico Volunteer regiment so completely that it was not heard from again.

Bitter cannonading was exchanged between the two sides as cavalry and infantry manuvered for attack. The battle hit a peak at noon, then slacked off until an hour before sunset when the rebels spotted a gap in the Union lines.

While Canby was unsuccessful trying to persuade five companies of New Mexican Volunteers to cross the Rio Grande, the Union batteries were charged by Texans armed with double-barreled shotguns and machetes. Canby had his horse shot from under him. The Confederates were quick to turn the captured batteries against the Northern troops retreating to Fort Craig.

Statistics of the Battle of Valverde term it proportionately the bloodiest of the Civil War in 1862. The bulk of the Union casualties were suffered by the regular Army and Colorado Volunteers; the re-

GUARDHOUSE was one of Craig's few stone buildings. It had two prison rooms, one for Negro the other for white prisoners, and in corner of guardroom was "trapdoor opening upon a stairway which leads down to the cells where prisoners are kept in solitary confinement," surgeon described. "The cells are six in number, three on each side of the passage way. Each cell is 5 feet 7 inches long, 2 feet 10 inches wide, and 4 feet 10 inches high." There was no light, and ventilation depended upon augur holes in the walls and chinks around doors. Due to sprinkling the earthen floors to keep the dust down, men had to sleep on moist ground and "colds and rheumatism are frequent among the inmates." One set of occupants for guardhouse probably was guard for July 4, 1863, which celebrated Independence Day by disposing of sutler's whiskey while on duty. Most of remaining troops were away on patrol. "The Indians were aware of this and attacked the post. Fortunately the yells of the attackers brought them to their senses enough to beat off the attack," reported contemporary newspaper account. "No doubt the internal fortitude helped give them a reckless daring that not only surprised the Indians but scared them off."

BARRACKS remains overlook mounds of Fort Craig's adobe breastwork that once reached 10 feet high. It had several breaks which would admit a man on horseback, but these were closed at night. Eighteen building ruins remained in 1964. Post was abandoned gradually and in 1878 Captain John Crawford, chief of scouts, took charge of government property there. A five-man detail reactivated it in 1880, but the 1881 Victorio uprising found 15 men in its garrison. Its troopers joined Fort Bayard detail and in an ambush lost popular lieutenant. He was so well liked, soldiers of both posts wore mourning badges for a month, and memorial services were held several years afterward at Fort Craig. By 1886, things had quieted down so that Crawford's daughter, Eva, decided to liven things up during dance in barracks. She climbed on roof, fired pistol several times, and amid frantic screams dropped a dummy through the air shaft onto the startled dancers. It took a round of drinks at the Crawfords to revive the guests. Army had abandoned post by 1885, and Crawford, who had bought most of the buildings, remained there protecting property from trespassers. His reputation as traveler was well known and during his absences vandals made nightly visits, aware that Mrs. Crawford was not as good an aim as her husband and just fired her rifle in air with the hope of scaring away thieves.

ports of Sibley's losses were minimized by the South and exaggerated by the North so that no source can be taken as wholly accurate.

Back under the protection of Fort Craig, Canby may have been in agreement with a Colorado Volunteer's discomforting description of it: "It contains quarters for two full companies of dragoons, and is surrounded by an adobe wall pierced for rifles. It would afford no protection against artillery."

The same Volunteer noted that the troops returned to the fort "in good order. An attack on the post was anticipated that night," and Canby "directed them in case of an attack to depend on their bayonets, that being the most formidable arm of resistance in use."

But the Confederates did not attack. Canby had mounted many so-called "Quaker cannon" of logs

in with his artillery to deceive them of his actual strength and perhaps this was one reason the fort was skirted.

In their subsequent retreat back to Texas, the rebels again by-passed Fort Craig. By this time it was a strong headquarters and depot. Kit Carson was in command, and, one trooper recorded, "He has kept his Mexicans at work. They dug a trench inside of the walls and have strengthened the walls some, but the plaza is full of rags and dirt. Canby will soon have this cleaned off. There is too much Injin in Kit to keep anything clean."

TO GET THERE: From San Antonio, N.M. take U.S. Interstate 25 about 20 miles south. On left side of highway is state marker. Turn left, follow gravel road five miles east where it terminates at ruins of Fort Craig.

OFFICERS QUARTERS were noted in 1872 report as being built of stone, but ruins suggest that adobe construction described in other reports is more accurate. Quarters were plastered on both sides, and each set included two bedrooms flanking 15-foot hall, a 20 by 20 foot dining room, a kitchen, and a servant's room. Fireplaces supplied heat. In its heyday, post saw almost continual Indian activity. In 1859, Apaches made uncommon predawn attack on nearby sheep herders and 47-man patrol was sent into pursuit. Twelve hours later soldiers returned without Indians, but driving 6,000 sheep. After another patrol later in year recovered more than 14,000 stolen sheep and killed 28 Indians, hostiles turned talents elsewhere, though patrols against them continued throughout Civil War.

"THE CEMETERY is near the fort, and anyone viewing it must be constrained to give General Canby credit for an uncommon share of humanity," described Colorado Volunteer about burials of Valverde dead. "Each is buried in a single grave, with a headboard stating birth place, corps and rank in the army, and place of death." Confederate dead were buried by Sibley on battlefield and "were in plain sight till high water obliterated their traces," Volunteer continued. Cemetery still is surrounded by stone wall, 200 feet square, but graves were moved to Santa Fe in 1876. Black Mesa, at foot of which Battle of Valverde was fought, is on horizon in background.

CAMP INDEPENDENCE, CALIFORNIA

Even 100 years later, Indians in California's Owens Valley still recall with bitter reluctance the darkest day in their relations with the whites.

The date was July 10, 1863, the place, year-old Camp Independence. Throughout the day tribesmen in the area had answered the summons to the post issued by Captain Moses A. McLaughlin, previously the relentless commander of Camp Babbitt.

When more than 1,000 Indians were gathered on the parade ground, McLaughlin called the chiefs to the center and ordered the others to sit on the ground. Through an interpreter, he informed them that they were to be up-rooted from their native hunting grounds and marched 200 miles southwest to abandoned Fort Tejon. He knew the Indians would react unfavorably and was prepared.

"I had taken the precaution to have the troops so stationed that their presence did not excite the suspicians of the Indians," he reported, "and yet at the time I made the announcement they were completely surrounded . . . During the night the troops slept upon their arms on the parade ground, ready at a moment's notice to prevent any attempt at escape."

The Indians knew it was hopeless, as expressed by their chief: "American capitan sabe much, Indian poco."

Seventy soldiers guarded the sorrowful procession when it started the next morning. Only a few wagons were available for some of the women and children. The mid-summer weather was unbearably hot. "The sufferings upon the route were intense" understated McLaughlin. The fact that only 850 Indians finished the trek spoke more eloquently of the hardships. Escape for some, death for others had taken their toll from the total.

Months later, most of the survivors had returned to the Owens Valley. Fort Tejon had been unbearable under McLaughlin and a disinterested Indian agent. By January, 1864, only 380 Indians were left.

"A ROW OF buildings stood before us, it was Fort Independence," wrote a visitor in 1865. He noted that there were 100 men at the post "who have been here about one year. They are retained as a safeguard for the settlers . . . a perfect understanding exists with the Indians, there are only a few of them left now, so that not the least danger is feared now. The fort is in complete order, the parade ground cannot be surpassed. Perfect good feeling exists between the officers and men." Peace still had not come to the Owens Valley, though. In 1867, First Sergeant F. R. Neale and 12 troopers trailed Indians for 80 miles, finally surprising them and killing or wounding a dozen. The patrol covered 250 miles in all, most of it through a heavy snowstorm. This plat shows fort after earthquake revamping. (Redrawn from McDowell Report, 1879.)

In another six months, department headquarters announced that because "there were no longer any Indians in the vicinity of Fort Tejon, that the post will be abandoned."

It was small consolation to the refugees that six months after their merciless march, McLaughlin would be relieved of his command and face court-martial. This was an old story to him; at least once before charges had been placed against him "for cruelly beating and maltreating" one of his troopers.

McLaughlin had come to Independence as a confirmed Indian hater, as a massacre of 35 while at Camp Babbitt attested. Local tradition places some of the blame for his actions on alcohol, and one story suggests that he did not confine his anger to Indians when his patience was tried.

On one occasion, the tale goes, his drinking was disturbed by general restlessness in the corral. He ordered two soldiers to shoot every horse that was moving around. When they refused to obey, he had them put in the guardhouse—from which they escaped by removing the hinges. Once they had put McLaughlin far behind them, they turned themselves in at another Army post.

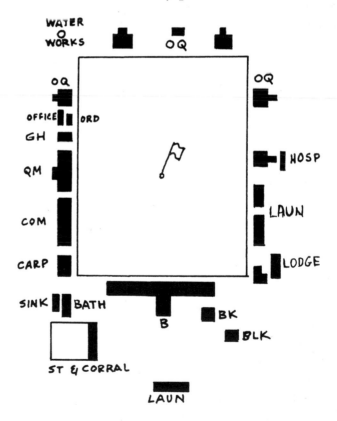

FORT INDEPENDENCE
CALIF. – 1877

CAMP INDEPENDENCE, probably after 1872 earthquake, had overcome complaint of 1870 surgeon: "The great desideratum at the post is shade during the winter months, as there are few shade trees, and no verandas around the buildings. A large number of trees have been set out, but as yet have not attained sufficient size to be of use." The 1875 Surgeon noted things had changed: "The present buildings are located on the four sides of a parallelogram, forming the parade ground and lawns in front of the officers' quarters. These grounds are set out with trees and covered with grass. A live hedge forms the westerly boundary of the camp." He noted the barracks was 164 feet long by 30 feet wide, "well lighted and well warmed with stoves." Most buildings were of frame except for storehouses which were former barracks and of adobe. The chimneys all were of adobe, but they were "carefully braced with wood and extended above the roofs by galvanized iron flues on account of earthquakes," he added cautiously.

The conditions at Independence may have had something to do with the unsavory situation. When it was established in 1862 a California cloudburst signalled the occasion, somewhat dampening the spirits of the men. Regardless, when a 50-foot flagpole was erected "and the old flag with all of the stars upon it hoisted to the breeze," Lieutenant Colonel George S. Evans could report there were "three times three given most heartily by the men, and a salute fired with small arms."

The day was July 4 and Independence was the logical choice for a name. This also may have accounted for the fact that within a few months there was at least one attempt at mutiny by the garrison.

The first quarters were rude huts and caves hollowed out of a nearby ravine. When the weather turned wintry in September, the troops took advantage of Evans' temporary absence by packing up and leaving.

Twenty-five miles below the camp he met them, "moving down the valley, bag and baggage, almost in a state of mutiny," he recounted. "The command are entirely out of provisions and clothing, and the weather is becoming very cold . . . The men are barefoot and naked . . . they have not been paid off for nearly nine months . . . and the men, volunteer-like, think they are badly treated at best in being left in this valley, and unless they are regularly fed and well clothed it will be impossible to keep them together."

EARLY SOLDIERS at Camp Independence lived in this cave, one of several at original site. Rooms have been hollowed out and there are overhead holes for chimneys. Walls bear soot traces from early fires . . . and from more modern ones of local campers and children. Visitors are cautioned to watch out for snakes.

ORIGINAL CAMP was here, with soldiers living in caves along side of ravine. These were used during first year of post. Ten years later, it was possible to report, "The post is a very healthy one; the duties of the troops being light, the air pure, and the food excellent." During slack time in hostilities, newspaper complained that there was nothing going on, "Not even an Indian fight. Uncle Sam's Boys in Blue are having an easy time of it, and are anxiously expecting a discharge or the paymaster."

COMMANDING OFFICER of Camp Independence once lived here, although building has been moved from original site to town. During Army days, post was scene of various events including an 1866 race riot. Contemporary newspaper tells that soldiers "were used the other day to quell a Negro insurrection. The darkies that came from New York to work the Cosco Mine are not well pleased with their new home whose deserts can offer no amusement . . . and they are threatening to secede, which is no approval of life in a sagebrush region." In 1873 troopers were used to guard telephone lines, to protect the town jail from a lynch mob, and in an unsuccessful bandit hunt.

SIERRA NEVADA mountains look down on former parade ground of Camp Independence. As soon as post was abandoned, settlers moved everything useable away; two buildings still are used as residences in Independence. Peaceful modern appearance belies early hostilities. First fight at site was in 1862 when expedition was sent to quiet 1,000 Indians who had "burnt every house and improvement" in the Valley, "have killed at least nine white men that have been found and buried . . . and killed at least 1,000 head of cattle."

The situation was resolved before the dead of winter set in. Adobe barracks were built by soldiers who had to divide their talents between engineering and Indian skirmishing. After the exodus of Redmen to Tejon, the post was abandoned over the protests of settlers.

Headquarters suggested the settlers organize a homeguard. As General Wright paternally informed them, what they needed were militia companies composed of "Loyal and true men . . . always ready to defend their own firesides and uphold the Constitution, the laws, and the Union."

The appeal to patriotism was not enough to quiet

the Indian raiding that followed the camp's abandonment. In December, 1864, Nevada Volunteers were ordered to re-garrison Camp Independence and it remained active for 13 more years.

TO GET THERE: Independence, California, straddles U.S. 395 about 45 miles south of Bishop. The former C.O.'s house has been moved to 303 Edwards Street, the town's name for U.S. 395, on the west side of the highway near the center of town. The camp site is two miles north of town. At Shabbell Lane (old 395) turn east one-quarter mile. The ravine with the original camp's caves is on the right at this point. The post side is on the left, a few hundred yards.

POST CEMETERY, an eighth of a mile from post, was 200 feet square with fence surrounding it. Today only townspeople's graves remain, with most legible markers having dates in 70's and 80's. This was lively period in local history. One incident involved soldiers who tried to crash New Year's Eve dance and were refused indiscriminately and many broken heads greeted new year. Later in post history temperance society made headway among garrison and by 1875 it was a rarity to have a prisoner in guardhouse.

CAMP BABBITT, CALIFORNIA

Secessionists were so active in 1862, "It is an everyday occurrence for them to ride through the streets of Visalia and hurrah for Jeff Davis and Stonewall Jackson, and often give groans for the Stars and Stripes," reported Camp Babbitt's first commander, Lieutenant Colonel George S. Evans.

He told departmental headquarters, "They do and say everything in the presence of soldiers to insult them by calling them Lincoln hirelings, and that they bear Abe Lincoln's livery, etc., and in one instance have gone so far as to draw a pistol and present it at a soldier, telling that he had a good mind to shoot the buttons off of his coat, just for fun."

His report cited several examples, including the killing of a soldier, and predicted that if the disloyal elements were not controlled, "all the officers between here and the Potomac, in my humble opinion, cannot prevent frequent collisions between the soldiers and the citizens, the ultimate result of which will be civil war."

Headquarters reacted promptly. "Under no circumstances will disloyal citizens be permitted to harass your troops or speak disrespectfully of our government," Evans was instructed. "If necessary to check conduct so unworthy of those seeking the protection of the government, you will arrest a few of the worst, holding them in close confinement, sending the leaders, if men of position, to Alcatraz Island."

Backing up the orders, headquarters rushed a company of California Volunteers to reinforce the post, even though the original garrison had only been there two months. The reputation of Visalia was well known, and the Army decided that immediate action was necessary.

Secession had been rife in this Joaquin Valley region as early as the 1850's when the citizens threatened to form their own republic if not granted a railroad line. In 1860, editors of the rival Union and rebel newspapers met for a duel, but tempers were so short that what was to be a shooting match ended with principals and seconds trading punches. The editors themselves faced down each other in one of the newspaper offices a few days later. The secessionist editor took a fatal bullet in his stomach. The Union man decided his popularity had waned so much he had better leave town.

Visalia was suspected of being a stop on the underground to the south, a role proved when Federal marshals intercepted a courier in 1861. The next step, obviously was to send in troops.

In October, 1862, Colonel Evans reported arriving at the site of Camp Babbitt after a forced march of 120 miles in four and-a-half days. The rigors of the march were obvious on the troopers, because the horses were too weak to carry burdens and, reported Evans, the men "were compelled to walk about two-thirds of way, and that, too, barefooted and naked, for many of them were as destitute of shoes as they were the day they were born, and had no pantaloons, except such as they had themselves made out of barley and flour sacks. . . Still the men plodded on and stood guard at night, leaving the blood from their feet upon the rocks and snow."

Evans selected a campsite a mile north of the center of Visalia and in General Orders No. 13, dated October 31, 1862, announced, "This camp is hereby named and shall hereafter be known and called Camp Babbitt, in honor of Lieut. Col. E. B. Babbitt, deputy quartermaster general, U.S. Army, Department of the Pacific." Despite the high sounding proclamation, the post was little more than a cluster of rude huts and tents amidst hugh oak trees.

Captain Moses A. McLaughlin succeeded Evans and on December 21 reported, "This command does not number more than 100 effective men, and the rebels can bring against it 250 men in 24 hours, and 400 in two days, all of them well armed." He had arrested three persons "who had the audacity to ride and drive in front of the battalion while on dress parade, hurrahing for Jeff Davis and Stonewall Jackson."

McLaughlin refused to acknowledge a writ of habeas corpus for the release of the prisoners, and predicted "the sheriff will summon a strong posse comitatus, trying to regain them by force."

Some of the dissension was quieted when the prisoners were released two weeks later after taking the oath of allegiance. One, the editor of the secessionist *Equal Rights Expositor* which had been banned from the mails, was kept in confinement when he balked at the oath.

In March, 1863, troopers took the newspaper question in their own hands. Thirty descended on the printshop after tattoo roll-call, "completely

(COURTESY COLONEL FRED B. ROGERS.)

TROOPS LEFT town site of Camp Babbitt in 1865 to put more space between themselves and townspeople. An 1864 killing of a civilian was over an age-old complaint: the citizen was stealing drinks. Although first post had become a social center, especially with the lure of blue uniforms on parade and at the periodic "grand balls," townspeople did not take kindly when the men practiced roping on the headstones in the town cemetery during cavalry drills. After the secession business had died down, the newspaper commented, "No big drunks have occurred, no shootings, Oh, how dull." The shooting of a soldier by another caused the newspaper to suggest the men be prohibited from carrying weapons off of the post because they were no longer needed. By 1866, this was obvious and the post was abandoned.

CAMP BABBITT in 1864 was sketched by Private George E. Young. By this time, troopers were preoccupied with Indian fighting. Babbitt's major action brought little credit to its California Volunteers when in 1863 they surrounded an Indian camp and, after settlers had identified 35 possible horse thiefs "for whom no one would vouch" they were "either shot or sabered," reported Captain Moses A. McLaughlin. "Their only chance for life being their fleetness, but none escaped, though many of them fought well with knives, sticks, stones, and clubs. This extreme punishment, though I regret it, was necessary, and I feel certain that a few such examples will soon crush the Indians and finish the war in this and adjacent valleys."

wrecked the office. . .breaking the doors and windows of the building, breaking the press, and throwing the type, paper, ink, etc., in the street."

A patrol was rushed into town to keep order, but the unorthodox means took effect. Other than the killing of a soldier by a rebel five months later and a rumor that "an outbreak may be looked for at any moment," public displays of disloyalty ceased.

It may have been because the townspeople organized two Home Guard companies—"To protect ourselves against the soldiers who came to protect us," one wag remarked after the war—or because the government rushed a howitzer to Babbitt with the orders: "Maintain your position at all costs."

Or it may have been that increased Indian depredations, caused both Union and secession sides to bury their political differences to face the common foe.

TO GET THERE: Original Camp Babbitt site is occupied by the Visalia ice plant with a sign at the corner of Race and Santa Fe Streets in Visalia. The second site is unmarked in the vicinity of Ben Maddox way and Houston Avenue.

IMPROMPTU BAND of Camp Babbitt probably provided entertainment of a sorts when it paraded at first site of post. Although some loyal townswomen organized a "Visalia Sanitary Association" as a forerunner of the Red Cross and provided food and entertainment for the bored troopers, usually they had to fend for themselves. Only one saloon in town welcomed them, an emporium operated by a Mexican War veteran. When they took their trade to the "Fashion" saloon and refused to pay for the drinks, they took offense when the bartender would not allow them cigars on the cuff, too. One soldier was fatally shot and another wounded in the events that followed. Forty armed secessionists patrolled the streets the next day to prevent further trouble, although the Army had confined the soldiers to quarters and promised to punish the guilty ones. They quickly vanished when the commanding officer announced he would not require his men to endure insults without retaliation, and hinted that unless the vigilantes disbanded, he would turn his men loose on them.

(FROM "LOS TULARES" COURTESY HAROLD SCHUTT AND W. R. PARKER)

FORT MILLER, CALIFORNIA

A hotbed of secession may have been what the new commander of Fort Miller expected to find in 1863, but he found a sickbed instead. What was more, no one seemed the least concerned that the Army had returned to this San Joaquin Valley post. To put it mildly, he reported, "The arrival of the command caused no excitement." Except for one thing: the officer had broken a collar bone and was viewing everything from a prone position.

Headquarters probably greeted the news with mingled sighs of relief and disappointment. According to earlier word on the Fort Miller area, it was flaming with rebellion, alive with "disloyal practices," and "had not a loyal man in the place."

The informant reported that when the townspeople received news of Lee's invasion of Maryland, "they celebrated the occasion by a public demonstration, in which all joined (of both sexes), by firing a Confederate salute . . . cheering for them and groaning for the United States government and its officers."

And, in addition, he noted, "This county is the resort of bad men. The people boast they have neither a common school nor a church in the county."

As a final insult, it was pointed out, "The fort is now occupied by the families of disloyal men, with one exception, using the buildings as dwelling houses."

"In my opinion the presence of a cavalry company would have a moral influence upon their conduct toward the government and its officers," was his recommendation. On August 11, 1863, orders were issued to carry out his suggestion, and then some. The headquarters and two companies of the

2d Regiment of California Infantry Volunteers were dispatched to the scene.

As General Wright explained to Washington, "There is a large element of disloyalty and the presence of troops in that quarter is indispensably necessary, at least until after the election."

Duty at Miller was nothing new to the military. Twelve years earlier, a detachment of 200 infantrymen under Captain Erasmus D. Keyes had camped at the site while escorting an Indian treaty commission.

"It was in the spring of the year 1851, and the San Joaquin Valley was in an absolute state of nature," Keyes later wrote in his autobiography. There was "no evidence of occupation by white men. . . Large troops of wild horses, many deer, antelope, and coyotes were constantly in view . . . The atmosphere was clear and wholesome."

As a forerunner of Fort Miller, a log blockhouse was built and named Camp Barbour after the chief commissioner. Here Keyes witnessed treaties being signed by 16 Indian tribes. He wrote that 1,200 Indians were assembled, "Many of whom had never seen a white man till they came to treat with us. I was impressed with the appearance of several chiefs and remembered the general aspect of all. . . while they amused themselves with football and other rough sports."

In 1858 he returned to Miller on court-martial duty and observed what civilization had brought to the Indians. "I was told that they were nearly all dead, victims to drunkenness, and that of the whole number I then saw in such full activity not above fifty remained. I took pains to see the wretched survivors, and was shocked with the spectacle of degradation and self-abandonment they presented."

The post was abandoned about this time. Life at the fort had been reduced to attempts by the officers to pan gold, gossiping over the quarrel between two settlers that resulted in the death of one, and the post surgeon's pickeling of the head of rob-

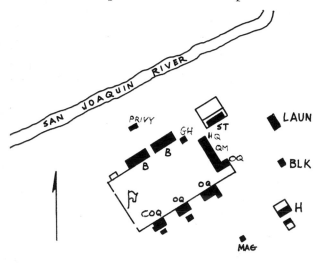

FORT MILLER
CALIF.-1864

SOME REBUILDING was necessary when Fort Miller was reoccupied in 1863. One storehouse had been burned down and the guardhouse had been carted off by an enterprising miner. In 1854, Army Inspector Mansfeld found post somewhat like this. The adobe officers' quarters were almost finished, but barracks row was vacant. Soldiers lived in log building at far end of parade ground opposite flagpole and canvas storehouses and kitchens formed a square behind it. Although the supplies were "As well stored as the buildings made of cloth would admit," Mansfield suggested, "it is apparent that supplies are not safe in such buildings." By 1864, the adobe storehouse was at the site of the old barracks. (Redrawn from plat in National Archives.)

CALIFORNIA
FORT MILLER
Latitude   Longitude
SKETCH
Approved by the Sec'y of War.

DEPARTMENTAL inspector in 1852 criticized Fort Miller location as "ill chosen . . . in a cul-de-sac, formed by a deep curve in the mountain range, the river passing through the apex of the curve . . . Fort Miller . . . 200 yards from the river bank." Although his criticism was in terms of poor circulation of air, ultimate result was disappearance of post when Millerton Lake was formed. This is Fort Miller in 1864, a quadrangle 350 by 200 feet, surrounded by a 5 foot high adobe wall capped with stone. Two howitzers were originally within the enclosure, plus two white oak trees— one of which was used as a whipping post, according to tradition. Camp Barbour blockhouse, not shown on plat, is square building with wide window across creek behind headquarters-storehouse building. Sketch is by C. F. Otto Skobel, talented soldier in 1864 garrison.

ber Joaquin Murietta in a barrel of whiskey.

About this time, too, in nearby Millerton a prisoner had picked his way out of the adobe jail on the same day the new edifice had been officially accepted by the town supervisors. Apparently the builder had begged the man to postpone his jail break until the rickety building was accepted and paid for. This the prisoner did, but not a minute more!

With the return of the Army in 1863, business in Millerton picked up. In 1855 it had boasted some 20 houses, "most of them canvas, two or three of them being shops and the majority of the rest drinking saloons and billiard rooms," wrote a visitor. It weathered floods in 1861 and 1862, and it weathered the Army's return in 1863.

"The Union men are undoubtedly in a small minority hereabouts," the commanding officer reported, "but the copperhead element shows no disposition to obtrude its sentiments by noisy demonstrations."

He had not had much chance to examine the situation personally, he admitted because of his broken collar bone, but "the surgeon assures me I shall remain hors de combat not exceeding two weeks longer."

This was about the only combat seen by the second generation Miller garrison. As the *Fresno Expositor* wrote later, "The mines of the river were rich and the county officials and officers and men at Fort Miller had a very agreeable time with the Millertonites and everything was conducted in a loose, devil-me-care sort of style."

Considering that Millerton usually conducted its official business by recessing trials so that the jury could attend the horse races, and the Board of Supervisors adjourned for 20 minutes per session for a thirst quencher at one of the many nearby saloons, it is small wonder that little came out of Fort Miller's second career!

TO GET THERE: In 1939 Fort Miller was described as "the best preserved of the forts erected after California became one of the United States." The Camp Barbour blockhouse, three officers' quarters, most of the other buildings, and even outlines of the stone and adobe walls remained. Construction of the Friant Dam spelled the end of Fort Miller forever, and it is now beneath the waters of Millerton Lake, northwest of Fresno. To reach the lake, take State 41 north 20 miles from Fresno, turning right on County 145 to Millerton Lake State Park, six miles.

FORT MILLER lies beneath this lake today. In 1852, inspector commented, "I consider maintenance of a military post in this section of the country very important and that the garrison should consist of two or three companies." This was agreed to in 1854 inspection. "This post is . . . well located for the present to overawe and restrain the Indians and protect the white settler, and should be retained some years." Latter inspector had only three critical comments. He said one company "was not instructed properly . . . were mostly recruits and could not drill mounted, and had but a few horses . . . marched indifferently . . . and there were but three pistols to this company." He found the musicians at the post "were indifferent and wanted instruction." And finally, "At this post are two 12-pound field howitzers which require painting, but a limited supply of fixed ammunition for them, say 130 rounds of all kinds." Today, Millerton Lake State Park surrounds watercovered site of Fort Miller.

FORT CHURCHILL, NEVADA

If the State of Nevada, with its motto "Battle Born," can credit the first days of the Civil War with granting it statehood, Fort Churchill was surely the supervising physician at the delivery. During the first ten years of Nevada's new status, hardly an event took place that did not have Churchill's troopers playing a key role.

Even before the Civil War, the site of Churchill was important. Ten miles from it the sparks of the Pyramid Lake Indian War were ignited in 1860 when two traders kidnapped two Indian girls and defied demands from the tribe for their return. After the Indians substituted fighting for talk, the trading post was leveled and its five occupants dead.

Word of the "massacre,"—that term used whenever the dead were white instead of Indian—resulted in 105 volunteers mustering at Buckland's ranch, almost where Fort Churchill would be established in two months. After these volunteers marched boldly to Pyramid Lake and smack into an ambush that cut their numbers almost in half, U.S. troops were called in. With 207 Army men and 750 volunteers, the next meeting with the Indians was more to the white's liking: something like 40 of the 300 Indians were killed while the white casualties totaled three.

After that "War of 1860," the volunteers were disbanded. Shortly the regular troops moved to the vicinity of Buckland's to build Nevada's first and largest fort. It was known for two months as "Post on the Carson River, Utah Territory" but in August, 1860, was officially named after Brevet Brigadier General Sylvester Churchill who was spending his last 20 of 50 years in the Army as Inspector General.

The establishment orders commanded, "Con-

struction to be of the simplest character with materials most easily procurred. Work on these structures to be pushed with vigor by the labor of the whole command."

It was not long before departmental headquarters cast a jaundiced eye on expenditures from the "simple" post. Pointing out that the estimates for Churchill "exceeded the amount appropriated for the construction and repair of barracks, etc. . . . for the whole army," headquarters called a halt to the work and sent a board to investigate.

They found 55 buildings in varying stages of completion, wagons carrying lumber from mills in California, 100 mules employed on the scene, $16,000 estimates for each of the six double-story officers' quarters, and stated requirements for $178,889.69 in order to finish the post. It was admitted that the labor market was high, what with new towns being built everytime a silver strike was made, and that everything but adobe had to be carted a great distance, but the board felt the officers' quarters were too elaborate. Other than this one extravagance, the board considered the other buildings "are rather less than what is necessary for the comfort of the men and preservation of public property."

By this time, war fever had overtaken events. Construction of the adobe building continued, but when the post was informed that it was to be enlarged by two more infantry companies, a cautious headquarters directed: "If buildings are to be erected they must be of the simplest character that will answer the purpose of temporary shelter; probably adobes will be the cheapest. Boards for flooring will be dispensed with, and shingle roofing also, unless it will cost very much less than heretofore at your post . . . All the labor must be performed by the troops."

This last comment invited a rejoinder from the commander as soon as some of his men were detailed on an expedition. He announced that he had to take some of the troop-laborers off of the adobes

(NATIONAL ARCHIVES.)

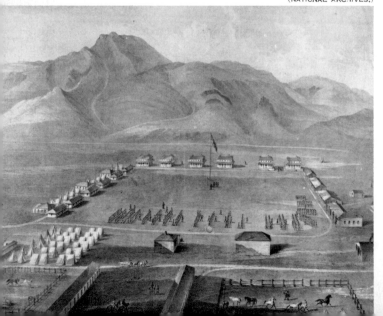

FORT CHURCHILL, as viewed by Army artist, was designed for 1,000 troops. It never had more than 800 while 300 was its average. Six barracks with messhalls in the rear were on left or west side of parade ground; six double-story officers' quarters across north side. Along right side, from north to south, were headquarters building, two warehouses, and hospital. Laundress quarters were behind hospital. Across near side were magazine, right, and guardhouse, center, with additional troop tents and stables to left. Corrals were in foreground, spread between parade ground and Carson River. River was expected to provide water for post, but it was found to be contaminated by mining wastes. Only after artesian well was drilled was acute water shortage solved.

to stand guard, "which will seriously impede the work on the soldiers' quarters and the shelter for the animals, and will render it almost impossible to get the work of building before the winter sets in."

A year later the new district commander, Colonel P. Edward Connor, arrived at Churchill and found "that matters at this post are being conducted with care and economy." The next year, after a 36-gun salute greeting, General Wright was to term it "in admirable order. I critically inspected all the departments and found the Government property well taken care of and economically used, and the officers zealous and attentive to their duties."

It was obvious that "economy" was a key question in the mind of every inspecting officer. But by this time, fort building had taken second priority to the more important matters of secessionists and Indians.

Churchill was the recruit camp for the 1,200 Nevada Volunteers called up during the war. Here, too, prospective officers were interviewed and given written examinations, something novel in officer selection of the period but which field experience was to show more effective than commissioning by popular vote.

Recruiting was carried on via drum and flag parades in the mining camps and saloons. When a southern-minded resident of Virginia City smashed a recruiter's drum, the latter retaliated with a right smash to the jaw. The resulting uproar brought in 75 recruits. Another group of volunteers is recorded as arriving at the fort "in an ambulance, jolly as lords and immensely patriotic."

The enthusiasm waned when it was apparent the troops were not to get in the big war in the East. Even though the governor volunteered to take a company to New York at no expense to the government, Washington turned the idea down. They felt Nevadans were more needed in the West than the East.

Secession activities were will o'wisps for four

LAUNDRESSES lived here, most of them wives of soldiers, providing both clean clothes and gentle influence to post. Each company was permitted to hire four laundresses who, along with wives and families of soldiers and officers were officially termed "camp followers." Other females near post included Indian squaws. In November, 1867, one squaw indicated her disapproval of her husband by poisoning him, but later was located by his brother who stabbed her to death. Piutes approved; this was their custom. An 1863 incident with Indians left everyone laughing when citizens of Como, Nevada, called for Army help, claiming town was besieged by blood thirsty braves. Twenty troopers rushed in and town was put under martial law with Home Guard assisting. In the darkness, two Home Guards, the password forgotten, blazed six-shooters at each other and town butcher, in his rush to man battlements, tripped over his shotgun. General melee was so bad that next morning, curious Indians came in to town to see what the row was about.

years. Frequently Churchill troops would be rushed to various towns to stop rumored plots and on at least one occasion the governor assumed personal command of a combined military-home guard force. Other than the occasional seditious loudmouth who found himself in the fort guardhouse or toting a sack of sand around the parade ground, the Southern threat came to naught. The state government, with the military at its right hand, had things under control.

TO GET THERE: From Reno, take U.S. 40 east to Alternate 95 toward Yerington. Eight miles south of its junction with U.S. 50 and Silver Springs, turn west on State 23. Fort site is now run-down and untended Nevada State Park at end of dirt road a short distance from the turn.

OFFICERS' QUARTERS drew criticism of Army board which felt two stories and $16,000 were too much. Six of these were built, only this one major ruin survives despite 1935 reconstruction of post by Civilian Conservation Corps under National Park Service supervision. Unaware of detailed historical and archaeological excavations conducted during reconstruction, souvenir and treasure hunters continue to probe ruins, accelerating deterioration.

EAST EDGE of parade ground included hospital, foreground, with storehouses and headquarters beyond. These were busy buildings, especially during period of 1865 Indian War when almost entire garrison was in field and three separate expeditions had to be supported. Soldiers suffered defeat when 65-man detail charged 500 Indians who were behind rock walls atop Table Mountain in northeastern Nevada. Indian aim was high and only two soldiers were killed, but they were unable to route hostiles in four hour exchange. Veterans claimed Indians had repeating rifles and that some white renegades were helping them. Later search of site located soldier bodies. Apparently one soldier was taken alive and tortured, shot in foot and torso and a fire kindled in his stomach; agony was so intense he had bitten off his tongue. Pursuing Army columns surprised one 200-man Indian camp, capturing 70 and scattering remainder. Twenty-five troopers chased chief's group until his horses collapsed and soldiers captured supplies but Indians escaped. A dawn attack on their new camp resulted in 11 dead, including chief. Other actions resulted in 26 more Indian deaths and war was about over when Lieutenant Colonel McDermit was shot from ambush by sniper. A final patrol three weeks later, lead by Captain Robert C. Payne, surprised an Indian camp inflicting an estimated 31 to 50 casualties. This same Payne after his discharge used his knowledge of territory to his advantage, gaining renown as a rustler.

SAMUEL BUCKLAND and his family are occupants of old fort cemetery. He was original owner of site, and successfully bid $750 for it when post was auctioned in 1870. During Army days, Buckland's trading post "one mile and one rod" from post provided refreshments and entertainment unavailable on military domain. Buckland also was participant in experimental use of camels by civilian entrepreneurs. In 1884, soldier graves were moved to Carson City and San Francisco, but only two could be identified. One was of Militia Major William Ormsby, killed in 1860 Pyramid Lake War, the other of most influential of Churchill commandants, Lieutenant Colonel Charles McDermit, killed by Indians in closing days of 1865 Indian War. Buckland family is buried in row along fence. Samuel Sanford Buckland, 58, died December 28, 1884, is commemorated by broken marker that once was erect at far left; his wife, 43 years old, is buried at upright marker. To its right are graves of two babies and three sons, 8, 2, and 1, an indication of high rate of infant mortality. Shaft is to 35-year old man and is dated 1876. Post ruins are in background; Carson River flows under row of trees.

CAMP DUN GLEN, NEVADA

"The soldiers have adopted the true method of Indian warfare. They neither wait for attacks nor hostile movements by them, but go and hunt them as men would wolves that prey on their stock."

In this fashion, the Owyhee, Idaho, *Avalanche* complimented Lt. Henry C. Penwell, 2d California Cavalry Volunteers, on his October 8, 1865, operation from Camp Dun Glen. It told how he and his troops had left this tiny outpost after a friendly Piute reported an Indian camp 25 miles to the south, "and slaughtered them all."

The Humbold *Register* of September 3 previously had described the exploits of another Penwell patrol from Dun Glen when he led 20 soldiers and some civilians in a surprise attack on a 10-man Indian camp. This was a period when all of Nevada was aroused by Indian looting and burning, and the *Register* could spare a few breezy phrases in its account of the bloody affair:

"The Pah-Ute guides led the party upon the camp at daybreak this morning," it recounted, "so cautiously that the entire gang was taken in, and ticketed for the happy hunting-grounds before they knew what was the matter. Seven bucks bit the dust, and one or two squaws were killed by accident."

Violence seemed to be the order of the day at just the time when the major bloodletting in the East had ceased. The Civil War demand for silver, could be answered in Nevada, Easterners learned, and the rush westward had continued to crowd the Indians from their homes and sources of food.

In 1865 the Indians struck back. In central Nevada, Army patrols found entire valleys abandoned by settlers and miners. Stories of massacres were common and, equally common, were stories of revenge by whites. In one incident in April, 1865, settlers attacked an Indian camp and "brought away with them 18 scalps as trophies of their work."

Almost in the middle of this holocaust sat the ranching settlement of Dun Glen, population 250. Founded in 1862, for a short time in 1863 it had quartered a detachment of Fort Churchill troops. But the soldiers were gone now. In March, 1865, the townspeople mustered all of their weapons, counted a total of only 19, and put in an immediate request: send the soldiers back.

"The general commanding deems that the best protection can be afforded by a movable body of mounted troops when the season is more advanced and the grass is grown," was the Army reaction about this time to Dun Glen's pleas. "No necessity exists for a permanent post."

By April 4, however, there must have been a change of heart.

"The citizens here desire me to express to you their thanks for having sent troops to their aid," wrote James A. Banks of Dun Glen to Fort Churchill. "The appearance and bearing of the soldiers are the subject of general commendation here."

Banks also noted that the work was ready for the soldiers as soon as they reported. "The troops you sent arrived here in good condition, and this morning started in search of a band of hostile Indians who three days ago stole a large number of stock,

DUN GLEN Canyon was described in 1881, "The hamlet is surrounded by high mountains, partially covered with stunted cedar trees, which furnish the wood of the settlement. It has a post-office called Dun Glen, but no telegraph or express office . . . Supplies are obtained . . . by way of Mill City, on the line of the Central Pacific Railroad, distant nine miles; freights being $9 per ton . . . The houses are mostly adobe and wood." Army camp was centered in vicinity of tall trees in background, but stone ruins and excavations dot entire length of canyon.

fired upon several men, wounding one man, and burned their house, at a point about 28 miles from this place."

Two days later, Indians shot a man 35 miles from Dun Glen and, it was reported, "set fire to the house, and as the men escaped and made for their horses they had their clothes cut with bullets, and one man had six bullets to through his overshirt; not hurt."

Camp Dun Glen was little more than a base camp for operations and its troops were on the move continually. In July a 65-man patrol scouted the entire area, taking off on various tangents after visible Indian trails but always coming across abandoned camps. Earlier, they had tried setting out an outpost 30 miles to the northeast to "scout night and day for the purpose of intercepting as well as punishing hostile Indians." Other than building themselves a camp of willows and bark and naming it Camp Overend after their lieutenant, the outpost accomplished little and was pulled back to Dun Glen.

In November, 1865, Dun Glen's detachment scored its most important victory. Once, again, needless cruelty had to mar the record.

By this time, the Piutes had decided to help the whites clean out the bad Indians, so that the destruction would end. A Piute chief, Captain Soo, agreed to take a Dun Glen patrol to the camp of Black Rock Tom, the leader of the year's depredations. After a 26-man detail under Penwell failed to dislodge Tom's forces from a mountain fortress, a patrol of 60 soldiers, four civilians, and 14 of Soo's men set out.

Within two miles of the hostile camp, the patrol leader's call pushed the men and their horses into a charge: "Come on boys, we can't go around, the best man will get there first!"

Although Tom and 10 cohorts escaped, 55 Indian bodies were counted after the fierce skirmish ended. Spotting a wounded squaw with a baby and a small child, a corporal told a private to take them to the camp. "It's a pity to leave her here to die and the little fellows to starve," he explained as he told a civilian to help.

A few minutes later the corporal heard several shots and the soldier rushed up to him, swearing. "That was a fine specimen you called to help me," he complained. "The damn bushwhacker shot the whole lot of them, babies and all, before I knew what he was up to."

Dun Glen's troops participated in one more hunt for Black Rock Tom and this time 40 braves were killed in a pre-dawn attack in deep snow. Tom escaped again, but finally gave himself up. While a prisoner, he was advised by some civilians that he was to be hanged and his only chance lay in escaping. He took advantage of the opportunity that conveniently made itself available and was shot dead in the attempt.

TO GET THERE: From Winnemucca, Nevada, take U.S. 40-95 south 28 miles to the few remaining buildings of Mill City. Turn left (east) onto the dirt road at the south edge of town. Follow this road, taking the left road at the fork in a half mile, and in six miles it runs into Dun Glen canyon. This is a narrow, sand-drifted track not recommended for the family car. Note: this is private property.

CAMP DUN GLEN was on this site in 1863 and 1865-66. Officers' quarters were under trees at left, commissary was in immediate foreground. Scattered rocks show some traces of locations, although historians would have difficulty in sorting Army buildings from those occupied by Dun Glen residents. Regular Army troops relieved Volunteers in 1866 when detachment of Company L, 1st Cavalry, was at Dun Glen. In 1867 citizens tried to get Army back, but officer scoffed at idea, said petitioners were either gamblers or merchants who wanted the military business. He said gamblers predominated, "I saw enough of this class in Dun Glen to exterminate all the Indians in Nevada." Both town and canyon were named after Scotsman, J. Angus Dun.

MOST PROMINENT ruins at Dun Glen are these double-deck remains of Essex Mill at mouth of Dun Glen canyon. Thompson and West's 1881 "History of the State of Nevada" described it as "one ten-stamp mill for extracting the gold from the quartz. The total amount of bullion so far is about $100,000. It is believed by many that thorough exploring would develop profitable mines." The 1908 gold boom saw some camp buildings torn down to provide material for new town of Chafey on same site and some went into high-sounding "Gold Mountain Hotel."

CONFEDERATE opponents had long quit New Mexico by the time Volunteers posed for this picture at 1864 Fort Sumner, N.M.

COLUMN FROM CALIFORNIA

"Men marching day after day through the burning sands and nearly suffocated with alkali dust required to be made of stern stuff—of such were the men composing this column. Men inured to mountain life in California, pioneers and miners; men self-reliant and enduring; men equal to any emergency, if guided by a firm hand and clear head. That they were equal to a great emergency is evinced by the fact that they conquered vast deserts, and accomplished a march not equaled in modern times, traversing a distance of nearly a thousand miles and almost the entire route over a sterile desert."

— Surgeon James McNulty's report on the California Column, 1863.

THE TEXTBOOKS ignore or hardly mention the feat of 2,350 men who marched across the wastes of desert from the Pacific to the Rio Grande in 1862, bringing with them a renewal of Federal authority and settling once and for all the matter of the Confederacy in the Southwest.

It was on December 9, 1861, that Brigadier General George Wright suggested to the War Department, "The proposition to recapture the forts in Arizona and New Mexico by a command to move from the southern district of this state." Nine days later, Major General George B. McClellan, a former soldier of the West who was then in command in Washington, D.C., approved the proposition with a single sentence: "If the movement in progress has not already been authorized, please do so at once."

James H. Carleton was placed in command of the project, "an officer of great experience, indefatigable and active," Wright commented. Wright did not include "meticulous" in his description, but he should have. Every fine point, from how to feed the animals to how to load the troops, from sending advance details to reconnoiter for Confederates to sending parties to clean out waterholes and to cache supplies, Carleton saw that every last bit of minutiae was resolved before the first soldier of the main body left the Pacific Coast.

His careful planning meant that the unit he termed the "Column from California" reached Arizona without a single casualty. It arrived in "rebel" territory fit to fight. And although it did not engage the Confederate force, the psychological effect of its arrival was sufficient to cause a Southern withdrawal deep into Texas.

Across Arizona they went. The entire First California Volunteer Infantry Regiment, five companies of the First California Cavalry, five companies of the Fifth California Infantry, a company of the Second California Cavalry, and a regular Army company from the Third Artillery moved eastward and reached the Rio Grande. Abandoned forts were touched, "the colors were put up . . . thus consecrating the ground anew to the country," and the Column established itself firmly in the territory between the Colorado and the Pecos.

After its sensational march, the affairs of the Column from California seemed almost anticlimatic. The rebels were gone in the main, but the Indian problems remained. It was to this matter that the men from the Pacific devoted themselves for the remainder of the Civil War. It was a task that was accomplished unsung in words, but appreciated in deed by the settlers to whom peace was brought by men of war.

DRUM BARRACKS, CALIFORNIA

Drum Barracks arrived on the military scene with a splash and hit its peak within its first few months. Everything that came after the rush of outfitting and dispatching the California Column was little more than anti-climactic.

No pun is intended by the reference to a splash at its founding, but this does describe its first days. A half mile from the port of New San Pedro—today merely one of many areas within the Los Angeles complex—the post first was "on a low, flat plain. . . sandy," described one occupant who added that the sand supposedly "mixes into mud after the rains begin to fall, until the roads are nearly or quite impassable."

When the post was moved to higher ground a mile from the town, the rains came and the place became a veritable island. Rain had prevented movement inland and "for nearly a whole week it was impossible to send an empty wagon one mile from camp, much less to bring in any loaded team," the post commander reported. "At the same time communication by water was entirely cut off."

Drum was located on property presented to the United States by Phineas T. Banning for $1. Banning was the guiding spirit of New San Pedro and he knew a good thing when he saw it. As the Army Inspector noted in 1866, Banning was "doing his

'level best' . . . and it was a big 'best' . . . to build up a nascent city . . . He was an enterprising Delawarean . . . wide awake and keen for business; had come to California a common stage-driver; but now ran stages and freight-wagons of his own over southern California and Arizona, for eight hundred and a thousand miles . . . was now state senator on the Republican side and talked of for governor . . ."

Banning seemed to have many fingers in the Army business at Drum. When it was noted that steamers could not tie up at piers in New San Pedro harbor because there were no piers, Banning installed himself in the lighterage business. His tugs and barges willingly ferried troops and supplies ashore at rates at least he felt were fair.

And when the post ran short of water, Banning enthusiastically acquired a right-of-way for a series of ditches and flumes to bring water 12 miles from the San Gabriel river. He provided 100,000 feet of lumber but the Army supplied 200 soldiers to do the work. After the Army took the water it needed, the remainder went to the town and, coincidentally enough, to irrigate barley fields owned by the same Banning.

Regardless of any machinations that were alluded to in reports, Banning drew the praise of the 1866 inspector. "A man of large and liberal ideas, with great native force of character and power of endurance, he was invaluable to Southern California and Arizona, and both of these sections owe him a debt of gratitude, which they can never repay," was the verdict.

The large and liberal business apparently entered into the Drum construction plans. An estimated million dollars were spent on the post, prompting General H. W. Halleck, in his 1865 report to describe it as "a very large and expensive depot and barracks." He complained, "I can perceive no good

DRUM BARRACKS
CALIF.—1871

DRUM'S DESIGNATION had its growing pains. Originally "Camp San Pedro," it was changed to Camp Drum to honor departmental adjutant. On May 21, 1863, commander recommended to that officer that post be redesignated "Fort Drum" to "better express the honor intended to the individual after whom it was named . . . it being a permanent post with barracks, quarters, magazine, depot, etc." After recommendation was repeated in September, question was settled by order of November 25, 1863: "From and after December 1, 1863, the official designation of Camp Drum, these headquarters, will be Drum Barracks." At this time, Drum Barracks included "quarters for officers and men of five companies, a commanding officer's quarters, hospital, cavalry stables, a stone magazine, ordnance store-house, brick bakery, guardhouse, stables, and offices" and was headquarters for District of Southern California. Post was surrounded by picket fence, 1,638 by 1,480 feet. (Redrawn from plat in National Archives.)

CAMELS CAME to Camp Drum as almost final chapter in pre-Civil War experiment. In 1863, Major Clarence E. Bennett, post commander, complained, "They had been kept at this post a long time on forage when in San Bernardino and various places within 100 miles of here they could have been subsisted without the expenditure of one cent for forage." He recommended the 36 camels at Drum be tested for service across Mojave Desert and be shipped to Fort Mojave because almost all grass at Drum was gone "and in little time the plains for miles and miles here will be perfectly bare." He advised they be carefully trained and tended by "an energetic officer whose conduct was characterized by sobriety and integrity." He blamed failure of previous camel use on fact government employees "regard service with camels extremely unpleasant." He said, "In appearance camels are extremely ugly, in gait very rough, in herding inclined to wander, and with their long strides they make haste slowly, keeping their herders on the go; they offer no facilities for stealing." The idea was not approved and camels were auctioned off at Benicia Depot the next year. Although this picture is identified officially as Drum Barracks, buildings resemble quartermaster and commissary storehouses at Wilmington Depot.

reason for the enormous expenses which have been incurred at that place."

When General Carleton was at Drum, extravagant construction was the least of his thoughts. He was devoting every minute, sheet of paper, and jar of ink to insuring that his California Column went forth promptly and in good order.

He issued detailed instructions for the amount of baggage his officers could take, setting a maximum of 80 pounds per company officer and prohibiting "mess-chests, or trunks, or mattresses on the march." He directed that each company would be allowed only two wagons for all of its equipment and, once loaded, "the weight of wagon will be in-

PROVIDING supply and storage facilities for Drum Barracks was Wilmington Depot, a mile away, a single block wide and two long bordered by C, Front, and Canal Streets. All buildings were frame. Two storerooms were 80 by 40 feet each, capable of holding a year's supplies for four companies. Wagon shed was 536 feet long, 15 wide, and included sadler's shop, harness room, and miscellaneous storage rooms. Barn was 270 by 70 feet, 16 feet high ceiling from floor that was five feet above ground; it could store 1,600,000 pounds of hay. In 1862, inspector complained of damp ground at depot, adding "The new buildings used for storehouses are admirably adapted for this purpose . . . I think they are raised sufficiently high to prevent any injurious effects." Site of depot was provided by Phineas Banning, donor of Drum site. (Redrawn from plat in Colonel Fred B. Rogers Collection.)

creased to 3,000 pounds by adding barley as forage for the mules."

His soldiers received a check list of what they should bring. Each was to wear the "uniform hat without trimmings," a blouse, pair of trousers, pair of stockings, woolen shirt, pair of drawers, and "a cravat in lieu of the leather stock." In his knapsack he was to pack a greatcoat, blanket, forage cap, woolen shirt, pair of drawers, pair of stockings, towel, two handkerchiefs, "one fine and one coarse

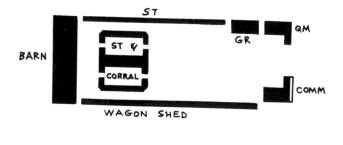

WILMINGTON DEPOT
CALIF. – 1871

LAST REMINDER of Drum Barracks is this former officers' quarters, now used as apartment house. It was a duplex, has 16 rooms each measuring 18 by 20 feet with 14 foot ceilings, and included four fireplaces and mahogany balustrades and two long stairways. All permanent buildings at post were elaborately constructed. "We were astonished to find Drum Barracks one of the finest we had ever seen," commented one California Volunteer. "Some of the men in our company who had seen service in the East said that they had never seen anything like it."

comb, one sewing kit, one piece of soap, one toothbrush," one fork, spoon, and plate. In addition, each was to have a canteen, haversack, tin cup and "wear a good sheath knife."

The reaction of one infantryman to this 50-pound load is quoted by Aurora Hunt in her book on Carleton: "I have often heard the groans of the heavily loaded pack mules moving past on their way to the mountains," he said, "but never did I sympathize with them until I threw the burden off my back and rolled in the desert sand after a 20-mile march."

Even as he rolled his maps and squared his "uniform hat without trimmings" to move out of Drum on April 13, 1862, Carleton penned parting instructions to the detail left behind. They were told not to spend a cent of public funds without Carleton's approval. "There are many teams here fitting up for the expedition," he added. "These are to be prepared in the most perfect manner possible for the service required of them."

And from Camp Wright, 120 miles away, Carleton sent a final word of advice for the troops to follow, plus a request:

"Have the troops walk at least half the time, and have at least two hours' halt to graze midday each day's march. The soldiers must be drilled at the saber exercise on horseback while marching at least an hour each day. The horses must be kept fresh and in good condition, even though the men walk most of the way. Please get from Mr. Banning two of Captain Moore's umbrellas and bring them on."

Umbrellas or not, military detachments were dispatched from Drum throughout the Civil War for the fighting posts inland. Even on the day that Lee surrendered at Appomattox, a unit of the Seventh California Volunteer Infantry left Drum for a year-long tour in Arizona.

TO GET THERE: From downtown Los Angeles, take San Diego Freeway (Interstate 405) south to U.S. 6 (Harbor Freeway). Take this south to Pacfiic Coast Highway (U.S. 6 and Alternate 101). In about two miles, Banning Park is on right, between Broad and Eubank Avenues. Banning mansion can be seen from highway. Only remaining Army building, former officers' quarters, is privately owned at 1053 Cary Avenue. This can be reached by going around park via Eubank Avenue and picking up Cary where it deadends at park opposite Banning house. Go further south on Cary two blocks to 1053, right side of street.

BANNING MANSION is memorial museum to original owner of barracks site. After Civil War, post activity dwindled though in 1866 Army inspector reported vicinity included "perhaps 500 inhabitants, more or less in his service, or employed at Drum Barracks." By 1869, post had permanent detail of only 20 men and, surgeon commented, it "is now in poor repair and the flume valueless, the water supply being carted daily from the wells at Wilmington. The buildings are seldom occupied and troops passing in transit to or from Arizona usually go into camp somewhere in the vicinity." Tiny garrison was used for "guard and fatigue duties, but is too weak to be able to keep the post in good repair." In 1873, Congress passed bill returning site to Banning and Wilson, his partner, and they bought most of the buildings at auction that netted government $6,357 for its $1,000,000 investment. The 16-room officers' quarters cost Banning $1,025; the 6,220 feet of picket fencing, $76. Mansion, Banning's home, stands at edge of former military post in center of Banning Park.

FORT YUMA, CALIFORNIA

"If necessary, defend your post to the last extremity, then if you are obliged to give way, which is not at all probable, destroy it and fight your way across the desert . . . Keep all of the time on the *qui vive*, yet do not be stampeded. You can whip any force that will menace you, having, as you have, command of the river."

The orders were to the point. It was 1862, rumors were out that 1,000 rebels were gathering at Tucson for a march on Fort Yuma, and the fort was to be held. "Surrounded as it is by a vast desert, if once in the possession of any enemy the key to the state is lost," was how one officer assessed the importance of the place.

A year earlier, the Sixth U.S. Infantry at the fort had been told, "the general considers that your command will be sufficiently strong to resist successfully any attack that may be made. At all events, under no circumstances whatever will any regular force in this military department surrender to the rebels."

In its location at the southeasternmost corner of California, Fort Yuma's importance was recognized even before its site was in the Union. Spanish priests had established missions atop its flat mesa, only to lose their lives and their converts in an Indian massacre in 1781. Early emigrants had built a pioneer fort nearby, naming it "Fort Defiance" to indicate their attitude to the hostile Indians.

An estimated 60,000 emigrants crossed the Colorado at the site in 1851—a figure that Bancroft, the historian, suggests might be overestimated. To care for "worn out and hungry gold seekers . . . emigrants, and the various bands of Indians," in 1849 the Army set up Camp Calhoun at the location of the ill-fated mission. In 1850 the post was shifted to the Colorado river ferry crossing not far away, renamed Camp Independence, and an assemblage of thatched huts made to answer for quarters, kitchens, guardhouse, and hospital.

This was too near the scene of Indian raids on the ferry, and to emigrant charges of exorbitant rates by the ferry keepers. A year later the Army returned to the Calhoun site and adopted a new name, after the Yuma Indians in the area.

Camp Yuma was marked for failure early in the game when the food supply was reduced to one barrel of flour. While the bulk of the garrison had gone to the coast for provisions, several hundred Indians surrounded the camp and put it under siege. The nine-man garrison held out for more than a month. Word that a relief column had been attacked and turned back was the final blow, and the scurvy-weakened soldiers cached the government property and abandoned the post.

Two months later, 150 troopers defeated a 300-man hostile band and re-established the post. They found that everything at the camp had been burned by the Indians. The hidden property had been dug up too.

When the Bartlett Boundary Commission arrived at the Colorado the next year, they were pleased to see that the Army was in possession. "We . . . pushed on towards Fort Yuma," Bartlett wrote in his report, "which appeared a few miles in advance, the stars and stripes waving from the flag-staff first greeting our eyes through the dense foliage of the valley."

CIVIL WAR redoubts still were visible in later years, but surgeon in 1869 doubted their value. "That which entitles Yuma to the designation of fort are certain unpretentious intrenchments scattered along the slopes of the bluff, which command the river and the bottom-lands adjacent," he wrote. "They are not visible from the river, and the spectator is not aware of their existence until he steps to the edge of the bluff and looks down upon their gabion revetments. They were constructed for barbette guns, but are now dismantled." In 1862, departmental inspector had this to say: "The tracing of the works is, to speak critically, defective, but when you recollect that the whole was executed by officers who had no previous experience and no military works to refer to, it is altogether one of the most creditable undertakings and executed in a manner worthy of commendation." Redoubts never were tested because, Yuma's war role became that of a supply and personnel depot. After the war, its small garrison provided security for supply depot and occasionally fielded patrols against marauding Indians. It was given up by Army in 1885. (Redrawn from Surgeon-General Circular No. 4, 1870.)

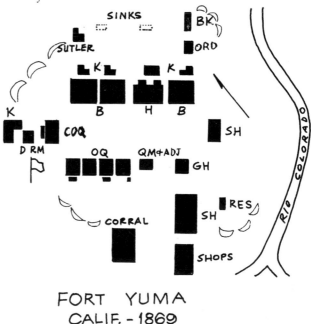

FORT YUMA
CALIF. - 1869

"FORT YUMA is popularly believed to be in Arizona, but is in reality in the extreme southeastern corner of California," wrote General James T. Rusling of an 1866 visit. "The fort itself stands on a high bluff, on the west bank of the Rio Colorado, which alone separates it from Arizona, and is usually occupied by two or three companies of U.S. troops." He added that opposite was Arizona City, "a straggling collection of adobe houses." "Here and at Yuma are located the government store-houses, shops, corrals, etc., as the grand depot for all the posts in Arizona. Hence, considerable business centers here; but it is chiefly of a military nature, and if the post and depot were removed, the 'City' as such would speedily subside into its original sand-hills." Arizona City became modern Yuma, Arizona. This view is from Arizona side. Commanding officer's quarters are at left with back walls of officers' quarters along center of mesa top, then guardhouse and storehouse.

He commented that the ruins of the old mission still were in evidence, though many of the walls had been removed and were used in building barracks at the fort. "The officers and men were living in tents, covered with sheds made of branches to protect them from the sun," he said. "The command was as comfortably situated as the nature of the place and its inaccessibility would allow; but long deprivation of fresh provisions and vegetables had

engendered the scurvy among the soldiers."

Bartlett noted that a few weeks before his visit, an entire patrol of eight soldiers had been clubbed to death by the Yumas. This caused the post commander to drive "them all from the banks of the Colorado for some eighty miles above, destroying their corn fields and their villages. They had been so cruel and treacherous to the various parties of Americans passing here, and had manifested so

FORT YUMA today resembles early appearance from across Colorado. This view was taken from Territorial Prison and presents slightly different angle than old picture. Rear view of former officers' quarters can be seen, although trees have been added to area. In 1870, surgeon said, "Shade trees are an impossibility, and grassed surfaces unknown." He described post as "a collection of substantial adobe houses, inclosed by deep verandas with venetian blinds, which shut out every direct ray of sunlight and exhibits an air of privacy unsurpassed by the surroundings of a Mormon harem." In 1861, General A. S. Johnson passed fort en route to join Confederacy, wrote of hearing gun salute in honor of July 4. His men were spotted by fort soldier who said he and others wanted to desert "and then seize the place and plunder it," Johnson's companion recorded. "But for the general's coolness on that occasion, we would in all likelihood have left Fort Yuma behind us a heap of smoking ruins. He objected to the procedure, on the ground that we were not in commission, and that an attack would be equivalent to piracy at sea."

GUARDHOUSE is now Indian Agency headquarters, but 4 by 8 foot solitary confinement cells supposedly are still beneath building. Tradition has it that tunnel once ran from here to Territorial Prison across river—but doesn't explain how it got under river. During Civil War, Fort Yuma guardhouse housed numerous political prisoners, including Sylvester Mowry, Arizona mine owner who was arrested because of secessionist actions. He had been lieutenant at Fort Yuma in 1850's and once served with Carleton. Later he accused Carleton of causing the arrest over past jealousies and in order to confiscate Mowry mine for personal profit. After four months in guardhouse, he was released and sued Carleton for more than million dollars. Senate investigation came to no conclusion and case died.

much hostility towards the troops, that it was found useless to attempt to conciliate them, or make any treaty with them unless they themselves were forced to come in and ask it."

Even while he was at the post, Bartlett found that the Yumas were on the watch. One morning he was told by the commanding officer, "From the peculiar barking of the dogs during the night, he believed the Indians had been near the fort." Herdsmen reported footprints in the bottomland below the place and signal fires during the night.

It was about this time that the famed "Oatman Massacre" took place. The Indians had killed Royce Oatman, his wife, and four of his seven children. A 14-year old son escaped to tell how the savages had kidnapped his two sisters, Olive, 16, and Mary Ann, 10. The Bartlett party came across the site 100 miles from Yuma, noting "numerous fragments of

NOT ONLY did some officers of California Column believe that fraud was involved in Yuma's supply dealings and "the officers at that post . . . are too much engaged (or at least the majority of them) consuming whiskey," but it was felt wasteful to land supplies by boat on the California side of the Colorado and ferry them across to Arizona. When a flood in 1864 damaged fort buildings and left it virtually an island, a supply depot was built across the river. It became principal forwarding depot up Colorado River and was important quartering place for mules, sometimes boasting upwards of a 900-mule population. Fire destroyed it in 1867, but it was quickly rebuilt. Large storehouse was 121 by 103 by 14 feet and corral was 146 by 216 feet. Adobe was principal building material. (Redrawn from McDowell 1879 report.)

trunks, boxes, clothing, wagons, with human bones and skulls" despite earlier attempts to cover the bodies with stones.

Five years later, a Fort Yuma carpenter, Henry Grinnell, suspected a friendly Indian knew something about the whereabouts of the missing girls. He pretended to read from a newspaper article that a large army was enroute to Yuma to rescue the girls and annihilate the guilty tribes. He noted that the Indian was impressed.

Twenty days later, having been given blankets and beads which he said he would need for bartering, the Indian returned to the post with Olive Oatman. While an officer's wife hurriedly loaned her a dress to cover a scanty Indian wardrobe, Olive explained that her younger sister had died.

Further details had to wait until the noise died down of the cannon fired in celebration of her rescue.

By 1858, a soldier was able to write home, "The houses and quarters are built of sun-dried bricks and with every effort and provision for making the summer's heat bearable for white inhabitants. Still though the post is but seven years old and is garrisoned by only two companies, a well-filled graveyard gives mute testimony of a most unhealthful climate for other than natives." He noted that in the summer it was so hot the soldiers had no duties, "even the sentries pace up and down under a roof built for that purpose."

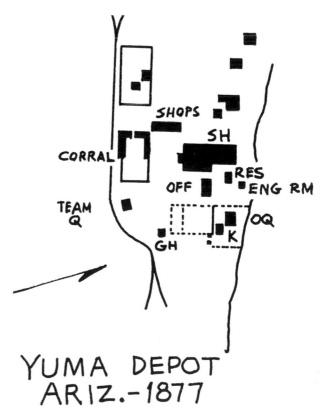

YUMA DEPOT
ARIZ.—1877

By Army traditions, Fort Yuma was the hottest post in the country. The surgeon once reported that his watch "felt like a hot boiled egg in my pocket," and the parade ground was so hot that—though he could not personally vouch for the story—a dog would run "on three legs across it, barking with pain at every step."

And, of course, every recital of Fort Yuma must include General George C. Thomas' anecdote of the veteran who in death had found hell so cool after the Yuma heat, that he returned to the barracks to requisition a few blankets as protection against the devilish chill.

Thomas was commander at Yuma in the '50's. In his *Memoirs*, the place is described as "one of the most disagreeable posts garrisoned by the Army . . . The hills around the garrison seemed to concentrate the excessive heat of the summer on the parade ground, and it was not an unusual circumstance to have . . . 116 degrees in the shade." Sleep before midnight was impossible "and then only on the rooftops."

When Thomas received orders to Texas in 1855, he "left Fort Yuma for the States without any delay whatever." In 1869, a major general, he made a quick stop at Yuma simply so he could revel in the fact he "would never again be compelled to become a permanent part of the garrison at that point."

Despite the secessionist danger in July, 1861, Yuma's commander warned against sending reinforcements "to the post during the present or next month . . . where the heat is excessive and exceedingly debilitating, and the supplies of water scanty and generally bad." A daily temperature greater than 108 degrees had been recorded for the past month, he added.

Regardless, the troops came. Rumors that the garrison was disloyal with a large number of soldiers who "will turn upon their officers the moment the attack is made," were added to tales that 250 secessionists were planning to take the fort. Although the authorities put little credence in the reports, they recognized the strategic location of the post and rushed reinforcements.

Within a few months, four companies and several cannon had been added to the camp. California Volunteers relieved the regular troops in 1811 and were ordered to examine every person who tried to pass the post. "All the crossing of the river must be done at one point under the guns of the fort," they were directed, and the oath of allegiance was to be required of any suspicious persons.

The appearance of a fortress was attempted and the troopers got out shovels. "I am throwing up one work 350 feet—faces on a low hill west of and adjoining the fort—and three smaller ones at different points," Lieutenant Colonel Joseph R. West described. "This gives us plenty of work. Also drilling all spare time, and artillery detachment at it continually. As Mose says, I shall 'spile' for a fight in about a week."

Reports came that Confederate pickets were within 50 miles of Fort Yuma. Civilians were employed as spies to locate them. West wrote at least one report to Carleton in Greek to baffle intercepters. He suggested that he could get the Indians to help, too, if he had $1,000 worth of blankets and leaf tobacco for presents to the principal chiefs.

Carleton arrived at Fort Yuma on May 1, 1862. He stayed long enough to gather his supplies and to admonish his men, "Have your sabers very sharp that they might readily cut through clothing . . . the cold steel will win against the pistol."

In two weeks, Carleton felt everything was ready. He led his troops across the Colorado and, in the words of one of his officers, "Crossed the Rubicon and emerged into the great field of labor" from which there was no "return without glory or disgrace."

FORMER HOSPITAL has been covered with wood exterior and double roofing is obvious. Verandas surrounded most buildings so that passage was possible from building to building without going into sun. Hospital was busy, despite overall good health at post, partly because of diseases prevalent in area. When whites came, as a private in 1858 wrote, some Indians began to earn living by begging "and by the profits of an infamous trafficking in their wives and daughters . . . I fail to see that civilization has profited them anything." General Rusling observed, "All seem corrupted and depraved by contact with the nobler white race. Then open and unblushing looseness and licentiousness of the riff-raff of Arizona City, with these poor Indians, was simply disgusting, and it is a disgrace to a Christian government to tolerate such orgies, as frequently occur there, under the very shadow of its flag." He put some of the blame on Army's earlier permitting of Indians to enter post. Official report in 1861 said there were no local diseases, "except such as arise from bad whiskey and diseased women."

TO GET THERE: Fort Yuma is on the California side of the Colorado River, overlooking the bridge of U.S. 80. It can be seen north of the bridge and can be approached through side roads across the bottom land after crossing the bridge. Site is now Fort Yuma Reservation and permission to visit should be requested from the tribal council at the fort.

FORT LOWELL AND TUCSON, ARIZONA

If the Column from California had known the real number of Confederates at Tucson, Carleton probably would have detached a flying company of cavalry, rushed the town, and taken it with ease.

But Tucson was rumored to have somewhere around 1,000 well-armed rebels entrenched behind its 150-year old walls. With that kind of opposition, Californians, or not, could see the dangers of rash moves.

Tucson had an early reputation as a military site. Early, is understating it, because some Tucsonites insist that their history goes back to 1555—antedating any other U.S. city. The military came about 1776 when 75 Spaniards established a Presidio within walls that missionaries had built in earlier days.

The Spanish military served to pacify the nearby tribes to a certain extent—usually by feeding and clothing them, teaching "them to drink intoxicating liquors, and to depend as much as possible on Spanish friendship for the gratification of their needs," a viceroy's order of 1786 proclaimed.

Laxity and what the historians term "official peculiations" weakened the Presidio's power and in 1828 the last troops were withdrawn. Mexican soldiers later garrisoned the walled town until General Philip St. George Cooke's Mormon Battalion came into sight in 1846. After Cooke rejected several attempts by the defenders to negotiate a surrender, the Mexicans hastily departed, taking with them 400 of the 500 citizens, and two brass cannon.

The Americans did not mourn the loss of either citizens or cannon, especially since the latter probably would have been greater threats to the gunners than the targets. They raised the Stars and Stripes about where Washington Street and Church Avenue intersect today. Then they confiscated all of the wheat they could find in the dilapidated fort. After noting with disgust the collapsing barracks

and crumbling walls of the town, they set up camp a half mile away.

For the next ten years, the Army apparently preferred field conditions to the conditions in town. As a Dragoon captain, Richard S. Ewell—later a Confederate general—was stationed in 1856 at what he listed as "Camp near Tucson, New Mexico." His main occupations here seem to have been patrolling for Indians, lobbying for funds to build a post, and trying his hand at animal husbandry.

In these he had varying success. In 1857 he went to Santa Fe "to try to get some money for our post" and was kept there two months "to await the arrival of money from the States." While he was in Sante Fe, he was dismayed to hear "the Indians have run off some 25 or 30 cows that I had near Tucson."

There were few, if any, Yankee troops around Tucson in 1861 when a Confederate constitutional convention was held there, a Confederate governor elected, and all of Arizona south of the 34th parallel declared no longer part of "the late United States." Colonel John Baylor and his Texas Volunteers held the military authority in the area until he fed some Indians poisoned flour, killed around 50, and was summarily relieved by President Davis.

Confederate troops took over Tucson in February, 1862. Despite rumors of greater numbers, interviews placed in the official records say: "The whole number of said detachment, including employees, did not exceed 105 men . . . three wagons . . . no artillery . . . the men were all mounted and well armed."

Thirty of the force were withdrawn when it was seen that all Unionists had departed and, according to Captain Sherod Hunter, the Confederate commander, "My timely arrival with my command was hailed by a majority, I may say the entire population, of the town of Tucson."

WHEN CALIFORNIA Column arrived in Tucson, they found town surrounded by 5-foot high adobe wall, supposedly the only walled city in United States. Originally Spanish Presidio, it had been used as fort by Mexicans, had lookout towers at each corner. Northeast corner was where U.S. flag was raised in 1846; California Column raised flag in front of "little fort" about where Pearl Street is today. Main enclosure had only two doors, both of heavy timber, which were closed at night. Mexican fort underwent at least two Apache attacks. One took place when they knew garrison and many civilians were away, but friendly Pima Indians counterattacked and drove Apaches off. Second attempt was spotted by alert sentry and defenders' muskets were successful against bows and arrows of Apaches. California Column and its supply depot occupied this area during Civil War. (Redrawn from Farish, *History of Arizona,* vol. 1.)

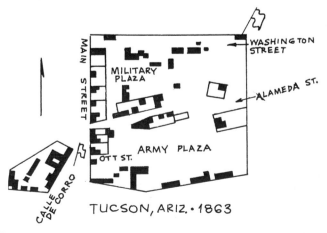

TUCSON, ARIZ. • 1863

BARRACKS were criticized in 1890 as old and in constant need of repairs. Climate was considered hot and disagreeable, and site unsuitable for permanent use. When post was to be abandoned, citizens realized they would lose estimated $65,000 annual payroll and attempted unsuccessful letter campaign to forestall closing. Attitude was different than in early days when fort was moved away from town because, official report said, "the proximity and attractions of gambling halls, saloons and other resorts of the early days are altogether too diverting for the welfare of the soldiers." Despite town's reputation, post surgeon in 1869, commented, "Veneral diseases have been rarely seen, although the dance-houses of the town are the chief resorts of soldiers on pass." One unusual encounter of Lowell troopers was in 1877 when 70 horses were being brought to fort for Apache expedition. Near Gila Bend, some camels—offspring of pre-Civil War experiment—appeared suddenly, stampeding horses into 50 mile run.

Hunter's 75-man force did not seem to over exert themselves. "His company was not drilled or disciplined during its stay in Tucson," said a citizen in a sworn statement later. "The horses of the said company were kept in the corral of the Overland Mail Company . . . the men . . . slept each where he liked, in any part of the town he chose, as a general thing . . ."

Hunter's company placed pickets along likely routes into Tucson and one of these skirmished with a California Column detachment on April 15, 1862. In what Arizonans term "The Battle of Picacho Pass," three Union and two Confederates were killed, and three Confederates captured. One Northerner was saved from death when the brass insignia on his hat deflected a bullet and left him with only an ugly scar.

After burying their dead "side by side, a few paces from where they fell," the Union detail pulled back. Fifty-six years later, in 1928, a railroader accidently discovered the graves. A marker now marks the final resting place for the dead of Arizona's only Civil War "battle."

Tucson returned to the Union on May 20, 1862, when Captain Emil Fritz, Company B, 1st California Cavalry, "dashed through the town at full speed and in five minutes had it surrounded," described a California Volunteer. They found that Hunter and his troops had left for New Mexico, taking along secessionist sympathizers who were, as a Volunteer put it, "That portion of the community, which could be best spared . . . and will be sure not to come back unless forced to."

The Army went into a tent camp at the Military

Plaza, about where the Santa Rita Hotel now stands. They found that prices were high for the few supplies available and that the absence of sutlers on the march had left everyone short of such items as soap, tobacco, and similar items.

Carleton proclaimed martial law. He required the oath of allegiance of all men, promised punishment for disloyal acts or words, and expelled from the territory any man "who does not pursue some lawful calling or have some legitimate means of support." He promised to serve the good of the people "so that when a man does have his throat cut, or his house robbed, or his field ravaged, he may at least have the consolation of knowing that there is some law that will reach him who does the injury."

Later the matter of vagrants was expanded to include beggars, confirmed drunkards, those who failed to maintain their families, and all who were in the habit "of loitering or sleeping in grogshops, beershops, outhouses, market sheds, stables, granaries, or unoccupied houses . . ."

Carleton was concerned more with outfitting his forces for the Rio Grande advance. "Clothing must be repaired as far as possible, arms, accouterments, and ammunition examined as to their condition, and all the camp and garrison equipage of each company must be out in complete order for the march," said General Order No. 17 on July 13. Ten days later they were on their way.

Left behind were the soldiers for the permanent Post and Depot of Tucson. Their job was to keep the area secure from invasion and to forward supplies to the Column and the forts that were to be established.

This turned out to be no small job. Indian activity frequently required the Tucson detachment to turn out almost to a man to keep peace in Southeastern Arizona. "My command is now very small, scarcely sufficient for garrison duty and to furnish necessary escorts," complained the post commander by the end of the year. He added that the Apache raids were so numerous and pursuit so difficult that sometimes "I could do nothing but bite my lips and let them go." In one incident, Indians stole two horses, complete with saddles and carbines from the quarters of none other than Captain Fritz, the rider who spearheaded the dramatic return to Tucson.

Amidst these troubles, Tucson found itself being accused of under-handed supply methods. It was described as "the sink that swallows up everything intended to come to the front."

In later years, one Tucson resident boasted of

FORT WAS in nearly final days when children posed in front of captain's quarters in 1889. By this time post had its history behind it: participation in Crook's and Miles' wars with Apaches; bandit hunting for renegado "Apache Kid;" and more trouble from townspeople who found fault with cavalry practice of racing mounts between city and fort, creating a "speedway" on one road. Modern Tucson still remembers this: road bears official name of Speedway Boulevard.

besting the government 10 times out of 10 in selling barley. As the quartermaster scales were set up in the plaza, 10 different times the consciousless settler presented wagon loads of barley to be weighed, collected his money, and drove the wagon in the direction of the corral for delivery. Except for one thing: he did not go to the corral, but went around the block and returned each time to re-weigh and re-sell the same wagonload. It worked so successfully, he said, that after the tenth time it seemed a shame to give the barley to the Army so he did not.

In fact, because the barley was only borrowed for the occasion, he returned it to its rightful owner and disappeared in the direction of the Mexican border!

At the time Carleton had instituted a system for taxes on businesses, saloons, and gambling parlors in order to support his hospital fund. One gambling saloon owner later claimed that one of Carleton's officers offered to grant him exclusive rights to the business for $500. He also had to promise never to serve drunken soldiers. As a political step, he set up a back room for the officers and provided them the best of his wares.

Suddenly, an officer was ordered to Tucson to "institute a thorough and searching investigation into the management of the affairs . . ." and, of the commanding officer, "a rigid investigation into the personal and official conduct."

Despite a furor, the investigation was fruitless and the commander reinstated. The routine returned to requests for at least a company of cavalry

BY CHRISTMAS, 1873, barracks at Fort Lowell were completed. On Sunday, December 22, General Carr and two officers' wives raised the flag, a 38-gun salute was fired, equal the number of states in the Union, and Star Spangled Banner played. Post was quarter mile long parallelogram described by *Arizona Weekly Star:* It "included a number of officers' quarters on the west lines built on a fine avenue shaded with cottonwood. On the east, men's quarters, mess room, stables, etc., while at either end were built the hospital rooms, sutlers store, quartermasters and adjutant quarters, including a roomy court-martial office . . . It is the supply or distribution point for all of Southern Arizona including the paymaster's quarters; is convenient to the coming railroad, healthfully located, and needs a sawmill and force to run it for a year or so to do up the camp as it really requires. There are now there about 100 men but it was built for 300."

to be stationed at Tucson, "loud mouthed complaints" about a ration of nothing but fresh beef, and the continual patrolling. An 1863 expedition of 25 troopers, 42 civilians, and 30 Indians marched five days, traveled only at night, lit no fires, and surprised an Apache rancheria. They lost one civilian and claimed to have killed 50 Apaches and wounded the same number. They brought back 10 prisoners and 66 cattle.

The California Volunteers stayed in Tucson when the war ended—20 were buried there, 13 in graves marked "unknown"—and an 1866 inspection was to find things still in need of improvement. Es-

corts still went on all wagons going to the east, draining 30 men from the 83-man detachment.

At the time the post was in the center of town, to which it had returned after two years on the outskirts. It consisted of three houses that had been confiscated and 10 buildings which were rented. Rent ran almost $300 a month. Added to the $184,942.31 debt already piled up, the inspector suggested, "The expenses of this post are quite high . . . at an early day the men should commence the construction of quarters, of the same material as those at the other posts, that is of adobe, at little or no additional expense."

The troopers weathered out the makeshift camp, even an 1870 incident when 20 of them overimbibed and let off spirits so wildly that even raucous Tucson was aroused.

The post had the Lowell name by this time, but only one permanent building, an adobe guardhouse. It must have been busy because in 1873, when General Eugene A. Carr was ordered to build a permanent post, the governor accompanied him on his searches for a site. "He wants it in a place not too near the town of Tucson, as do I," Carr wrote his wife, explaining that he wanted to insure a location that provided "distance from the temptations of town." He found the spot seven miles east of Tucson and here built an adobe post that served Tucson and the Indian Wars until 1891.

TO GET THERE: Downtown site of Army post is Santa Rita hotel. Original Presidio was bounded by modern streets of Washington, Main, Pennington, and Church. To get to Fort Lowell ruins, take Broadway from downtown east 55 blocks to Craycroft Road. Turn left (north), go 30 blocks to Fort Lowell Park, right side. Visitor's center, picnic facilities, parking lot are available to visitors of fort ruins.

THIS ADOBE post had taken shape by 1881, mainly through efforts of soldiers. Blistering 120 degree heat and need for constant patrolling against Indians, prompted 5th Cavalry Commander Carr to appeal to headquarters for funds "to relieve the soldiers to a great extent, from the labor of building. As it is, what with the necessary guards, fatigues, gardners, and detachments, and the work on the quarters: the soldiers are kept constantly busy, at work, or on military duty, an average of 10 to 12 hours daily and often more, besides having to keep their areas in order, and to be always ready to fight." The appeal did no good, but by fall post began to take shape. Then when orders were received to stop work on barracks and build storehouses instead, Carr remonstrated: "I thought that I had reason to suppose that I was ordered here to build the shelters for troops at this camp. It seems to me, nothing more than is required by humanity and justice to the troops then to build first the Hospital and the Company Shelters." Priority was shifted to barracks building. (Redrawn from plat courtesy Jack Redmond, Tucson Chamber of Commerce.)

FORT LOWELL
ARIZ. - 1881

DEPOT RIO GILA & FORT WEST, N.M.

"Originating in the bombastic folly of a silly old man already in his dotage, and thus far conducted with a degree of stupidity almost asinine," was the caustic fashion in which Lieutenant Henry M. Lazelle described the start of the Gila Expedition of 1857.

"Our slow motioned and heavily laden Infantry, toilsomely dragging its lengthy and sluggish columns over the burning plains, its troops choking with dust finer than ashes, and its animals suffocating, and dying under their heavy burdens from want of water," Lazelle continued.

It was into the mountains of southwestern New Mexico, and its neighboring areas of Arizona, that Colonel William Bonneville led his two-pronged column. The objective was to punish the Apache murders of an Indian agent.

In his fortieth year of Army service, and 20 years past the apex of his career when he was an explorer, Bonneville commanded his forces from an ambulance. Even Captain Richard S. Ewell—later the Confederate general—had unenthusiastic words for Bonneville and his associates:

"I am very tired of chasing a parcel of Indians about at the orders of men who don't know what to do or how to do it if they knew what they wanted," Ewell wrote in a letter home. "I would prefer the less romantic but hardly less inhuman business of

raising potatoes and cabbages—I say hardly less inhuman because as we now are about starting in a 'solumn' (solid column) of 600 men we will NOT be apt to see Indians, and mules and horses will be the only sufferers."

Bonneville established a base camp and supply center on the east bank of the Rio Gila. From this rendezvous he organized his columns. The place was known by various names but generally Depot on the Rio Gila was accepted for the entire site. Fort Floyd, "as 'Old Bonne's' (Col. Bonneville's) stronghold is designated," was listed by Lazelle as the location within the depot for the expedition's headquarters.

THIS IS A guess of how Fort West may have been laid out, based on a study of ground remains. Post apparently burned after Army abandoned it in early 1864. In November, Army patrol used "the quarters not yet destroyed by the fire," records show. Local tradition is that remains were leveled in 1890 by cattle baron, Tom Lyons, in building his 25-room ranch house and outbuildings a mile away. Remaining adobes were used in construction of what is probably the last of the lavish headquarters houses of the Western feudal-style cattle empire. Former opera star Artur Ocheltree began restoration of headquarters complex in 1964 and intended to encompass Fort West history in his project. (Drawn from surface remains at site.)

ANCESTOR OF Fort West, this depot was at curve of Rio Gila; actually river flows from north and makes sharp turns at this point, and post site was on eastern side. This location is believed to be about five miles south of Fort West site. It was "situated upon a very level plateau of the broad prairie bluff; is contiguous to water, wood, etc., with excellent grazing in its vicinity . . . The encampment is well arranged, and contains the usual large and commodious storehouses, the hospital, workshops, and quarters which are generally established." (Redrawn from plat in National Archives.)

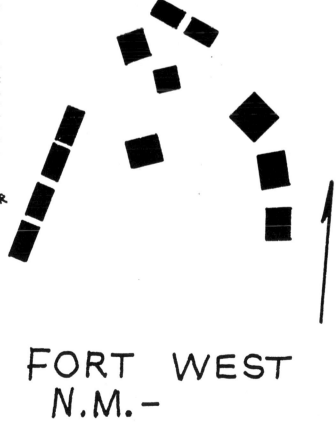

FORT WEST
N.M.—

DEPOT ON RIO GILA
N.M. —1859

POSSIBLE HEADQUARTERS area, at apex of triangle, includes large mound of rocks. Rifle shells and other military artifacts are scattered over area, further suggesting this is Fort West site. Town of Gila is in valley to rear. At its heyday, Fort West had two companies each of cavalry and infantry; after few months, cavalry were transferred and a 10-man mounted detail left behind to escort mails from Tucson to Rio Grande.

Across the Gila and a mile downstream was "Camp Union," the troop location, characterized by Lazelle as "better situated, and possessing more advantage and conveniences."

Prairie grass surrounded the camps. Frequently troop details had to turn firefighters to beat out flames generally credited to Apache marauders. Nightly raids on the depot property were blamed on Indians supposedly hidden at a rancheria 20 miles away. The civilian guides claimed to have seen the Indian camp but Lazelle had his doubts, "the general character of our guides being too well known to warrant much faith in their statements."

The harassments strained Bonneville's patience. He said he could care less whether the depot was burned to the ground; he wanted to get his expedition into the field. On May 21, five days after arrival, the expedition moved out.

Contrary to the predictions of Lazelle and Ewell, the Gila Expedition was to be at least a temporary success. One column killed a half dozen Apaches and a leading chief, and captured 1,000 stolen sheep.

On June 27, Bonneville's main force fought from mid-afternoon until sundown across a mile-wide battlefield on both sides of the Gila in Arizona. The Apaches lost 24 dead and 27 prisoners against an Army toll of a half dozen wounded. Not long afterward, the tribe appealed to the Army for peace.

When war of a different nature began four years later, the New Mexican veteran, Carleton, remembered the Gila Depot location. He directed that a post be established in its vicinity and, early 1863, troops occupied the site temporarily. They had just completed a patrol that resulted in the death of the Apache chief, Mangas Colorado. A few raids by Apaches followed, but were costly to the Indians. One raid in which two soldiers were killed cost the hostile 20 dead and 15 wounded.

In February, 1863, the final site of Fort West was selected a few miles north of the depot, "well advanced into the Indian country, enabling them to operate to advantage against the Indians, and at the same time to perfect their knowledge of the surrounding country," the official report explained. It was also more convenient to the cross-country routes, both for mail and Carleton's probable advance.

If the troopers had any idea of a palatial post, they were quickly discouraged. The district commander decided that none of the officers in the Fort West command had the ability "to make plans and estimate for the work" of the "erection of buildings at the post."

Admonished not to "undertake the construction of any permanent buildings until further orders," the post commander was authorized "full liberty to provide temporary quarters for your men, should such be necessary and their construction not interfere with an active pursuit of the Indians."

Other "not to interfere" matters were added: planting corn, cultivating a garden, and gathering hay. Plows and seed were to be issued, but, still, "On foot or mounted, your troops are to make war against the Indians. That must be the business of your command . . . Indian women and children are to be taken captives when possible and reported to these headquarters, but against the men you are to make war and war means killing."

The discovery of gold in the Gila area intensified settler interest and further disarranged relations with the Indians. Establishment of a post, rude that it was, encouraged settlement. Apparently it temporarily discouraged the Indian because 20 days of West scouts "moving in all directions" in April, 1863, failed to note any fresh sign.

This condition did not last long. After a patrol from Fort Craig was ambushed and the patrol leader's head severed as a trophy, Fort West's commander was told to "leave only a sufficient force to protect the stores at your post," and "to scour every foot of ground and beat up all their haunts" in order to insure that the band is "exterminated to the last man."

Not long after this patrol—the Indians ran off 400 horses and mules from the post. As the post surgeon said of Major William McCleave, post commander, "There is a devilish look in Mac's eyes that foretells stiff work for us. He will have those horses again or give good reasons why."

Seventy-two hours later, McCleave and 100 Volunteers had cornered the Indians. The troopers had rested four hours in the 72, eaten only cold rations, and left 70 mounts dead from exhaustion. A 15-minute attack killed 40 Indians and recovered 300 horses. One soldier died later from his wounds.

As it turned out, this was the last combat action from Fort West. A month later, the post commander was directed to "observe vigilance particularly

WESTERN ROW of building sites at supposed Fort West location could have been barracks. Outlines of rectangular buildings extend as far as pole in this view to south.

against a surprise at night" because the district commander was worried about "the exposed position of your stock corrals."

But on Christmas Day, the word came: "The post of Fort West is hereby ordered to be abandoned, and the following disposition of troops will be made without delay . . ."

TO GET THERE: From Silver City, N.M., take U.S. 180 west about 25 miles to right fork onto County 211. Continue on 211 four miles to crossing of Gila River. At dirt road that runs beside airstrip, turn left and follow this road to base of hill, then as it winds up to private residence of George Harsh. Fort West site is believed to be on top of hill immediately behind his house; permission to cross private property should be requested.

FORT THORN, NEW MEXICO

"Hats off, cheers were given. It was impossible to express our feelings . . . We now knew that friends were at the fort. Our California comrades came to meet us."

So wrote Captain William McCleave of his approach to Fort Thorn after his release as a Confederate prisoner in 1862. He had been exchanged in El Paso and as he headed north toward the end of the Mesilla Valley, "Fort Thorn was seen in the distance and our glorious flag—the dear old stars and stripes—waving in the breeze." He added that this was a "grand and unexpected sight."

The Stars and Stripes had been at Thorn only a few days when McCleave arrived. An advance party of Californians had arrived at the Rio Grande three miles above the fort near sunset on the 4th of July, 1862.

Other than it signalled a dropping back of the South's lines, the capture of Fort Thorn was little more than psychological. Carleton arrived at it on August 7 to find, as described by one of his privates and quoted in Aurora Hunt's *The Army of the Pacific:*

"It was in a horrible condition as it had also been abandoned. The walls and roofs of the quarters were almost torn down but the flagstaff was still standing and we were rejoiced to think there would be nothing but the glorious Stars and Stripes raised from it."

The oft-mentioned flag first flew here in November, 1853. The departmental commander figured that the "extensive and fertile" valley could support at least 4,000 settlers and "all that is necessary to make it a thriving settlement is the presence of troops to repress Indian depredations."

Per usual, the troops were put to work as laborers, following the admonition to construct "comfortable quarters having due regard to the economies of the service."

In addition to the usual peck of Indian troubles, Thorn had its problems with commanding officers. Its founder, Brevet Major Israel B. Richardson, known as "Greasy Dick" out of his hearing, was pressured into resigning because he "had become obnoxious to a majority of the officers of his regiment." His successor, Brevet Lieutenant Colonel Joseph H. Eaton went the same resignation route after a series of rebukes from headquarters for his curt reactions to orders he disliked.

Both Richardson and Eaton compiled Civil War records as Volunteers to indicate their sides had merit, too. The former was a brevet major general when he was killed at Sharpsburg, his twenty-second campaign. Eaton ended the war as a brevet brigadier.

Young Lieutenant Henry M. Lazelle—later a brigadier—was with the Gila Expedition when it

(FROM DAVIS, "EL GRINGO," 1857.)

WALLED FORT in traditional fashion actually not too common in Southwest, Fort Thorn was not symmetrical, running 600 feet along its southeast wall, 520 along southwest. Buildings were of adobe. Post was centered in a six-mile square reservation. Settlers disregarded reservation and commander complained "None of the citizens at Santa Barbara have any right other than squatters to occupy the land." He explained that he had to post round-the-clock guard on acequia that brought water to post from three and a half miles away because citizens threatened law suits and would shut off water "for some days and nights . . . for a week at a time," although 25 soldiers spent a month building acqueduct. Fort apparently had a measure of culture if Dragoon Sergeant Bennett is correct in diary entry of January 24, 1856: "By invitation, recited Plato's 'Soliloquy on the Immortality of the Soul' at a kind of a theatre established here. Officers were all present."

FLOOD in 1884 washed away last trace of adobe Fort Thorn which was located somewhere in this area at northern end of Mesilla Valley. Site is closer to Rio Grande than it was in 1850's due to shift in river's course. In this picture from western hills, river flows across center, marked by occasional tree. When California Column arrived here in 1862, most companies stayed only long enough to rest their animals and build boats with which to cross flooded river.

camped four miles from the post. He found Eaton's successor "a person of very brilliant imagination" but noted that there was a fondness for liquor "which his nose and my eyes told he partook of freely."

This must have been routine, though. "At about 9 a.m." Lazelle commented, "visited the post and found most of the officers in the sutler's store, a filthy hole, drinking or preparing to do so."

The society at Thorn he found "constrained, hurried, uneasy, and without style" and he was pleased when he left the place after a five-day stay.

"It is a crowded, contracted, united sort of place, in its construction," he remembered. "Its officers with their families, are exceedingly hospitable and entertaining, but entirely too neighborly, almost to a common brotherhood, to conform to my views of constant happiness and domestic comfort."

An officer's wife who stopped at the post for a short visit had similar appreciation of the fort when she departed. "We were delighted it was not to be our station and were glad to leave," she said.

Despite the social comments, Fort Thorn performed well under fire. Sometimes the situation bordered on the ludicrous, as when Indians made off with 68 mules from the post corral, and Lazelle was led to call it "a beautiful burlesque upon the dignity of our much talked of great expedition."

On other occasions, everything was all business. The previously mentioned Sergeant Bennett was present as interpreter in 1855 when treaties were signed with the Mescalero Apache and Gila In-

dians. "Met in council," he wrote. "250 Indians made a treaty. Received from them 40 stolen horses, 10 mules, 3 Mexican boys, and a girl. The children were taken by them a few months ago."

With Mangas Colorado as one of its wards, the fort became the headquarters of the Indian Agency. This set the stage for a dangerous incident in 1858. While at the agency camp a mile away, Apaches suddenly were attacked by a gang of Mexican cutthroats who called themselves the "Mesilla Guards." Several Indians, mostly women and children, were killed before agency employees could drive the marauders away. Soldiers captured 36 of the men, and on orders of the Federal judge, sent them to Socorro for trial.

This incident took place during another of the perennial problems with Thorn commanders. The chase of the Indians was led by a lieutenant; his commander—a brevet major—accompanied him but was unable to issue orders because he was under a six-month suspension from command!

Thorn's official life as a military post ended in 1859. The surgeon termed it the "sickliest post in the territory" and departmental headquarters informed the War Department that the post was to be broken up because it "has been so unhealthy for the troops."

In 1861, there was a short skirmish near abandoned Fort Thorn between Union and Confederate patrols. After the rebels had occupied the area, they used it as a base of operations, fielding the march to Tucson from it. General Sibley spent three weeks there in 1862.

The bulk of Sibley's force—3,000 strong, 15 cannon, and a heavy supply train—left Thorn on February 7, 1862. The remainder pulled out when Carleton's advance was observed five months later.

Although Carleton originally planned to station four companies at Thorn, usually a single company was used to provide security along the route from Craig to Mesilla. By mid-1863, even this was eliminated when the Column's mission was re-oriented.

"With a view to operating against the Indians south of Cooke's Springs . . . You will accordingly move with your whole command to Cooke's Springs," was the order on August 5, 1863, that closed the book on Fort Thorn.

TO GET THERE: Take U.S. 85 north from Hatch about 1.2 miles. Turn left on improved road. Follow this about two miles to Oak Road, an angle to the right. Almost immediately, go left at the next fork. At next intersection, about a half-mile, turn left. Road tapers off in about a mile. This is general site of post as determined from surveyor records in 1960 by Colonel George M. Ruhlen, USA (retired) and his son, Major General George Ruhlen, USA, during a detailed search of Mesilla Valley.

FORT BAKER, NEVADA

By doing nothing at all, Fort Baker performed its mission for the California Column. It did it without the loss of a life, without a single fight, and even without a single trooper. It appears, in fact, that Fort Baker, adobe walls and all, was a fort in name only.

The fact that it was on the maps of both Confederate and Federal commanders and fresh in the memories of Confederate leaders lately of the Union Army, put it in a strategic position to do a job. This it did by doing nothing.

Its history antedated the California Column by some six years when it was founded in 1855 by 30 Mormon settlers. They had been sent from Salt Lake City by Brigham Young with orders "to go to Las Vegas, build a fort there to protect immigrants and the United States mail from the Indians, and to teach the latter how to raise corn, wheat, potatoes, squash, and melons."

John Fremont had first located the site of Las Vegas in his 1844 expedition. His journal told of two "narrow streams of clear water, four or five feet deep . . . The taste of the water is good, but rather too warm to be agreeable." He did not like 70 degree drinking water, but found that it "afforded a delightful bathing place."

It did not take the Mormons long to establish themselves once they had arrived amidst what they termed, "a nice patch of grass, about half a mile wide and two or three miles long." Within three months, work was well along on an adobe fort 150 feet square. The post was completely surrounded by a ten foot wall, two feet thick at the bottom and one foot at the top. Adobe was used throughout the construction because the closest timber was 20 miles away.

Although the plan was to run the walks to 14 feet, this had not been done by the time Young summoned the faithful back to Salt Lake City in 1857. His capital was being threatened by General Johnston's Utah Expedition, and Young mustered every Mormon for its defense. By 1858, both the fort and Las Vagas settlement were deserted, but Overland Mail stages and military patrols frequently stopped at the springs.

The Civil War beckoned California troops to the Rio Grande and the established presence of the Mormon Fort at Las Vegas proved valuable to Carleton. Conscious of the speed with which his every move was learned by the Confederates, Carleton announced on December 19, 1861, plans for "important field service connected with the re-establishment of Fort Mojave and Fort Baker at Las Vegas, on the Salt Lake road."

In case the Baker name was confusing, four days later Carleton explained, "The new post at Las Vegas will be known as Fort Baker." It was to be set up by four companies of the First California Volunteer Infantry, part of a total of seven to move up the Colorado River from Yuma to bring to terms the Navajo Indians who "obstruct the route from Albuquerque to Los Angeles."

The remaining three companies of the Mojave Expedition—for that was Carleton's name for the enterprise—were to "reoccupy Fort Navajo and re-establish the ferry." By this time he was getting confused himself, it appears, because obviously in this case he was referring to Fort Mojave.

Plans for the expedition were leaked conveniently. Stores shipped in public wagons were prominently marked with destinations of Fort Mojave or Fort Baker. Somehow the quartermasters knew

FORT BAKER was prominent landmark in this view of Las Vegas in 1876. It had been purchased from Mormons when they rushed to Salt Lake City. Periodically it was occupied by settlers or travelers. This view is to east; Frenchman mountain is on right, Sunrise mountain on left. Las Vegas Creek flows in middle of sketch.

that "Mojave Expedition" was another way of saying "Column from California" and destinations of Baker or Mojave meant only one thing: Fort Yuma and the supply points enroute to and beyond it.

Although some accounts say that the Army was at Baker in the Civil War, the official records indicate otherwise. Even in unofficial accounts of visits to Las Vegas during the period, there is a complete absence of reference to the fort or its garrison. The springs and the grass come in for comment; the Army post is ignored.

As with diversionary tactics employed by other armies in other wars, there is no way to learn whether the Confederates were fooled by the proclaimed plans to garrison Fort Baker. Even so, it did its job and, most likely contributed its share of camouflage and confusion to the Confederacy while Carleton pushed his efforts eastward.

TO GET THERE: From downtown Las Vegas, Nevada, go north on Las Vegas Boulevard nine blocks to 908. On east side of street and next to Elks Lodge is site of Fort Baker. A marker is next to sidewalk; remaining adobe building is under trees at southeastern corner of area. Original springs are near Elks Lodge, next door.

ONLY ONE adobe "barracks" remains at site of Fort Baker. Local tradition attaches barracks identity to this building but more likely it served as home for Mormons who built building and by their successors. Original adobe is in walls, enhanced by modern latching and rain-deflecting roof. Defense of fort was anticipated by Mormon builders who placed peep holes in the walls—apparently for tall men or short men on high stools. They were seven feet from the ground. Las Vegas springs nearby are more than 60 feet deep. Building is owned and tended by Daughters of the Utah Pioneers, and caretaker lives in this building—a combination museum and private dwelling.

(EARL OLSON, HISTORIAN, CHURCH OF JESUS CHRIST OF LATTER-DAY SAINTS)

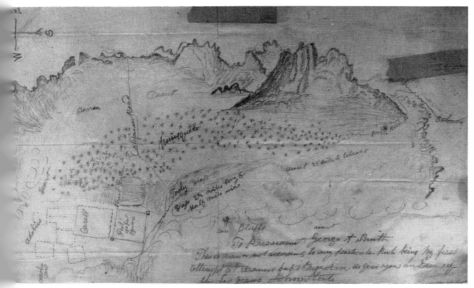

CRUDE LAYOUT of "Las Vegas Fort" in 1850's was submitted to Salt Lake City, showing shape of fortified post and locations of corral and adobe buildings outside of walls.

71

FORT CUMMINGS, NEW MEXICO

After crossing the Rio Grande and moving up the crumbling cliffs to the wide flat-lands that lay beyond, the emigrant of yesteryear was beckoned forth by a cone-shaped hill, 8,400-foot high Cooke's Peak. Near the base of it occasionally stood what the Army called, "Fort Cummings."

Occasionally is the proper word, as applied to Fort Cummings. "The place had been abandoned by the Army no less than three consecutive times, and yet it had always been found necessary to reoccupy it," explained Brevet Brigadier General George A. Forsyth, a former commanding officer, in his *Story of the Soldier*.

The California Column was the first official Army occupant of the site, although in pre-Civil War days the Butterfield Stage Line had a station here. Despite a fortress-like stone corral for protection, the station was victim of a seven-man massacre in 1861.

"SMALL, compactly built, and inclosed by a wall, 10 feet high, composed of adobe," is how the post surgeon described Fort Cummings in 1869. "The buildings are one story high, built of adobe and covered with earth." Post was about 350 feet square with all major activities within adobe wall. Barracks provided 223 cubic feet of air per man for average post strength of 80 troopers, but in late 1860's smallpox epidemic hit a quarter of post. Surgeon blamed this on stagnant water in Cooke's Well "impregnated with a large amount of organic matter, animal and vegetable, dead and alive, so as sometimes to become really obnoxious to health." He also blamed refuse piles, especially behind the post-trader's building, and large pools of water that caused ground to become marshy. (Redrawn from Surgeon-General Circular No. 4, 1870.)

SINKS · COQ · B · OQ · OQ · H · OFF · QM · SHOP · SH · CORRAL · SHOP · GH · PR · CORRAL · SHEDS

FORT CUMMINGS N. MEX. — 1870

When Carleton pushed his forces across sandy wastes to the Rio Grande, the notation "Cooke's Springs" was an important one in each itinerary. Here the troops and their mounts could find water in a slight depression that was named after Phillip St. George Cooke of the Mormon Battalion who had passed there in 1846. In later years, the Cooke name was to be retained, even though the spelling was not.

Protection of the springs by the Army dates back to August 22, 1863, when a company of the 5th Infantry California Volunteers was posted there "with a view to striking at the Indians whenever and wherever it can be done."

A 20-man detail was kept at the springs to escort the semi-monthly mail run and a company was located a half mile north to build Fort Cummings. Except for the general advice to watch for Indians, at first this detachment had no instructions other than "be in readiness for field service."

Cummings was the rendezvous point for a 90-trooper expedition in April, 1864, that sent detachments from nine New Mexican posts into Apache land. The soldiers and their civilian guides and teamsters were sent to "scour over the country to the southward" with orders, "All Apache men large enough to bear arms who may be encountered in Arizona will be slain wherever met, unless they give themselves up as prisoners. No women or children will be harmed; these will be taken as prisoners."

The men were permitted to carry one blanket and basic rations in their haversacks because, as Carleton believed, "To be encumbered with more is not to find Indians."

Apache hunting did not confine itself to this one

(NATIONAL ARCHIVES.)

BY 1882, tents had taken over most of Cummings site although romantic adobe fortress remained in near-ruins. "The renewed activity of the Indians under Victorio caused the Government to regarrison the post in 1881," wrote Surgeon Parker. "During its period of abandonment, the fort fell into ruins; so that when it was regarrisoned, the barracks and quarters were uninhabitable and the troops lived in tents outside the walls. The old barracks inside the fort were used as the Q.M. corral, and the old officers' quarters were patched up to serve as storehouses and workshops. The old Commanding Officer's quarters became the guardhouse."

expedition. A few months later, a patrol was sent into Mexico to determine whether dealing with the tribes was going on south of the border. In a 1,200-mile scout, the conclusion reached was that there was no illegal combine; the Mexicans had as much to lose at the hands of a well-armed Apache as did the Americans.

This patrol had to be interrupted in order to send a detail back to Cummings for "infantry shoes, sole leather for repairing the same, horse and mule shoe nails, etc."

When wet weather finally brought the expedition

to a bogged down end, Lieutenant Colonel N. H. Davis, had to summarize it. "The scout was long, hot, and in many respects a hard and tedious one . . . Many night marches were made and every effort taken to surprise Indians at these various places, should any be living or encamped there, but contrary to the general belief and report, this vast section of country, with one exception, was deserted by the wily Apache." And that one exception, an Apache rancheria, Davis said he was unable to attack in time because his guide had misled him with falsehoods and treachery.

"FORT CUMMINGS was built of adobe and surrounded by a high adobe wall, with a sally-port on the southern side," Surgeon Parker recorded. "For many years, it was in a state of almost perpetual siege; and anyone who poked his head out of the sally-port or showed it above the walk took the chance of having it shot off." This is Cummings today although identification of buildings is difficult due to later use as stage station and emigrant camp. One thing is certain; cone shaped mountain in center background is Cooke's Peak.

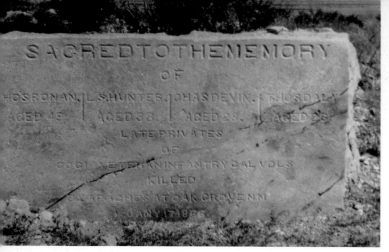

IN 1867, Surgeon W. Thorton Parker returned from scout and "found the post more vigilant than ever, the sentries doubled, front and rear. Later when the morning and evening gun no longer saluted Old Glory at Reveille or Retreat, we learned that we were reduced to three rounds per man for ammunition. A desperate situation." But no last stand came to Fort Cummings, despite Parker's dire description. This sketch from his sentimental account of the old days purports to show front wall of Cummings. Sally port is in center, flanked on left by guardhouse and right by prison. Shops were next to guardhouse, storerooms next to prison, and corrals with their sheds running to each far corner. Cooke's Peak is to right rear.

WOOD CUTTING ended fatally for this foursome in 1866, only four and a half miles from post. Marker is at Fort Cummings site, although soldiers' bodies probably were moved in 1892. At that time, 74 graves were taken to Fort Leavenworth; 25 were marked "unknown." Post returns of Cummings for January, 1866, show that all were privates who were "surprised and killed by Apache Indians . . . while on daily duty cutting wood for this garrison" and that Private Nathanial B. Goldsberg "received a slight wound in the left hip" in the same fight. On January 17, 1866, First Lieutenant Jonathan D. Slocum, post commander, ordered, "The troops of this post will be paraded tomorrow at 8 o'clock p.m. to attend upon the last sad rites" of the men. Post cemetery was outside of walls, was surrounded by four foot high stone wall, 150 square.

It was at this time that General Forsyth was in command of Cummings. After a patrol had made contact with Apaches, the bulk of the garrison was sent in pursuit. The Apaches were driven from their positions toward the Mexican border.

Ordinarily this would have provided sanctuary, but in 1882 this was not the case. Picking up details from other posts along the way, Forsyth drove into Mexico, despite orders to the contrary.

Pushing close on the Apaches and capturing stragglers, the Cummings expedition finally met a Mexican Army contingent. The Mexican commander informed them that as far as the marauding Apaches were concerned, "My command fought, routed and scattered them."

Forsyth examined the battlefield, noted that the Mexicans had suffered 21 dead and 16 wounded, and offered the services of his surgeons. He counted 78 dead Indians on the field and decided that Fort Cummings had played a critical, albeit second-hand, role in the chastisement.

Patrols from Cummings continued frequently, but the Indian threat did not seem to materialize. The bulk of the post—one officer and 30 men—patrolled in May, 1865, but with no result. Considering that the fort ranged from two officers and 41 enlisted in 1864, to one and 58 in May '65, this was a hefty slice of the men available for adobe making and stage escorting.

Post-war events at Cummings included a number of Indian engagements before the post was abandoned in 1870. By this time the surgeon had complained that the adobe barracks built seven years earlier were "poorly built and badly ventilated."

The second phase of Cummings operations opened in 1881, although a corporal's guard had kept watch over the crumbling adobes in the interim. The adobes were so crumbled, however, that the new garrison used little of the old post and, instead, camped next to it. From this tent camp, the detachment fielded one of its major expeditions.

TO GET THERE: From Deming, N.M. take U.S. 260 north one mile, turn east on State 26 for 15 miles. Turn left on dirt road at historical marker and black tanks marked "Florida." Follow this for five miles, then turn left on road to Hyatt ranch. After obtaining permission to visit, at ranch take right fork in road, continue along fence line, open and close cattle gate, and continue on dirt road to fort site, one mile.

NORTHERN EDGE of Fort Cummings shows remains of two officers' quarters. In 1882, post suffered from major typhoid epidemic. Surgeon Parker noted that more than 50 men died and "some weeks there was a funeral every day." Epidemic was blamed on water and surgeon tried to purify water with pinkish permanganate of potassium. He found everyone was as afraid of fever as of the pinkish spring, but, "There was nothing else to drink; and they had to choose between the typhoid, the poison, and the thirst."

FORT BASCOM, NEW MEXICO

Rebellion may have brought the California Column to New Mexico, but Indian trouble and white renegades kept it there. At least that was the story for Fort Bascom, a place once condemned by its commander as the most neglected, abandoned, and forgotten fort in the West.

Kit Carson as a Volunteer colonel figured in the history of Bascom, but it is a page that some Carson biographers would like to forget. This was the "Battle of Adobe Walls," and according to some versions, the Great Scout did not come away from it with his usual amount of glory.

It was on November 12, 1864, that Carson led 335 troops and 75 Indian allies from Fort Bascom and into Texas. After contending with a raging "norther," the snowstorm for which the Texas Panhandle is famous, the expedition came upon a large Kiowa camp and attacked.

The Kiowas fled in the face of the soldier attack. While the troopers stopped to destroy the village, the Indians gathered reinforcements at another camp and counterattacked.

From the ruins of an adobe trading post built 20 years before by the Bent brothers, the expedition held the line against determined Indian charges. Then as they pulled back, they found that the only way to keep the Indians at a respectful distance was to shower them with howitzer shells.

Later, Carson admitted that without his artillery he would have suffered disastrous results. He lost two men killed and 21 wounded; the Indian losses were officially estimated at 60 killed and wounded.

Carson reported two complications in the battle. One was the fact that the Indians fired the high grass around the column and then used the smoke to cover raids on the column. The other was a tal-

ented Indian bugler—some say Chief Satanta himself, known to be a bugler—who blew conflicting calls through out the day. Army calls to "advance" would be echoed by Indian "retreat" notes.

The Carson expedition was part of the larger strategy for which Fort Bascom was designed. "While Fort Bascom will be an outpost to New Mexico during the present rebellion, its advanced pickets watching the roads from Arkansas and Texas, it will be of the greatest importance in preventing the predatory incursions of the Comanche and Kiowa Indians," was how Carleton's General Order No. 20 described the mission.

The site of Bascom was astride the Comanche War Trail, the cattle drive route, and what later was called the Fort Smith-Santa Fe route by railroad engineers. The Whipple Survey of 1853 had camped at the spot "along the valley of the Canadian . . . where a low ridge of hills from the south impinged upon the river."

Here Whipple first encountered the so-called "Comancheros," the American and Mexican renegades who joined with Indians to barter in what-

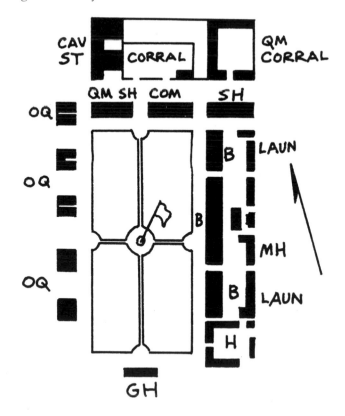

FORT BASCOM N.M.-1869

BY 1931, only the barracks adobe remained. Mrs. Lillie Gerhardt Anderson of Tucumcari, N.M., took this picture during a 1931 visit to line camp where she lived in 1914 with her husband. They revisited it again in 1940's and noted oblong mounds marking where these walls had been. Cycle is finished now and no trace remains. These barracks were roofed with poles and earth and divided by four covered passageways into rooms, each 100 by 13 feet.

(MRS. LILLIE GERHARDT ANDERSON.)

ever items could not be obtained legally. The Comancheros provided the Indians with guns, ammunition, and whiskey; they reciprocated with rustled cattle and anything else that would be accepted in trade.

This trade was to become a scourge that involved the Bascom garrison before it was stamped out. To counter the illicit business, Carleton decreed all traders would have to have licenses issued by him and which prohibited guns and whiskey. Enforcing this, the Army searched all trade wagons passing Fort Bascom, and put pickets 15 miles out from the fort to prevent attempts to bypass the post.

Until scandal put pressure on the Bascom area, the check-point system had only token success. One Army wife wrote later that trading with the Comancheros for cattle was common, although there was little doubt that the cattle were late residents of Texas ranches. She remembered receiving 12 head of cattle in return for a copper kettle and a Navajo blanket.

The commanding officer of Fort Bascom was rumored to be in league with the Comancheros and it was suggested his officers were encouraging rustling so that they could buy the cattle. Frequently the videttes would confiscate the goods and sell

them, the proceeds going into a post fund for the purchase of incidentals not provided in the Army issue.

On at least one occasion, not all of the contraband was sold. Mules laden with whiskey were diverted and the capturing patrol took care of the contraband itself. They wound up in the guardhouse for sobering up and disciplining, but Bascom's commander said that the merchants trading in the illegal liquor were the real guilty ones.

One commander made a determined effort to stop the Comancheros. He asked for the authority to deputize every settler with the authority to make arrests, but was refused. A concerted drive by his troopers netted 20 traders, but these were freed as soon as they were turned over to Santa Fe authorities.

Then the Navajoes made two raids within 20 miles of the fort, and two other tribes ransacked a house near the fort, killing a woman. The last straw was when they fired at a sentry at the post and stole five Army horses.

The commanding officer complained to headquarters that he was unable to destroy the Comanchero trade, protect the settlements, quiet the Indians, and provide wagon train escorts with only 88 men.

Headquarters agreed. They abandoned the post.

TO GET THERE: Although Fort Bascom is only nine miles straight north of Tucumcari, N.M., locked fences make it necessary to make a 40-mile detour. From Tucumcari, take U.S. 54 east to Logan, 22 miles. Turn left on State 39 at the eastern edge of Logan. At first mailbox on right in three miles, take first turnoff to left. Take this dirt road about 14 miles. At second mailbox, turn left and in about a half mile this road deadends at ranch house. The fort site is about one mile further to southwest, but permission to visit must be requested at ranch house. Site is privately owned. There are no remains.

TUCUMCARI MOUNTAIN looks down on Fort Bascom general area on south side of Canadian River.

FORT SUMNER, NEW MEXICO

"Send all captured Navajos and Apaches to Fort Sumner and there to feed them until they have opened farms and become able to support themselves," was General Carleton's summary of his final mission east of the Rio Grande.

As a less-senior officer in the pre-Civil War Army, he had seen the results of continual warfare with the Navajos—treaties made and broken, campaigns carried on to the death, settlers and Indians alike writing finis to the story in their own blood. Carleton felt he had the answer.

"Fort Sumner," he commented in the *Congressional Globe*, was designed to "be a chaplain post so that the chaplain there could educate the Indian children." There they could learn kindness away from their customary haunts, Christianity away from their tribal superstitions, habits and modes of life of a new world away from the old Indians and "all latent longings for murdering and robbing."

The obvious merit of the scheme won it fairly quick approval. In November, 1862, a board of officers had been detailed to "select the exact site of Fort Sumner, the new post recently ordered to be erected."

They inspected a spot east of the Pecos River known as the Bosque Redondo—Round Grove of Trees—but they felt that building material was too distant to be convenient, the water was impure, and the valley was subject to inundation by the periodic floods. They added that it had good grazing and a fine view.

Although an alternate site was proposed, Carleton had made up his mind already. Memories of visits to the area in the 1850's convinced him that this was the place for his sanctuary, and here was where Fort Sumner was built. Not only was it convenient to the tribes intended to be located there, he reasoned, but it was astraddle the Indian raiding route and would offer a salutory effect on the depredations.

Although hints were offered that Carleton was anxious to relocate the Navajos in order to examine the mineral potential of their traditional hunting

grounds, by and large the opinion was that he had only humanitarian motives in mind. This was tempered, of course, with thoughts of advancing the mineral and transportation future of New Mexico which would be dormant as long as hostile tribes monopolized much of the territory.

The post was established in 1862. Within a year Carleton could count 400 Mescalero Apaches "contented and happy. They planted . . . some large fields of corn . . . have their acequia dug, will next year raise quite enough to support themselves." With the Mascaleros quiet, Carleton could concentrate on the Navajos.

Forts Wingate and Canby were established on or near the sites of pre-war Forts Lyon and Defiance, the troops were gathered, and on June 23, 1863, Carleton was able to order all Navajos to move to these locations. As for those choosing not to move, Carleton had but one announcement: "Every Navajo that is seen will be considered as hostile and treated accordingly; that after that day the door now open will be closed."

Aggressive execution of Carleton's orders resulted in more than two million pounds of Navajo grain being destroyed, many dollars in bonuses being collected by settlers for livestock recovered (at $20 a head for horses and mules), and, finally, a plea for peace from the tribe before the winter snows came in October, 1863.

Only 180 braves surrendered in this affair, but it was a start. The detachment at Fort Sumner found

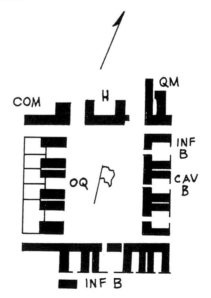

FORT SUMNER
N.M. - 1865

IN 1863, Fort Sumner was wind-blown tent and hut-camp amid cottonwoods along Pecos River. Navajos had not completely accepted idea of farming and in early 1864 post was alerted to Navajo raid on horse herd. During pursuit that followed, estimated 65 Navajos were killed or wounded while Army command of soldiers and Apache scouts lost only two wounded—both scouts. Commander of pursuit believed he could have taken entire force of raiders if weather had not been so cold "that it was with great difficulty that the men could load and fire their pieces."

itself harassed to provide shelter and food. By order of General Carleton, the old and very young were provided with at least the bare essentials, tents, old Army blankets, and clothing.

Some "tame" Navajos from Sumner were sent back to their tribes so that they could describe the wondrous pleasures awaiting them if they surrendered. The answer was written in the number of depredations that followed and the columns of smoke in the air.

In early 1864, a detachment of nine troopers and 40 Apache scouts met one recalcitrant band of 150 Navajos. After a momentary sizing up period, "We went at them on the full charge," a trooper wrote later, "discharging our carbines in their faces at about 40 yards . . . The fight was too close and too warm to last long; as usual, superior arms and discipline prevailed and the savages broke and fled. After that it was a running fight for ten miles."

This engagement is only a hint of the desperate attempts of the Navajo to retain his native land. With winter cold on the land, however, most tribes had no choice. By March 4, more than 2,500 had arrived in the Canby-Wingate area for disposal at the whims of the Army.

Despite the good intentions in mind, Carleton's deputies had less than maximum success in moving the Navajo tribes to Sumner from the rendezvous areas. Within a week 126 Navajos had died of dysentery or exposure. Many more were sick because they did not know how to cook the raw flour issued them by the Army—and the watered down gruel they made with it doubled them over with cramps.

Carleton eyed the casualties unhappily, but predicted, "This will be the last Navajo War. The persistent efforts which have been made and will continue to be made can hardly fail to bring in the whole tribe before the year's end."

The worst march in Navajo history took place in April, 1864, when 2,400 stumbled through snow and

FORT SUMNER today is southeast of town of Fort Sumner and along Pecos River—which flows behind trees in background. After fort was auctioned off, buildings became headquarters of Maxwell Ranch. In 1884, a Colorado cattle syndicate bought site. Ten years later, buildings were abandoned. In 1941, Pecos flood covered site, removing last traces of historic post. Diligent searcher today can find traces of foundations, especially on side of eroded river bank.

ADOBE IMPROVEMENTS changed appearance of Fort Sumner by 1865. By this time, post included more than 8,000 Navajos and 400 Mescalero Apaches, not a happy combination in view of traditional rivalries. "That place at Fort Sumner was what is now called a concentration camp," Apache survivor of boyhood days at Sumner was quoted in 1958 *Frontier Times* article. "There was nothing there for us except misery and hunger . . . They put men and women to work digging ditches and digging up ground with shovels to plant corn. And once a week the soldiers gave us enough food to last perhaps two days . . . To add to our misery, the soldiers brought in many Navajos . . . They fought us; they stole our horses and our food. And worst of all, they got a sickness from the soldiers . . . smallpox, I think. They died by hundreds, and the soldiers made those who were left throw the dead bodies into the Pecos. They drifted down past our camp, where we had to get drinking water. There were worms in the water, many, many worms." Although his memories of Sumner days may have been colored by time, Apache was correct when he added that in 1865 the Apaches deserted post and later were settled on another reservation. Work shown here apparently was on infantry barracks at southeastern corner of fort.

over the frozen corpses of their tribesmen. This is the "Long Walk" now traditional legend in many Navajo families.

Success was too much for Carleton's experiment. Before he knew it he had 6,000 Indians under care at Fort Sumner. He had to put the troopers in his department on half rations in order to eke out even a bare ration for his Indian charges of a pound of meat, corn, cabbages, or flour a day. Then he found he had to teach them how to cook the rations because many had never encountered "white man's food" before.

The Indian Bureau threw up its bureaucratic hands at all of this, and the Agent rushed to Washington for guidance. Meanwhile, Carleton followed his policy, "We can feed them cheaper than we can fight them." He set his Indians to plowing and planting for 25 miles up and down the Pecos, even if the proper tools were unavailable at the moment.

Harvest time the next year promised a yield of 84,000 bushels of corn until a worm afflicted the tassels and an unseasonable frost ruined what little remained. Carleton cut back once again on the rations. He directed that the next year's planting would be diversified so that the tribes would have a

MUSEUM of Billy the Kid in town of Fort Sumner has collection of fort relics, including letters from General Sumner's wife regarding post's name, general's sword and field blanket. Desk in museum once was used as postoffice at fort, then in town. Locked drawer which was jimmied open in 1899 robbery when postmaster was killed still is obvious in desk.

chance of success regardless of the pest or weather that visited.

Congress had tried to come to the rescue with a $100,000 appropriation. When Army Inspectors checked the 1864 allotment provided by the Indian Bureau, however, they felt some items were completely unnecessary and others, well, "the purchasers were either culpably negligent, or entirely regardless of the interests of the Government and of the Indians." Noting that Indian Bureau blankets cost $18.50 while Army blankets of better quality cost $5.85, the Army estimated that the $100,000 in goods could be retailed for $30,000; the post sutler gave the Bureau a slight edge with a $50,000 estimate.

What had started with bright hopes quickly evaporated. Several of Carleton's officers were found to be misappropriating Indian goods and were court-martialed, the Indian Agent was declared persona non grata on the reservation, and the bulk

YANKEE UNIFORM USED AT THE OLD FORT

THE FLAG THAT FLEW OVER THE OLD FORT

DIAGRAM OLD FT. SUMNER

PARADE

NOTORIOUS Billy the Kid came to Maxwell ranch, former Fort Sumner, because of a girl friend. Deputy Sheriff Pat Garrett heard of the visit and was waiting for outlaw when he entered Maxwell's son's room. "The moonlight streamed in through the open window, but . . . Garrett was able to partially hide himself in the shadow," Silver City newspaper reported. "The figure advanced to the bed with a butcher knife in his hand . . . He asked, having noticed the strange figure, 'who is that?' . . . Receiving no answer to his query, Billy jumped away from the bed, at the same time drawing his self-cocking revolver . . . Garrett . . . rose up and fired. The shot struck 'the kid' in the heart and he fell on his back, a dead man." Wire fence has been erected to prevent defacement of grave marker of killer of at least 11 persons . . . some stories say 21, one for each year of his life.

of the 400 Apaches deserted. Indians trained in the manual arts such as metalworking showed an ingenious talent in counterfeiting rations tags—earlier fake cardboard rations cards had been replaced because the wards could duplicate them, too. Then the harvest of 1865 fell far shy of the six million pounds of food needed, the result of bug infestation, again.

The crop in 1866 failed similarly. Bayonets had to be waved to force the 1867 planting by the Indians remaining, although by this time many had disappeared, returning to their native haunts. Finally in 1867, territorial politics reached as far east as the White House and General Carleton was relieved with hardly a note of appreciation for his half-decade of efforts in the territory.

Then the end of Fort Sumner and the noble experiment came in 1868. With the volatile Carleton shifted to duty in Texas, and the Army out of the

LUCIEN MAXWELL once owned area shown on his grave marker. It was three times size of Rhode Island, totaling 1,714,765 acres. In addition to data given on stone, Maxwell was a major supplier of beef to Army posts and unsuccessful gold mine investor. His grave was unmarked for 50 years until Denver monument company donated this stone.

picture, no one knew what to do at the combination fort and agency. The Army garrison felt that it was out of their hands, but the Indian Bureau had no orders to take over. Then when the Bureau got the word, the Army commander said he had no orders that he was to surrender responsibility.

Red tape snarled the whole situation until a commission that included General William Tecumseh Sherman visited Sumner in May, 1868. They saw the destitution and starvation, the degradation and defeat of a once proud people.

Two weeks later, the Navajos marched in a column ten miles long back to their home territories. It is from this day of their deliverance that modern Navajo tribal history is reckoned.

TO GET THERE: Town of Fort Sumner is in eastern New Mexico at junction of U.S. 60 and 84. Next to town on U.S. 60-84 is Billy the Kid Museum where artifacts of Fort Sumner are displayed. Site of fort is further east. Take U.S. 60-84 three miles from town, turn right on State 212 for four miles to Old Fort Sumner Museum, where artifacts are on display. Behind museum is graveyard. Fort site is half mile to west in privately owned fields next to river, approachable by driving along irrigation ditch road that leads from farmhouse at museum. Permission should be requested; guide is recommended.

FORT GOODWIN, ARIZONA

Putting it mildly, the news out of Fort Goodwin was bad in May, 1866: the post had been overrun by 2,000 Apaches and 100 soldiers massacred. Only one trooper lived to tell the tale.

Leading newspapers on both coasts recounted the gory details. There was just one hitch in the whole thing: it was pure fiction. The only Indians around Goodwin at the time were 800 White Mountain Apaches camped convenient to the periodic ration issues of the post quartermaster.

That seems to have been the mission of Goodwin from its founding in 1864. Originally it was established as a depot of supplies "in a central position" from which troops "will march in every direction to points where the enemy will be found." But by 1868, Goodwin was considered in a different light. Orders then called it "a post which protects those Indians which come in and give themselves up."

Before it acquired this peaceful mission, Goodwin was blooded in several expeditions in southeastern Arizona. Every one seemed to have a white flag of truce somewhere in its scenario, however.

In July, 1864, a patrol to the Gila mountain area patiently tried to move in on an Indian gathering, but found that they would retreat one hill every time the soldiers advanced one hill. A truce flag lead to a supposed agreement to surrender, but the Indians took off in directions opposite to those agreed upon. An estimated five Apaches were wounded when the soldiers tried to stop them.

Soon after this patrol returned, another departed for the Pinal Mountains. They planned to surprise the Indians and even had blackened their rifle barrels to reduce reflections. The scheme was a partial success, but with one drawback. Both the Indians and soldiers were equally surprised one night when the latter blundered into a hidden Apache camp.

More flags of truce were displayed on this adventure, but to no avail. This three-week expedition became a near-comedy of errors. One of the lieutenants fell victim to what is now politely termed "combat fatigue." He "was wandering through camp perfectly wild" and "imagined that he was followed by an Indian . . . and that the guide want-

ALTHOUGH records have not yielded any views of old Fort Goodwin, post was reputed to have been extensive adobe establishment. In 1865 district commander said it was "well located, and controls a large area of Apache country . . . I do not think it a good post for cavalry, and will, as soon as I can do so, replace the company there by infantry. It is too expensive in the first place, and the surrounding country too rugged for them to operate." Other changes he made were to relieve the post commander and the surgeon, both of whom he did not consider "fitted for their positions, owing to their constant use of intoxicating liquors." At first, fort consisted of brush houses, but these were replaced by adobes. Today, a row of mounds is hidden under trees along what is believed to be edge of old parade ground. Scraping at edges of mounds reveals adobe bricks underneath.

ed to kill him." He was "put under guard for fear he might do some injury either to himself or someone else."

About the same time, a 14-year old Indian boy asked the Army if he could stay with them. In his enthusiasm to adopt this lad, the expedition commander somehow lost sight of his mission. He devoted more time to parleys and hostage-taking so he could keep the boy than to the questions at hand. When the boy was kidnapped by other Indians and the tribe would not return him, at least two Apache hostages were hanged by the Army.

The final incident of the expedition occurred three hours after it had abandoned its last camp. Thirty men had been hidden at the site "with instructions to kill any Indians coming into camp after the command moved out." They were able to kill five of the 15 Apaches who fell into the trap.

The Army included a "scorched earth" policy with the Indian hunting. Soon this began to pay off in tribesmen turning themselves in at the fort. It paid off so well, in fact, that on March 22, 1865 the post commander said he "was placed in the position of the man who drew the elephant in the lottery."

He had 400 Indians under a white flag, but "With nothing to feed them, no transportation to send them to the reservation, and no orders to do so if I had."

The periodic surrenders of Indians at Goodwin did not appear to have much effect. As one group turned itself in, another would waylay the express coach or attack settlers. "The locating of Fort Goodwin has settled the reign of murdering Apaches who have held it so long," was the boast in 1864.

When the post was abandoned in 1871, the reign of murder still was not settled. The major Apache Wars were yet to come.

TO GET THERE: From Globe, Arizona, take U.S. 70 about 48 miles east to Geronimo. Take dirt road to west about one half mile to ranchhouse. Cotton field west of ranchhouse was site of post and adobe mounds are under trees across field. Permission should be requested to drive around field on irrigation dike.

FORT GOODWIN parade ground, now completely leveled by agricultural use, once was scene of 4th of July celebration in 1864. Even though every soldier was involved in building new post, all labor was suspended on holiday. "At 8 a.m., the troops were paraded, and in the absence of heavy ordnance a volley of muskets was fired, as the flag of our country was elevated on a temporary flag-staff, after which Lieut. John Lambert, Fifth Infantry California Volunteers, delivered an appropriate address." Actually this site was second one for Goodwin. At first, supplies had been dropped 32 miles southeast at a "Camp Goodwin." Within a month everything had been moved to final site and ambush detail was left behind at camp to greet any Indian scavengers. Although post was in pleasant valley and strategically located, it was extremely unhealthy. When almost every soldier and family was hit by fever in 1870, Goodwin was quickly abandoned, a move enthusiastically seconded by entire garrison.

FORT MASON, ARIZONA

When the exiled governor of Sonora appeared at Fort Mason, the Californian Column found itself right in the middle of an international incident in 1866.

All of this was unusual to the Californians, but they were used to the unusual. They had arrived in Arizona after the Civil War had ended, and Fort Mason also dated from the postwar days. Even the vicinity of Mason, the Santa Cruz valley of southeastern Arizona a skip or two from the Mexican border, had a strange history.

Under the name of Calabasas, the site of the fort had been an eighteenth century mission and then presidio. When gold mines were discovered in the area, it became a mining center. In 1855, Dragoon Sergeant James A. Bennett noted that the rancho included two Germans whose brother had been killed by livestock-stealing Apaches. He had one comment on the duo: "These two brothers kept an awful old 'bachelor hall.' "

General Carleton entertained the idea of locating at Calabasas in 1862, even though it was rumored to be the headquarters of 900 Confederates. By

May, 1862, his advance guard announced, "Inquiry makes me of the opinion that the Calabasas Ranch will be a desirable locality for the full cavalry command of the column. Its occupancy is generously offered by Governor Guadara, who represents the grazing fine and buildings sufficient to quarter 400 men."

When the Army moved to Calabasas and established what was to become Fort Mason, it was located on a gently sloping plain at the base of a hill. Lookouts could observe the countryside from the hill. Although the first plan was to build of limestone, an 1866 Inspection found "one company is now quartered in small huts built by the men at the fort, the other occupies the abandoned buildings at Calabasas."

Erection of buildings had stopped when the Army's right to the land was challenged. It had reserved to itself "two miles extending in every direction from the flagstaff which is ⅓ miles from Calabasas." The inspector said the condition of the men and their quarters was excellent but that with settlement of the ownership question work could be

FORT MASON area was between marker and mountains. During Civil War, troops occasionally outposted Calabasas area—an 18-man detail was there in 1864—and 1865-66 it was Headquarters for Sub-District of Arizona and of 7th California Infantry. Major expedition against Apaches was attempted in January, 1866, but snowstorm forced infantry to turn back; by the time cavalry had reached Indian camp, they were out of rations and had to return to post. Faulty supply system was blamed. Post went months without salt, sugar, and salted meat. Shoes did not last in rough terrain, and homemade buckskin was substituted by troopers. On September 6, 1866, post was renamed Camp McKee, in memory of 1st Cavalryman, but lasted under this name only until October 1 when it was abandoned.

resumed on the post. He was especially unhappy at the "rude structure of adobe" used as a storehouse and at the $61,439.92 debt run up by the quartermaster whose affairs were "in a very mixed condition."

Fort Mason was victim of a major epidemic in 1866. Included in the 30-some deaths were the quartermaster's baby and his two assistants. The inspector agreed that this may have had a bearing on the state of affairs—the quartermaster himself had just recovered—and he drew the two surgeons in for criticism. One he labeled "incompetent" and the other he said "was reported of intemperate habits and neglectful of his duties. His appearance does not belie the report." He recommended replacement of both.

This inspection took place shortly after the altercation over the border. At that time, in fall of 1865,

the post had a battalion of infantry and cavalry and two 12-pound Napoleon cannon. When the governor appeared and asked for sanctuary near the fort, the commander "offered him the hospitality and protection of the post," a Volunteer wrote later.

The governor camped with his retinue in the nearby ranch and the Volunteer's opinion was, "It is reasonable to suppose that he has money." This was hinted by the fact he had 1,000 cattle, 100 horses and mules, many sheep and goat, his family and servants." Shortly after, Juarez took the lead over Maximilian. Sonora became safe for the governor and he left Fort Mason.

TO GET THERE: From Tucson, take U.S. 89 south 56 miles to marker for Calabasas ghost town. Actual town site was two miles east (turn left on dirt road), site of Fort Mason was between highway and town site. There are no remains.

PICKET POST for Fort Mason was at Tubac, 12 miles away, reputedly the oldest town in Arizona. Dating from 1526—according to some sources—Tubac went through periods of occupation by both Spanish and Mexican troops. It was completely abandoned several times and in 1862 was demolished by Apache siege. Soon after, California Volunteers outposted town. In 1863, it was considered as possible site for Arizona supply depot. Throughout Army career, Tubac quartered troopers in houses around town at no cost to government. Protection soldiers provided was considered adequate payment, though 1866 Whittier inspection report had this to say: "The company occupies adobe houses, the proprietorship of which is doubtful. No rent is paid." General Whittier inspected both Mason and Tubac on same day, noted that hospital for both was at Tubac "as a sanitary measure," although he disapproved of hospital surgeon's intemperate habits. Tubac received supplies three times a month from Mason he noted, and "a small amount of grain is kept at Tubac for use of government animals passing through." With Army providing protection, settlers began to return to Tubac after Civil War. Whittier estimated there were 40 males in town, not counting troops, and correctly predicted that soon there would be no need for detachments at either Mason or Tubac. Town now is artists' center and subject of extensive restoration program. Adobe ruins shown here date from Army days and have been stabilized to prevent further deterioration.

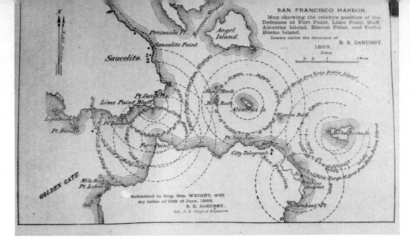

PLAN FOR San Francisco's defenses was submitted in this fashion in 1863 by 73-year old Colonel Rene E. DeRussy, builder of many East coast forts and superintendent of San Francisco harbor defenses throughout Civil War. Most of the defenses ultimately were adopted, but long after DeRussy's death six months after end of war. This is his plan as it appears in the *Official Records of the War of the Rebellion.*

RING AROUND THE GOLDEN GATE

"In view of a possibility of a hostile force threatening this city I have desired the chief engineer, Colonel DeRussy, to submit to me a plan for temporary defensive works. I shall then throw up field-works to command the approaches, but we may be somewhat embarrassed for the want of a sufficient number of heavy guns. The forts at Fort Point and on Alcatraz Island have in position about one-half of the guns required for their complete armament. I deem it of importance that the balance of the armament for these forts should be sent out as soon as practicable."

—General Wright to the Adjutant General of the Army, Dec. 19, 1861.

WITH secession on the land, Pacific Coast fears of a Confederate invasion were centered on its most important harbor, San Francisco. But the priority was in the East. It was to take far more than the four years of Civil War to make San Francisco safe behind bulwarks and gun batteries.

In 1861 an inspection of the harbor's defenses was so dismaying that it was not made public; it "showed much which should not be made public at this moment." The Bay was short at least 200 guns and the appropriate ammunition, needed at least 1,550 artillerymen to man its defenses, and most of the defenses still had to be built.

Eighty-nine guns were offered by the Navy at Mare Island, but these had shipboard mounts and would require new carriages. At Benicia Arsenal, the only available carriages had been used by a New York Regiment in 1846 and they were considered obsolete at that time.

And in the city, there was open talk of taking sides with the South or of setting up a Pacific Republic. The San Francisco *Bulletin* might editorialize that before this came about, "There are 100,000 men in California who would have to be put to the sword," but still it took mass parades and completion of the intercontinental telegraph line before the Legislature would pledge its alliegance to the Union.

Plans for the defenses were sent to Washington. Action was so slow that General Wright wrote bluntly to the adjutant general. "I fear greatly the masterly inactivity system and the time consumed in planning and deliberating as to the best points for our batteries, and then going to work with our permanent fortifications, slowness may be fatal," he complained. "While we are meditating some morning, the first thing we shall know will be the enemy's guns thundering against the city."

It was feared that the privateer could use fog as a cover to steal past the defense lines and imperil the city. The fear was well founded. The Confederate privateer Shenendoah, 25 sinkings and five captures to her record, planned to do just this. The surrender at Appomattox was the most effective single reason this did not come about.

The slow fortifying of San Francisco had one advantage. Bancroft's *History of California* says: "Vast sums have been saved by the neglect, for such has been the improvement in war vessels and heavy ordnance that expensive changes must have been made every few years."

THE PRESIDIO OF SAN FRANCISCO, CALIFORNIA

Back in 1849, the arrival of 86 soldiers, "all fine looking and in good discipline," was good news indeed to the new commander of the Presidio of San Francisco, Captain Erasmus D. Keyes, 3rd Artillery. But '49 was the year of the Gold Rush. When "We began having dress parades, and doing garrison duty strictly according to Army regulations," Keyes found that within a week he had lost two-thirds of his men.

Desertion to the gold fields turned out to be one of the major problems facing the military installations in San Francisco. For Keyes, it almost wiped out his entire command.

"One night the whole guard, including the corporal, went off," he wrote in his memoirs. An officer was sent in pursuit, overtaking the guard 15 miles away, "shot a couple, but brought back only one wounded soldier, as all his escort joined the deserters."

William T. Sherman, a young lieutenant at the time, also was stationed in California. His *Memoirs* note that pursuits of deserters had to be composed wholly of officers because the enlisted men were more apt to join the deserters.

The reason for desertions was that a man could earn more in a day at the mines than in a month as a soldier. Prices were so high that when the Headquarters for the Department of the Pacific were set up in San Francisco, an old adobe custom house was used as an office. The commanding general and his wife lived aboard the USS Ohio as guests of the commodore.

Sherman was adjutant general to the commander, General Persifor T. Smith. Smith succeeded Colonel Richard B. Mason who had asked to be relieved because the war with Mexico was over and, "The soldiers nearly all deserted." Even his cook had left and the colonel had to prepare his own meals.

The Smiths found themselves in the same situation. All but one of their servants disappeared and, to quote Sherman, "The general, commanding all the mighty forces on the Pacific coast, had to scratch to get one square meal a day for his family. . . . Breakfast would be announced any time between ten and twelve, and dinner according to circumstances." Finally the married officers gave up and sent their families back to the East.

To make ends meet, and, as Keyes noted, "The garrison being too much reduced for proper military service, the officers were allowed by General Smith to do something to increase their pay." Keyes took up surveying and real estate and within a year was receiving $1,000 a month in rentals. In 1856, Congress authorized additional pay for officers and men stationed in California.

Although Lieutenant H. W. Halleck, an associate, also invested in city property, Sherman rejected a suggestion that he buy, too. "I felt actually insulted that he should think me such a fool as to pay money for property in such a horrid place," Sherman noted in his *Memoirs*.

WHEN HE VISITED San Francisco in 1792, English Captain George Vancouver was permitted to visit Presidio. He found it "a square area, whose sides were about 200 yards in length, enclosed by a mud wall, and resembling a pound for cattle. Above this wall the thatched roofs of their low small houses just made their appearance. On entering the Presidio, we found one of its sides still uninclosed by the wall, and very indifferently fenced in by a few bushes here and there, fastened to stakes in the ground . . . It is about 14 feet high, five in breadth, and was first formed by uprights and horizontal rafters of large timber, between which dried sods and moistened earth were pressed as close and as hard as possible; after which the whole was cased with earth made into a sort of mud plaster, which gave it the appearance of durability . . . Houses were along the wall, within the square, and their fronts uniformly extended the same distance into the area." He said the church was small, whitewashed with a lime made from crushed sea shells, and extended deeper into the parade ground. He added that the Presidio was "totally incapable of making resistance against a foreign invasion," its only cannon being a three pounder mounted on a carriage that was beginning to fall apart. When Vancouver's visit was discovered by Spanish authorities, commandant was reprimanded for permitting too close an inspection of the place. (Redrawn from plat in Bancroft, *History of California*; north arrow is as shown in Bancroft but it actually points west.)

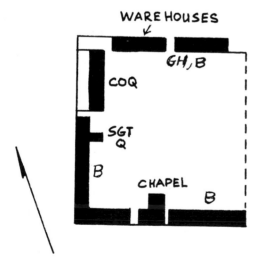

PRESIDIO OF SAN FRANCISCO
CALIF. — 1792

This "horrid place" had a military history that dated back to 1776 when a 63-man expedition of Spanish soldiers, priests, and settlers arrived to establish a presidio. They brought with them the authority of Spain, in answer to English and Russian overtures from Canada and Alaska. At the same time, Father Junipero Serra established a mission nearby, calling it San Francisco de Asis. Later it was known as Mission Dolores.

The primitive palisaded Presidio was not designed to fend off Indian attacks, because the Indians were considered friendly. As time passed and adobe replaced the rough stick and stone construction, it became obvious that it was not even designed to ward off the changeable San Francisco weather. Throughout the period of pre-American occupation, the Presidio was in a state of continual construction. As fast as new adobe would be built during the dry season, it would be attacked by the rain and atmosphere in the rainy season. Twenty-five years after work started, the fourth wall still had not been completed.

Thirty soldiers founded the Presidio. Twenty years later, a detachment of 35 more arrived. Patrols and escorts, plus a guard at the mission, usually left the Presidio almost vacant and the small garrison was unable to cope with the deterioration of the post. In 1800 the magazine was covered by drifting sand while a hurricane tore off several roofs. By this time, most of the available labor was being directed to Fort San Joaquin, on the future site of Fort Point at the Golden Gate.

Isolated from Spain, there was no hesitancy about changing allegiance to Mexico when the garrison heard about independence in 1822. The Presidio continued in operation, but the deterioration could not be prevented when the garrison was reduced to seven artillerymen in 1835. A year later, all regular troops were recalled. A few retired soldiers and their families remained at the ruined forts.

The United States moved in with little effort in 1846. The decrepit defenses offered no resistance when Marines of the USS Portmouth landed at Yerba Buena and raised the American flag. Yerba Buena soon was renamed San Francisco, and the plaza of the flag raising, Portsmouth Plaza. In the latter years of a wide open city, the Plaza was to be a vice center.

Above the principal landing, in 1846 the Navy placed "a couple of Navy guns," Sherman remembered. He said the site was named the Battery and, from that, the street received its name. Marines manned the Presidio at the same time.

A few months later, a regiment of New York Volunteers relieved the Marines at the Presidio. Two companies were designated to repair it. Stores and ordnance were landed at the city wharf, but the heavy guns, mortars, and carriages had to remain at the docks for several years because they could not be moved across the sand hills.

An 1854 inspection was critical of the place. "The quarters for the soldiers were miserable adoby (sic) buildings, the leavings of the Mexican government," it said, "but were kept in good police and order." A temporary wooden barracks was added.

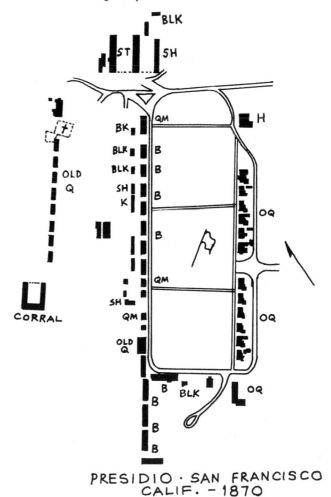

PRESIDIO · SAN FRANCISCO
CALIF. — 1870

PARALLELOGRAM, 550 yards by 150, was shape of Presidio by 1870, completely swallowing up original site. Barracks at southwestern corner of parade ground was original commandant's house. Officers' quarters included 12 31- by 18-foot story-and-a-half frame cottages and one three-story frame building, 114 by 32 feet plus a 44- by 30-foot wing, that had 39 rooms for bachelor officers. Barracks for 900 men included nine frame buildings; laundresses and their families lived in the adobe barracks. Because of strong winds from Golden Gate that blew into front of officers' row, a lattice screen of lath, 12 feet high, was built across front of row. Picket fence surrounded entire post on city side. (Redrawn from plat in Surgeon-General Circular No. 4, 1870.)

OLDEST BUILDING in San Francisco, this is original Presidio commandant's quarters, now used as Officers' Club. It was built between 1776 and 1778, remodeled in 1850, altered again in 1900, 1912 (when electricity was installed), 1915, and in 1934 when it was restored to original architecture. Vancouver visited it in 1792, later gave this description: "The apartment in the commandant's house into which we were ushered was about 30 feet long, 14 feet broad, and 12 feet high; and the other room, or chamber, I judged to be of the same dimensions, excepting its length, which appeared to be somewhat less. The floor was of the native soil raised about three feet from its original level, without being boarded, paved, or even reduced to an even surface; the roof was covered in flags and rushes, the walls on the inside had once been whitewashed; the furniture consisted of a very sparing assortment of the most indispensable articles, of the rudest fashion, and of the meanest kind; and ill accorded with the ideas we had conceived of the sumptuous manner in which the Spaniards live on this side of the globe."

With desertions and frequent demands for special details, it was difficult to pursue the matter of construction effectively.

Devices to minimize desertion included General Bennett Riley's shift of his command to Monterey where they would be farther from the gold fields. The Navy, having lost several crews, took no chances when USS Oregon arrived. She was anchored alongside USS Ohio and her entire crew sent aboard as prisoners until ready to sail.

San Francisco owed her early buildings to crew desertions. In 1849, the Presidio saw 549 vessels pass by and within the next five years the harbor had more tonnage than any other port in the world. In 1851, desertions had resulted in the abandonment of 148 ships in the mud along shore. As these were tightly closed in by sand, they became business houses and residence. The Apollo became the Apollo saloon; the Euphema was bought by the city as a

FRONT WALL of Commandant's House includes about 75 per cent original construction, but with alterations from 1792 Vancouver description. He said that walls "are a sufficient security against the inclemency of the weather, yet the windows, which are cut in the front wall, and look into the square, are destitute of glass, or any other defense that does not at the same time exclude the light." He suggested that buildings "in winter, or rainy seasons must at the best be very uncomfortable dwellings."

PRESIDIO in the Seventies matches ground plan. Triple-story bachelor officer quarters is on right, original Presidio building is left of center in picture (behind horse-drawn wood cart). Alcatraz Island is at right edge of picture in this view to north-northeast down center of parade. At right of flagpole in background is hospital, dating from 1854 and still at original site. Post was inspected in 1866 when it had 1,156 officers and men in 16 companies, 14 of them preparing for duty in Arizona. Brevet Brigadier C. A. Whittier, the inspector, had few good comments to make. He noted regarding drill, "Movements not known to the Regulations of the Army or the approved tactics were being continually ordered by the commanding officer. The review so far as it depended upon simultaneous movements of all the troops was a failure and would have been discreditable to a first sergeant commanding." He found quartermaster records a mess. Condition of post indicated "little or no attention being paid to policing," with no toilet facilities in guardhouse huts occupied by 59 prisoners. The quarters of men being mustered out were "very dirty." His recommendation was to remove or reassign post commander who had "almost complete lack of knowledge of the fort and who is incompetent."

jail and was moored next to the Apollo on the spot now occupied by the Federal Bank Building.

The expansion of the city brought with it squatters on government lands. Captain Keyes led one "expedition" to clear squatters and, though successful, was brought to court and sued for doing his duty. Presidio troopers also were called out to preserve law and order in the days of Vigilance movements.

These problems stepped to the background in 1861 when a flag of secession was raised for a few moments in San Francisco. Doubts about the status of General A. S. Johnston were relieved when General Edwin V. Sumner arrived on April 24, 1861. "I hereby assume command of this department," he proclaimed. "All concerned will govern themselves accordingly."

Sumner found 500 troops in San Francisco, 115 at the Presidio. He made all three Bay posts independent—Presidio, Point, and Alcatraz—and pushed completion of the fortifications. For good measure,

PRESIDIO TODAY shows changes from 1870 surgeon's comment: "There are no shade trees in the vicinity." Barracks row, left, is about 100 yards to rear of 1870 row; original Presidio building is in center foreground, on line with single tree on parade ground. Alcatraz Island is at right edge of picture. Far shore is partly obscured by perennial Bay fog, described in 1866, as providing climate that "can scarcely be called inviting. . . . Her continual rains in winter, and cold winds and fogs in summer, must be very trying to average nerves and lungs. . . . It did rain there sometimes the easiest of any place I ever saw. . . . As a rule nobody seemed to mind a perpetual drizzle." In 1889, Anson Mills was stationed at Presidio as executive officer, found it "the most enjoyable station we ever had. . . . Numerous balls, dances, and other amusements in additional to strenuous duties kept us all busy and healthy." A 1935 report said, regarding climate; "There is nothing else but. Never cold, never hot. Always cool. Rains are heavy during the winter season." It found City of San Francisco, "than which there is no better post town" which agreed with 1866 comment that Army officers were no better esteemed or better treated than there. Post has been headquarters for Army west of Rocky Mountains continuously since 1857.

he renamed the quartermaster's brig the General Jesup, after the Army quartermaster general, instead of its previous name honoring John Floyd, former Secretary of War who had gone south.

During the Civil War, as it did in later conflicts, the Presidio was the command post for the Bay. As the inspection report of 1854 stated, the Presidio site was "the only spot about here suitable for a command of troops, either for the forts or for instruction, and is ample and convenient."

TO GET THERE: From downtown San Francisco, take U.S. 101 (Van Ness) north and then west (on Lombard) to main gate. Original site of Presidio is reached by following Lincoln Boulevard through main gate about four blocks west to Graham street. Southern end of this large parade ground was original Presidio; former Commandant's house, now Officers' Club, is at south end of Graham Street.

MAGAZINE, 28 by 23 feet, dates from 1863. Presidio was point from which troops were dispatched for many Indian expeditions, including San Joaquin Valley and Rogue River Indian War in 1851 and Snake River campaigns of 1856. Latter took six companies into Oregon and Idaho and culminated in Battle of Steptoe Butte. During Civil War, in order to augment Presidio garrison, 80 rifles were issued to San Francisco police. Mayor requested 500 troops be sent to city to help preserve order after Lincoln's assassination. One of hardest fought battles of Presidio was on paper in 1850's between General Wool and Secretary of War. Latter wanted to abandon post in favor of Benicia; Wool's reaction was to revamp the post and to propose building a plank road the three miles to city's center. He pointed out that abandonment of valuable Presidio property would touch off violent squatter war.

OLD STABLES now serve as offices and storehouses. By 1890, frontier version of Presidio had been replaced by this permanent brick construction. At this time, post included six artillery batteries, a cavalry troop, and two companies of infantry. It could accommodate 39 officers and 562 enlisted men. In 1889 it was scene of one of Army's first boards to examine officers for promotion. Thirty-three were tested and "It was a very lively and, I think, an efficient board," commented Anson Mills, a member. Canteen was established at Presidio in 1889 when annual admission rate for alcoholism was 114.05 per 1,000 men; by 1891 rate had dropped astoundingly to 8.68.

HOSPITAL BUILDING was built in 1854, is oldest Army construction at Presidio. Its brick foundations and pine and hemlock girders were shipped around Horn. Inspection in 1866, although critical of remainder of Presidio, found, "The hospital was in all respects in good condition." In 1870, surgeon reported hospital was arranged for 50 beds with average occupancy of 17, and the sick list has been mostly composed of venereal diseases contracted in San Francisco." His statistics showed 141 cases out of mean strength of 319.5 men in 1869. City's notoriety was mentioned in U. S. Grant's *Memoirs*. In 1853 he found, "Eating, drinking and gambling houses were conspicuous for their number and publicity. They were on the first floor with doors wide open. At all hours of the day and night in walking the streets, the eye was regaled, on every block near the waterfront, by the sight of players at faro." In 1854 he noticed, "Gambling houses had disappeared from public view. The city had become staid and orderly." This was disputed by General Rusling's 1866 visit to Barbary Coast. "Here in narrow, noisome alleys are congregated the wretched Chinese women, that are imported by the ship-load, mainly for infamous purposes," he wrote in *Across America*. "They are not more immodest, than those of our own race, who ply the same vocation in Philadelphia and New York . . . San Francisco owes it to herself—to obliterate, to stamp out this plague spot." San Francisco *Call* had this to say of Barbary Coast at the time: "That sunk of moral pollution, whose reefs are strewn with human wrecks, and into whose vortex are constantly drifting barks of moral life, while swiftly down the whirlpool of death go the sinking hulks of the murderer and suicide . . . The coast where no gentle breezes blow but where rages the sirocco of sin." Reform movement of 1917 ended vice reign in San Francisco.

FORT POINT, CALIFORNIA

The situation truly was well in hand when John Fremont, a few Marines, and some settlers made an amphibious assault on the Golden Gate back in 1846. It was midnight on July 1, when the small party crossed from Sausalito in a launch, scaled the 100-foot height, and swarmed into the adobe fort of Castillo de San Joaquin.

Ten cannon quickly were spiked and the attacking party waded back to their boat and returned to Sausalito. There was only one thing that detracted from the glorious success: Fort San Joaquin was completely undefended, the garrison having been withdrawn more than a quarter of a century before.

"In the absence of a garrison with no powder," is the caustic comment in Bancroft's *History of California,* "it is not surprising that, as far as can be known, not one of the ten cannon offered the slightest resistance."

The site of San Joaquin, at the southern side of the Golden Gate, was to become Fort Point ten years later. It was the logical location for a key defense of the San Francisco harbor, and as early as 1793 construction had begun on a fortress there.

At that time, the point of land was about 100 feet above the waterline. The post was of adobe but with brick facing and had dimensions that ranged between 100 by 120 feet to 140 by 140 feet, depending upon the authority consulted—and the time period concerned. As with the Presidio, the fortress apparently underwent considerable modification, especially when each rainy season took its toll of the adobe foundations.

A dozen cannon went into the finished castillo, the heaviest aimed toward the ocean and the Golden Gate. The wall along this side was 10 feet thick. The shore side was only five feet thick and mounted only light guns.

With the place completed, the authorities seemed content to devote their efforts to keeping it from falling apart. By 1836, however, all regular troops had been withdrawn, and San Joaquin had nothing to prevent it from washing away.

It was in this decrepit condition when Fremont and company seized it 30 years later, although in his *Memoirs* Fremont tells of spiking "large handsome pieces" there. Seven years after that, the U.S. Congress decided that the Golden Gate needed fortresses in more than just name, and appropriated $500,000 to build them at this site and on Alcatraz Island.

At the time, no one bothered with a name for either place. Although in 1865 General Irvin McDowell suggested that Fort Point be named Fort Reno, the matter was let die.

The first problem was to chop off 90 feet of the bluff so that cannon in the fort could bear on to attacking ships. The level was brought down to 10 feet above the waterline and then a fortress similar to Fort Sumter, S.C., was erected. While the work was underway, General Wool had 10 24-pounders mounted on the high ground to its rear for use until the post was complete.

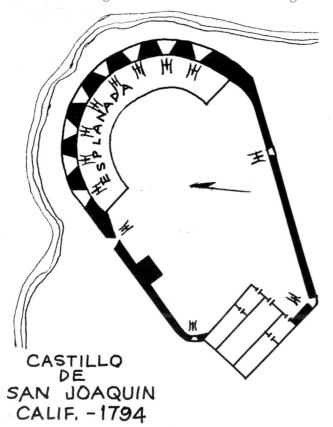

CASTILLO
DE
SAN JOAQUIN
CALIF. – 1794

ONE VERSION of Fort Point's ancestor, as it appeared in Bancroft's *History of California,* measured about 240 by 140 feet. An earlier sketch of fort put it 120 by 180 feet with the buildings in center rather than against rear wall. Still another version had it 120 by 100 feet. Probably all were correct for periods described due to constant remodeling, especially in 1799, 1805, 1808, 1810, 1816, and 1818. "The structure rested on sand and decaying rock," a 1796 report said. "The brick-faced adobe walls crumbled at the shock whenever a salute was fired; the guns were badly mounted and for the most part worn out, only two of the 13 24-pounders being serviceable or capable of sending a ball across the entrance of the port. The whole work, protected by an adobe wall with one gate, was commanded by a hill in the rear, and the garrison of a corporal and six artillerymen was altogether insufficient." Soon after Mexico took over California, visitor wrote, "I found St. Joachim on his ricky throne, truly a very peaceful and well disposed saint; no one of his cannon in condition to fire a single shot." (Redrawn from Bancroft plat.)

(NATIONAL ARCHIVES.)

CIVIL WAR appearance of interior of Fort Point is shown by this view of southern side which included quarters and office casemates. On first floor were shops for wheelwright, blacksmith, carpenter, and other utility services. Three prison cells were next to sally port—which is flanked by cannon in center of first floor; cells were on left of this entrance. One cell was lighted from opening on outside of fort, another had light from opening to inner court, but middle cell was unlighted "solitary confinement" room. Second floor had officers' quarters and barracks were on third floor. Eleven 32-pounder sea coast guns, commanding hill behind fort and road approaches from wharf, can be seen on this part of fourth tier. Apparently temporary wooden shelters protected them from elements.

Thirty-six foot thick walls, a shot tower, places for upwards of 200 guns, guardhouse cells, living quarters, all were included in what was to become the most elaborate fortification on the Pacific coast. The original appropriation soon was used up, and by 1854 a request was sent to Washington for another $750,000 for the next fiscal year.

In all, upwards of three million dollars were spent on Fort Point, $400,000 of it on a 2,000-foot long granite sea wall. Quarters, barracks, storehouses, and workshops were built along this sea wall to the east of the fort.

"FORT POINT is a permanent work, built of brick and granite," said report of 1879. "Has four tiers and two flank defence towers for guns on the water side. 126 guns can be mounted in it. Soldiers quarters and hospital on land side, officers quarters on outside." The 20-some buildings outside of fort were built between 1854 and 1862. Commanding officer's quarters dated from 1858, had two stories with single story office attached. Both officers' quarters were double-story duplexes, six rooms per set, built in 1862. Barracks also dated from 1862, were described as "mere shells . . . one story, rough boards and batting sides, shingle roof and pile foundation. Windows and doors destroyed; used as lumber and storerooms." Post was not garrisoned for ten years after 1868 but underwent repairs and refurnishing upon reoccupation in September, 1878, when two companies of 4th Artillery moved in. Cluster of unindentified buildings south of low row of "permanent" fortifications probably were engineer and construction workers' quarters. The fortifications were earthen barbettes begun in 1870. None of these buildings remains. (Redrawn from McDowell Report, 1879.)

A visitor in 1855 noted that the granite block foundations were being laid in a trench nine feet long and 10 to 20 feet wide. A cistern was being dug within the enclosure. By 1856, the first floor had been completed and four 32-pounders were added for defense while the work was in progress. The second tier of gun arches was completed in 1857 when 240 men were in the work force. A year later, 200 men were pushing work on the arches for the fourth tier. Three spiral staircases went up at this time to a lighthouse on top.

In 1861, the War Department sent word to suspend work on the fort and the labor force was discharged, leaving unfinished a small portion of the defenses and the living quarters. With orders on

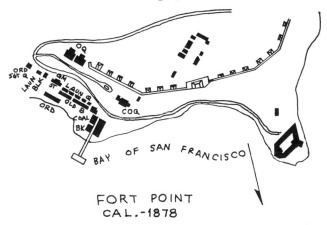

FORT POINT
CAL.-1878

INTERIOR OF Fort Point stands mute and littered, not having been fully active since garrison left it after earthquake in 1906. German prisoners were kept there in World War I and in World War II it housed a 75-mm recoilless rifle battery and searchlight detachment. In 1861, its first troops were issued series of orders by General A. S. Johnston. He required round-the-clock sentinels on barbette battery atop fort and at main gate. Officer of the day was told to be present whenever gate was opened or closed, "in whose hands the keys must always remain." Before gates were opened, exterior was to be examined by patrols with guard under arms while patrol was absent. Officer of day was required to inspect lower shutter fastenings at retreat, main magazine was to be entered only under direct supervision of a commissioned officer, garrison was to be under arms whenever stores or ammunition was being moved from outer store houses, and cartridges and loaded shells were required to be next to all guns. This view looks at northeastern corner of fort.

February 15 to occupy "the fort at Fort Point," General Albert S. Johnston decided that this included "of necessity the authority to do all such acts as are necessary to render the occupation secure and the place inhabitable." He ordered the work to resume.

Two companies of the 3rd Artillery garrisoned Fort Point with 160 men. The California State Militia of the National Guard volunteered to man the place, but this was politely rejected. The Army said it had enough men to do it. Three years later McDowell asked the War Department for authority to form a regiment of civilian artillerymen to man Fort Point, but was told to use the troops that he had, even if he had to put infantrymen to work on the cannon. An 1864 estimate said that 700 artillerymen would be necessary to defend the fortress, but the garrison never approached that size.

General George Wright inspected the place on November 9, 1861. "The armament of the fort, al-though incomplete, was found in handsome condition and ready for any emergency," he reported. A month later, he added that he had "found everything in the highest order" and "by the industry and activity" of the commanding officer "the fort has been put in the best possible condition to guard the passage of the Golden Gate."

In 1862, Wright reported that there were 140 guns mounted at Point, but that this was only half the number needed. He explained that if war from a seagoing opponent ever should come, "this is the only point on the Pacific Coast where effective resistance could be made."

During the Civil War, the garrison at Fort Point was alerted whenever a ship was sighted at the Golden Gate. A revenue cutter challenged visitors under the frowning gun ports of the structure, and cannon was rolled out and ready to react at any hostile act.

Nothing came from the seaward side of Fort

CASEMATES along sea side of Fort Point look like this. All guns were removed in 1897 and offered to permanent posts for ornamental purposes. Those remaining were bought in 1901 by Herman White for scrapping. Denying that the many-thousand pound weapons were "White elephants," he was able to break them into manageable pieces of scrap. In this section of third tier, Civil War garrison had 8-inch Columbiads mounted along this casemate where traces of traversing tracks still can be seen on floor. This was a cast-metal, smooth-bore, bronze cannon with range upwards of one mile.

BY 1908, disappearing cannons were mounted at Fort Point's successor, Fort Winfield Scott. Reinforced concrete installations were started in 1893 and were not finished until 1908 when this picture was taken. They obliterated earthen revetments dug during and after Civil War. Three 15-inch dynamite guns, 12- and 16-inch mortars, and disappearing guns ranging in calibre from 6- to 12-inches covered bluff above original fort. This cannon was in Battery Cranston overlooking Golden Gate; Lime Point is in background. Gun is in firing position, crew is traversing carriage at direction of gun-pointer who is on platform.

Point, and any military commitments placed on the garrison came from disorders in San Francisco. They were on alert at every election, the entire garrison armed and ready. The Volunteers who were California citizens were taken unarmed by boat to their voting precincts to cast their ballots.

With peace, the defense of the Golden Gate was not forgotten. More batteries were built along the 100 foot contour line on the hill behind Fort Point. Gradually the defense line worked itself back until Fort Point was left alone out on a point. In 1882 the post was officially renamed Fort Winfield Scott,

LIGHTHOUSE atop Fort Point was built in 1856, circular stairway is in round tower at right. This shows northeastern barbette where 8- and 10-inch Columbiads were mounted to bring fire on any ships entering Golden Gate. Bay entrance is obscured in this picture by perennial San Francisco fog. For two years after Civil War fort was manned, and in 1866 inspector reported there were seven officers and 158 enlisted men stationed there. Eighty guns were mounted and 15 unmounted. "Guns are being continuously received at the posts and new works being erected," he noted. He was impressed by post, especially when they demonstrated their ability to fire artillery over channel.

GOLDEN GATE dwarfs Fort Point. Bridge was completed in 1937 at cost of 35 and a half million dollars. Its tallest towers are 746 feet above water and center span—1,125 feet long—is 220 above water. Cables are a yard in diameter. Below its southern end is Fort Point, 150 feet wide, 250 feet long on its longest side and 45 feet high. Bastions extend out 40 feet on northeast and northwest sides to provide flanking fire. Battery to protect rear of fort was placed on hill behind it. Even when Castillo de San Joaquin occupied this site, danger from land was noted. "To render the fort tenable in case of approach to it by land, it is indispensable that a work be thrown up on the eminence which commands it, about four or five hundred yards immediately in its rear," 1846 inspection report commented, "otherwise it is at the mercy of an enemy on the land side."

a term applied to the entire system of coastal defenses west of the Presidio.

By 1906, Fort Point—for it never really felt comfortable with the Scott name—was declared obsolete and its garrison moved to the Presidio. Its batteries were abandoned in 1914. Fort Winfield Scott remained, its modern coastal defense for the World Wars obliterating the positions on the bluff. And in 1937, the Golden Gate Bridge crossed above Fort Point, dwarfing what once had been the most magnificent edifice and most powerful defender on San Francisco Bay.

TO GET THERE: Lincoln Boulevard, at entrance of Presidio, goes under Golden Gate Approach at McDowell Avenue. At this point, take right fork away from Lincoln Boulevard, go under Approach and follow McDowell and Long Avenues past Fort Point Coast Guard Station and Fort Point Mine Dock to boarded up fortress under Golden Gate. Admission to interior is restricted to groups and arrangements should be made 30 days in advance with Community Relations Division of the Sixth Army's Information Officer at the Presidio.

SALLY PORT was protected by set of heavy doors studded with large nails and closed with iron bar that pivoted on one of doors. Small doorway permitted access without exposing entire entrance. Passageway inside leading to second set of doors had loopholes in its walls from which small arms fire could be brought against enemy forcing outer doors. Officers' bedroom windows are above entrance. Most bricks were made in yards set up on hill behind by George D. Naglee, whose name was pressed into each brick and still can be seen.

BATTERIES overlooking Golden Gate now are deserted, their gun pits and magazines last used in World War II. This battery is atop bluff overlooking Fort Point, immediately next to the toll booths of Golden Gate Bridge, obscured in immediate background by fog.

FROM GOLDEN GATE Bridge this is how Fort Point looks. Positions along top tier barbette remain for Civil War armament that included nine 10-inch and 17 8-inch Columbiads and 11 32-pounder seacoast artillery. Remainder of ordnance in fort included six 24- and 28 42-pounders and 56 8-inch Columbiads. "The fortification from which Fort Point receives its name, is a brick structure modeled after Fort Sumter," 1884 description reads, "and, before the recent improvements in naval warfare, was considered an impregnable work; but before the arms now in use, it is asserted, it would not stand one hour." Compared to Sumter, Point had only a third the number of men, a quarter more number of guns but of smaller sizes. Sumter had 15-inch Columbiads that weighed 49,100 pounds and fired 320-pound shell 5,730 yards. In 1863, two of these were to be sent to Point.

FAR CRY from its Fort Point ancestor, this is modern headquarters of Fort Winfield Scott. Post was completed in 1912 after old brick fort was condemned. Eleven concrete barracks in Spanish decor cost $700,000 and were described in 1924 recruiting circular, "There is no group of buildings in the public service that presents a more uniformly beautiful appearance, in a setting equally attractive." In 1935 it was headquarters for Harbor Defense command and housed bulk of coast artillery regiment. It is now a sub-post of Presidio.

SURGEON worked in this room, area near windows being partitioned as kitchen and steward's room and near part of room as office. Partitions were torn down long ago. Exterior walls were seven feet thick at this point. Post was inspected in 1866 and report took special note of the fact fort had "52 gallons superior whiskey on hand"—presumably for medicinal purposes.

FORT MASON, CALIFORNIA

Nine points of the law or not, possession had little effect in 1863 when the Army decided that it needed Point San Jose. Squatters who had moved into the reservation within the past decade, building, renting, mortgaging, and selling the property without regard for legal titles, were told they would have to go.

Fresh in the memories of some Army men was the furor when Captain E. D. Keyes cleared squatters from Rincon Point in 1853. That episode had resulted in a civil trial. Although the suit was dismissed by the judge, Keyes was told by a juror that the jury probably would have found Keyes guilty in sympathy for the "underdog" squatters.

This had subdued Army enthusiasm for clearing Point San Jose. As General Irvin McDowell summarized the situation, "Combinations of land-grabbers and land-jumpers so harassed this officer that he wrote in despair that he could not protect the government property, and in one of his letters reports: 'They have seized on Point San Jose and have it in complete possession.'"

The military value of the point was admitted as early as 1797. That was when "Bateria San Jose" was constructed at the tip of the point. It was also known as "Battery at Yerba Buena." Five brass 8-pounder cannon were put in earthworks that were hastily dug and covered with brushwood fascines. Instead of a permanent garrison, a sentinel was to visit the place every day.

By 1806 this practice must have stopped. An inspection by the governor noted that the battery had been neglected. "There was not even a hut for the gunners and the guns were rendered useless by exposure," it pointed out.

The sandhills and scrub brush gradually reclaimed the area. By the time that Mexico took over San Francisco in 1822, the site was known as Black Point because of the dark underbrush that covered everything.

Although the United States quickly asserted its ownership of the Point as early as 1850, nothing in the military line was done to use it. An 1856 report on Bay defenses suggested that a permanent battery should be constructed at Point San Jose. It should be "in barbette, with earthen parapet, breast height of bricks, a small magazine, and a brick building for ordnance stores and a guardhouse," the report recommended. "It should mount 20 guns."

This recommendation was repeated in 1862, but it was with some hesitancy that the Army took action. Large, well-built residences had been erected by citizens on Black Point, shrubbery and fences had been laid out, and taxes had been paid to the city in accordance with their assessments. Even John Fremont had paid an estimated $40,000 for a frame cottage and 12 acres on the Point. He had rented the place to a friend in 1861 when he went East for Army service.

Then at 6 a.m. on October 3, 1863, General George Wright received a telegram from the War Department. "The Secretary of War directs that you take military possession of Point San Jose," it said, "and erect the battery proposed for its defense. The question of ownership will be determined later."

A few days later a company of the 9th Infantry was ordered to Point San Jose to "take and hold military possession of such land as necessary for the erection of batteries." Almost immediately com-

FORT MASON
CALIF.—1877

AS POST POINT SAN JOSE, and Fort Mason after 1882, this ground plan remains basically correct to modern times. An 1870 report said, "The officers' quarters are five frame cottages of different sizes and plan, but all are comfortable and pleasantly situated on the sheltered brow, with a luxuriant flower garden around them. They were cottages of citizens before the point was taken up as a government post." It noted that above battery "are built two sets of company quarters, of which only one at the present time is occupied. They are each of wood, 90 by 30½ by 13 feet . . . furnished with a double row of bunks, two tiers high . . . two tables and four benches complete its furniture." Reservation included 67 acres with a small parade ground on the crown of the point. (Redrawn from McDowell report, 1879.)

"SAN JOSE is a rocky point which, with an elevation of 80 feet, projects into the bay northward," reported surgeon in 1870. "It is steep and bare on its western face, less so on its eastern or sheltered face; and on both sides it falls away into low sand mounds." This 1865-era painting shows entire Point. Officers' quarters are in foreground across road, headquarters is long building with porch across front.

(JAMES A. SULLIVAN. ARMY TERMINAL COMMAND)

plaints were heard from occupants. The first was that the soldiers had destroyed some shrubbery.

Shrubbery removal was not the least of the Army efforts, however. The houses were commandeered and those in the way of the engineers' plans were removed or leveled. Fremont's cottage was razed, touching off a series of legal disputes that went as far as the United States Supreme Court.

When the Court determined that the property belonged to the United States "whether or not they were by sufficient authority appropriate for public use," the Fremont family brought suit for damages. From a $250,000 claim in 1866, the suit was re-filed for a million dollars in 1893. When nothing was done on it for 14 more years, it was thrown out of court.

The 10-gun battery was placed on the western brow of the point, in position to intersect the fires from Alcatraz. An estimated need for 100 artillerymen to man them was made in 1864. One company of infantrymen from the 9th Regiment was the garrison until late in 1864 when a battery of the 3rd

Artillery was transferred from Alcatraz. In March, 1865, the post became the headquarters of the 9th Infantry Regiment, a non-artillery role that was to hint of the future.

Along with the other Bay forts, San Jose's troopers devoted more of their attention to settling civil problems than with defending the harbor from Confederate attack. And as the Civil War ended, the squatter problem once again raised its head.

An inspection on June 6, 1865, revealed, "Certain citizens have possession of a part of the military reservation at Point San Jose (Black Point) . . . If the present occupants are allowed to retain undisputed possession of this highly valuable property any longer, it may cost the government a large sum to dispossess them."

TO GET THERE: Called Fort Mason since 1882, the Post at Point San Jose is on Van Ness Avenue at Bay Street. Although its transportation depot functions were closed in 1964, its historic residences have been retained by Army and have been marked.

CIVILIAN DESIGN is apparent in Brook House No. 2, its appearance hardly unchanged from its 1855 construction date. Two other 1850-era houses also are left, along with a row of family houses erected when post first was established. After fort's artillery functions ended, it became quartermaster depot, then a supply and transportation center through which 23 million tons of cargo and a million troops were deployed in World War II. In 1906 it was a refugee camp for victims of San Francisco earthquake. Hundreds were fed and housed. In a single night six babies were born in the camp.

OFFICIAL RESIDENCE of Commanding Generals of the Department of the West from 1865 to 1943, McDowell Hall has been occupied by Generals Irvin McDowell, E. O. C. Ord, Phil Sheridan, John Pope, Nelson Miles, and Arthur MacArthur. During visit to his father, Lieutenant Douglas MacArthur participated in 1903 pursuit of guardhouse escapee, finally finding him hiding on brush-covered hillside of post. Building was first known as Brook House No. 1, after one of civilian owners. It was originally a larger building, but was split into two—thus the No. 1 designation.

CAMP YERBA BUENA ISLAND, CALIFORNIA

Although it always seemed to be in the middle of things whenever schemes for the defense of San Francisco were devised, Yerba Buena Island finished the Civil War as nothing more than a paperwork fortress.

It was in 1861 that the first recommendation for garrisoning the island was made, and by the Navy rather than the Army. Fearing that a ship could sneak by Fort Point and Alcatraz in San Francisco's fogs, the Mare Island Navy Yard commandant recommended "earthworks be thrown up on Yerba Buena Island and a battery of guns planted on Point Rincon to bring a cross fire on any vessel that got past Alcatraz on the city side."

The Army engineers agreed. They included this plan in their recommendations in 1862, proposing a gun on the island would "command the anchorage and protect the city."

When the final engineer plan was submitted a year later—spurred on by rumors of a Confederate plan to invade the harbor—two batteries were recommended for Yerba Buena Island. One would be on the eastern shore mounting heavy guns, the other on the southern shore for eight 32-pounder guns. "A temporary redoubt or block house to protect the rear of the two batteries" was proposed for the northern portion.

San Francisco businessmen provided $20,000 so that work could start immediately there and at Rincon Point, and an official request for $100,000 was dispatched to Washington. On August 11, 1863, orders directed the immediate preparations "for constructing temporary quarters near the works about to be established on Yerba Buena Island. The command will consist of one field officer and four companies. It is desirable that work should be done as rapidly as possible."

No sooner had this decision been made than a telegram was received from Washington: "Works on Rincon Point and Yerba Buena Island will not be constructed at present," ordered General Henry W. Halleck, himself a veteran of the 1850's in San Francisco.

The reason for the cancellation: both points "are of too secondary importance to justify their construction while the external lines are incomplete." And, besides that, by the time a vessel came within reach of their guns, it could fire on the anchorage and the city, and the defenses would be useless.

Rincon Point was dropped without much argument. Engineers had noted that a battery there would have meant tearing down a dozen buildings. Any practice firing would have toppled a warehouse and a hospital below the proposed earthworks.

But Yerba Buena Island was another matter. When General Irvin McDowell took command in 1864, the deposed hero of the Army of the Potomac reopened the battle. He mentioned Rincon Point again, but was particularly positive regarding the island.

"I wish some of the same enlightened judgment in this matter which gave us such a number of heavy guns for our Eastern works may do the same for the harbors of the Pacific coast, where they are more needed than on the Atlantic," he summarized

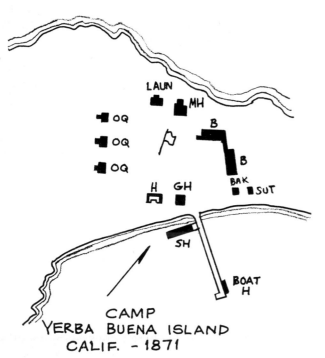

CAMP YERBA BUENA ISLAND CALIF. - 1871

CALLED BOTH a "post and depot" when this ground plan was made, Yerba Buena had facilities for four officers and 150 men. Barracks were two buildings connected by walkway, each 95 by 30 by 16 feet, "built of rough boards, set upright and battened . . . ventilated by the ridge, each lighted by 10 windows and warmed by coal-stoves," surgeon reported in 1870. "They are furnished with iron bedsteads, and give 750 cubic feet of air space per man of average occupancy," considerably more than the 600 cubic feet considered by Army to be minimum for health of soldiers. Each barracks had first sergeant's room and washroom partitioned from main dormitory. Except for officers' quarters, all traces of these buildings have disappeared; a few pilings remain to show location of wharf at which government boat stopped every other day in 1870's. (Redrawn from plat in National Archives.)

OAKLAND BAY BRIDGE, eight miles from end to end and with 4.5 miles in bridge proper, was completed in 1937. It enters double-deck tunnel at Yerba Buena Island, the 76-foot wide by 50-foot high passage being largest bore tunnel in world. In days before bridge, an 1884 visitor described island by its earlier name. "'Goat Island' is its homely American name," tourist wrote. "It stands 376 feet above the water; is inhabited by the keeper of the light, and serves as a fog-signal station, as well as a place for the manufacture and storage of buoys, numbers of which lie scattered about on the other side." Original Army plan to put batteries here never came about. Had they been completed, one battery would have been about where bridge meets island; second and heavier battery would have been at far left. Later Army camp is behind hillside at right. Picture was taken from harbor boat on San Francisco side of island.

his feelings. Remembering that previous recommendations had been vetoed by boards in Washington, he asked for permission to start at once and "require them to be carried with as much dispatch, consequently as little reference back to Washington as possible."

It was not until three years after the war that McDowell's plan was approved. A company of engineers was sent to the island and a post began to take shape on a low plateau near the eastern edge, the only area level enough for a camp. In the peacetime era, progress was slow. Two years later the camp still was "in an unfinished condition," the surgeon reported.

After an uneventful career as a "sometimes Army post," the island was turned over to a most appropriate occupant. Considering that its use had first been suggested by the Navy, it was to this service that ownership was passed and the Army days ended.

TO GET THERE: From San Francisco or Oakland, take Bay Bridge to turn off for Yerba Buena Island. This flanks the bridge on the east, man-made Treasure Island flanks it on the west. After leaving bridge, proceed to road fork. Take lower road after checking for permission at sentry box here. Lower road is narrowed, steep, and winding and leads out peninsula shown in old photograph.

101

BY 1870'S Camp Yerba Buena Island had been completed as is shown in this view by pioneer San Francisco photographer Edward J. Muybridge. Photograph matches ground plan exactly. Lighthouse was on point beyond camp. Although parade ground appears level, actually there was a 30 foot difference in elevation between its center and officers' row. Muybridge titled this stereo view "Military Post at Goat Island," name given island in 1841 when a half dozen of the quadrupeds were placed here and quickly multiplied like goats.

OFFICERS' ROW in modern times is used by Navy as residences for senior officers stationed in San Francisco area. Not shown in picture is residence of Fleet Admiral Chester Nimitz, only five-star World War II admiral still alive when photograph was made in 1964. Considerable improvements had been made in what were described in 1872 as hard-finished and sided buildings, "each two rooms, 18 by 20 feet, with rear 18 by 21 feet, built with attics." In 1872, Yerba Buena Island was center of controversy over where terminus should be of Central Pacific railroad. Oakland wanted it on island, putting it only mile and half from their waterfront; San Francisco pointed out that this would place it at least two and a half from her waterfront and, besides there was no good reason to give railroad gift of island worth at least six million dollars. Although in 1880 sale of island was authorized by War Department, as late as 1890 a custodian was paid $25 a month to take care of buildings.

TREES AND BRUSH obscure parade ground of modern Yerba Buena Island, looking from officers' row toward lighthouse point. Supporting tower and trusses for Bay Bridge are in right background, overshadowing area once occupied by guardhouse and messhall. Concrete Navy storehouse occupies center of parade ground. Island included 116 acres, five of which were used in 1870 as garden "cultivated by enlisted men," surgeon reported. "Potatoes, turnips, cabbage, lettuce, tomatoes, peaches, etc., are raised." He said diet at post "has been of regulation quantity and variety, and the articles of good quality. Extras are purchased in the San Francisco market and from the commissary by the funds of the company, and vegetables are furnished in their season by the garden." He said garrison had been "occupied in building quarters, engineer duties, drills, and police. Baseball and other open-air exercises, with occasional visits to the city, have constituted their amusements." Visits to city also contributed to main sick-list item: in 1869 there were 46 cases of venereal disease out of a mean strength of 99.25 men.

POST OF ALCATRAZ ISLAND, CALIFORNIA

Alcatraz Island's heavy guns may not have fired a shot in anger in her 81 years as a military post, but they came mighty close to it on October 1, 1863. That was when a suspicious ship was noticed approaching Raccoon Straits and the ensuing confusion included firing between the ship and the island with Fort Point chiming in.

Routinely during the Civil War a Revenue Service cutter greeted every arriving ship at the Golden Gate, but on October 1 she left her station to help a wrecked Russian ship. Captain William A. Winder, commanding at Alcatraz, was asked to challenge all ships before permitting them to enter the port.

"The officer of the day reported an armed ship towed by small boats in the direction of Raccoon Straits," reported Winder. After he was unable to recognize her colors—there was no wind and the flag fell in folds—Winder decided her course was so unusual, "I deemed it my duty to bring her to and ascertain her character and the reason . . .

"I therefore fired a blank charge, which apparently not attracting her attention, I directed a gun to be loaded with an empty shell and to be fired 200 or 300 yards ahead of her," he said. His two boats were busy inspecting other ships, but while waiting for one to return so that the newcomer could be inspected, "The ship commenced firing." He thought it might be a salute, but could not be sure because she was firing broadside and was "entirely enveloped in the smoke of her guns."

As soon as he decided it was a salute, he started to return a 21-gun answer. Before he was finished, "Fort Point commenced firing."

Finally everyone stopped. The letter exchange that followed was even more pointed when the ship was identified as Her Majesty's ship Sutlej, the flagship of Rear Admiral John Kingcome. The admiral did not take kindly to the unusual welcome, Captain Winder did not appreciate the Sutlej's "unusual course," and in the final outcome, the departmental commander suggested a mild reproof to Alcatraz.

"It is expected that the delicate duty devolving on military commanders will be exercised with prudence," he announced in a letter dated five months later.

The embarrassing international situation was all part of the game to Alcatraz, however. With her position recognized as the key to San Francisco Bay, she was in a sensitive situation throughout the war. In 1864, in fact, an even greater reaction set in

EXCEPT FOR shape of 12-acre island, this version of Alcatraz bears little resemblance to later period of Army or prison use. Almost all of these buildings had been replaced by time prison was closed in 1963. As Army post in 1870's, Alcatraz had room for 300 men in two frame barracks. Officers' quarters, hospital, offices, and storerooms were in citadel that was two-storied, plus basement, measuring 200 by 100 feet. Prisoners were kept in three buildings that had total of 113 cells which averaged 8 by 6 by 3 feet. Bowling alley, gymnasium, and theater provided amusement at isolated post. At start of Civil War, commander officer complained that island had no place to keep prisoners and that both guard and prisoners were jammed into casemates overlooking wharf. He noted that temporary wooden store sheds could not contain required three months' supplies, and much had to be stored outside wall of fortification. Island was supplied with fresh water by barge "which a besieging force might cut off," and he asked authority to bore a well. Later, a 50,000 gallon cistern was built. Work on post continued even after war and 1866 inspection noted the men were constructing earthworks. At that time, its redoubts had 105 guns manned by eight officers and 146 men and condition of post "reflects great credit on the commanding Officer." Only improvement 1866 could suggest was refinishing of bunks in barracks. (Redrawn from McDowell Report, 1879.)

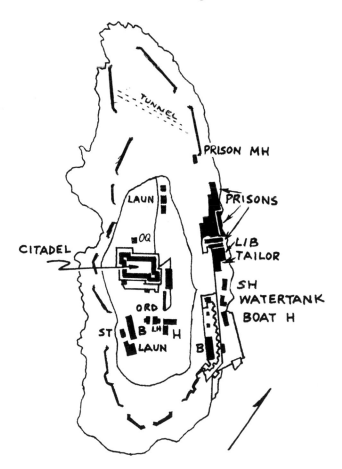

ALCATRAZ ISLAND
CALIF. – 1877

"FROWNING ALCATRAZ, Key of San Francisco," was 1866 description of fortress, expanded by 1884 comment: "It commands the entrance to the Golden Gate, and forms an effectual defense for the harbor of San Francisco." It "is 450 feet wide, 1,650 feet long, irregular in shape, and encircled by powerful batteries, in which are said to be mounted some of the heaviest guns ever cast in America." This view dates from military prison days, was taken from new parade ground level east of lighthouse. In modern times, lighthouse and quarters remained, but were surrounded by other quarters. An 1890 report complained, "Sanitary defects of the prison are especially apparent at this season of the year. The ventilation of the buildings is very faulty. The corridors, kitchen, and mess rooms are disagreeably and dangerously drafty . . . The prisoner when locked in for the night is virtually boxed in for so many hours . . . The means available for solitary confinement are such as have long been discarded in the better class of civilian penal establishments."

when commercial photographers were permitted to make 30 photographs that showed every road and battery.

The War Department heard about the photos, ordered them supressed, and demanded to know who had authorized them. As department head, General McDowell reported to Washington that the photos had been approved by the area engineer and authorized by Winder, whose "motive was one of pride and interest in his important command and a desire to have himself and the command have pictures of the place."

McDowell denied any disloyal motives on Winder's part, including rumors that he was influenced by the fact his father was in the Confederate Army. If he wanted to be disloyal, McDowell suggested, as an officer of intelligence he would not "have acted so openly and undisguisedly as he did."

The real losers in the proposition seem to have been the San Francisco firm that claimed it took the views on a $400 contract from the Army, and had spent $1,500 in the process. They hoped to recoup the difference by selling their photos for a ru-

mored $100 to interested soldiers. Instead, the pictures and negatives wound up at the War Department.

Had Confederate agents obtained and interpreted the photographs, they would have found that Alcatraz had not changed materially from 1861 when she had 85 cannon and 130 men. In one of his last acts before resigning to join the Confederacy, General Albert S. Johnston had rushed 10,000 muskets and 150,000 cartridges to Alcatraz. His successor, General Sumner, had proposed posting 400 men on the island. And in 1864, an official estimate was that 600 artillerymen were needed to man the works.

This was not to be. In fact, details from Alcatraz were siphoned off frequently. Thirty men spent months guarding Mare Island Navy Yard until they could be relieved by Marines from the USS Lancaster. Another detail was dispatched to man a battery on the south end of Angel Island—later the location of the vegetable garden tended by Alcatraz troopers.

Rumors of election riots placed the entire garrison on alert frequently. The bulk of the force was shifted to San Francisco to keep order in 1865 in the unsettled days following Lincoln's assassination. The Bay area's official half hourly gun salute on the day of Lincoln's funeral was fired by the batteries of Alcatraz.

Alcatraz' important position was recognized as early as 1849 when it was bought in the name of the United States by John Fremont, acting governor of California, for $5,000. Despite charges that the $5,000 never was paid, the government moved in and by 1853 a construction detail had arrived. "Temporary buildings for the accommodation of workmen have been erected, excavations made, masonry commenced," reported an 1854 inspection, and "The batteries on this island might be completed in about one year."

General Wool ordered six 8-inch and six 32-pound guns to be mounted on Alcatraz, despite the inspection report characterizing "Alcatrazes Island" as "a highly important point in the water defences, where 200 guns . . . should be mounted."

The initial work at Alcatraz was finished in 1858. By 1861, the post included a belt of encircling batteries, a massive brick guardhouse, and a three-story barracks that could hold 600 men. Then, with rumors of seccession, came rumors that Kentucky-born Johnston planned to take over the city from headquarters on the island.

"There is treason on Alcatraz," reported one contemporary account of a message sent to the White House. "To insure success of the scheme, Albert Sidney Johnston was placed in command at Fort Alcatraz," the version continued. "It was arranged that the leaders in San Francisco with a force of picked men sufficient for the purpose, should surprise and capture the fort."

The fact was Johnston was in San Francisco and not on the island. "As long as he held his commission he would maintain the authority of the United States to the last extremity," intimates insisted. And when General Sumner relieved him of his command, Sumner was able to report, "It gives me pleasure to state that the command was turned over to me in good order. General Johnston . . . was carrying out the orders of the Government."

As the war progressed, these orders involved Alcatraz in a variety of duties. In 1863, a suspicious clipper schooner was towed to Alcatraz when inspectors from the USS Cyane found 15 armed men and unmanifested cannon and ammunition hidden below her decks. The crew was questioned in separate cells on Alcatraz. A plot was revealed for the schooner to take on other military stores elsewhere, then to act as a Confederate privateer against the coastal ships.

Another plan to capture the California mail steamers was uncovered in 1864 by the arrest of plotters when they arrived in San Francisco. A result was an order for all steamer passengers to be searched for concealed weapons and for all ship officers to be armed in order to discourage attempts to commandeer the vessels.

Political prisoners were imprisoned at Alcatraz during the war, a hint of things to come. In 1868 it became a disciplinary barracks and military prison. During the seventies, troublesome Indians were sent to Alcatraz; in 1900, Philippine prisoners arrived at Alcatraz. Conscientious objectors were kept there during World War I.

The Army need for the Alcatraz prison was gone by the 1930's just when the rise of organized crime called for a maximum security penetentiary. In 1934, the Federal Bureau of Prisons took over San Francisco's prime fortress for a 30-year occupation that carned it a reputation dreaded by criminals as "The Rock."

TO GET THERE: Regular boat runs to Alcatraz stopped when the island was dropped from the Federal Prison system in 1963. At that time visitors were prohibited, but hourly tours of the bay from Fisherman's Warf closed to within 100 yards of the island.

SWIFT CURRENT around Alcatraz was element of its protection in Army days, and prevented escape later. Few escapes were tried during Federal prison days; two mass attempts were stopped, one in 1947 by combined forces of guards, Coast Guardsmen, and U. S. Marines. Early day prisoners included Indian chiefs, some of whom enjoyed visit, especially Piute Chief Naches who was sent in 1874 after supposedly inciting depredations in Nevada. "There he was treated with much consideration, shown the 'sights,' and the power of the whites, and went home rejoicing after a short detention," is commentary in 1881 *History of Nevada*.

CAMP REYNOLDS, CALIFORNIA

Dueling, smuggling, titles, and escaping prisoners all had a hand in the slow progress made by the Army in turning Angel Island into a military post. Occupying a square mile in San Francisco Bay, the wooded and hilly island had obvious strategic values, but the Civil War was half over before these were exploited.

The story of Camp Reynolds is the story of Angel Island, and that goes back to the earliest days of Spanish exploration in the Bay of San Francisco. On August 13, 1775, Lieutenant Don Juan Manuel Ayala dropped the anchor of his packet boat in a northern cove of the island, named the place "Neustra Senora de Los Angeles," and used it as his base of operations while he explored the rest of the Bay.

"Our Lady of the Angels," shortened to "Angel Island" survived as the name of the island, although Richard Henry Dana's *Two Years Before the Mast* calls it Wood Island in telling of fueling operations there in 1835. There were other operations, too, it seems, and not anywhere angelic. Russian, French, and English merchantmen used the island to smuggle cargo past the customs man at Yerba Buena—early San Francisco.

In 1853, with the United States in control, Angel Island had a short life as a prison. While San Quentin Prison was being built, the island watched over the territory's convicted criminals as they languished in hulks of ships anchored off shore. The ease with which these prisoners either bribed or forced their way to freedom won for Angel Island an unfavorable reputation. The prison status was short-lived.

Then in the Fifties the hot bloods of San Francisco determined that this relatively inaccessible island would make a good dueling ground. That so-called gentlemen's sport being illegal, the island shared the notoriety whenever the duelists' pistols rang out. The high point came at 5 o'clock of a hot afternoon in August, 1858 when State Senator William I. Furguson dueled with George P. Johnston, clerk of the U. S. Circuit Court. Johnston had been a proponent of severe punishment for dueling when he was an assemblyman five years earlier. The question was over slavery and an estimated 100 small craft brought an audience to see the settlement. Both men were wounded, but Furguson later died while his shattered leg was being amputated.

When the Army cast its eyes island-ward for a secondary defense line in the Bay, Angel along with Alcatraz were the logical selections. Angel Island could prevent passage through Raccoon Straits,

CAMP REYNOLDS
CALIF. - 1877

"THE CAMP is situated on the western extremity of the island, in a triangular depression between three hills, which leaves it exposed to the westward fronting the entrance to the harbor, the base being a pretty sand beach of about 1,000 feet in length," reported Reynolds surgeon in 1869. Site was 800 by 1,000 feet, with officers' quarters on one side, enlisted on other. Most construction dated from 1864. Wooden barracks were designed for 100 men each. There were six sets of frame officers' quarters, each including two rooms plus kitchen. Most quarters buildings remain under vine and brush cover, but barracks row had been removed by time of visit in 1964. Next to Camp Reynolds—renamed Fort McDowell in 1900—were two batteries. Battery Steward was at north corner, with armament of three 32-pounders and one 10-inch howitzer. Battery Knox was a short distance to south, boasting seven 32-pounders, two 10- and one 8-inch Rodman guns. The commanding officer placed five 32-pounders at wharf at head of garrison valley over objections of engineers who wanted these for Point Blunt, but these still were in place in 1869. (Redrawn from McDowell Report, 1879.)

CAMP REYNOLDS near turn of century was elaborate post. Barracks, built in 1864, were considered by surgeon, "Well ventilated, and well warmed by large stoves, but imperfectly lighted. They are not lathed or plastered nor ceiled, a very great mistake in this windy climate, and detrimental to the health of the men." Barracks row is along foreground of picture, officers row parallel to walk in center; chapel, later schoolhouse, is on hill to right center. Cemetery is in fenced enclosure behind officers' row and to right of flagpole; in 1879 it contained 32 graves. When 1866 inspection took place, post had three officers, 60 men, and 28 guns. Inspector said he found post in "Remarkably good order. There was nothing in the management of it to which exception could be taken."

could neutralize any enemy anchoring at Sausalito, and could intersect across the Bay with fires of Alcatraz, an 1856 Engineer Board concluded.

"Batteries should be constructed with the facility of ordinary entrenchments revetted with sandbags," it said. "This position being more isolated, it should be held by a keep or defensive barrack; the latter should be prepared for 25 guns."

The island had been set aside "for public purposes" by presidential order in 1850, but 12 years earlier Antonio Osio had been given permission by the Mexican government to use the island "for the advancement of the mercantile and agricultural branches." The condition was that, "whenever it may be convenient, the government may establish a fort thereon."

CAMP REYNOLDS TODAY is overgrown by vines, brush, and trees. This view was taken from about same position as old version, but foliage obscures remaining buildings. Enlisted barracks would be along foreground, but they have been removed; officers' quarters are under trees in background. Identity of single wooden building in center is uncertain. In 1890, post surgeon criticized "The crowded condition of the barracks. As the companies are now recruited to their full strength," he said "very little floor space is left between the bunks. As yet I have observed no sickness in consequence, although there have been much inconvenience and discomfort."

HOSPITAL of turn-of-century Camp Reynolds stands vacant at site of 1869 frame hospital. In leveling area for previous hospital, workers found evidences of early Indian use. According to surgeon in 1869, "Several skeletons have been exhumed, together with stone mortars and some trinkets, showing they were burial places for the Indians, and that the island was originally inhabited by them." Digging also revealed another hidden facet of island: "Some mining has been done," surgeon added, "silver ore taken out yielding about $14 to the ton, and gold is said to have been discovered." One soldier thought he had discovered his own version of gold when he took possession of an abandoned seven-room house near Point Blunt. It had been built by Pacific Mail Steamship Company and later was used by representative of island's owner in 1850's. After it was owned by discharged soldier, an enterprising man named Rafferty, it became what one authority described, "The shelter of uncertain parties of both sexes." A nuisance to the military authorities, the place "became the subject of a conflagration in 1867 without detriment to the morale of the locality."

A year later Osio was granted the island as his property in order to check any "foreign adventurers" who might want to use it. While he put on the island cattle and some overseers to watch them and built several houses, his ownership was not finally

COAST ARTILLERY storehouse is most prominent ruin at Camp Reynolds site, mainly because it stands at mouth of valley, is not obscured by vegetation, and is within view of San Francisco across Bay. Golden Gate Bridge can be seen dimly in left background, Squsalito in right background. By 1869 coast artillery defense of island was second rate when parapets at Point Blunt slid into water and were abandoned. In 1884, tourist commented, "Angel Island is strongly garrisoned, and the powerful guns of its three fixed batteries defend the harbor in all directions, insuring the safety of the Navy-yard and of the towns and cities lining the shores of the bay. Unlike Alcatraz, it is abundantly supplied with good water from natural sources, and at the season is carpeted with flowers." Three years later, San Francisco paper quoted artillery officer, "It is sufficient to say that with the defenses of San Francisco as they are, one English iron-clad can capture and hold the city, its superb harbor, our only Navy yard, and our only arsenal on the Pacific coast." It was noted that all three batteries on island were decayed and useless: "It is possible to fire all of the guns once as they are now pointed," it said. "The result must be conceived to be a final dissolution of all that remains of the platforms and the seven wood carriages."

recorded. Unfortunately for him, the Mexican Assembly never got around to formally approving the title, and on this technicality the United States was able to take it over free and clear.

When this happened, Osio sued. He pointed out that there were many tenants on the island who paid him rent and that his representative maintained large flocks and herds, even though the Navy had killed his cattle for military and naval uses "until there were none left" during the Mexican War.

Although the Osio claim ultimately was disallowed, later opinions suggest he may have had a case. The two critical questions were over the fact that the Assembly never approved his title and he never lived on the island. He was an occasional visitor but was represented by a tenant.

In 1860, Angel Island was declared a military reserve but it was not until 1863 that an inspection took place. At this time several houses were noticed there, but their occupants—it was reported—agreed, "The land has been acknowledged indisputably to be a government reserve."

On September 1, 1863, the order was announced to, "Proceed with the preparations necessary for constructing field works." Eleven days later Lieutenant John L. Tierson led Company B, 3d Artillery, in landing in a valley on the west side of the island. A camp was put up and named in honor of a former member of the regiment, Major General John F. Reynolds, a hero of Gettysburg.

The company moved to obey the War Department's orders to erect "ten or 12 guns on Angel Island so as to unite as well as possible the defense of Raccoon Straits with a cross fire toward Alcatraz."

The immediate success was not overwhelming. A year later General Irvin McDowell complained that the Raccoon Straits battery was so small and was so high above the water "that ships could pass close in to shore with impunity." He made the same objections to the batteries on the south shore.

In September, 1864, the engineers reported that batteries at Point Blunt, on the southeastern edge of the island, were complete. Except for one thing: the guns intended for Blunt had been landed at Camp Reynolds where the commander there immediately appropriated them for the defenses in front of the camp.

"Nobody ever said that any of these guns were sent here by accident or intended for another post," he commented, adding that he felt they were of more value where they were. And to move them would cost at least $400 in gold.

As the Army gained experience at Angel Island, it realized that a single post could not manage the whole layout. Supplies and ordnance landed at Camp Reynolds, but intended for Blunt, for instance, had to be re-shipped by water because roads were impassable. That was both costly and time-consuming, the delay usually amounting to a couple of weeks. In 1865, a company of infantry was landed at Blunt, told to bring their tents for temporary shelter, and established themselves to mind the eastern side of the island.

In 1864, the Army had estimated it needed 150 artillerymen to man Angel Island and the arrival of the infantrymen gave it almost that number. But by June, 1865, the results were not too pleasing. Although an inspection revealed all other batteries in serviceable condition, the position at Blunt had deteriorated.

The guns were all there "mounted and ready for service," but the parapet "in front of three of the 32-pounders has settled so as to leave a thickness of only three feet of earth . . . The portion of the parapet left standing above the slide would not afford protection against ordinary field guns." The infantry were not to blame, though, because it was established that the work was done on civilian contract. Camp Reynolds also was innocent; the bat-

DOUBLE-STORIED officers' quarters can be easily located in old photograph as largest building in row, third house from left. It dates from 1864 and was in continual use until island was abandoned by Army in 1946, except for six-month period in 1866 when post was temporarily abandoned. Headquarters of 12th Infantry Regiment was located on island from 1869 to 1879. First Infantry was located there until Spanish American War, but twice were ordered on field duties. In 1890, it was rushed to Division of the Missouri for Messiah War which ended in Battle of Wounded Knee. Four years later, they went to Los Angeles when strike had interrupted mail service. Presence of troops and their commanding officer, Colonel William R. Shafter, was credited with speedily settling difficulties. Shafter was commander at Angel Island for 12 years, a record ended when he assumed command of Department of California and then later, as major general, went to Cuba to lead Army in Spanish-American War. In World War II, both Italian and Japanese prisoners of war were imprisoned on island. Immigration Service also used island. When finally abandoned, a total of 235 buildings existed at various sites there.

tery at Blunt was the responsibility of the commanding officer on Alcatraz.

With Camp Reynolds as headquarters of the island, it was noted that there were 13 guns at the post, two barracks, a bakery, small hospital, 7,400 pounds of powder, and about 2,000 rounds of shot.

Although the post never had a reason for firing a shot in anger, it did have chances to test its armaments. The post commander unhappily reported that the 10-second fuzes received from Benicia Arsenal averaged between four and seven seconds. Long storage at Benicia was suggested as the reason, but the explanation pleased no one at this vital though peaceful post.

TO GET THERE: Angel Island is part of California Beaches and Parks System and its picnic grounds can be reached by a daily boat from Fisherman's Wharf or, on weekends and holidays, a more frequent one that leaves from Tiburon.

SCHOOLHOUSE overlooking Camp Reynolds served at first as chapel. As such it can be located immediately above flagpole in old picture, apparently from period before steeple was shortened. In 1900 post was re-named Fort McDowell, a term gradually used for entire island while Camp Reynolds was referred to as "West Garrison." A larger post, known as "Eastern Garrison," was built on east side of island with Alcatraz prisoners doing much of work. By 1935, Army report on island described this "one of the Army's most beautiful posts; the officers' line is most splendidly situated to overlook the bay . . . Flowers bloom the year through." It said that it was "one of Army's most important peace-time posts. It handles more men a year than any other post." Boats made nine trips to a day to San Francisco, an improvement over alternate day schedule in 1879. By this time schoolhouse was outmoded and children took 8 a.m. boat to Fort Mason where busses took them to city schools. Post had 12-car garage at Fort Mason because private cars were not permitted on island, causing report to term personal vehicles "not exactly a nuisance but almost."

OFFICERS' QUARTERS, though altered by addition of dormer windows, can be located in old photograph in center of officers' row where it was the only story-and-half set. Building was duplex, housing two families. Trees that were young saplings now tower over building, almost hiding it. Rich soil on island made it possible for company gardens to be maintained but by 1875 it was found to be cheaper to buy vegetables in San Francisco. Alcatraz garrison took over gardening duties and military prisoners from island maintained vegetable plots. Other uses for post included detention camp for several Indian prisoners of Arizona campaigns in 1869. In 1898 a caretaker detachment took charge of remaining artillery and a year later post began period of greatest activity as quarantine and replacement camp for Pacific bases. Soldiers exposed to contagious diseases were kept there for short period after return from Philippines. Those due for discharge were processed there away from the "dives of vice and saloons of a low order" that crowded Presidio's boundaries, so that the returning soldiers would not "become the prey of the unscrupulous" or "lured into temptation while awaiting final orders and pay. By 1905, more than 87,000 men had been processed through Angel Island facilities.

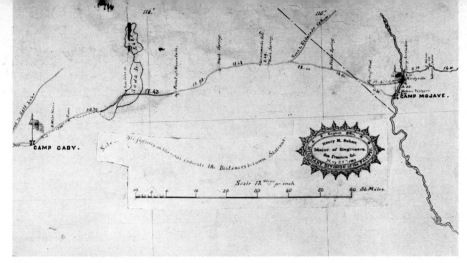

ROAD ACROSS THE MOJAVE

*"Major Carleton built these strong redoubts on the line of emigration,
which will be of essential service in the future. Each redoubt is capable of
accommodating a large company with their animals and wagons, thus affording protection to those traveling the road. They are all, of course, in
the immediate vicinity of springs which were opened up and reservoirs
constructed capable of containing a large supply of water."*

—Los Angeles *News*, July 14, 1860.

IT WAS AN early day in the story of California, one hardly a dozen years after she became a
part of the United States, when politics and economics joined to put the military on the Mojave.

Across the shimmering sun-beaten and sand-swept wastes of desert due east of Los Angeles
was the door of the future for Southern California. The routes of emigration most commonly
traveled were of little value to Los Angeles; either the trails funneled the pioneer into San Diego
to the south, or San Francisco to the north. Los Angeles needed a route that would bring the settler directly to her.

The Military District of Southern California, headquartered in Los Angeles, bowed to the
pressures. The Mojave's 130-some miles of torture were first traveled by the Franciscan Friars in
1776, then by traders and trappers in the 1820's, and, by late 1850, hardy emigrants willing to
brave the dangers of desert and depredations.

Major—later General—Carleton laid out military posts at the springs across the desert: Cady,
Hancock (at Soda Lake), Rock Springs, Beale (at Piute), Mojave; and Bitter and Resting Springs
on the northeastern trail to Las Vegas. In 1860 these informal redoubts—only Cady, Mojave, and
Rock Springs ever achieved official status as military posts—watched over lumbering wagon
trains.

In the Civil War, sporadic Indian troubles required sporadic patrol activity. By the end of the
war, or a year later, the Army was back. Troops of Cady, Soda, Rock Springs, Piute, Mojave
helped fend off depredation and death. Garrisons either manned or visited these places and,
when water finally showed Rock Springs inadequate, the water hole of Marl Springs was added.
Plans were made to form a company of Indian troopers to guard the road; 100 muskets and 100
red blankets were shipped out for issue, but nothing came of the idea.

More than 2,000 wagons used the road in its peak years of activity. But keeping it safe in the
face of few men, many Indians, disagreeable conditions, and other commitments was an objective
not truly realized in the road's heyday.

By the end of the 1860's a shorter and less dangerous route had been opened to the south.
The "Government Road" across the Mojave became the "Old Government Road." The traffic
shifted southward and a page in history was turned.

Data and Precautions for Visits to the Mojave Desert Forts are on Page 6.

FORT MOJAVE, ARIZONA

Discomfort, disease, discord, and disaster made up the four-edged sword that almost spelled defeat in the earliest days of Fort Mojave.

One visitor complained that it had "mosquitos by the bushel." Another said it "was a rude post, most uncomfortable every way." Everyone seemed to agree that, speaking mildly, the place was unpleasant.

It was on the east bank of the Colorado River at Beale's Crossing, the place where Lieutenant Edward Beale forded his camel caravan in 1857. The main post stood on a low bluff overlooking the tangled mass of underbrush and immature trees that covered the river's bottomlands. This was the only green in what was otherwise, as described by a surgeon's report, "A waste . . . a sterile plain."

An Indian massacre of an emigrant train in 1858 was the catalyst for Mojave, but it made a false start before it became a reality. The first detail of 50 Dragoons and eight infantrymen under Colonel William Hoffman found the Indians inhospitable hosts when they got to the site.

"The Indians objected to his passage through their lands and continually encircled his party, shot arrows into the camp at night, and so on," recorded Sergeant Eugene Bandel in a letter home. "These Indians have neither horses or firearms. Their arrows, too, still have the points of stone instead of iron. They were dangerous, therefore, only by reason of their numbers."

Hoffman took his command as far as the river, "passed a sleepless night," and decided to return to San Bernardino, his starting point. The Indians fell behind after 20 were dropped by a volley of carbine fire.

"Since that engagement, however, the Indians refuse to allow any white men in their domain," Bandel wrote in February, 1859, "and have more than once made raids quite near us to steal cattle from the neighborhood."

Far from cowed by the hostility, Hoffman formed what was to be called the "Mojave Expedition of 1859" and returned to the scene via the steamboat Uncle Sam and Fort Yuma. Although shipwreck delayed final formation of his column, by March 26 he headed up the Colorado with 760 men and 500 mules. Seven companies of the 6th Infantry and a detachment of mountain howitzers made up the command, plus two river steamers on which supplies and reserve ammunition were carried.

On April 20 the expedition arrived at the site of the future fort. "The heat by day is unbearable, the soil mostly sandy, and, except in places on the river level, very dry," Bandel wrote. The line of march was littered by "many a good coat and other articles of clothing" thrown away by the unmounted soldiers "in order to lighten the weight of the knapsack if only by a pound."

Rumors were that the Indians, "alarmed by the warlike preparations they know we are making, will seek peace," Bandel said, something which turned out to be correct. On April 23, a peace conference was held at the site of the future post. Upwards of 500 Indians entered the camp while the soldiers stood by with loaded weapons. The artil-

FORT MOJAVE
ARIZ. -1877

AT LEAST twice Fort Mojave suffered defeats from nature. In 1876 building row along south was destroyed by fire. In 1880, a 20-minute "furious tornado" inflicted considerable damage. A musician and three privates were killed by falling walls in barracks, later were buried in single grave. Original camp was built of logs and poles stuck upright in ground, jackal or stockade fashion. They were rebuilt in similar fashion after being burned when post was abandoned at start of Civil War. In late 1860's new buildings of adobe were started. By 1870 troops could move into first of two new barracks, 35 by 90 feet, while old quarters were torn down for their materials. At time, officers' quarters were two four-room stockade buildings termed "much dilapidated" by surgeon. Enlisted families lived in adobe buildings "contiguous to the barracks . . . erected and formerly occupied by citizens." Hospital in 1869 was "an old, dilapidated stockade building, not worth repairs, with dirt roof and floor" but was replaced. In 1872, hospital grounds were "enclosed by slight fence, thus securing privacy." (Redrawn from McDowell report, 1879.)

lerymen surrounded the delegation, loaded revolvers at the draw.

"Three interpreters were necessary to conduct the proceedings," explained Bandel. "Our colonel spoke English; the first interpreter, the captain of the artillery company, translated his address into the Spanish language; the second interpreter, a Yuma Indian, put this into the language of the Yuma Indians; the third interpreter, a Mojave Indian who had lived among the Yuma tribe, finally translated this into the language of the Mojave; and this order was then reversed."

Despite the unwieldy language situation, Hoffman was able to convince the Indians that, given the alternatives of peace or war, they would be better off with the first course. Hoffman later reported, "After all was amicably arranged . . . each of them expressed the happiness it afforded them that I had permitted them to have peace, and their gratification that a post was to be established in their country. They said that the country was mine, and I might do what I pleased with it; all they asked was that they might be permitted to live in it."

Six chiefs were turned over to the Army as hostages to prove the good intentions of the Indians. Two companies of infantry and an artillery detail were left at what Hoffman called "Camp Colorado." The remainder of the expedition returned to other posts, the hostages being taken to Fort Yuma.

Enroute, Bandel wrote, he passed the site where the Indians "attacked and murdered a party of 30 or 40 immigrants. There still remained to be seen the ironwork of the burned wagons, the hair from a torn mattress, several pages of torn books, and the dried blood of a child on a tree, under which the murder must have taken place. The tree still held the stone points of several arrows and other evidences of their cruelty."

Fort Mojave became the official name on April 28, by order of the first commander, Major Lewis A. Armistead. At first the Indians seemed content

with the new residents, visiting the place to trade food for clothing. This peaceful situation lasted until mid-summer when word came that the hostages had fought their way free from the Yuma guardhouse.

Mojave was hit from all sides. Coast newspapers had condemned the Hoffman treaty for not chastising the Indians "for their former misconduct. Past experience is worth nothing, if this treaty does not prove utterly valueless," said a San Francisco paper. "The Indians know no restraint, save the fear of a superior power; and until they are made to feel the ability of the United States to punish the outrages they will repeat them as often as the temptation to do so arises."

While the soldiers labored on their log and mud buildings, they were harassed continually from the surrounding hills. A patrol near the post was fired on and the stage was attacked less than three miles below the camp. Finally, the Indians overran the fort, trampled the gardens, and killed a sentry.

Armistead retaliated. Twenty troopers forded the Colorado on August 2 and destroyed an Indian farm. Remembering that destroying their crops would only lead the hostiles to ever greater desper-

FINAL CHAPTER in story of Fort Mojave was written in 1941 when site was sold to Mrs. Mabel LeClair on condition she level all buildings. Bulldozers and wrecking bars were doing job when this historic picture was taken of former administration building (left) and barracks. River and California are in background. Army left post in 1890, a day long awaited by soldiers who almost unanimously agreed with General Rusling's description in 1866. "We found it hot, and dusty, and miserable . . . Here were a handful of troops, and two or three officers, all praying for the day when they might be ordered elsewhere, assured that fortune could send them to no worse post, outside of Alaska."

ation, Armistead then shifted his attention to the tribesmen themselves.

Under cover of darkness, Armistead took 25 men across the river the night of August 4. They worked their way silently until they were in position below a suspected rendezvous, 12 miles from the fort.

At dawn, Armistead saw three Indians planting beans in a field. The first sounds of firing brought quick reaction and shortly the command was surrounded. A bitter half-hour fight broke off suddenly when 30 more soldiers arrived.

In 15 minutes the Indians counterattacked "and fought more deliberately then ever," Armistead reported later, "but were finally driven from the field with a loss of 23 killed." Three soldiers were slightly wounded.

On August 24, Indian runners appeared at Fort Mojave. They carried an appeal for peace from the chiefs, and this time they meant it.

Once the immediate Indian problem had been settled, attention at the fort was concentrated on its construction. The loss of the garden meant no vegetables to supplement the meagre salt meat rations left behind by the spring expedition. Scurvy felled most of the garrison. Eight troopers died of dysentery.

Further deaths were prevented by the arrival of 10 eight-mule teams with supplies after a 20-day trek across the desert. They had been dispatched by Captain Winfield S. Hancock, district quarter-master, disproving the theory that it was impossible to make major supply shipments across the desert.

While his revitalized men continued the work on the fort, Armistead took 60 days leave. In his absence it was planned to finish eight buildings, all to be of cottonwood pickets placed upright in the ground and chinked with mud. Three officers remained to direct the work.

Discord appeared within two weeks. The first lieutenant in acting command took offense at the manner in which another first lieutenant was handling the outposts and had him put under arrest. Court-martial charges were preferred. District headquarters did not take kindly to having two-thirds of Mojave's officer strength tied up in legal proceedings, so they took direct and effective action. A captain was rushed to the post to assume the command.

Red tape being what it was, the lieutenant remained under arrest for five months. A few months after his release, he was compensated for the ordeal with transfer from Fort Mojave. He left on an assignment to recruiting duty in parts far distant from the lieutenant formerly in command.

The Civil War meant abandonment of Fort Mojave. The buildings were burned on May 28, 1861 and on June 18 Captain G. O. Haller could report that he had arrived at New San Diego Barracks, Calif., the day before, "having a total of 52 enlisted men, aggregate 53, being 21 days out from Fort

Mojave, N. Mex., (sic) and having marched in 18 days 387 miles."

By 1863, settlers near the fort were clamoring for protection. One wrote that they were "surrounded by howling wolves, starving Mojaves, and thieving Piutes." He told friends at headquarters, "Strain every nerve to get the place garrisoned by a few soldiers."

In April, two companies were ordered to the post to "cultivate the most friendly relations with the Indians, at the same time . . . prevent them from commiting depredations on the whites."

The Indians greeted the soldiers by appropriating any stock that strayed from the post and occasionally jumping small parties and unescorted trains. By 1867, however, General McDowell could report, "Many of the Mojaves have been living quietly in the vicinity of Fort Mojave . . . raising food for themselves and for sale, procuring wood for the steamers plying the river, transporting the supplies for the government and the miners and other settlers in the territory."

A Mojave expedition into Arizona in 1867 resulted in a dozen Indian casualties. By 1870, the climate—Indianwise, that is—had so improved that a peace conference could be called. The results this time were permanent.

There is a postscript to the story of the rescue of Armistead's command by Hancock's supply train.

Both went on to become Civil War generals, Armistead on the Southern side. At Gettysburg, he was a brigade commander in Pickett's famous charge. He lost his life in storming a Union position manned by troops whose commander was Major General Winfield S. Hancock.

TO GET THERE: Fort Mojave appears on the Davis Dam 1:62,500 Quadrangle—although it goes by the Mohave spelling (the official Arizona spelling for it although almost every War Department record prefers Mojave). From Las Vegas, Nevada, go southeast on U.S. 95 about 75 miles to State 77. Take State 77 east across Colorado River and Davis Dam until it intersects with State 68 in about 1.5 miles. Turn back to west toward Davis Dam town where hard surface road turns southward and parallels river as it passes through Davis Dam town and Bullhead City. One mile south of Bullhead City, at fork of dirt road labelled "Rogers Landing," jog right. (Going left would take visitor past site of Hardyville on right side, one mile.) Follow main course of dirt road as it curves around river bend, cuts southward down small peninsula, and then comes to river again. About eight miles south of Roger's Landing, road has fork, one route going directly south, the other straight west. Follow westward fork until it disappears in rolling bluffs overlooking river, possibly marked by small signs indicating this is site of "Fort Mohave." Private property.

ONLY SIDEWALKS and remnants of drainage ditches and water system remain at main site of post and nearby Mohave City. By 1889, water was supplied to post via series of iron pipes from two 7,000-gallon tanks kept full by steam pump at river's edge. Sidewalks in this picture appear to head straight into California. Old Government road can be seen faintly in background as it winds across southernmost tip of Nevada, climbing gradually from Mojave's 541 feet to 2,680 at pass on horizon. Pass, and mountains on left, are in California in this three state picture. River was crossed by ferry started in 1852 which served both fort and only town in vicinity, Hardyville, eight miles to north.

FORT PIUTE, CALIFORNIA

Indian fights were common enough around Western forts, but not many of them could claim one that involved three tribes and not a single white man.

This was the case in the vicinity of Fort Piute, if local legend is to be believed. Apparently the battle started when a party of Piutes were attacked in their traditional hunting grounds by a larger group of Navajos. Included in the observers drawn by the clatter were several Apache scouts.

One of them hustled off to his main camp and led his cohorts back to the battle area. When it appeared that things were quieting down with the Navajos the winners, the Apaches moved in and claimed victory over both tribes.

The story continues that a resultant peace treaty between the tribes restricted the right to eat meat to the Apaches. It prohibited the Piutes from eating anything but fish. The Navajos were permitted any diet they desired so long as it did not include meat. Supposedly this tradition still is observed—but no restraunteer in the desert area will vouch for it!

Fighting among themselves should not be construed to mean that the Indians did not fight the white trespassers in the Piute area. Only 22 miles west of the Colorado and on the flank of a valley but once removed from that of the river, the Piute area was considered their personal property by the redmen. Its planted and irrigated fields were commented upon in the report of the Whipple Expedition of 1854.

Scattered traces of petroglyphs abound in the area, suggesting occuation long before Whipple, perhaps as early as the prehistoric days before the Mojave was a desert.

Colonel William Hoffman passed through the site and probably watered at its spring in 1859. It was not far from Piute that he was harrassed by the Indians and finally discouraged pursuit by firing on them. Although he had only half of his 60-some men shoot, the range was so close that he estimated 20 Indians were dropped.

When the then Major Carleton established his chain of desert redoubts in 1859 and 1860, the first one west of Fort Mojave was what Carleton named Fort Beale. This was in honor of Edward Fitzgerald Beale, the ex-Naval officer who was involved in the camel experiment and whose charges passed the place in 1857.

Rock with which the area abounds was used in building the fort. Ground remains indicate at least three buildings or units were erected, the largest being a main building of several rooms. Measuring 60 feet long by 25 feet wide, it included rifle ports in the thick walls, deflecting shields in front of each door to prevent direct fire through the opening, and rock breastworks at strategic locations immediately outside.

There was a rock corral and a rock walkway to protect persons moving between the main building and the corral.

Another building, considerably smaller, may have been for a sentry or a cannon or as a shelter for users of the spring—the main reason for the post's existence. The water was cool and fast flowing within the canyon where it formed the creek, even if it was swallowed up by a thirsty desert within half a mile.

This was a lifesaver for the Price Expedition in 1864. Fielded with orders to find the best supply route for Salt Lake City, Captain George F. Price had suffered many reverses in crossing the rough desert terrain. His mules had worn out, cavalrymen and their horses were hitched to the wagons, and he found the desert wells dry.

By the time he reached the Piute vicinity, half of

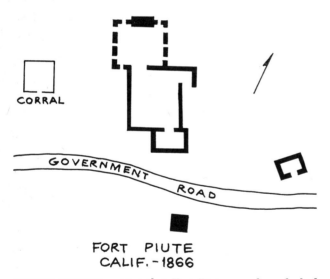

FORT PIUTE
CALIF.—1866

GROUND REMAINS suggest that Fort Piute may have looked like this. All ruins are of rock and walls are several feet thick. Center building apparently was headquarters; it may have included three rooms or smallest of three could have been fireplace. More likely it was guardroom from which mouth of canyon and entrance to building could be observed and, if necessary, covered by fire. Its walls are not high enough to show whether it had rifle loopholes as did room on opposite end. Corral was formed by rocks and was connected to main building by rock passageways which protected movement between both places. Tradition says that cannon covering entrance to canyon was mounted in small building. Creek in canyon parallels trace of road. (Redrawn from site inspection.)

ROCK PICKET POSTS surrounded Fort Piute from between 50 and 100 yards away, covering entrances into canyon and approaches to crest. In this view of general area from corral, corral wall can be seen in foreground; main building of fort is in center, virtually camouflaged by its blending in with surroundings; crest of hill in rear suggests at least one rock outpost, right center. Outpost is about 3,080 feet altitude and has views of California, Nevada and Arizona.

his men were barefoot. Only 20 of the original 89 horses and mules were serviceable. More would have given out had they not been able to quench their thirst earlier at Government Holes, and then drink their fill at Piute.

Fort Beale was abandoned during the Civil War but was outposted frequently. The Indians continued to consider it their property, taking with impunity whatever happened to pass through. In 1864, two incidents were reported of Piute Creek Indians making off with settlers' stock. In the second case, the stolen cattle did not go far; they were slaughtered nearby. "A part of the meat had been taken away, and a piece of Indian arrow was found near the horse—fresh tracks were found near the camp," a citizen reported.

When the Army returned after the war, Beale became Fort Piute. In reality, it never had an official status, other than as an outpost of Fort Mojave. Under the name "Piute Springs" it also was a relay station where the Overland Mail changed horses.

When Brigadier James T. Rusling passed it in 1866, he made no mention of any military outpost in the rock buildings. In *Across America* he did have critical comments to make on the area.

"Pai-Ute hill, so-called . . . is really a sharp and ugly little mountain up which we toiled slowly and wearily . . . It was a wild and desolate canon, barren and rocky, miles away from every human habitation," he wrote.

It may be that his impressions of the place were colored, however. In rounding a turn in the road, one of the ambulances which had served him for thousands of miles in his inspection tour of posts, struck a rock.

"There could hardly have been a more thorough collapse of spokes and felloes—everything seemed to go to pieces—and it could hardly have occurred in a worse place," was how he summed up his stop in Piute Canyon.

TO GET THERE: From Searchlight, Nevada, take U.S. 95 south 12 miles to dirt road on right. Turn right and go three miles west to dead end at power line. Turn left and go south on power line road about 12 miles to George Erwin Ranch on right. Turn right onto ranch road, private property. If permission to visit is obtained, fort ruins can be seen about two miles west of turn in canyon. Road is for good weather, rough-duty driving only.

FIREPLACE in main building still is serviceable, and blackened interior suggests frequent use recently. Wall in foreground is "partition" between this room and larger center one in headquarters building. One rifle loophole can be noted in wall at left of fireplace; another one is barely visible at right.

HEADQUARTERS building had rock breastwork outside of loopholed room for additional protection. Piled rocks in foreground suggest breastwork was connected to building. Loopholes are noticeable every five feet on wall; fireplace is at right. This view is from northern slope of canyon, looking toward southwest.

CAMP ROCK SPRINGS, CALIFORNIA

"No glory there, nor much for military fame; but true patriots and heroes were they, to submit to such privations," wrote Brevet Brigadier General James T. Rusling in 1866 of Camp Rock Springs. "Too many of our frontier posts are akin to this, and little do members of Congress east, who know only 'the pomp and circumstance of glorious war,' imagine what army-life out there really is.

"It is a poor place for fuss and feathers, gilt epaulets and brass buttons, and our 'Home Guard,' holiday Militia east, so fond of parading up and down our peaceful streets, with full rations and hotel quarters, would soon acquire for soldiering there a rare and infinite disgust. Yet these are the nurseries of the Army, and from such hard schools we graduated a Grant, Sherman, Sheridan, and Thomas."

Rusling wrote this way in *Across America*, his unofficial account of an 1866 inspection tour of western forts. In his official report to the Congress he did not go into these same flowery details—nor the barbed comments. "Not considered of much importance," he said of Rock Springs, "and the general route for troops and supplies . . . roundabout, unadvisable, and bad."

Rock Springs' military status began in 1860, as part of the Carleton guard. During the Civil War it was frequently outposted. In 1863, while an outpost of Fort Mojave, its detachment was to keep the fort informed "of any hostile movement that may be made within your knowledge." Rock Springs was to send out "detached scouting parties" in order to "keep the road clear and open for travel in your vicinity."

A one-officer, 20-man patrol made two round trips a month between Fort Mojave and Rock Springs in 1864 "to keep a watch upon the road and see that order is maintained and travelers protect-ed," district headquarters directed. It appears that the camp was not occupied at this time and this was a substitute measure to protect the road.

Frequent complaints along the road kept the Army busy. In 1863 a citizen at Rock Spring reported seeing 80 to 100 Indians in the area plus another 300 to 400 at a camp 30 miles to the south. In 1864, Indians reportedly were terrorizing the few citizens in the area, making off with 24 cattle and threatening "their property and personal security." The report was cancelled two days later when it turned out to be a false alarm.

In late 1865, two men built a hut and began mining operations near the site of the post. During their absence, Indians or white—no one could be certain as to which—"burnt the roof from their hut and stole what they could carry off," reported Brevet Brigadier Charles A. Whittier during an inspection trip.

"These two men have been loud in their complaints that while they were developing the resources of the country for the benefit of the government (?), the government does not afford them the protection to which they as American citizens are entitled—and have considered it proper that a full or at least half a company should be sent to this point."

He added, "The removal either of their roof or their mining prospects has caused the two above mentioned citizens to sortie from Rock Springs."

Soon after, a detachment was sent to Rock Springs and it became an official post. "On the desert . . . very disagreeable place for the troops," is how the Secretary of War's 1867 *Report* describes it.

"CAMP ROCK SPRINGS itself was a forlorn military post, consisting of one officer and perhaps a dozen men, guarding the springs and the road there. The officer was quartered in a natural cave on the hillside, and his men had 'hutted' themselves out on the sand the best they could," was General Rusling's description in 1866. Although local legends credit certain ruins with being remains of Army redoubts, identity is uncertain. This ruin is probably typical of redoubt construction, half of it being a dugout, the other half a stone wall high enough so that a man could stand inside. Storehouse was a cave, both dry and secure.

SOLID HOUSE at site of Rock Springs hints how early fort buildings may have looked, or, with time, could have looked. Supposedly built partly with remnants of old fort ruins, this three-room house has walls almost two feet thick. The Whipple Expedition camped at the springs on March 5, 1853, reported that they found "a spring of water oozing out of a rocky ravine . . . a few pools were found among the rocks."

Building material came easy to the place, and stone buildings and breastworks were built quickly. The lack of forage along the road dictated that infantry replace the cavalry, although some mules and horses were sent to mount the mail wagon escort. The decision was bitterly fought in the light of the relative immobility of an unmounted infantryman versus a mounted Indian, but the facts of life were there. Grain cost $8 a bushel at Rock Springs compared to 80 cents at less isolated posts!

Rock Springs also was to serve as a secondary supply point and even had a post office for a short time. It was supplied from Drum Barracks and San Pedro Depot 250 miles to the west and was advised to "make timely requisitions."

Water was a problem at the post. The spring was poor and irregular and wells had to be sunk a mile westward at "Government Holes." It was to here that a Utah expedition went in 1864 when they found the Rock Springs dry.

The Secretary of War 1867 report told the future: "Camp Rock Springs is to be broken up due to lack of water." By 1868 this had taken place, with roving patrols and the Camp at Marl Springs watching over the area.

TO GET THERE: Rock Springs shows on the Mid Hills 1:62,500 Quadrangle. From Baker, Calif., take Interstate 15 east 28 miles to Valley Wells turnoff. Follow this blacktop road to south through Cima, 17 miles. Continue to south about 4 miles where a gravel road deadends from east. Turn left (east), going up Cedar Canyon. In 10 miles, on right will be site of Government Holes and in another mile, site of Camp Rock Springs. This is a good road throughout.

PROOF OF Army visit at Rock Springs is cut into stone there. Most likely a member of the 4th Infantry California Volunteers, soldier "Stuart" probably carved this between 1863 and 1866 when that regiment provided many of the troops to protect Government Road. Records show at least one Stuart in regiment during that period. Among scattered rock groups in area is one known as "Morgue" where tradition says bodies were kept in until burial wagon arrived to take them to civilization.

CAMP MARL SPRINGS, CALIFORNIA

It may have been the last of the desert redoubts to be established, but Camp Marl Springs' history indicates it was one of the most important.

Location had a lot to do with the importance. It was about halfway between Camp Cady and the Colorado River. And, more so, it was flanked on the east by a 12-mile valley that had a 1,400 foot elevation change—a torturous trail of loose gravel and sand repeatedly crisscrossed by dry washes. To the west, it was even worse. Devil's Playground was the nickname pinned on a 17-mile stretch of drifting sand that had neither tracks to follow nor water to drink.

Especially for the eastbound traveler, Marl Springs was a welcome sight. In 1852, John Brown—later the ferry owner at Fort Mojave—found the springs a life saver. When his party had become exhausted in the blowing sand dunes of the playground, Brown had struck out ahead for Marl Springs. The peaks of the Old Dad Mountains showed him the way out of the windswept bowl, then he marked his desperate route between the bare, rocky wastes of the Kelso Marl Mountains, on his right, and rolling lava hills on his left.

He dropped into Marl Springs without ceremony and filled his belly. After the life had returned to his joints and veins, and a keg had been filled with water, he returned to the wagon train. His keg provided enough refreshment to get the travelers and their stock to Marl Springs and a new life. A couple of dozen Piutes met Brown at the spring both times, but "they behaved well."

Marl Springs was not one of the original Carleton redoubts across the desert. The intention was that roving patrols between Rock Springs and Hancock Redoubt (at Soda Lake) would keep the area clear of roving Indians.

The springs was an important water source on the road. The Whipple Survey party of 1854 spent a night at the site on March 7, reporting "excellent grass . . . scant wood . . . windy . . . cold." They found the springs "small, not half enough water for the mules, but it constantly flowed and after a while there was enough to satisfy the mules." The flow was so regular that they were able to refill their kegs and also have enough for the camp's use.

The water that drew the traveler also drew the opposition. Fifteen or 20 Piutes were reported harassing wagon trains on the western half of the road in 1863. "It is said that they killed one of the mules belonging to a citizen at Marl Springs," the Fort Mojave commander wrote to headquarters.

A year later, rumors of Indian depredations again were heard. The Mojave commander received a letter from a civil officer "stating that four horses and a bullock had been killed and eaten by Indians at Marl Springs." But this was a false alarm; two days later the official reported that the stock had been found, neither killed nor eaten.

With traffic on the road increasing, the Army put token protection at Marl Springs in order to provide some type of cover from attack. The tiny post sat at the foot of a spur of the granite Marl Mountains. Commanded on two sides by high ground, it had to sacrifice defensibility in order to command the spring. The facts of desert life were bluntly a matter of defending from a poor spot that had

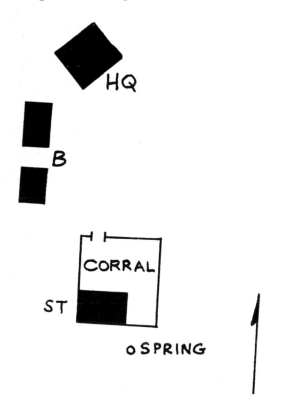

CAMP AT MARL SPRINGS
CALIF. - 1866

MARL SPRINGS' military post might have looked like this; at least this is how ground remains look today. This plat is based on a studied guess of traces present in 1964 which may have come from old Army site, or from later use. Corral apparently was square area surrounded by rock wall with rock building against southwest corner. Two "barracks," a guess as to use, are suggested by dugouts in hill side while "headquarters" is at location of outlines of stone building. (Drawn from site inspection.)

CAMP MARL SPRINGS is in immediate foreground in this view looking east toward Providence Mountains. In center foreground, rectangular watering trough at spring can be seen between posts. Corral is to immediate left with corral building most obvious. In immediate left foreground, side walls of possible headquarters building can be seen against side of slope. Dugouts were in row to right, obscured by brush. Government Road across valley to east goes 12 miles before reaching foot of mountains. Valley is 300 feet below level of Marl Springs. From low point in valley to pass leading to Rock Springs, road increases in elevation 1,200 feet in eight miles. Although it is only 18 miles from Marl to Rock Springs by Government Road, six miles of it in this valley have eroded away and direct route is impassable.

water instead of a good but dry location that could prove a trap.

In 1867, the post was surrounded by hostile Indians. During a 24-hour siege, the station had a full test of its position. There were only three men there but they came out with their scalps intact. In the true spirit of the romanticized West, just at dawn a rescue column of soldiers cut through the besieging circle of Indians to save the post.

TO GET THERE: Marl Springs shows on the Kelso 1:62,500 Quadrangle. The private road passing through Rainbow Wells is usable; pick it up east of Baker from U.S. 91. Two and a half miles south of Rainbow Wells, take right set of tracks toward Marl Mountains. Site of camp is at foot, next to spring. A U.S. Geological Survey marker is about 25 yeads from spring. Do not attempt to proceed to other fort sites west or east directly from here; traces of the Government road have been eroded and the way is impassable.

TWO DUGOUTS of this type probably served as living quarters, a use suggested by holes and primitive chimney for smoke escape. Dugouts probably were caves hollowed out of hillside next to corral, and roofs have collapsed since use. Fireplace was inside, as suggested by soot-blackened hole and smoke traces. Pile of rocks surrounds ceiling hole and served as chimney.

FORT SODA, CALIFORNIA

Things at Soda Lake almost got out of hand back in 1863, but "prompt action and determined manner" convinced the Indians they had picked the wrong set of opponents.

This was in the interim period between Army posts at what an Army inspection termed "a dried up lake, or sea, whose salts of soda efforesce and whiten the ground like snow for miles in every direction."

In 1860 it had been the site of Hancock Redoubt, a series of breastworks and corrals constructed to protect travelers on the Government Road. It was 35 miles from Camp Cady, the nearest post to the west, and 75 to Fort Beale in the Piute Mountains to the east.

After 1860 most of the posts were not manned, an encouraging situation as far as the Indians were concerned. The scene was set for them, they figured, on July 30, 1863, when a band spotted two government teams with wagons at Soda Lake. The teams were bringing potatoes to Fort Mojave.

FORT SODA may have looked like this, based on ground remains. Stone buildings were used by travelers in years after Army left, then by German chemical company in 1910's. Company rebuilt buildings so that modern inspection of site cannot be certain whether buildings date from that period or earlier. Layout and building identifications are based on local legend. Site is 930 feet above sea level, quite a drop from 5079 feet only 42 miles to east near Rock Springs. (Drawn from inspection of ground remains.)

"The Indians demanded flour and tobacco as the price of peace," the commander at Fort Mojave reported. "Not having these articles supplied them they commenced climbing into the wagons to help themselves, when the men with the teams seized their muskets, drove them from the wagons, and by their prompt and determined manner induced the Indians to lay down their bows and arrows and forego not only the above-mentioned luxuries, but the luxury of a fight also."

Apparently the natives had forgotten the lesson administered to them at Soda Lake three years earlier.

That was during the period of construction for so-called "Fort Soda." While Carleton and his men devoted their main effort to building Camp Cady, a detachment was sent to locate the Indians believed to be in the vicinity of Soda Lake.

Here, in their temporary homes from which they could plunder and ambush travelers, the Indians were surprised by an Army patrol. A desperate battle followed in which the scales of victory tipped to the Army because of the primitive weapons used by the tribe. The Indian casualties were three killed, one seriously wounded, and one woman prisoner. Not long afterward, the Indians asked for a truce.

Hancock Redoubt did not remain in action long after that. Less than a month later, the post was abandoned. It had been intended only as an over-

SPRING

OQ

HQ

GH

B ROCK

LAKE SHORE

CAMP SODA LAKE
CALIF. — 1866

GUARDHOUSE'S original walls can be detected for first couple of feet above ground. Original construction was without mortar, but was so solid that it could be built upon with only minor improvement. Unchinked portion of walls is original part; obviously roofs, window, and painted area are new. Building now serves as dining room for resort.

SODA LAKE from Fort Soda was described in 1866 by Army Inspector Rusling as "a vast basin, rimmed around with desolate hills and mountains, and during the rainy season a considerable body of water, indeed, collects here. Soon, however, evaporation does its work, and the lake proper subsides to little or nothing, worth speaking of. When we were there, it was said to be 20 miles long, by four or five wide, though of course everything very marshy or shallow." This was before Fort Soda was re-established and "there was no house or even hut there; no person or living thing; and what with the heat, and glare, and awful desolation—I think it was about the most wretched and miserable day I spent everywhere." Rusling suggested situation was complicated by presence of Indian fires in hills during night, suggesting possibility of attack. Even more so, he noted that a rattlesnake had crawled into blankets of member of party, causing uproar when owner arose in morning. "After this," Rusling added, "we usually retired with all our clothes and tallest boots on." This view is across Soda Lake toward Cowhole and Old Dad Mountains and Devil's Playground. In 1871 officer's wife passed here, wrote, "I had no idea that such a forlorn district was comprised within the limits of the United States . . . We traveled 18 miles through deep sand, which is the hardest thing imaginable on the poor mules, for their feet being very small sink deep in, the last few miles being through choking dust." Lake was last full in 1937 when it flooded entire area.

night camp although an officer with the Boundary Commission credited it with a higher stature.

"There is a small fort at the sink of the Mojave and another 35 miles above known as Camp Cady, neither of them are garrisoned. They have both been constructed of mud and willow brush and a half dozen resolute men could hold them against all of the Indians combined inhabiting the Great American Desert," he said.

"I am told they were built to afford shelter to small parties of whites travelling through the country who were apprehensive of Indian activities," he added, "but it would seem to me that a party of Indians meditating on attack would have the sagacity to occupy the fort in advance."

When the posts were re-opened in 1867, Hancock Redoubt became Fort Soda or Camp Soda Springs. The name is uncertain because it never got into official records. It served in anonymity.

One of its most serious incidents occurred in 1867 when an Army ambulance was jumped by 15 Indians between Soda Lake and Camp Cady. The first shots dropped the escort's horse. The soldier jumped into the ambulance and it broke out for Soda Lake after an hour's fight.

Despite the heavy fire being conducted out the rear of the ambulance, the Indians kept up the pursuit. Every likely ambush spot was manned to Fort Soda, but the ambulance got through. A surgeon who was a passenger in the vehicle was fatally wounded in the fight. He lived only long enough at the fort to write a final letter.

Incidents of another calibre highlighted the history of this short-time post. During the period when the chain of redoubts were being abandoned, the officer in charge at Fort Soda had to report that a private had deserted, "taking the best horse at the post."

The horse was not given a chance to prove himself, apparently, because the private was caught a few months later. He had turned gold miner and had located himself at Eldorado Canyon. He didn't know that the same unit provided men for the Mojave Desert forts and various Nevada camps . . . including Eldorado Canyon, only a few miles upriver from Fort Mojave.

TO GET THERE: Soda Springs and Soda Lake show on the Soda Lake 1:62,500 Quadrant. From Baker, go west six miles on U.S. 91. Turn on Road 466 to the south. In five miles, turn in to Zzyzx Springs, privately owned non-profit health and rest resort. This is only fort along chain which is convenient to visit.

CAMP CADY, CALIFORNIA

"Half a days pull through heavy sandy and gravelly wastes brought us to this God-foreseken Botany-Bay of a place," wrote Elliott Coues when he visited Camp Cady in 1865, "the meanest I ever saw for a military station, where four officers and a handful of men manage to exist in some unexplained way in mud and brush hovels."

The comparison of Cady to the notorious Australian convict colony was apt, although not calculated to raise the morale of the troopers manning the desolate outpost. It had been built in early 1860 by then Major Carleton at the site of a "Depot on the Mojave," a temporary camp of the preceding September.

Carleton's men had no intention of staying at the spot and were content to live in a scattering of adobe and brush huts, half underground dugout-style. There was a central building which could lay some claim to fortresslike attributes, a 40-foot adobe square that stood man-high and was surrounded by a ditch.

From here, Carleton vigorously scoured the countryside for traces of Indian marauders. Surgeon Jonathan Letterman—the originator of the Army's ambulance service and after whom Letterman General Hospital is named—was with Carleton at the time.

An officer "killed two Indians on the 19th in the mountains southwest of our camp," Letterman later wrote. "In the affray two men were seriously wounded, one in the neck and one in the abdomen, by the Indians. Both are doing well, but the one wounded in the abdomen is out of danger yet."

The Los Angeles *Star* carried news of a Carleton expedition in May, 1860 in which he destroyed a Piute rancheria 50 miles from Cady, "bringing away several trophies highly prized by the Indians." A civilian teamster was missing "and it is supposed that he was killed by the Indians. These Piutes must get a thorough drubbing."

Rather than a drubbing, Carleton held a peace conference at Camp Cady with 24 Piutes spokesmen —one of them a woman. He told them that the white man and his "Great Father" was powerful and wanted to be a friend of the Indians. The chiefs agreed, gave their pledges, took their gifts, and—for the moment—keep the peace. Camp Cady was abandoned.

Two years later the post was temporarily reactivated, but this time as an early warning outpost against feared Confederate attack. Orders were issued on April 5, 1862 for an 11-man detail to go to Camp Cady "and there shelter yourself and party in a field-work which was thrown up at that point by Colonel Carleton two years since. It is reported that there is a large body of men east of Beale's Crossing on the Colorado River, and it is possible, though not probable, that they will attempt to enter California by the Mojave route.

"The object of sending you to Camp Cady is to give the colonel commanding timely notice, if such be their purpose, and to send to him any intelligence which you may receive of their movements.

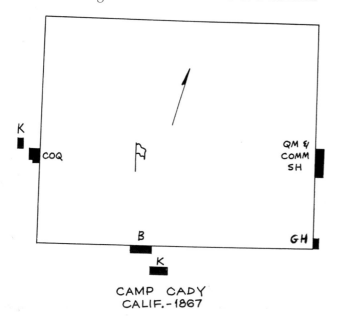

CAMP CADY
CALIF.-1867

THIS IS HOW Camp Cady looked after it was moved in 1868 in order to give it parade ground. It measured 360 yards east to west and 300 north to south. All buildings "are of adobe, floored, and shingle-roofed, plastered outside and plastered and whitewashed inside," surgeon reported in 1869. "The officers' quarters is the only building ceiled. . . . The barrack building is 86 by 26 by 12 feet, but has the northwest and southeast corners partitioned off as temporary dispensary and saddler's shop respectively. It is heated by stoves when necessary, lighted and ventilated by 12 windows and three doors. . . . The officers' quarters is one building, 36 by 18 feet, divided by a hall into two rooms. There is a wing in rear, 14 by 12 feet, and a small out-house as kitchen." Surgeon and his family lived in guardhouse, 26-by 18-foot two-room building. Hospital tent was used for prisoners. So-called "hangman's tree" was next to guard-house, but there is no record of it being used. Each building had double slanting shingle roof and floors, a far cry from first fort. Rock foundations were quarried four miles away and hauled to site. Soldiers did all construction, used 35,000 adobe bricks, 32,000 feet of lumber, 30,000 roofing shakes. No permanent bunks were in barracks because men were on alert to move at moment's notice, but 30 temporary bunks were made by soldiers on which to put their bed-sacks. There was no hospital; hospital at first camp was used. Before post was abandoned, second officers' quarters was added, according to 1872 report. (Redrawn from plat in National Archives.)

ORIGINAL CAMP CADY "fortress" stood next to Government Road, was photographed in 1860's by R. D'Heureux. Army inspector in 1866 was not enchanted by desert area. "There is little probability of the post being long occupied," he reported. ". . . The country for miles around is not of such a character to induce any sane man to settle. . . . The country is a desert and to my mind there is no possibility of it ever being settled." He found three officers and 63 enlisted men, noted district commander had "wisely" directed reducing post to 15 men to preserve the buildings and supplies enroute to Arizona—but this token force was not long maintained. Fortunately post quartermaster had no outstanding debts because he had only $2.50 on hand. Inspector recommended that meat ration be increased to make up for the fact that 450-pound cattle bought in Wilmington lost 100 pounds by the time they got to Cady.

By putting your men and animals inside of the work, spies or a small number of scouts from such a party, coming up the river, would not know of your presence until they come so close that their escape would be impossible."

The officer commanding the detail was told to stay out 11 days, "when if you receive no intelligence of the body of men alluded to above, you will return by easy marches to your proper station."

A month later, the patrol was back. It had stayed at Cady from April 14 to 24 "seeing and hearing of nothing unusual." Enroute they had heard of wagon loads of powder and small groups of armed men moving on other routes, but their direction was generally northeasterly and did not seem to pose a threat to California.

The Indian depredations finally caused Cady to return to the official orders on July 26, 1864. Captain John C. Cremony and his B Company of the Second California Cavalry were ordered to patrol

from Cady to Rock Springs and "to protect travel, clear the road of thieving, troublesome Indians."

A year later, the murder of two men 18 miles from the post, and activities of Indians who "come down from the mountains on either side of the road, steal stock, rob houses, lay forced tribute on travelers, threaten lives" forced the reopening of Camp Cady by a company of cavalry.

They were told to maintain a camp guard of 15 men. "The balance of the men will patrol the road constantly . . . keeping it clear . . . and particularly to keep Indians away from the watering places," was the guidance to the first detail sent out in March, 1865.

While reestablishing the post, three soldiers were wounded and government stores burned in an Indian attack. The camp was officially reactivated on April 23, 1865, when Company C, 4th California Volunteer Infantry arrived.

They manned Cady until July, 1866, rebuilding

CAMP CADY SITE today is bare of evidences of early use, flood in 1938 having washed away all adobe traces. Barracks and sutler store are in ruins, used for stock purposes; rocks mark hospital site. John Fremont was at site in 1844 and prepared for desert trip here. Three fatigued cattle were killed and their meat jerked. During stay, two Mexican refugees told him of being ambushed by 100 Indians at Resting Springs, to the north on the Las Vegas-Salt Lake City trail.

PART OF ORIGINAL barracks now serves as stock barn. Schedule for soldiers when living in barracks included reveille at 5 a.m., breakfast at 5:30, drill at 6:30, fatigue call at 7. Due to heat that hit 118 at times, men were permitted to rest from 10:30 to 2:30, with dinner at noon. Taps was at 9:30 p.m. Monotonous duty meant a full guardhouse, severely weakening tiny garrison. One man, an experienced soldier who had been in three Indian fights in as many weeks, still was bored, finally deserted. At least one soldier was knifed to death by fellow trooper and, in final years, soldiers broke into sutler's store, then burned it down. Commanding officer accused sutler of peddling cheap whiskey to men, ordered, "No man henceforth will receive more than one glass of wine or half bottle of ale in the same afternoon." After store was burned, owner sued post commander and, ultimately, officer was dismissed from service.

its collapsed buildings. "The quarters are made entirely of brush and are intended for shelter from the sun only" wrote an observer.

On January 10, 1866, Inspector Brevet Brigadier C. A. Whittier visited the post. "Great credit is due to Captain West for the construction of neat and comfortable houses with the means at his disposal save the adobe and at no expense to the government," Whittier reported, "for the cleanliness and good order prevailing through the camp and for the care of his command and general good administration of affairs."

The following day, the Cady garrison was officially commended by General McDowell for building 35 adobes at the post.

An attempt was made to abandon the camp in 1866, but public and political pressure was too great. Hardly was the post back in business again when a party of Indians approached the fort in a hostile demonstration. Twenty troopers charged after them. Five soldiers were killed in an ambush set up in the dense undergrowth along the river.

In the aftermath, a posse arrived from San Bernar-dino to reinforce the fort and chase the Indians, but the enemy had disappeared.

Attacks continued on the road. With requirements for pursuit patrols and train escorts, upwards of 120 men manned the fort at times.

In 1868 the post was moved a half mile to the west. Here was sufficient level ground for a parade field, something missing at the first cramped site.

A more formal post was built in a rectangle, but a year later the garrison was cut to a token force. By this time, the trail was known as the "Old Government Road" for it had been supplanted by a more direct and safer route.

In 1871 the buildings were sold to civilian stockmen. The mission was finished and the unsentimental Army no longer had any use for shanties reported to "be of adobe and . . . of little value."

TO GET THERE: Camp Cady site appears on Newberry 1:62,500 Quadrant. From Barstow, Calif., take Interstate 15 east 21 miles to Harvard station, nothing but a signpost alongside railroad track. Turn right (south). Local directions and permission should be asked in order to find site which is between this point and mountains. Area is so criss-crossed by jeep tracks through loose sand that guide is essential in order to maintain proper direction.

WHITE RIVER Agency was burned by rampaging Utes in 1879 and Agent Nathan Meeker and nine employees killed. Meeker's wife, daughter, and another girl were taken captive and held for 23 days. After both guilty and innocent Utes were moved away, traces of massacre disappeared; today only grazing cattle are on site. Sketch of agency in October, 1879, from *Frank Leslie's Illustrated.*)

THE MILD MISTER MEEKER

"I have been assaulted by a leading chief, Johnson, forced out of my house and injured badly, but was rescued by employees. It is now revealed that Johnson originated all the trouble stated in letter Sept. 8. His son shot at plowman, and opposition to plowing is wide. Plowing stops; life of self, family, and employees not safe: want protection immediately: have asked Governor Pitkin to confer with General Pope."

—Telegram from Nathan C. Meeker to Washington, D.C., Sept. 13, 1879

NATHAN COOK MEEKER at age 62 had no small reputation as a newspaperman and agricultural editor, nor did he have less notoriety as a dabbler in socialism and do-goodism.

One had led to the other until at his sixtieth year, Meeker was appointed the agent for the White River band of Ute Indians. Sixteen months later, Meeker was dead, a log chain around his neck and a barrel stave driven down his throat.

Several bands of Ute Indians were served by the agency which Meeker controlled in 1878. Their acknowledged leader was Ouray, a striking and enlightened chief who lived on the Uncompaghre river in western Colorado. While he planned the gradual conversion of his tribe from the old ways to those of the white man, he had close ties with the White River branch through its chief, Douglas, and the head medicine man, Johnson. This is the same Johnson whose wife, Susan—Ouray's sister—, was rescued by the Army in 1863.

It was Ouray's proud boast that never in recent years had a Ute taken the life of a white man. The white man might rustle the Indian's cattle, trespass on his land, short him on his annuities or just fail to pay him, but the Ute would not resort to physical protest. In the main, this was the situation for the tribe after the Civil War.

But they were being crowded in their hunting grounds of western Colorado. White men ringed the borders and coveted the mineral and natural wealth of the mountains and valleys and rivers alloted to the Utes.

Trouble was stirring, much of it caused by an Indian Bureau that fumbled its management and delayed its payments. Then in 1878, Nathan Meeker took charge of the most troublesome agency, that of the White River Utes. Called "Father Meeker" alternately affectionately or derisively, the deceptively mild ex-reporter and author had been the founder of Greeley, Colorado, an experiment in a socialistic-like cooperative community in northeastern Colorado.

The Greeley experiment—named in honor of the newspaperman who advised everyone to "Go west!"—was a success, but not until after several false starts. It was to repay debts incurred in these false starts that Meeker policied for the $1,500-a-year agent's job. He also thought he could bring prosperity to the Indian.

Death was his reward and the Ute War that terrorized 1879 Colorado the result.

FORT COLLINS, COLORADO

The soldiers who galloped out of the new Army post at Laporte, Colorado, in 1863 little knew that their patrol would have far-reaching effects on the peace of Colorado. As far as they were concerned, all they were doing was saving an Indian girl from being burned at the stake.

At the moment, the new post was merely a guard detachment for the Overland Stage Station. Amid signs of increasing Indian agitation against the main route of the line, in September, 1863, Company B, 1st Colorado Volunteer Cavalry, had been sent up to keep watch. They established themselves on the bank of the Cache la Poudre river, just west of the center of town. Log cabins and stables were built hastily in view of the evening chills that foretold a cold winter.

It took no time for the soldier carpenters to shift into military roles when a Yampa Ute head medicine man interrupted their labors. His wife had been captured by Araphoe cattle rustlers, he reported.

The troopers were able to pick up the trail without much trouble. Since the fate of an Indian woman of another tribe was similar to that of a captured white woman, the soldiers could sympathize with the Ute. This sympathy drove them in desperate pursuit.

A mile from modern Greeley, Colorado, the chase ended. As the soldiers charged into the Arapahoe camp, they saw the woman. Next to her, several Arapahoes were trying to light a pile of sticks and brush under her feet. They intended to burn her at the stake because a white settler had refused to trade an old hat and a mirror for her.

The Arapahoes took off for the hills and the Army took custody of the squaw. In years later, the full story came out. The squaw was Susan, the younger sister of Ouray, chief of the Uncompahgre Utes. Her marriage with the medicine man, generally known as Johnson, was a political machination of Ouray to unite his tribe with the newly-organized White River grouping of Utes.

To the troopers at Laporte, however, the rescue was something to tell about in old age, perhaps even to write about back to the "States," but it was not of much concern otherwise. Many historians since have credited this enthusiastic Army action with keeping the Uncompahgre and White River Utes on the "peace path" many years after other branches of the tribe had broken loose. Even when the Sand Creek Massacre of 1864 pushed most of the Ute clan into fearsome reprisals, the parent tribes of Susan and Johnson kept the peace.

In 1863, high level Indian tribe politics was far from the minds of troopers who were trying to find themselves a home for the winter. When the spring thaw of 1864 arrived, they found that they had not been too successful. Their camp went underwater when the nearby Cache la Poudre river overflowed. This was no particular problem to the Colorado Volunteers however; by May, 1864, they had been relieved by two companies of the 11th Ohio Cavalry.

The Ohioans were disenchanted by the whole idea. In casting about for a new location they hit upon a plateau that stood safely above the river only a few miles to the southeast. By this time they had attached a name to their soggy encampment, honoring their regimental commander, Colonel W. O. Collins.

When the good colonel saw his namesake in summer, 1864, he reported back to headquarters, "I became satisfied that the good of the service required a change in the location of the post. The present site is within the town of Laporte, where the claims of lot holders seriously interfere with military interests, the ground is subject to overflow, the whole having been under water and much public property

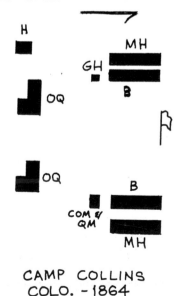

CAMP COLLINS
COLO. - 1864

THIS IS HOW Colonel Collins ordered that new Fort Collins was to look. Barracks were to be 20 by 90 feet, facing each other from opposite sides of 300- by 300-foot parade ground. Each barracks had two 20- by 40-foot dormitories and one 10-foot wide orderly room, and each had its own kitchen and mess hall in a 60-foot long building to rear. Officers quarters had two rooms and a kitchen apiece, while square hospital was to be moved to opposite corner of post, not far from Cache la Poudre river north of fort. (Redrawn from copy of original plat displayed in Fort Collins Museum.)

destroyed about the 10th of June last, and the space being too contracted for military purposes."

Before the troopers could move, they were summoned by a rancher for more Indian chasing. He reported that six Utes—tribal branch unknown or, more likely, unimportant to him—had jumped his horse herd, killing one herder, and causing the settlers in the area to flee. The Ohioans were able to pick up the trail and recover the horses, killing one Indian and wounding another in the process.

But on October 23, the Ohioans moved and the new site took on the more distinguished name of "Fort" Collins.

Four months later men of Company B were with Colonel Collins on an expedition that was attacked by 2,500 Sioux. Seven of the Ohioans were in a 16-man volunteer patrol that charged 50 Indians to clear them from a spot 350 yards from the camp.

The Ohioans stayed at Collins until June, 1865, then were relieved by elements of the 21st New York Cavalry. A year later, so-called "Galvanized Yankees" of a Missouri Regiment garrisoned the post until it was abandoned in 1867. These were former Confederate soldiers who had enlisted for the western duty. One departmental commander, General John Pope, officially commented, "They answer well for such service, and relieve regiments which can be sent elsewhere."

Although by and large the Collins garrison found it had quieted the Ute dangers, they found this had little effect on the problems generated by other tribes. Nor did it affect the local problems. In time-honored fashion, settlers had immediately located next to the post when it moved. In equally time-honored fashion, the relations were not too amicable.

The settlers resented the assertedly "overbearing" attitude of the troopers, especially when the commanding officer issued orders which he felt should be obeyed with equal speed by military and civilian alike. The fact that non-Coloradoans manned the post—especially "Easterners" of the Ohio and New

(HARRY SMILEY, CURATOR, FORT COLLINS MUSEUM.)

FORT COLLINS in 1865, as painted by soldier named DeLennep, did not quite match original plans for it. This view is from north bank of river, looking toward south. Modern Jefferson street is the path in foreground above stables. Two small cabins on other side probably were Aunty Stone and sutler's houses. Stables were partial dugouts under bank of river. In this painting, barracks face each other across parade. Only complete mess hall was behind western barracks. Log officers' quarters apparently were augmented by two more buildings behind flagpole, possibly headquarters and commanding officer's quarters. Corrals, store houses, laundress quarters, and citizens' cabins were other buildings. Many civilians came to vicinity of fort, partly to trade and partly for protection. In year before Army arrived, area was scene of frequent Indian attacks. One was discouraged by stageline employee who mounted segments of stovepipe in rock barricade. Indians pulled back when they saw fearsome barrels of black "cannon" aimed at them.

York variety, plus ex-Confederates—undoubtedly contributed to the mutual disenchantment.

And as a continuing source of discontent, the Army found much of its time devoted to guarding its unfenced haystacks from depredations of civilian-owned livestock. Tradition still has it that protection of their valuable hay was more vital to the Fort Collins garrison than protection of the civilians—but that is local "civilian" traditional.

TO GET THERE: Fort Collins is a city 65 miles north of Denver. Museum and restored "Aunty Stone Cabin" are in Lincoln Park, 219 Peterson Street, just east of downtown area. Original site is covered by Union Pacific railroad yards but a stone marker is next to Power House on College Avenue north of downtown.

ONLY REMAINING building of Army days is so-called "Aunty Stone Cabin," built in 1864 as mess room for Fort Collins officers by Judge Lewis Stone. After his death in 1866, his wife continued taking care of officers. "She has a very comfortable home for this country," schoolteacher niece who stayed there in 1866 wrote in her diary. "There are three large rooms below and chambers for sleeping rooms. . . . She already has eight officers as regular boarders." After Army left in 1867, Aunty Stone used house as Fort Collins' first hotel. After later career as kitchen, cottage, paint shop, and —at a different location—Pioneer Museum, it was moved in 1959 behind city museum. It was first private building erected in Fort Collins, although built with Army permission to serve Army.

CANTONMENT ON WHITE RIVER, COLORADO

The story of Camp on White River is anti-climactic to that of Nathan Meeker and his massacre. To tell of the former cannot be done without at least touching lightly on the latter. In fact, because of the over-riding nature of the massacre and its allied events, the important history of Camp on White River had taken place before the post was established.

The proverbial barn door was closed belatedly when the Army came to the White River valley of northwestern Colorado. Then the 10-company, rambling "Camp on White River" came into being for a brief tenure of less than four years.

When Meeker became the agent at White River in 1878, he found the situation was not the happiest. The Indian Bureau owed the Utes $112,000 for land cessations. The past winter the White River group had almost starved because its supplies lay rotting in Rawlins while the bureau unraveled red tape.

Settlers were unhappy with the Utes because they ranged beyond the reservation hunting for food. The Utes were equally unhappy with whites who killed reservation game and cast covetous eyes on the natural resources. It was well known that the state politicians of the day had been elected on the platform, "Get the Utes out of Colorado." Ouray knew that it would not take much provocation to abrogate the treaties and force his people from their traditional homes.

Meeker came fired with an enthusiasm to prove that his charges could be self-sufficient and easily adaptable to the ways of the whites. He felt that agriculture was the answer. He soon learned that his predecessors had described farming as squaw work so they could recruit Utes for the post-Custer expeditions against the Sioux. The Utes who did go with the Army as scouts brought back with them the seamier side of soldiering, whiskey and disease included.

Meeker pressured the Indian Bureau into shipping the back annuities which he distributed fairly and efficiently. He pushed through an allocation of $20,000 to start his agricultural project, envisioning the day when Ute-produced corn, cattle, milk, chickens, and produce would be shipped to the outside world.

But as the farm machinery moved in and the braves saw themselves being tailored for farm life, the signs of discontent appeared.

An article of Meeker's in the Greeley *Tribune* aroused the chiefs who then claimed he was the author of other critical pieces on the tribe. A white posse invaded the reservation and it took the combined vocal talents of Meeker and the chiefs to eject them. The crowning blow was when Meeker announced that the 2,000-plus ponies with which the Utes figured their wordly wealth would have to go. He emphasized his ultimatum by plowing up a pony pasture and the tribal race track.

Events tumbled one after the other. The Indians refused to work. Bullets stopped the plowing. Meeker was assaulted by Johnson—of the 1863 Camp Collins incident. A telegram for help was dispatched. The troops at Fort Fred Steele, Wyoming, were on the move.

When Ute scouts reported soldiers had entered their reservation, the White River tribe burned the agency, killed Meeker and his employees, and kidnapped three of the women. Eighteen miles from the agency, they met the Army column of 153 soldiers, 25 civilians, 220 mules and 150 horses. In the confusion, firing started and the Battle of Milk Creek began on Sept. 29, 1879.

CAMP ON WHITE RIVER
COLO. – 1882

LOGS, BRICK, and adobe were used in buildings of Camp on White River and year before it was abandoned it was a sprawling, elaborate post that cost almost $300,000. Bordering the 450- by 775-foot parade ground were seven officers' quarters, most of them duplexes; new hospital; and nine barracks, two of them 25 feet wide by 150 feet deep. Other officer and enlisted quarters were scattered south of main post, with stables and yards near White River. Elaborate post trader building was 100 feet across front, 25 feet deep, with wing 50 feet deep. (Redrawn from plat in National Archives.)

CAMP ON WHITE RIVER was town of Meeker when this picture was taken in 1887, four years after Army left. Settlers bought all buildings, giving them ready-made town. This view is from north with officers' row in foreground and long, narrow barracks on other side of parade ground behind bare flagpole. Although false fronts had been put on many buildings, their Army design still is obvious. Brick buildings have replaced barracks row in modern Meeker, county courthouse stands in middle of parade ground, but three log officers' quarters remain. About time this picture was taken, so-called "Second Ute War" took place. Two Utes of band led by Chief Colorow—veteran of first war—were accused of selling stolen horses in Meeker. More than 70 "deputy sheriffs" pursued them. Firing resulted when they met 50-Indian Colorow band. Rumor got out that Meeker was under siege and seven brigades of National Guardsmen were rushed to town. Colorow tried to escape into Utah but was cornered near border. In three hour skirmish, eight Indians and three whites died. Fight ended when ammunition was exhausted. "War" proved to be political and publicity-seeking fake, cost Colorado taxpayers $80,314.72.

Thirteen men were killed—including Major Thomas T. Thornburgh, the expedition's commander—and at least 42 wounded. Most of the animals were killed. Their carcasses formed a circle of rotting breastworks behind which the soldiers crouched. Later, 35 Negro cavalrymen from Fort Lewis, Colorado, broke through the Ute lines to reinforce the expedition. They were greeted by one officer, "You men of the Ninth Cavalry are the whitest black men I have ever seen!"

Soldiers, black and white, still were behind putrifying horses and broken wagons on October 5 when the main body of reinforcements arrived under the command of Brevet General Wesley Merritt. The besiegers disappeared.

"Other troops were hurried forward . . . reinforcing Merritt to about a thousand effectives," General Sherman later reported. Then he moved to the agency, "finding it burned down, and the murdered bodies of Mr. Meeker and six employees, having buried three others on the road . . .

"As soon as the reinforcements enroute overtook him, Colonel Merritt began his pursuit south . . . but before he had reached the crest of the first mountain, he was overtaken by a dispatch . . ."

The dispatch was from Sherman, relaying a report that Chief Ouray had telegraphed the Utes to stop fighting. They promised to obey "and will fight no more unless forced to do so."

Merritt returned to what was to be the site of Camp on White River and "there awaited the result of the negotiations." He had upwards of 1,500 troopers by this time. They divided their time between setting up a camp and patrolling.

A tragic postscript to the period of massacre marked the end of armed conflict. While on patrol,

a lieutenant and a scout were killed by an Indian party. They, in turn, claimed that the scout had first killed a member of their band.

The official report of Camp on the White River's only combat casualties could have been applied to many conflicts in the west. The Indians, it said, "insist they had no purpose to fight; that they were simply watching the movements of Merritt's troops."

TO GET THERE: Meeker is at the junction of State 64, 789, and 13 in northwestern Colorado. Courthouse stands in center of old parade ground; three log cabins north of it formerly were officers' quarters. Massacre marker is on south side of State 64, 3.2 miles west of Meeker.

CHINKED LOG construction of officers' quarters is obvious in these two buildings remaining from Army days. Museum building, also a residence, is flanked by quarters which still are occupied. After Army took command in area in 1879, Utes involved in massacre were brought to trial, but with inconclusive results. Chief Douglas wound up spending year at Fort Leavenworth, finally was released quietly after no charges were made. He remained in vicinity of Meeker and in 1885 was killed while returning to reservation from drinking bout in Meeker saloons. Ralph Meeker, son of murdered agent, also returned to Meeker, was last there in 1921 shortly before his death.

CANTONMENT ON THE UNCOMPAHGRE, COLORADO

With Nathan Meeker dead, along with 64 other soldiers, settlers, and hostile Utes, an uneasy calm closed on western Colorado. The next logical step was to punish the guilty. Logic had little to do with the outcome, however.

Rumors of Ute massacres throughout all of Colorado widened the scene momentarily, but as these were found to be false the spotlight narrowed to one spot: the Los Pinos Agency on the Uncompahgre river. This was not far from where Chief Ouray lived as a gentleman farmer and tribal elder. Here Ouray became a member of a three-man commission convened to determine the facts of the Ute uprising and the names of the guilty braves.

As far as Coloradoans were concerned, the entire Ute world was guilty. Let those with blood on their hands be hanged, the rest taken lock, stock, and tepee out of the state, popular sentiment and politicians thundered. The destination of the Utes was immaterial so long as they were uprooted from the valuable agricultural and mineral areas that they occupied.

Danger was obvious when the commission had its first hearing on November 12, 1879. There were 25 white men present, only 15 of them soldiers, while the entire valley was covered with tepees of Ute families. Bordering the valley was the greater danger: the camps of the white men who planned to jump the Ute claims the minute they felt they could get away with it.

The commission sat 41 times until January 7, 1880, but had its full membership present only 20 times. A dozen Utes were pointed out as leaders in the massacre, but identifications were so hazy that

little stock could be put in them. One of the kidnapped women complained, "With no whiskers and nothing but mean looks," all of the Indians looked alike.

General Ranald S. Mackenzie suddenly appeared, six companies of cavalry and nine of infantry behind him. They were the answer to two rumors: one that the Utes would refuse to be dislocated, another that the whites planned to move into the reservation by force.

General of the Army William T. Sherman was convinced that the Army was necessary to keep the peace. The Secretary of War was asked for $100,000 "for a considerable post, one that will insure peace in all that region. . . . With a good strong post on the Gunnison. . . I feel certain that the Army can enforce peace in that mountain region for sometime to come."

A supply camp was established about four miles from the Los Pinos Agency on July 21, 1880. In August, the Utes signed a treaty providing for their removal to Utah the next spring.

The half-year delay in opening up the area drew the wrath of the white squatters. A drunken freighter killed a Ute on "Son of a Bitch" hill east of Los Pinos and then, in turn, was killed by a Ute posse.

The approach of winter had a calming effect on the area, and the bulk of Mackenzie's troops returned to their home forts. About 250 men of the 23rd U. S. Infantry remained. Their attention was directed immediately to replacing their rows of tents with log buildings.

"The first winter at Cantonment on the Uncompahgre River, Colorado, was in tents," remembered an officer's daughter later. "The weather was so

FORT CRAWFORD
COLO.—1889

RE-NAMED IN 1886 in memory of Captain Emmet Crawford —who had been killed while pursuing Apaches in Mexico— Cantonment on the Uncompahgre was elaborate post around 575- by 150-foot parade ground. Barracks, headquarters, guardhouse, bakery, hospital ward, and one ordnance store house were frame construction, remainder of post was of log pickets "chinked in with clay and are lined with old canvas or cotton cloth." Each barracks, capacity one company, was one story, measured 70 by 40 feet across front with 40- by 25-foot wings to rear. Post commander's picket quarters was 58 by 15 feet with wing 62 by 15 feet. Hospital measured 115 by 15 feet, plus 22- by 41-foot picket ward to left and 24- by 40-foot frame ward to right. Corral had room for 100 animals in its stalls around square 200 by 178 feet. Headquarters building, 75 by 35 feet with 50- by 42-wing served extracurricular function, officer's daughter later wrote. "Notwithstanding the discomforts and primitive mode of life, there was quite a bit of entertaining, with crude service," she said. "Also certain hops were held in the headquarters building, the largest house in the Cantonment" (Redrawn from plat in National Archives.)

CANTONMENT on the Uncompahgre in 1886 was virtually as complete as it was to be when it was abandoned in 1890. This view is from southeast, headquarters at left edge, commander's quarters beyond it, officers' row in background. Two unusual buildings are shooting gallery and gymnasium at far end of parade ground. Southernmost barracks burned and was rebuilt by troops, the original builders of post. Caretaker watched buildings after Army left and until they were auctioned off in 1895. James A. Fenlon, former sutler, exercised his right as resident and claimed 160 acres of post proper, paying $1.25 an acre. He operated store near railroad for many years.

cold that the officers had to be up and down all night stoking the Sibley stoves to keep their families from freezing to death, and oftentimes where there had been a snowstorm they would find the cots covered with snow."

After the winter, the matter of moving the Utes was paramount. Chief Ouray had died the previous August, following a desperate ride with his wife and a white doctor over the "top of the world" to muster Ute votes for the removal. He had left a death bed to carry out his final mission of peace for his tribe.

In August, 1881, the Ouray power was but a memory, and the Utes refused to be budged. Troops from the Cantonment were drawn up. Mackenzie told the assembled Ute chiefs to decide within 24 hours to move, or be driven out by force.

"The next day the Indians submitted and pledged themselves to go quietly and at once," the district commander later reported. "They moved off in a day or two thereafter peaceably, but manifesting the greatest grief and regret at being obliged to abandon, in this manner, the homes of their tribe for so many years."

On September 1, 1881, the 350-mile trek to Utah began. Almost 1,500 men, women, and children; 8,000 ponies; 10,000 sheep and goats; countless wagons and travois of tepees, food, clothing and equipment slowly moved, single file, under the watchful and protecting wing of the Army.

The squatters had won. "Sunday morning the Utes bid adieu to their old hunting grounds and folded their tents, rounded up their dogs, sheep, goats, ponies and traps, and took up the line of march for their new reservation," editorialized a local newspaper. "This is an event that has long and devoutly been prayed for by our people. How joyful it sounds and with what satisfaction one can say, 'The Utes have gone'."

The Cantonment troopers noted one last bit of resistance. Suddenly Chief Colorow and 50 of his painted braves wheeled their ponies and charged at the 600 assembled troopers. Mackenzie gave a few sharp orders. The line of soldiers erupted in a volley of rifle and cannon fire aimed to impress rather than injure.

The desperate charge of the Utes reined up. For a moment, Colorow gazed hopelessly at the opposition, then he and his braves turned their mounts and headed for Utah.

TO GET THERE: From Montrose, Colorado, take U.S. 550 south for four miles. On right side is Ouray-Chipeta Park, state maintained area which included burial place of Chipeta, Ouray's wife; monument to Ouray; and museum. Continue on U. S. 550 another four miles south to ranch of Harold Flowers, right (west) side. This is site of Cantonment on the Uncompahgre, but only stately cottonwoods along fenceline remain from Army days.

"THE LOGS of the cabins were erected in an undried state with the pitch oozing from them," former resident wrote. "These were covered with condemned canvas tent flies. The canvas was used on walls and ceiling to keep the pitch from dropping on, or coming in contact with the occupants." This picket building is possible solitary remnant of fort days at site; if not dating from Army period, it comes close to that era and matches construction of bulk of post.

FORTS DUCHESNE & THORNBURGH, UTAH

The blood of red, white, and black man that mingled in the Battle of Milk Creek was almost a prophecy of the future for the Ute Indians and the Army.

Driven from their hunting grounds in Colorado and re-settled on the Uintah and Uncompahgre reservations in northeastern Utah, the Utes were party to an early and relatively successful experiment in integration. It was in 1886 at newly established Fort Duchesne that it began.

Midway between the two reservations, the post was established to "discipline and control" the occupants of both. To do the job the Army sent four companies of infantry plus two troops of Negro cavalry—men of the Ninth Cavalry. This was the same regiment from which the first reinforcements at Milk Creek came; the Negro troopers termed "the whitest black men" they had ever seen by the besieged Thornburgh command.

Despite the presence of both Negro and Caucasi-

an soldiers to keep the peace, few incidents occurred. In 1886 a newspaper noted that the Indians called the Negroes "Buffalo soldiers because of their wooly heads," but this was a nickname common throughout the West. "The dislike is not sufficient to cause apprehension," it added.

It may be that part of the credit for the smooth relations was owed to the founder of Fort Duchesne and the commander of the Negro troops, Major Frederick W. Benteen. Best known for his heroism at the Battle of the Little Big Horn, Benteen was known throughout the Army as a combat commander who fought "where a leader should be —in the front." For a year after the Civil War he commanded a Colored Regiment before joining the Seventh Cavalry.

The Oriental race added to the situation at Fort Duchesne when Wong Sing, a Chinese immigrant, set up a makeshift laundry on the banks of the Uintah river near the post. Ten years before, Congress had eliminated the venerable tradition of the post laundresses, so Wong Sing found himself much in demand. Soon he was able to expand into a general store, having picked up enough English and Ute words so that he could serve both the soldiers and their wards. A restaurant then was added to his enterprise.

The prosperity of the laundryman-turned-entrepreneur aroused the ire of several white merchants. They pointed out that Wong Sing was illegally trading on a government reservation, and there was no alternative but to move him.

Wong Sing's popularity with the Indians fol-

FORT DUCHESNE
UTAH - 1888

ADOBE was important ingredient in most buildings at Fort Duchesne, but frame ultimately was used to cover them. First troops at fort spent most of their time in hauling logs and building barracks, officers' quarters, commissary, storehouse, and hospital at cost of about $22,800. When General George Crook visited in 1887, he said that the buildings were not all he hoped for, but they were all which could be built due to cost and late season. Except for commanding officer's residence, officers' quarters were duplexes that measured 32 feet across front of building and 56 feet in depth. Six barracks each were 120 by 30 feet in main section with wing that was 70 by 30 feet. Top two on each side of parade were for infantry, lower ones were for cavalry. Hospital apparently was group of three buildings —ward, surgery, and steward's quarters or office. Amusement hall and administration building at south side of parade—top of plat is north—was 120 by 32 feet while building used temporarily in 1888 as headquarters measured 70 by 16 feet. Parade ground was 653 feet wide and 900 feet long, not counting arc at officers' row. Corral, cord wood enclosure, measured 466 by 300 feet. (Redrawn from plat in National Archives.)

FORT DUCHESNE in its heydey showed that most adobe construction had been covered by frames, although some picket-log buildings remained. View is from southwest looking at rear of post trader's buildings with barracks on left, officers' row in background, shops and granary on right. In 1890, post surgeon reported, "The quarters are good except that several of those occupied by married men leak badly. . . . Very poor accommodations for bathing. Lack of bath tubs, lack of conveniences for warming water, and room, and lack of privacy makes bathing uncomfortable, so I have no doubt it is frequently neglected."

lowed him to his new store just off the reservation. Not only did the Indians refuse to patronize the white traders who had reported Wong Sing, but it was not long before mysterious fires leveled the traders' businesses. Loyally supported by his Utes, Wong Sing continued in business for many years. In 1929, the immigrant who had started with a riverside laundry had a $70,000 inventory on his shelves.

The far-reaching example of racial equality may have been one of the more important and lasting contributions of Fort Duchesne, but it was little noted in the 1880's when the fort was started. Actually, the Army came to the Duchesne area five years before Benteen's "buffalo soldiers," but it did not stay.

When Ranald Mackenzie's Colorado Caravan headed into Utah, the open wounds of Ute hostility indicated that an Army post would be needed at their new home. Four companies of the Sixth Infantry came from the Cantonment on the Uncompahgre and set up a tent camp in August, 1881. They named it Fort Thornburgh after the fallen leader at Milk Creek.

Near Ouray, about 15 miles southeast of the ultimate site of Fort Duchesne, the new post was considered by the Indian Bureau to be too close to the agency. Under pressure from Indian Agents who feared trouble if troopers and Utes were in too close proximity, the Army packed up its tents and shifted to a new site 35 miles northeast. Here, a few miles north of Vernal, the Army made plans to

PARADE GROUND today shows Army-planted trees prospered although Fort Duchesne buildings have been razed. Modern house in background is at approximate site of commanding officer's quarters. Houses were occupied until removal in recent years. Most barracks still remain, though much altered in use. One of those on eastern side of parade is now a garage for school busses; one on western side has been remodeled into shower and locker room for swimming pool. Up to 1890, post had average of 300 men, but this was halved for remaining years until abandonment in 1912. Of Negro and white units serving there jointly, 1886 comment was, "The white infantrymen and the black cavalrymen at the fort fraternize without any . . . discrimination as to color. They associate, eat . . . and sleep and fight the festive bedbug together."

MAGAZINE of Fort Duchesne recalls days when soldiers guarded tribal annuity shipments from railhead, especially in 1898 when rumor was heard that notorious Butch Cassidy "Robber's Roost Gang" planned to ambush wagon train. In addition, troopers protected 16-steer bi-weekly beef allotment and officer from fort inspected it, attesting to its quality before it was turned over to Indian Agent for issue. In early days, garrison devoted considerable labor improving road and telegraph from Salt Lake City and railhead to fort.

build an elaborate $84,000 fort.

The money was slow in arriving. The first winter was spent in tents. When no money came in 1882, the garrison was removed to more permanent and warmer quarters for the winter. In 1883, the magnificent sum of $1,500 was allocated for the fort. Eight adobe buildings erected by the troops resulted.

Finally the Army gave up on Fort Thornburgh, defeated not by Indian battle but by squatter pressures.

"Owing to the individual sharpness and avarice of squatters and land-owners within the limits of new Fort Thornburgh Reservation it became impossible to secure a valid title to the land, so that the War Department very wisely gave up the building of the post," General O. O. Howard, the departmental commander, wrote in his annual report for 1883.

The last garrison at Thornburgh considered itself merely at what Howard described "a summer encampment." Most of their labors were concentrated on improving the road and telegraph network, projects of value regardless of the post's future. A sergeant and a telegraph operator manned the adobe installation during the winter of 1883-84, and then the place was abandoned to squatters who took immediate possession.

The question of who owned the reservation probably was little more than academic, as far as the Army was concerned. It was felt that the Indians "are not liable to any outbreak during the winter," Howard said. "Should necessity demand it another encampment can be made next season," he added, but the theory was that troops could more efficiently remain at other posts and rush to the area if required.

Although in 1884 the Uintah Agent boasted of having "the best lot of savages in America," the Utes could not resist the temptation to visit their old Colorado haunts. Amid settler charges of Ute depredations, by 1886 the various bands of Utes began fighting between themselves, shooting "one another with that pleasing freedom so characteristic of the noble red man."

An 1886 change in agents suggested a condition as potentially dangerous as that at White River in 1879. Because by treaty the annuities of the White River band had to contribute $3,500 annually to the families of those killed in the Meeker Massacre, their per capita shares amounted to less than $7. When the new agent tried to assess the $3,500 equally from the allotments of all the Utes—the innocent along with the guilty—the fuse was set for another Ute explosion.

Fortunately by 1886, communications were more rapid and officials more enlightened than in early days. Investigators were rushed to the agency by both the Interior and War Departments. The unfair situation was corrected by the former, and its enforcement guaranteed by the latter with the recommendation that a fort be established.

The Utes did not take kindly to the arrival of blue-coats on their reservation. When Benteen's six companies arrived, they were confronted by "about 700 Indians. . .in full war dress and paint, and hostile, as hostile as can be," an infantryman later wrote.

While the soldiers hastily posted pickets and dug rifle pits, the Army officers, the Indian Agent, and the chiefs conferred. Promised that they had nothing to fear as long as they kept the peace, the Utes agreed that the Army could build their fort.

The painted braves looked deeply into the faces of the assembled military. Slowly their ranks parted, then in small groups the Utes returned to their tepees. Fort Duchesne was the immediate result; the citizen who is proud of his Ute ancestry and the heritage of Ouray was to be the ultimate achievement.

TO GET THERE: Site of "New" Fort Thornburgh is reached from Vernal, Utah. Take State 245 west to Maeser, 3 miles. Turn right on improved road which heads to north. At point before it crosses Ashley creek, about 3 miles, is site of fort, left (west) side of road. There are no remains. Fort Duchesne still is Indian Agency 22 miles west of Vernal and a mile south of U.S. 40.

FARMING was one of many attractions of the West put before the eyes of a restless East at the close of the Civil War. Illinois may not seem west to modern Americans, but it was the portal to a better future in 1865.

(ADVERTISEMENT IN HARPER'S WEEKLY, APRIL 22, 1865).

PATHFINDERS AND SETTLERS

". . . Go into the heart of their buffalo country and build and hold forts until the trouble is over. A hasty expedition, however successful, is only a temporary lesson, whereas the presence of troops in force in the country where the Indians are compelled to live and subsist would soon oblige them to sue for peace and accept such terms as the Government may think proper to impose."

—Lt. Col. William O. Collins' Indian Problem Solution, 1865.

THE LURE of the West was unceasing. The initial trickle of the trapper and trader soon became a flood of emigrants following closely on the tracks of the trail breaker.

Trails cut wide swaths through prairie grass, deep ruts across sandy wastes, treacherous tracks over mountain tops. Nothing, it seemed, would stem the tide.

Red men soon realized that the whites had no intention of passing through without leaving an indelible mark on the land. When this mark began to crowd aside the Indian and to destroy his means of livelihood, he fought back.

The Army had a role from the very beginning in westward expansion. First it pioneered the explorers' paths, either in the principal role of scientist or as protective escort. Then as the routes and the Indian opposition to them became firmly established, the Army manned the protective forts along the way.

What follows are a few of these places, ranging from the rough, makeshift huts of Cantonment Far West to the permanent brick construction of Fort Logan. Forty years separate the extremes that were far deeper than the mere symbology of architectural difference. But they mirror the changes that saw the disappearance of the frontier.

CANTONMENT FAR WEST, CALIFORNIA

Gold rush days in early California posed a series of contradictions, as far as Captain Hannibal Day was concerned. As commanding officer of Cantonment Far West, a temporary camp that lasted three years, he noted that the hardy and well armed miner was being defended by an under-fed and scurvy-weakened soldier from "a miserable race of savages. . .armed only with the bow and arrow."

Despite his post's mission to protect the emigrant trails and wagon roads to the mines, Day reported, "So far as the defence of the territory is concerned, no better force could be needed than the present population of the mines, armed and equipped as they very generally are."

At least two problems were at the root of the situation, however. Desertion that weakened every California fort of 1850 touched Far West equally. One captain and 27 enlisted men had taken off for the mines in the last half of 1849. Then the entire teamster detail followed suit, first hampering pursuit by driving off the post's mounts. Day asked department headquarters what they had in mind for the officers to do, "when we shall have no rank and file left, which, I fancy, will not be a very distant period of time."

One staff officer at headquarters commented that the California regiments soon would be at the stage characterized by a senior officer as "terrestial happiness: an Army without soldiers."

The second problem faced by Day was the makeshift situation at Far West. "As for hard service in this territory with all imaginable deprivations and uncomfortable position," he complained, "I will not yield to anyone of the regiment."

His place at Far West was a small plateau of high ground near Bear Creek, a tributary of the Sacramento river. It was founded in 1849 as an overnight camp on land owned by a cousin of William T. Sherman, then an aide to the departmental commander, and was considered as little more than temporary during its whole career.

Northern California's autumn being less than tropical, however, within a month Day reported four soldiers had died. He said that the post surgeon predicted more fatalities unless "we can shelter ourselves from the winter rains" and noted that a saw mill 20 miles from the post would sell lumber for buildings. He thought the Army should take advantage of this source of shelter, not only to do "justice to a command already reduced by desertion," but because "more attention is due to the comfort of those who 'stand by their colors.' "

On December 16 he was able to report that a log cabin hospital was finished "and other similar structures are in progress of completion for the two companies."

No sooner had the first of the log cabins been finished that Day was told that his lumber requisition had arrived and was at Vernon, the head of navigation of the river. "I was somewhat apprehensive that our previous outlay for log cabins and a beginning of shingles might prove unnecessary and extravagant," he commented, "but on discharging the transport, it was found that we had but about 12,000 feet of boards. . .some 8,000 feet were landed at Vernon and in use there for building but for whom and by whose authority does not appear."

Work was pushed on two 20- by 40-foot barracks. Winter set in before both could be completed. One with a shingle roof served for troops while one with a canvas top was appropriated as a supply

DAUGHTERS OF GOLDEN WEST placed this marker to commemorate pioneers buried in Far West graveyard. Papers and other souvenirs put inside were stolen long ago, and this plate is only one of four remaining. Its accuracy is open to question. Captain Day's official correspondence file shows that Private "Newton Barrs" died on 10 July 1849, "Harbor of San Fancisco Cal. on board transport," and it is unlikely remains were taken to new cantonment for burial.

warehouse. Officers' quarters were log cabins or floor-boarded tents while a tent had to serve for a guardhouse.

By mid-January, 1850, Cantonment Far West was becoming more comfortable. "By extraordinary exertion between the heavy falls of rain," the commander reported, "we have succeeded in completing our main cabin with shingle roof, and said stores are this moment being placed therein, being the first moment such a thing has been possible and the companies are ordered to occupy their cabin."

Scurvy continued to harass the garrison. In February a boat arrived but it turned out whatever was aboard was private property. It was for sale "on private account of some one." Of course the post had no money or authority to buy.

When the winter of 1849-50 began to break up in March, Day immediately sent his quartermaster with requisitions for vinegar, sugar, garden hoses, scythes, and a half dozen ball and chain sets. He found that many of his requisitions had been filled, but without boats to negotiate the creek he had no way to get them over the primitive road to his post.

By April, the soil was firm enough for supply movement—and other movement. Miners and other settlers reported Indian skirmishes, but the miners' rifles outmatched the Indians "in which their skill in archery was found quite inefficient." Day said that at one point the miners planned to send a deputation to petition for Army protection, "but probably a 'sober second thought' seemed to shame them of the transaction. . . . From all the information I can gather, the aggression was rather on the part of the whites towards the natives."

His theory was reinforced the next month when two settlers were attacked by Indians, despite a reputation of having "been all winter on the most friendly terms with the Indians and even more have treated them kindly and hospitably." Apparently some white men had attacked an Indian camp earlier in the belief that missing cattle had been rustled by

them. The return of the accidently strayed stock did nothing to resurrect two slain braves, and the tribesmen struck out at the nearest white men "as the most available victims and considering after such outrages all white men were equally at fault."

Day's comments, made in 1850, were appropriate for the remaining two years of the post:

"With the present reduced state of my command," he said, "a military station here or at any other point in this valley seems but as the merest pretense of protection or aid of any kind to the inhabitants, as I have not the force or ability to send ten bayonets a mile from camp on any duty whatever. So far as the mining population is concerned, they are competent for their own protection. . . ."

He suggested that the Indian agent visit the tribes and notify them "of what will be their probable fate unless they discontinue their thieving and submit with a better grace to being shot down, although it may seem strange to them to be thus intruded upon by the whites. . .and they must vacate their hunting grounds in favor of our gold-diggers."

TO GET THERE: From San Francisco, take U.S. 40 143 miles to Roseville. Turn north on U.S. 99E. Go 21 miles to Wheatland. Turn right in center of town toward east, go 1.5 miles to E. Clemens Horts ranch. At dirt road follow signs to right toward "Camp Far West Reservoir," recreation area; at first fork in dirt road, veer right. This road leads in about one mile to site of post and cemetery.

SLIGHT SLOPE marks site of Cantonment Far West and stone-fenced cemetery on location. Post commander considered it a "Botany Bay" place, after Australian convict colony, in his official correspondence, but he defended it in letters to subordinates. When lieutenant asked for reassignment, C.O. rejected request with comment, "Wiser heads than ours, or at least those of superior rank, have placed us in this peculiarly uncomfortable position and we must take care of ourselves with such means and appliances as are available." Discipline at post was continual problem, records of 1850 showing that private was found guilty of stealing gold dust from civilian. Sentenced to 200 lashes, he confessed after 20 and told where $1,200 worth of dust was hidden. Commander asked permission to dishonorably discharge him, "branded as he is with infamy and disgrace by the lashes, so deservedly inflicted." Settlers were not lily white either. Post commander in 1851 complained he could not re-enlist soldier because local justice of peace was "obliged to run from the sheriff under an indictment of grand jury." This left the area with no one to give the reenlistment oath.

CANTONMENT FAR WEST site is marked by graveyard and vandalized monument. Reportedly monument stands on original location of flagpole for Army post. Far West was known variously as camp, fort, and cantonment, but last appears most frequently in official correspondence from post.

POPE'S CAMP AND WELLS, TEXAS

Water rather than Indians was the objective of one of the most unusual projects of the Western Army, the artesian well-drilling adventuring of Captain John Pope along the Texas-New Mexico 32nd parallel boundary.

Politics was at the root of the idea, of course. It was Southern desire for the transcontinental railroad route that caused Pope and upwards of 150 men to spend four years and $160,000 in drilling for water along a proposed railroad route. Southern desires may have started the whole thing, but it was continued to a great extent on the strength of Pope's almost fanatic belief that it would work.

"The only obstacle on this route, and one which alone has prevented it from becoming the great and only highway across the Plains, is the want of water on the Llano Estacado, over a distance of 125 miles," Pope reported, "and this difficulty, as will be exhibited hereafter, is obviated so easily and at so little expense, that it cannot weigh as a feather in the balance against the unrivaled advantages of this route."

Originally assigned as a Topographical Corps engineer to the Post at Albuquerque, Pope was detached in 1853, given eight wagons, 50 herders and teamsters, and 25 soldiers as an escort, and told to check the "military capabilities" and "properties for a railroad" of this route.

On February 12, 1854, the contingent struck out on what later would be part of the route of the Butterfield Overland Stage Line. After several narrow escapes from water shortages, it arrived in Preston, Texas, in mid-May. Pope headed for Washington, D. C. to trumpet his success.

Ignoring the fact that the route crossed one of the most desolate and God-forsaken areas of the West, Pope pointed out that it was level, would require minimum grading, had timber and fertile soil along the way, was near to the "navigable waters of Texas rivers," and, with artesian wells, would be ideal.

The general theory of the Topographical Engineers of the period was that water underlaid most of the Llano Estacado, so Pope was not alone on his belief. He came up with an estimate of $35,932 to drill four wells along the route to the depth of 700 feet. The final estimate was $28,532 after selling the mules, wagons, and boring instruments when the project was complete.

Urged by Jefferson Davis, the Secretary of War, and with Pope's enthusiastic report at hand, Congress appropriated $100,000 for the experiment. They went far beyond Pope's idea for four wells. Included were a total of five wells across the Llano Estacado, eight between the Rio Gande and the San Pedro, and four to six across the Colorado Desert in Arizona.

The first matter was to build a headquarters. An engineer company and a quartermaster unit did this about seven miles south of the New Mexican boundary on the east bank of the Pecos river. Two

POPE'S CAMP
TEXAS - 1855

"QUARTERS AND shops, with several smaller structures, were constructed of stone and adobe; a breastwork of stone surrounded the whole and flat native stone was extensively used to build foundations, walks and floors; a flag pole was provided and a nearby spring furnished water, that of the Pecos being so brackish as to almost deny its use for human consumption." This is how Historian Lee Myers has described Pope's Camp. Month after Army left, post was used as relay station on Butterfield Overland Stage line for a year and later was on route of famed Goodnight cattle trail. Camp was 300 feet east of Pecos river and about 50 feet higher than it. Building within walls was 80 by 40 feet, of stone or adobe; main area measured 200 feet along northern wall, 100 feet along southern. Shops actually were 300 feet from wall, cemetery 500 feet. (Redrawn from sketch of Roscoe P. Conkling in "Butterfield Overland Mail," copyright 1947 and used with special permission of the Arthur H. Clark Company, Glendale, Calif.)

companies of the Fifth Infantry garrisoned the post.

"This camp was well and solidly built; in fact when one considers the isolation and nakedness of the location, it was almost luxurious," comments New Mexico Historian Lee Myers who has made a detailed study of the project and reported his results in several articles. "Located as it was, close to water and the wagon road from San Antonio and Fort Davis, this camp served mainly as headquarters and quartermaster supply depot for the expedition."

Pope's drillings often-times were rewarded with finding water, but at a level far below the surface. Without modern power to push the water above ground, these wells were of little use. Frequently Pope despaired of success when his borings reached hundreds of feet only to end when the tubing caved in.

The first well was about 14 miles east of the junction of Delaware creek and the Pecos. The mule-driven equipment, brought from the East and laboriously dragged across the plains and deserts from Indianola, Texas, was not as effective against razor-sharp Pecos strata as it had been in the East. At 640 feet, with all of his tubing used up, Pope had to stop until more could be shipped to him. He had struck water, but it was far below the surface.

About this time, rumors got out that Indians had attacked the detachment. "He is said to be hemmed in by Comanche Indians upon the Rio Pecos and has lost seven men, killed by Indians," recorded Sergeant James Bennett, a member of a Fort Stanton patrol sent to rescue Pope. "Brought with us a howitzer, a 12 pounder. . . . The soil is filled with vermin. Thousands of rattlesnakes, tarantulas, and centipedes are running over the ground throughout this region. . . . The thermometer was about 121 degrees above zero."

The patrol found the Indian rumor was false. Pope was in good health, "boring artesian wells on the Llano Estacado, or Stake (sic) Plain, which is dry sandy route through Texas."

Work was resumed in spring, 1856, five miles from the 1855 site. At 450 feet the tubing collapsed and the site was abandoned. A third site nearer the river was started in May. Water was struck at 676 feet and rose to within 110 feet of the surface. At 861 feet, drilling at this location was suspended in August because Pope found he had run out of tubing again.

New equipment, including a boiler and a steam engine, was obtained by Pope during a trip East in the winter of 1856-57. Drilling resumed at the third site in September, 1857. As if to make up for his late start, Pope pushed the work despite the dual difficulties of a severe winter and the appearance of scurvy in the command.

At 1,050 feet, with a winter and summer of dogged drilling behind him, Pope found that the patience of Congress had run out. In August, 1858, with Pope's latest suggestion that perhaps it would be necessary to drill to 2,200 feet, Congress ruled the project was too expensive. "Pope's Folly" was a favorite newspaper term for this production that somehow had garnered $60,000 in additional appropriations on top of the original $100,000.

Tentage, equipment, and other belongings were packed up at the well site and the main camp in 1858. The detachment marched away, leaving, as Pope described it, "this great plain to its pristine solitude and desolation."

TOP OF Pope's Hill includes ruins of stone quarters believed to have been Captain Pope's headquarters. Site is half mile south of New Mexico border; New Mexico is in background, Texas in foreground. Boiler brought one hundred years before by Pope was at site until hauled away for scrap in 1957. Rectangular scatterings of rocks atop hill and around its base suggest that they were used as walls to support soldiers' and workers' tents.

POPE'S CAMP next to Pecos River is marked by area of upturned flagstones and this solitary wall from corral. Seldom exposed to view because of waters of Red Bluff reservoir, corral wall happened to be high and dry during 1964 visit. It is most definite indication that at this site Pope and his 150-some men once camped and drilled.

POPE'S CROSSING

USED BY EMIGRANTS AND THE SOUTHERN (BUTTERFIELD) OVERLAND MAIL WHICH LINKED ST. LOUIS AND SAN FRANCISCO WITH A SEMI-WEEKLY MAIL, 1858-1861 • HEADQUARTERS IN 1855 OF CAPTAIN JOHN POPE, SUPERVISOR OF THE DRILLING OF THE FIRST DEEP WELL WEST OF THE 98TH MERIDIAN • THEY STRUCK WATER AT 244 FEET BUT SANK TO 1140 HOPING TO STRIKE ARTESIAN FLOW • THE WELL CAVED BEFORE ITS VALUE COULD BE DETERMINED • THIS $100,000 EXPERI- MENT POINTED THE WAY TO DEEP WELL DRILLING IN THE GREAT PLAINS

Erected by the State of Texas
1936

STORY OF Pope's experiments is told on this marker next to U.S. 285 just south of Texas-New Mexico border. Marker originally was at actual crossing site several miles to east, but seldom was seen due to isolated location. Location next to highway may not be historically accurate, but it is practical.

TO GET THERE: The major ruins are of Pope's Third Well and Pope's Camp, but it is virtually impossible to find them without a guide. However, to get to the well site, from Orla, Texas (18 miles south of the New Mexico line on U.S. 285), take dirt road east in direction of Jal, N.M. 15 miles to cattle guard of Ohio Camp. From Ohio Camp, take unimproved road north toward old Ross Ranch, turning left in seven miles on rough trail. Take this to where oil well site has been cleared, then turn left again and head south about two miles. Follow trail to right until it circles to right, then left and ends on top of Pope's Hill. To get to Pope's Camp, from Orla go north on U.S 285 about three miles to turnoff to right to Red Bluff Dam. After turning right, proceed about four miles to Red Bluff Dam recreation area office where permission to enter should be requested and, if required, a nominal fee paid. They can direct visitors to site of Pope's Camp (or, as it is sometimes called locally, "Engineer's Camp"). Site is about three miles north of Red Bluff Dam on right side of reservoir.

POPE'S HILL, site of third well, is littered with remnants of hundred-year-old drilling. Blacksmith and repair shop area is believed to have been in this location at base of hill; excavation of dugout is next to rusted-out can with soldered seams that bespeak early manufacture. Top of hill is in background.

FORT McGARRY, NEVADA

The isolation of the western fort—overtaken by civilization at almost every site—still exists at Fort McGarry, Nevada. As the crow flies, it is 40 miles to the nearest hamlet. It is half again that via crude, dirt tracks that wind through mesquite, lava-like rock, and drifted sand in this desolate corner of northwestern Nevada.

Neither electricity nor telephone disturbs the silence of this little-known, seldom visited former home of two companies of troopers. Centered in a 75-square mile reservation, McGarry was near the shore of Summit Lake, a reed-fringed, half-marshy body of water that contributes more to the mosquito population than to irrigation.

California Volunteers established the post originally as a field camp on November 23, 1865, while they protected the stage road from California to Idaho. At first it was simply called Camp Summit Lake. As part of the Army's policy "to make the posts as temporary and cheap as possible," it was decided it would be sufficient to use "tents and huts constructed by the troops."

Regulars of the 9th Infantry relieved the Volunteers in 1866 and the post took on a permanent look. Rock buildings were laid out around a rectangular parade ground. Even more status was achieved when headquarters for the District of Nevada was shifted from Fort Churchill to McGarry, a more central location. About the same time the area was reorganized and then McGarry became headquarters of the District of Summit Lake—a two-fort district that included Fort Bidwell, just across the California line to the west.

This distinction was short-lived. An inspecting team, probably after a dusty ride across the inhospitable High Rock Canyon wastes, decided that McGarry was too isolated. The headquarters shifted to Bidwell.

Regardless of these administrative rearrangements, the troopers at McGarry still had their share of activity.

The matter of protecting the stage meant that soldier escorts had to go along whenever the coach had "no passenger who could provide protection." According to the departmental orders, this meant an escort of one or more men between McGarry and Camp C. F. Smith, 40 miles to the northeast. Similar escorts had to be provided in other directions.

GROUND REMAINS provided the data for this plat. Ruins are at the approximate locations shown here. Identifications are based on arrangement and nature of remains.

In 1866, the post was directed to determine the shortest route to Fort Bidwell, and then "use working parties from either or both camps to open the road for wagons." Even today, the road is hardly more than a primitive wagon road!

Although the post was built of rock, many of the supplies had to be kept in tents. Records tell frequently of boards of survey convened to study the matter of missing or ruined stores. In 1866, a board announced that "the strength of the garrison being inadequate to furnish a guard of the necessary strength," it was no one's fault for the loss of 106 pounds of flour, 453 pounds of bread, 175 pounds of coffee, 69 pounds of candles, 18 pounds of rice, and, strangely enough, one pair of infantry trousers.

Two months later a board had to drop from the records 1,000 pounds of barley "damaged and wasted from the ravages of rats and mice."

Patrols kept the troopers busy, with minimum results. An 1867 foray took ten men away for six days but all they got for their trouble was a mess of Indian tracks. They had been alerted by miners that 15 Indians were holed up in caves, so the troopers crept two miles on foot to find the caves empty.

Thirty-five men went out for six days to chase stolen horses and reported "no Indians whatsoever."

The report was even more blunt a year later

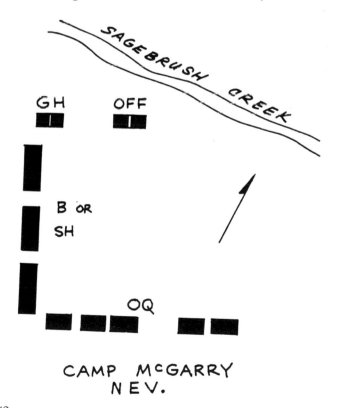

CAMP McGARRY
NEV.

PARADE GROUND of Camp McGarry as it appears from officers' quarters row. Probable guardhouse is at far left, roofless headquarters building at right. McGarry also provided detachments at outposts, including detail at Soldiers' Meadows, 15 miles south, and Camp McKee, 50 miles south. Former included stone buildings connected by underground passageways. At Camp McKee, sergeant in charge complained "The tents the men are quartered in here are no longer fit for use being in a worn out and torn condition and we have no tent to cook in." He added that the cook house was built of borrowed lumber and the owner wanted it back to use for fencing. In 1867, McKee messenger brought following report from corporal: "July 24, 1867, 2½ o'clock p.m. Sweeny of the 9th Infantry was killed by Jackson about 10 minutes ago. Bates was with him. Sweeney was in the act of raising his gun at the time Jackson fired. Mr. Elliott was present. I have Jackson and Bates under arrest. What shall I do with the Body and prisoners? The weather is very warm." McKee was abandoned in 1868 when the stage road was re-routed.

GUARD HOUSE—if such an identification can be guessed from bars on windows of its second room—now serves as line camp for cattle company. Lone cattleman lives in it during warm season. Discipline was a problem at McGarry, as elsewhere. In 1866 post surgeon lost his contract "for disobedience of orders and conduct unbecoming a medical officer of the Army." In 1867, sutler—a former California Volunteer lieutenant—charged a captain with peddling articles to enlisted men "and camp women in opposition to what he considers his right as sutler, he having to pay a tax for the privilege of sutling on this post," official report stated. Departmental headquarters demanded to know "the date and place of sales, what was sold, who bought, what price, conditions of sale—that is, how he happened to sell them." Record does not tell results of investigation. Probable post headquarters building is beyond guardhouse.

OFFICERS' QUARTERS at far end of row still have man-high wall left. Other quarters can be seen to rear. When post was ordered to be abandoned in October 1868, commanding officer announced he still had a year's supply of stores on hand and it would take some time to move it. He must have moved fast; post actually was abandoned on December 18 of that year.

after the men hunted horses through three-and-a-half-foot snows. They were helping a civilian, but he refused to accompany them, even though offered a mount and rations. Progress against the wind averaged a mile an hour and the pack mules had to be led when they refused to face the wind. The officer in charge reported that all he found were some Indian huts, which he burned, and that he did not believe there were any Indians in the area. He said that the canyons and valleys were impassable because of the snow, his horses would not be fit for a month, and furthermore, "in my opinion, the horses reported stolen were lost through carelessness."

A patrol that did achieve an objective of sorts was in October 1868, when nine civilians joined a detail of 15 men, a second lieutenant, and a surgeon. After a 20-mile tail, a base camp was set up when a patrol announced meeting the Indians. The braves were chased for four miles through timber after they abandoned their horses. Snow turned the pursuers away.

Back at the Indian camp, the Army captured nine horses, a rifle, a pistol, seven saddles, and other supplies. The Indians had shot five more horses before leaving. The camp was estimated to have had 50 braves and squaws in it. One souvenir found by the Army was a letter signed by the Indian agent, which reported:

"There has not been any body of armed Indians on the river. If the whites would speak the truth as well and act with as much fairness as the Indians, there would be no danger of trouble."

TO GET THERE: This is almost 200 miles round trip, fair weather only, and not for the family car! From Gerlach, Nevada, take State 34 for ten miles north. When it crosses rise of Granite Peak-Division Peak range at sharp left, take dirt road to right across alkali flat. Continue along this vague dirt road through many gates to Soldier's Meadows, 61 miles from Gerlach. (This was once an outpost of McGarry). Through the corrals, follow dirt road up into hills until it levels off and Summit Lake can be seen to right front. At first intersection to right after passing alongside lake, turn to right. After a mile, rock ruins can be seen on private grazing property to south (right side of road) across Sagebrush creek.

BARS CANNOT BE seen in this picture, but this is interior of prison room of guardhouse. Window slit on opposite wall has solid bars. Even interior walls were of stone. McGarry was scene of 1867 example of a second lieutenant getting at the base of the question. Post records contain official letter from him to post commander in response to order that he explain the reasons for not appearing "at guard mount with my uniform coat on. I would respectfully state that my only reason being that it was quite warm." Unquote.

CAMP PENA COLORADO, TEXAS

Confusion seems to have characterized the story of Camp Pena Colorado throughout its career. First, its founding date is uncertain because official records refer to it by different names in the same report. Then, it seems to have belonged at various times as a sub-post to three different permanent forts. It was even an independent fort of its own for a short period—but the term "fort" never was official.

Finally, with clerks and printers habitually wanting to insert a comma between the "Pena" and the "Colorado," the place found itself re-located geographically. Even when it was first established, the Secretary of War report for 1879 tells of the 70-man expedition from Fort Concho, Texas, under Colonel Benjamin Grierson that went 1,000 miles for: "Tour on inspection of commanding officer district of the Pecos, to Pena, Colo., to locate a camp at that point and occupy and scout the country and open a wagon-road from Fort Davis toward Fort Clark."

Regardless of the typographical errors, the fact was that Pena Colorado was located in Texas and in one of the most rugged parts of Texas, for good measure.

Apparently first a temporary camp known as "Rainbow Cliffs," the post was formalized in August, 1879, and given the Pena Colorado tag. Spanish for "red bluff," the name came from such a

landmark overlooking the site. At first the post was near a spring at the base of the bluff, but frequent flooding of the spring forced a half mile move.

Although the departmental commander complained in 1879, "It is very disheartening to the officers to be compelled, through the cold winters and hot summers of West Texas, to keep their wives and children in tents, shanties, or brush huts," that is exactly what faced the garrison at the new post.

Tents and hastily built adobe and stone shanties housed the two companies of the 25th Infantry first located at Pena Colorado.

As late as 1886, the quartermaster could point out, "The buildings at this post have been constructed without expense to the government except for the little brick used."

The previous year an official report suggested that perhaps the soldier artisans were less than overwhelmingly successful in their labors. "The roofs of the officers and men's quarters are of bush and dirt covered with canvas and all leak," the quartermaster complained. "They are all ill constructed and most involve continual expense to keep in habitable order. . . . Some of the buildings are not worth further labor in repairs, certainly not to the extent of shingling, but their stone might be advantageously used in adding to the height and in repairing others."

As far as peace-keeping was concerned, Pena Colorado was founded at almost the same time that Texas' last Indian war ended. With the death of Chief Victorio in 1880, large-scale marauding ceased in Texas. The arrival of the railroad in the mid-eighties brought a greater element of civilization. One legend tells about a famed chieftain who turned himself in after a raid when he saw the "iron horse" apparently pursuing him.

CAMP PEÑA COLORADO
TEXAS –

RUINS AND excavations at site suggest that Camp Pena Colorado may have looked like this. Apparently post was built gradually and without formal plan—at least none has been located so far—and this is how National Park Service historians found site when they surveyed it. Identifications of buildings are based on appearance and local tradition. In 1886, official report described post as including one commanding officers' quarters of "stone, mud walls inside, condition fair;" two adobe officers' quarters with mud walls and canvas and mud roofs, "condition very poor;" a stone surgeon's quarters, "mud walls, no ceiling, rough board floor;" one room stone mud and canvas headquarters; stone quartermaster office; a 35-foot by 25 stone storehouse, "capacity insufficient;" a stone 34- by 15-foot guardhouse with canvas roof, "capacity ample;" a stone and adobe barracks 169 by 18 feet, of "insufficient capacity;" and other buildings. (Redrawn from NPS plat.)

PARADE GROUND of Pena Colorado, viewed from surgeon's front porch toward commanding officer's quarters (rear), was subject of 1886 request that it all "should be enclosed by a barbed wire fence to exclude stray cattle or hogs from the interior of the post, officers' quarters, and barracks." Estimated cost: $201.47.

By 1891, Fort Davis had been closed but Pena Colorado's mission remained. "Camp Pena Colorado is a cantonment, on a leased site, occupied by one troop of cavalry, which is kept in active employment looking over the large uninhabited country between the Southern Pacific Railroad and the Rio Grande, 150 miles distant," Brigadier General D. S. Stanley reported.

As the only post in the vast Big Bend area, Pena Colorado found that it was the peacekeeper on the Rio Grande. "The only safe way is to regard all or any person coming from the right bank as an idler; with arms in his hand, and no visible means of support as an intruder," Stanley said. "We find that the very presence of troops is a restraining influence."

Regardless of the influence, however, Pena Colorado was abandoned a year and a half later. Hardly had the Army left than bandits overran the area,

OLD-TIMERS in Marathon, Texas, helped Mrs. Frank Wedin to picture how Pena Colorado looked. As boys, several men worked for fort and prior to their deaths they described post to Mrs. Wedin. Stone corral was 190 feet long and 120 wide; despite guard shacks at entrance, stock once was run off from it.

(MRS. FRANK WEDIN. PEG THEOPOLIS & PAUL HARTLE.)

COMMANDING OFFICER'S quarters now is occupied by Seminole Indian, Blas Payne, whose grandfather helped build house "with his fingers" because there were no tools available. In 1886 report it was considered in fair condition, had two rooms and hall in 42- by 15-foot main area with wing that added two rooms. A 16- by 14-foot lean-to was on one side and a 30- by 18-foot adobe kitchen added. Officially, government had built only one room, according to report.

stealing 1,200 cattle only 40 miles from the post. Cattlemen gathered a posse and chased the rustlers into Mexico, rescuing the stock after a two-day running fight.

TO GET THERE: From Marathon, Texas, which is on U.S. 90, turn west across tracks at railroad depot. Follow this gravel road four miles. At point where road crosses small bridge, look to right. Pena Colorado site is a quarter of mile from road on privately owned property of Combs Cattle Company. Half mile further on gravel road is site of original post within picnic and swimming area, identified by marker.

SURGEON LIVED here although present use is as harness and blacksmith shop. This is rear room of quarters that measured 40 by 14 feet and included two rooms and hall. Roof was of mud and canvas, walls were of mud. There was no ceiling, but building had rough board floor. Canvas porch was in front. Hospital next door was wooden building sold to rancher after fort was abandoned. Until recently it was used as saddle barn. During most of Pena Colorado's active days, garrison was a single cavalry company rotated from Fort Davis. Duty was monotonous and troopers were hardpressed for entertainment. Local tradition tells of soldiers entertaining themselves by playing impromptu "water polo" in dammed-up creek, each man floating in his washtub until it overturned or filled with water.

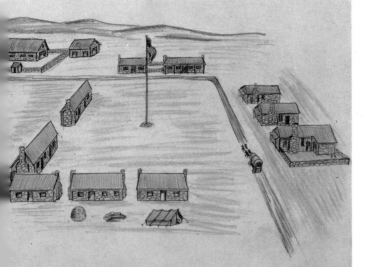

FORT LOGAN, COLORADO

Snow was early in the fall of '87 when troops of the 18th Infantry put up their tepee-like tents on Bear Creek south of Denver, and started to build a fort. As far as Denver politicians were concerned, early snow or not, the Army was late.

The main play had ended and only a sketchy epilogue remained from the drama of Indian fighting, and the Denverites sensed this. Their Congressional voices long had argued for troops in a fort near Denver "whence they could be ordered to suppress Indian troubles." But they knew that the Army consented to the location because the need for small posts was over, and it was desired to concentrate the soldiers in large, centrally-located, well-built, permanent posts.

For almost 30 years, Denver spokesmen had lobbied for a military post. In 1859, the Army had built a small arsenal in the Auraria section of the new city. It served as a warehouse during the Civil War and, during the Indian Scare of 1864, as a refuge for women, children, and, most likely, a few males.

Colorado Volunteers had built themselves imposing Camp Weld, not far from the Arsenal. This is discussed elsewhere. In 1864, about the time that Weld was abandoned, Colorado Volunteers set up a tent-post a few blocks to the northeast and called it Camp Wheeler. Another, Camp Evans, was located near the city.

But all of this was temporary. With the Civil War over, freight rates going up because of Indian troubles on the stage lines, placer mining outputs leveling off or dropping, and things generally in a bad state, the business men of Denver knew the solution was to lure the Army and its payroll to the city.

General Sherman was besieged with petitioners to this effect when he visited in 1866. His recommendation to General Grant—then commanding the Army—was unequivocal.

"The question of this as a Military Post I decide emphatically No," he wrote Grant. "Denver needs no protection. She should raise on an hour's notice 1,000 men, and instead of protection she can and should protect the neighboring settlements that tend to give her support, and business."

He even rejected the idea of a supply depot. The small post-war Army had no need for a Colorado dispenser of goods and foodstuffs and, besides, nothing could be bought in Denver that was not cheaper elsewhere.

Sherman was skeptical of the motives behind the request for a fort. Every Colorado town seemed to have the same request. Some petitions, he noted, carried more signatures than he had soldiers in his department. His reaction to the petition in Colorado Springs, as recorded by a settler's son, could be applied to Denver, too:

"General Sherman received the appeal with utter indifference, and replied that he thought we were unnecessarily alarmed, since there were no hostile Indians in this region. He then sarcastically remarked that it probably would be a very profitable arrangement for this community could it have a force of government troops located near here, to whom the farmers might sell their grain and other products at a high price."

Sherman's visit to Denver was at a propitious time. Just before his arrival, an election for Congressional delegate had been decided by the governor contrary to the recommendation of the official Board of Canvassers.

"There was breezy time in Denver for awhile," wrote Inspector General Rusling who joined Sherman's party there. "The papers savagely denounced

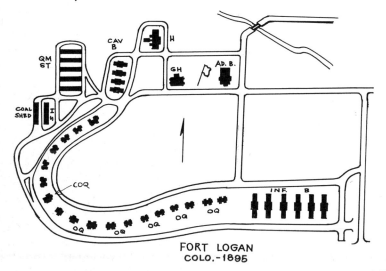

FORT LOGAN
COLO.-1895

ORIGINALLY known officially as "Post Near the City of Denver" and unofficially as "Fort Sheridan" and "Sheridan Post," final name was designated by War Department at request of Sheridan. He asked that new post near Chicago—unofficially called Fort Logan—be named after him, so unofficial names were traded. Logan was considered greatest civilian combat general in Civil War, won Congressional Medal of Honor at Vicksburg, and later served in both houses of Congress and was unsuccessful Republican candidate for vice-presidency. He was founder of Memorial Day. His namesake post was built of brick at cost of more than half-million dollars, could accommodate 29 officers and families, two troops of cavalry, eight companies of infantry, and a regimental headquarters staff and band. Except for barracks and hospital, buildings shown here still exist. (Redrawn from plat in National Archives.)

FORT LOGAN construction was completed by 1894 but its landscaping still was wanting, as indicated by this photograph of southern side of officers' horseshoe. End of double-story infantry barracks can be seen at far end of row. Post was major attraction for Denver, especially at Sunday evening dress parade. This was described in newspaper: "The band made its appearance and the troops wheeled into sight to the inspiring strains of a martial air. Battalion drill was rapidly gone through, with the regularity of a machine—the bugle sang 'goodnight,' the evening gun saluted the sun just disappearing behind the distant mountains—the flag fluttered earthward, and the spectators spread along the roads for home."

the governor's conduct . . . The saloons were filled with excited crowds . . . The governor wisely appeared in public but little, and for several nights found it convenient to sleep elsewhere than at his home.

"Finally it was given out that the military were on his side, as in duty bound, and the storm presently blew over. Subsequently it appeared that said military consisted of only two officers, without a single soldier . . . General Sherman's arrival immediately after was just in the nick of time . . . and was a good salve to the public sore."

A year later, when the Denverites renewed their appeals for military protection, Sherman suggested that the state raise a battalion of mounted men

"ready to be called into the service of the United States . . . if an emergency should arise." Denver reaction to this was to burn Sherman in effigy during his next visit to the city, six months later.

With difficulties increasing in the matter of moving the Indians to reservations, Sherman agreed in fall, 1868, that some tribes were in the wrong and "I will not prevent your people from chastising them if they are really in earnest, but it is more than our small Army can do to defend every ranch in Colorado, Montana, Nebraska, and Kansas. The settlers should collect and defend their own property, leaving the regular troops to go after the Indians."

This philosophy pertained as long as Sherman

GUARDHOUSE at Fort Logan shows sign of age in pockmarked bricks. One of first buildings completed, it was subject of immediate criticism. "In the new guardhouse," surgeon complained in 1890, "the bathing facilities are of but little use in cold weather, there being no means for heating water. The cleanliness of the prisoners is a sanitary necessity, and a hot-water supply should not be regarded as a luxury. All deserters who have been brought to this post have been exceedingly dirty and generally infected with vermin." Administration building can be seen behind guardhouse.

COMMANDING OFFICER had elaborate residence at Fort Logan. One of most famous occupants was General Arthur MacArthur, post commander in 1901 and 1902 while his son, future General Douglas MacArthur, was cadet at West Point. In 1903, a private in Second Infantry was given permission to build study room at his own expense at one end of barracks, later won appointment to West Point as result of diligent studying. His success caused study rooms to be included in all barracks at post. By World War II, he was Air Corps General Rush B. Lincoln.

was a maker of Army policy. By 1882, however, he had begun to mellow. He recommended abandoning all small posts in favor of permanent barracks strategically located so that troops could be rushed by railroad to trouble spots.

Hardly three years after Sherman turned command of the Army over to General Sheridan, Denver found that it had finally won its battle for a fort. The politicians convinced the Army by emphasizing the central location of Denver, the fact that seven railroads served the city "for speedy transfer of troops in all directions," and that Denver had a healthful and temperate climate.

After receiving Sheridan's agreement, the Congressmen found they had to overcome pro-labor objections that the fort would be used to put down strikes and "over-awe" the new labor unions. This had temporarily vetoed a new post near Chicago; only through vigorous cloakroom maneuvers was the way cleared for approval of the legislation.

It was not a complete victory for Denverites, however. They were required to contribute at no cost to the government at least 640 acres on which to locate the fort. And when General Sheridan selected the site, it was not the one favored by the Denver backers.

The city fathers wanted the post near the town where "it would be easier to keep away the saloons and other nuisances." Sheridan did not see it that way. He picked a site eight miles from downtown, described in 1887 by the Denver *Republican:* "As sightly an eminence as could be wished for . . . where the Stars and Stripes will wave from graceful buildings in another year, Sheridan Post, U.S.A."

Unhappiness with the choice still did not prevent the citizens from quickly coming up with $33,619 to finance giving it to the government. With equal

speed, the Army moved in on October 22, 1887, with 26 tents along the creek north of the site. On October 25, Major George K. Brady assumed command and had the camp moved to the actual post location the next day, the official founding date.

Temporary frame barracks were put up for $2,000 to house the troops for the coming winter. Contracts of the hundred-thousand dollar category were signed with civilian builders for the permanent post, a building project that took seven years to complete.

Construction and field training were the main occupations of the post, interrupted only twice by operational pursuits. Six companies were rushed in 1890 to the Dakota Badlands to suppress the so-called "Messiah War." This ended in the "Battle" of Wounded Knee before they arrived.

They helped round up some 300 "hostile" Indians, but returned to Denver a month later without having engaged in any skirmishes.

In 1894, the garrison was moved to Denver when the city fire and policemen barricaded themselves in the City Hall. Their commissioners had refused to stop gambling in the city and rejected demands of the governor that they resign. He trained loaded cannon on the building and ordered the militia to remove the officials. The intervention of cooler business heads—and the presence of the Logan regiment—caused the "revolt" to be settled without bloodshed.

TO GET THERE: Denver Arsenal site is now a parking lot on northeast corner of 11th and Larimer streets. Camp Wheeler is now Lincoln Park at 13th and Osage, only about 10 blocks south. Fort Logan can be reached by taking U.S. 85 (Valley and S. Santa Fe drives) south from downtown about eight miles to Sheridan suburb and turning west on W. Oxford avenue. This deadends at post site, now Fort Logan Mental Health Center.

(NATIONAL ARCHIVES.)

CAMPAIGNING WITH CROOK

"The Apaches in Southern New Mexico and Arizona are . . . a squalid, untrustworthy people, robbers and thieves by nature, and with less form of government that any Indians in this country . . . They require to be hunted down by small detachments over a large region of country, and give the troops more hard service and the government more expense than tribes ten times more formidable both in numbers and warlike capacity."

—Brevet Major General John Pope in his Department of the Missouri *Annual Report*, 1879.

BEFORE the white man, the Apaches fought their fellow Indians. With the advent of the settler and the traveler, the miner and soldier, the Apache widened his horizons. When the white man retaliated with equal cruelty and dishonesty, the Apache knew that here was truly a natural enemy.

The decade that began in 1860 was marked in Arizona by the Apache murders of 1,000 men, women, and children. About 150 soldiers and 2,000 Apaches died. The loss to live-stock and property was incalculable.

In one Arizona county in 1868-69, the Apaches killed 52 and wounded 18 settlers. The next year, they killed 47 and wounded six. In 1870, the Congress received a list of 144 citizens recently murdered by Apaches.

Finally General George Crook was ordered to Arizona, his record of successful dealings with Indians before and after the Civil War speaking for him. At the same time, Vincent Colyer was sent out as a civilian emissary of the Indian Bureau. Crook held up on his military plans while Colyer preached his message of peaceful settlement. Forty-one citizens died in 54 raids after Colyer left. Then General Oliver O. Howard appeared as a new peaceful agent.

Regardless of the good intentions of Howard and the momentary calm that settled over the Apaches, the fact was that no one was ready for peace—least of all white men who wanted the Apache lands and money. Finally Crook was able to pursue his aggressive campaign and by the mid-1870's the Apaches were generally at peace. Crook was the hero and Indian-fighter acclaimed by all.

He was ordered back to Arizona in 1882 after a series of Apache outbreaks. This time he carried his campaign across the border into Mexico's Sierra Madre mountains, fielding marches of long duration with ingenious use of pack trains and Indian scouts. But his fame was too much for the politics of the Army, and his efficient, unassuming, unpublicized expeditions not fast enough.

Finally, exasperated by Army criticism of his methods—especially when he lost Geronimo after capturing him—Crook asked to be relieved of Arizona duty. General Nelson A. Miles replaced him and with a mighty ego and 3,000 troopers ended the Apache Wars shortly after.

CAMP WALLEN, ARIZONA

With the Civil War over and attention directed to disciplining Apaches who had run at will for four years, logic dictated the location of Camp Wallen. As it turned out, the site was too logical. It was so much in the center of Apache Land, that fighting Indians and nature left little time for fort building and the place had to be abandoned.

Long before the southeastern corner of Arizona entered the Union, it was a hotbed of Apache unrest. In the 1830's one of the largest cattle ranches in Mexico was located here on what was known as the Babocomari Grant. "The cattle roamed the entire length of the valley," commented Boundary Commissioner John R. Bartlett when he camped at the site in 1851, finding only the ruins of a large hacienda.

"At the time it was abandoned, there were not less than 40,000 head of them, besides a large number of horses and mules. The same cause which led to the abandonment of so many other ranches, haciendas, and villages, in the state, had been the ruin of this. The Apaches encroached upon them, drove off their animals and murdered the herdsmen . . ."

When Brevet Brigadier General Mansfield inspected the area in 1854, he relayed a recommendation that "one station of two companies would be well located . . . near the destroyed Ranch of Babocomari . . . where wood, water, grazing, tillable land, etc. etc., are abundant; with a healthy and good climate."

Out of his recommendation came the establishment of Fort Buchanan about a dozen miles to the west. In 1857, James Tevis—a guest of Captain Richard S. Ewell, Buchanan's commander—accompanied a horse-hunting expedition to a "Fort Babocomari," probably the same ruined hacienda noted by Bartlett.

"The fort, which consisted of adobe buildings, covered about an acre of ground," he wrote later. "A wall about 15 feet high encircled the entire fort, with only one entrance, on the east side, large enough to drive a wagon through; and the rooms for quarters were built on the east, south, and west sides of the enclosure, with lookout posts at each corner on top of the walls. The remaining part was a plaza.

"The first night we were there, we put on a regular guard, and, besides that, we pulled one of the wagons up before the entrance, blocking it up effectively."

The second night, two Indians were spotted lurking near the "fort." The following day the horse herd was stampeded "with about 15 Indians whooping them up."

After the Indians were chased away, Tevis and a companion fought their way through an ambush in order to summon reinforcements from Buchanan. Ewell led 75 Dragoons to the Babocomari the next day and "received a most hearty welcome from the men."

When the Army decided to stop permanently at the Babocomari in 1866, it took possession of the ruined hacienda as a corral. The troops lived in tents outside of the enclosure at first, and cavalry horses were driven into it at night to prevent stampedes.

The fort had deteriorated, but the watch towers at the corners still were prominent. A Mexican cowboy taught the soldiers to make several thousand adobe bricks for use in rebuilding the hacienda. Lumber for rafters and window frames was cut and brought from a timber stand nine miles away.

The work went slowly in the hot Arizona summer. "The camp was established May 10th and yet up to September nothing seems to have been done by anyone in Arizona towards providing these shelters for the men such as have been hitherto throughout the country, from Washington Territory to the Sonora line," General Irvin McDowell complained officially in his Annual Report of the California Department for 1867.

"The troops, wherever sent, have always soon made themselves comfortable by their officers' direction, and by their own labor hutted themselves in the same way prospecting miners have done and are continually doing, by the use of either stone, wood, adobes, poles placed upright and filled in with clay turf sod, reeds, willows, etc., and this

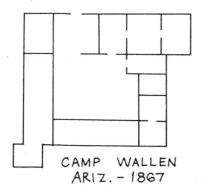

CAMP WALLEN
ARIZ. – 1867

ADOBE RUINS at site are in this design. Uses of rooms and, in some cases, even locations of doorways cannot be estimated. Rooms that jut out from opposite corners obviously had watch tower mission. (Drawn from site inspection.)

WATCH TOWER of Camp Wallen was connected to remainder of fort by one wall, but had three clear walls with apertures through which entire valley and approaches could be observed.

in places more destitute than at Camp Wallen . . .

"If the officers and men, like at Camp Wallen, prefer to suffer rather than exert themselves, as those before them have done, and had rather live under a shelter tent than to make themselves comfortable as they have been authorized and ordered to do, their discomfort merits reproaches rather than sympathy."

With the departmental commander's criticism ringing in their ears, the Wallen garrison could take small comfort in the fact that their first winter found them snowbound for several days. Many sheep and cattle died of exposure. The summers were the other extreme and periodically most of the command was stricken with an intermittent fever that incapacitated the post.

These bouts with nature and officialdom did not minimize the Apache picture, however. The horse stampeding sport resumed and at least three patrols then inflicted damage on the Apaches. In December, 1866, a 39-man detail pursued a band that had ambushed a party of travelers. After the band was overtaken and killed, it was identified as part of Cochise's tribe.

Six months later a patrol struck an Apache rancheria in a mountain hideout, killing three Indians and destroying supplies and weapons. Another patrol entered the mountains in December, 1867,

tracking the Apaches until shooting started. Twenty hostiles were killed.

By the time the camp was abandoned, its official reports boasted that its forays against Cochise had checked the Apache threat. The next 20 years would show how temporary this was.

TO GET THERE: Camp Wallen is on property of Babocomari Ranch in vicinity of Elgin, Arizona. It is not open to public ordinarily and permission to visit must be obtained from headquarters in Phoenix.

FRONT WALL of old ranch was under complete observation from watch tower at far end. Any approach by hostile force could be interdicted with flanking fire. As shown in background, area is one of rolling mesquite-covered hills. Babocomari Creek bottomland in rear is fertile, spreading its irrigated wealth throughout entire valley.

INTERIOR of post shows little is left. Banks of dirt scattered around area suggest locations of walls of interior rooms and of other buildings outside of post. Circle of rocks in foreground shows that isolated location occasionally has visitors.

FORT GRANT, ARIZONA

"Camp Grant was situated on a little plateau. Underneath and about 50 feet below ran the San Pedro river, a stream about 10 or 15 feet wide. On the banks of this stream, and under the shade of some large cottonwood trees, General Howard and I spread our blankets."

In his *Autobiography*, General Crook thus sets the scene for an 1872 council between the Apaches and the government—Howard and Crook representing the latter at Camp Grant.

Crook's aide, John G. Bourke, tells in *On The Border With Crook* of life at this "most forlorn parody of a military garrison," but with more sarcasm than enthusiasm. "There would be very little use in attempting to describe Old Fort Grant, Arizona," he wrote, "partly because there was really no fort to describe . . . It was recognized from the tidewaters of the Hudson to those of the Columbia as the most thoroughly God-forsaken post of all those supposed to be included in the annual Congressional appropriations.

"Beauty of situation or of construction it had none; its site was the supposed junction of the sand-bed of the Aravaypa (sic) with the sand-bed of the San Pedro, which complacently figured on the topographical charts of the time as creek or river respectively, but generally were dry as a lime-burner's hat excepting during the 'rainy season' . . ."

The post was "a rectangle whose four sides were the row of officers' 'quarters,' the adjutant's office, post bakery, and guardhouse, the commissary and quartermaster's storehouses, and the men's quarters, and sutler's store . . . There were three kinds of quarters at Old Camp Grant, and he who was reckless enough to make a choice of one passed the rest of his existence while at the post in growling at the better luck of comrades who had selected either one of the others."

Bourke's quarters were that of a bachelor officer. He said that he made them snug with a paint job, a hard dirt floor over which the paint had been spilled accidently but liberally by the soldier painter, cheery Navajo rugs, a row of bottles filled with specimens of poisonous insects, and a suit of armor that contained the bones of a man when first found. Bourke theorized that it dated from the 16th century Spanish conquistadors, and it provided a homey atmosphere to his place.

It is likely that Crook felt the decor of the Bourke quarters was right in keeping with the confused atmosphere. "There was more or less feeling against me amongst the officers at this post," Crook wrote. He believed it was mainly because he had preferred charges against a lieutenant "who had deserted his colors and gone over to the 'Indian Ring' bag and baggage, and had behaved himself in such a manner" that he was courtmartialed for being a drunkard.

The Indian feeling was no better. "The Indians had assembled in quite large numbers, and a more saucy, imprudent lot of cut-throats I had never before seen," recorded Crook. "Many of them were armed with lances and guns. They would walk through our camp in that defiant, imprudent manner, as much as to say, 'I would like to kill you just for the fun of it, just to see you kick.'"

Aware that Howard was the spokesman for a soft policy, the Indians paid attention to him and then promised to move to certain reservations where the government would take care of them. One of the Apache spokesmen was Eskimotlin, a chief who once boasted that he had killed the only white friend he ever had because "anyone can kill an enemy, but it takes a strong man to kill a friend." He was showing his people "that there must be no

CAMP GRANT
ARIZ. - 1877

NEW FORT GRANT was decided improvement over earlier version even though most buildings still were made of adobe. So-called "Lake Constance" was dug about in the center of this ground plan. In 1890, post drew criticism in Secretary of War report: "The quarters for the enlisted men at this station are of inferior construction, contracted, and uncomfortable. The stables for the cavalry are in bad condition, needing much repair for the proper protection and comfort of the animals occupying them." Fort Grant included 42,341-acre reservation, had three troops of cavalry and two companies of infantry. Twenty-three officers and 240 men were stationed there. Although post was abandoned in 1896, in 1908 Colonel William F. Stewart and his cook arrived to be its garrison. With 40 years of service behind him, Stewart had refused to retire. President Roosevelt determined this near-exile would speed him on way. (Redrawn from McDowell Report, 1877.)

"**FORT GRANT** was beautifully situated at the foot of Mount Graham," wrote wife of Colonel James Biddle of duty there in 1880's. "The climate was perfect . . . The life at Grant was very simple and very healthful. I have never breathed such invigorating air." Indians were close, however. "They used to come prowling around our house trying to see my little children, Nicholas and Alice, whom they thought very beautiful, on account of the light hair and blue eyes." Once she found "eight or 10 Indians sitting in a circle on the floor" of her kitchen, playing with the children. This view is of officers' row with "Lake Constance" behind troop formation. This was installed by Brevet General Anson Mills, commander in 1888, and named after his daughter. His predecessor had recommended abandoning post because of water lack, but Mills took over with orders from General Miles to "get water from the mountains and make Grant one of the best posts." "At a cost of $16,000, I put in a most excellent water and sewage system, with a cement-lined lake in the middle of the parade ground, 60 by 200 feet," Mills wrote in *My Story*. "We put fountains all over the post, capable of throwing water 100 feet high, as the reservoirs had 400 feet pressure." This drew Miles' compliments, and resulted in green landscaping, even though in 1892 post was criticized for "a complete lack of personal cleanliness, owing to the absence of proper bathing facilities." Olympic-size swimming pool now occupies part of old parade ground.

OFFICERS' ROW today, as taken from approximate spot as old picture, shows trees have matured, most buildings are modernized, but Mount Graham, rear, is unchanged. Fort Grant figured prominently in 1880-era Apache War, fielding numerous patrols and participating in Crook's campaign into Mexico. Indian Scouts who mutinied at Battle of Cibicu were tried by courtmartial at Grant. Dead Shot, Dandy Jim, and Skitashe were sentenced to hang. Gallows was built on parade ground in front of guardhouse. Dead Shot attempted escape after filing through shackle chain. He ran from guardhouse, was brought down with two bullets that lightly wounded him. Hanging took place on schedule, guardhouse prisoner springing the trap in exchange for freedom. Bodies disappeared from post cemetery the same night, later post surgeon admitted he had paid three soldiers $25 apiece to bring cadavers to him. Surgeon also had his share of work along disease line because of nearby "hog ranch" of Bonita where 1,000 people and 10 saloons provided off-post entertainment. Anton Mazzanovich remembered that "some of the men would stroll down to the settlement at the edge of the reservation for a 'shot' or two, and a whirl at the dance hall with 'senoritas.' . . . Several years previous, when the settlement was started, a small plot of ground was selected for a graveyard. It was fenced in and the fence was whitewashed; but the place was so healthy that no one 'bit the dust.' After waiting two years for someone to 'kick in' a Mexican was killed to give the graveyard a start." Mazzanovich stayed in area after Army discharge, worked for awhile for post sutler as bartender. Here he introduced mixed drinks, simulating unavailable ice with small pebbles that at least sounded like ice in shaker.

OFFICER'S QUARTERS remaining at Fort Grant can be noted at left edge of old photograph. Mrs. Biddle tells of strange coincidence in 1880's when post flag became tangled and flew at half-mast for 30 minutes until pulled down. After it was re-raised, "the Colonel told them never again to allow a flag to remain at half mast, when not for a death." Later in morning, captain breakfasting with Biddles excused himself, walked into bedroom and in a few minutes was found "dead, lying across the bed on his face, where he had fallen and died, from apoplexy." "Of course, we were all impressed with the fact that the flag had floated at half mast for 30 minutes," Mrs. Biddle added.

friendship between them and the white man."

Crook knew this Apache as "Skimmy." "Finally the council drew to a close with Skimmy giving General Howard a stone," wrote Crook, "saying that when that stone melted, he would break his word and not before. The rascal had gone through this same operation so many times with other persons that he had it pat. He hadn't promised anything, and didn't intend keeping this promise if he had. When we left, he was very profuse in his demonstrations of friendship towards General Howard, but he scarcely noticed me, didn't even offer to shake hands with me."

The peace lasted but a short time. Not long after, Crook "was again allowed to commence hostile operations against these wretches." Expeditions were fielded from Grant, McDowell, and Apache, usually with Crook present wherever they started.

The 1872 conference was one of the last events in the history of what Arizonians call "Old Camp Grant." Within a year the site was abandoned and the post moved to a more healthful location.

A neighboring plateau was chosen as a new site and the post described by Bourke was built. "All the roofs are liable to leak in rainy weather," the surgeon reported in 1870. Tents supplemented adobe, stockade, and reed buildings.

The post reportedly had room for 180 men in quarters that by 1872 were described: "Those built of stockade, timber partly rotten, roofs leak badly,

are totally unfit for quarters. Those built of adobe require constant repairs." The officers' quarters were all of adobe and required constant repair. An 1872 report said, "The officers have not sufficient room for either comfort or health."

Two cavalry corrals for 150 horses were built "of logs on the principle of a stockade," the report said. "This was done more for protection against Indians than weather."

In 1871 it might have been for protection against white men, too. A band of about 300 Apaches had settled temporarily near Fort Grant, were treated and fed as prisoners of war, and helped with haying and other chores of the post.

Tucson citizens charged that the Apaches also continued their depredations, returning to the fort after raids. In April, a mob of 40 citizens and 100 Papago Indians descended on the camp and killed 85 Apaches. "The bucks being mostly absent," Crook wrote, "they killed mostly women and children."

Only eight of the slain Indians were men. Another 30 children were captured, some becoming slaves of the Papagos, others entering Tucson homes. One reason for the Howard-Crook council was to arrange for the return of these hostages.

Regardles of whether the Apaches were responsible for continued depredations, popular sentiment was against the perpetrators of what became known as the "Camp Grant Massacre." A year later 108 persons were tried for murder in the massacre, but by this time popular opinion had been swayed by more Apache raids. The accused were acquitted.

About the same time, Crook ordered removal of the post to the new site because of unhealthiness of the location and its bad reputation. The 250-man garrison was pleased to move to a grass-covered plain in the shadows of Mount Graham even though construction of a new post was "with the labor of troops."

They did have some help. Among the Apache captives taken to the new site was Crook's friend "Skimmy." He and his band were in irons, but that did not hinder them from making adobes for the new post.

TO GET THERE: Old Camp Grant site has been obliterated, is about 40 miles northeast of Tucson. From Tucson go north on State 789 to State 77. Go on 77 about 10 miles north of Mammoth where dirt road enters from right. Fifty yards southeast of this intersection is privately owned site of first fort. New Camp Grant site is 45 miles to southeast. From Safford, Arizona, go south on U.S. 666 about 17 miles to State 266. Go west 22 miles to Arizona State Industrial School, present occupant of fort. Permission to visit should be requested.

FORT McDOWELL, ARIZONA

Varied were the official theories on Apache subduing, ranging from General Crook's stern-but-fair program to the General Oliver O. Howard plan of peaceful, by-the-Bible settlement. The garrison at Fort McDowell was closely identified with the former because of a key location amidst the Indian troubles and along the routes of travel.

It came very close to being exposed to the Howard policy, too, when Howard came West as a special commissioner to investigate the Indian troubles. Along with a civilian who was to become Commissioner of Indian Affairs, and a Captain Wilkinson—his aide—Howard stoped at McDowell in 1872.

Never fond of Howard who had graduated from West Point two years later than he, but wound up with higher rank after the Civil War, Crook was especially critical of the Howard solution to the Indian question.

"General Howard was fond of public speaking," Crook wrote in his *Autobiography*. "His themes generally were 'How He was Converted' and 'The Battle of Gettysburg.' At McDowell, on his way to Prescott, he told the commanding officer that he had been requested to deliver a speech to the soldiers. The C.O., not being an admirer of his, and at the same time pressing him on the point as to who had asked him, he finally had to acknowledge that it was Capt. Wilkinson."

Of course Howard's memoirs carry a different version of his journeys in Arizona, but, regardless, the men at McDowell were spared his speechmaking.

Considering their other problems, the McDowell

"THE POST as planned and built in 1865 consisted of a parade ground 525 by 435 feet, with its center one-third of a mile from the margin of the river . . . The buildings were arranged along the sides of the parade grounds as follows: on the west and furthest from the river, the quarters of the commanding officer, a comparatively large square building, with a hall and two rooms on either side . . . On the south a line of quarters for officers; four houses facing the parade, each divided into four rather small rooms . . . On the north, immediately opposite the officer's quarters, four sets of company barracks . . . 187 by 24 feet long . . ." That was how the surgeon reported McDowell looked originally. If this plan does not resemble it, the surgeon added, "All the buildings were of adobe, with earthen floors, mud roofs, and open fireplaces . . . But, however carefully built by the California troops, the buildings proved unequal to the heavy washing showers of the summer and the penetrating rains of the winter months. The roofs leaked almost from their first exposure, and the walls cracked and washed away in place after place, until, in spite of constant repairs, many of the houses became almost untenable." By 1869, three of the barracks were abandoned and the troops lived in tents. By 1877, the width of the parade had been reduced from 435 to 250 feet and this is how the post looked then. (Redrawn from McDowell Report, 1877.)

garrison may not have taken kindly to a sermon on being nice to the Apache. Their key position meant that they were continually on the alert for Apache raids. In September, 1871, Indian Bureau representative Vincent Colyer declared the post to be a temporary reserve for the Tonto Apaches, giving them official status at it.

This nearness resulted in the rustling of the post herd in February, 1872. So when Crook and Howard arrived for their conference six weeks later, the McDowell garrison was not at all open to suggestions of "turn the other cheek." Six months later, Howard abolished the Indian preserve and the post went back to its normal Indian-fighting routine.

At this time, the routine required greater talents in the building trades than soldiering. Commencement of the Apache campaign had increased the size of the garrison and a construction program resulted, the troops doing the work, per usual.

"This 'labor of the troops' was a great thing," wrote Captain John G. Bourke, Crook's adjutant and biographer. "It made the poor wretch who enlisted under the vague notion that his admiring country needed his services to quell hostile Indians, suddenly find himself a brevet architect, carrying a hod and doing odd jobs of plastering and kalsomining."

The work was so demanding that Brevet General Eugene A. Carr, the post commander, had to discourage requests for protection of the supply trains. "As I am using all the strength of my men in building quarters, I do not wish to give escorts unless absolutely necessary," he announced.

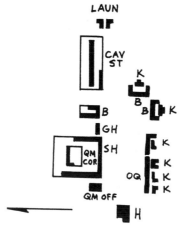

CAMP McDOWELL
ARIZ. - 1877

FORT McDOWELL prior to abandonment in 1890 had few of original buildings left. Officers' row is in foreground, barracks in background. Wife of Colonel Andrew Burt wrote of her stay at McDowell in 1884, "But few pleasant memories remain of that isolated spot. Its desolation was relieved only by the green of the cottonwoods that grew luxuriously along the acequia which carried a stream around the parade ground . . . Of the unpleasant memories there are unfortunately many . . . the rattlesnake killed after quite an exciting battle; the numerous scorpions and centipedes that overran the old adobe walls of the kitchen; the monstrous tarantulas that were killed every now and then in the vicinity; and how our shoes each night were carefully filled with paper or other material to prevent an invasion from these repugnant and venomous creatures."

OFFICER'S QUARTERS is only building remaining from original fort. In 1871, quarters were occupied by Captain Anson Mills and his wife. "Our quarters are very comfortable; the houses are built of adobe and have three rooms and a kitchen," Mrs. Mills wrote in a letter quoted in Mills' *My Story*.

A similar situation existed when McDowell was established in 1865 by five companies of California Volunteers. Under Lieutenant Colonel Clarence E. Bennett, they embarked on a grandiose scheme of construction using stone from the ruins of an ancient Aztec structure on the site. It was intended to be a six company post, but when Brigadier Rusling inspected it in 1867, he found accommodations for only four.

"The work has been done chiefly by troops, and the cost apparently has therefore been small," Rusling reported. "The buildings bore marks of haste, and the roofs were all reported as leaking more or less during severe rains . . . The post as a whole, however, is a fine one, and with some little work on the roofs, etc., will become all that could be expected in Arizona."

Aside from minor criticism of the design of the post, Rusling's main complaint was about the former supply officer and that officer's pet project, the post farm. Rusling found shortages of forage, leather, stationery, iron, copper rivets, potatoes, and vegetables. All of this he blamed on the recently relieved quartermaster. "He impressed me as a visionary officer inspired by ideas that unfit one for the practical duties of the QM department," was Rusling's sarcastic comment.

The quartermaster: Lieutenant Clarence E. Bennett, former lieutenant colonel of California Volunteers and founder of McDowell, who was appointed a lieutenant in the regular Army when he left the Volunteers in October, 1866. He served for a short time as quartermaster of the post he founded before reassignment in Texas. "I apprehend the ser-

vice in Arizona will not suffer by his transfer to Texas," Rusling commented.

The pet project was derisively called "Bennett's Big Farm" by the citizens of Arizona, Rusling claimed. It was the post farm that filled the entire valley. It "seems to me to be defeating the chief objects the Army has in view in establishing military posts," reported Rusling, "namely to encourage and protect settlements. If we had no farm there, and the reservation was of reasonable size, settlers would probably occupy the valley of the Verde, and soon supply the post with all the grain needed at reasonable figures.

"In doing so they would, of course, do away with the necessity for a post there altogether. . . So, I think, troops are enlisted and paid to scout and fight Indians—not to dig ditches and farm."

Bennett had used both his privates and noncommissioned officers to build a four-mile long ditch for irrigating, with "commissioned officers being stationed over the parties to see that they worked faithfully."

When the protests grew too loud, Bennett relieved the soldiers of this duty. Then he moved them to the farm, an undertaking finally operated by 24 civilian employees. Rusling protested that this resulted in excessive costs and finally the farm was leased to a civilian contractor.

TO GET THERE: From Phoenix, Arizona, take State 87 (Bee Line Highway) northeast. About 12 miles from intersection with U.S. 80-89-60-70, Bee Line Highway crosses improved road that heads almost straight north. By taking this road, route will go through McDowell Pass, favorite ambush point. "The soldiers were not partial to McDowell canon (sic)," officers' wife wrote, "they knew too much about the place; and we all breathed a sign of relief when we emerged from this dark uncanny road . . ." Both this road and State 87 pass entrance to Fort McDowell Indian Reservation, left turn. Follow road to dead end at former officer's quarters, about two miles.

FORT VERDE, ARIZONA

When Crook's first Apache campaign drew to a close in 1873, most of his command was mustered at Fort Verde, Arizona, to witness the surrender ceremony. As befitted the rough field conditions, the troopers stood in ranks without ceremony or special costuming.

"A dirtier, greasier, more uncouth-looking set of officers and men it would be hard to encounter anywhere," commented John G. Bourke in *On The Border with Crook.* "Dust, soot, rain, and grime had made their impress upon the canvas suits which each had donned, and with hair uncut for months and beards growing with straggling growth all over the face, there was not one of the party who would venture to pose as an Adonis; but all were happy, because the campaign had resulted in the unconditional surrender of the Apaches and we were now to see the reward of our hard work."

Crook heard the Indian surrender pleas from the porch of the commanding officer's quarters. "Had it not been for their barbarities," he wrote in his *Autobiography,* "one would have been moved to pity by their appearance. They were emaciated, clothes torn in tatters, some of their legs were not thicker than my arm. Some of them looked as if though they had dropped out of a comic almanac."

The reason for the surrender was summed up by one chief.

"You see," he was quoted by Crook, "we're all nearly dead from want of food and exposure—the copper cartridge has done the business for us. I am glad of the opportunity to surrender, but I do it not because I love you, but because I am afraid of General."

The conditions required by Crook could be summed up: go to the reservation and live in peace, the Army will protect you. He insisted that the Apaches realize "they must not take upon themselves the redress of grievances but report to the military officer upon their reservation, who would see that their wrongs were righted," Bourke reported.

"They should be treated exactly as white men were treated; there should be no unjust punishments. They must work like white men; a market would be found for all they could raise, and the money should be paid immediately; idleness was the source of all evils, and work was the only cure."

More than 300 Apaches were present at Verde and Bourke estimated that they represented 2,300 hostiles. At least for the moment, it appeared that the Apache War was over.

Verde's selection for the surrender council was more than coincidental. Occupying a location in mid-Arizona, the post had been harassed continually by Apaches in its short history. Even before the Army arrived, the ancestor of Verde carried on continual warfare with the hostiles.

This ancestor was a small stone fort built in 1865 by a group of Prescott pioneers led by a Doctor J. M. Swetman. Walls of an old Indian ruin were used in building the enclosure on the north bank of Clear Creek. The assassination of President Lincoln supplied a ready-made name for the civilian post: Camp Lincoln.

Some 200 acres of grain and vegetables were planted. By August, a load of barley was bought by the Army at Fort Whipple in order to support the new enterprise, even though it was of poor quality. This set the stage for military protection of the farms and farmers when harvest time found the Apaches stealing more than the settlers could gather.

A 16-man detail was located at Camp Lincoln in fall, 1865, and in January, 1866, the post was established officially. Companies A and E of the Arizona Volunteers provided its garrison. A detail

NEW SITE of Verde was occupied in 1871 and this post was built. It was on high mesa overlooking Verde Valley and was protected naturally from attack on three sides. Parade grounds measured 480 by 690 feet, was surrounded by adobe buildings. Water pipe connected almost all buildings. Some officers' quarters were destroyed by fire in 1881. Although in 1882 General Sherman recommended disposing of post, it was not abandoned until 1890. Indian reservation lands at Verde were relinquished to Department of Interior at 1884. Designation was changed from Camp Verde to Fort Verde in 1879. (Redrawn from McDowell Report, 1877.)

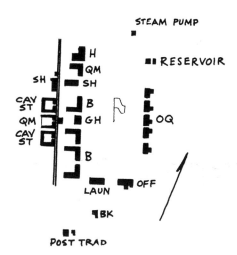

CAMP VERDE
ARIZ. –1877

VERDE in 1880 era presented this sight. Corrals are in foreground with rear of barracks behind them and to right side. Barracks are the three L-shaped buildings; guardhouse is rectangular building with chimney, partly hidden by corrals.

from the latter company was attacked near the post, several soldiers and Indians losing their lives. The mutual slaughter is commemorated with the name Grief Hill.

The Indians kept the troops busy, blocking most of the roads north of the Gila and terrorizing the ranches and settlements. A poor supply system, half-rations, tattered clothing, no pay, and the end of their one-year enlistments caused half of the garrison to resort to a most unusual step: they went on strike on August 3, 1866. The post commander, also an Arizona Volunteer, had to agree that under the conditions he could hardly blame them.

By the end of August, the commander reported that the entire garrison of Camp Lincoln consisted of himself and five ill enlisted men. Two weeks later, three of these were mustered out. The post commander had only one alternative; he called on the settlers to man the fort and protect the government property.

A regular Army company arrived on September 29 and the crisis ended. Pauline Weaver, the famous male scout with the female-sounding name, served as civilian scout for the command at this time. Upon his death in 1867, he was buried in the post cemetery.

The fort was re-named Camp Verde in 1868 in deference to the fact that the Lincoln name had been adopted by several other posts, including another one in Arizona. Until this time the soldiers lived in quarters described by the surgeon as "of the most primitive character." They were the original construction of the settlers and Arizona Volunteers "consisting of excavations on a hill-side, completed with logs and shelter tents."

In 1868 work began on "better and more permanent quarters." Two barracks of adobe, 100 by 26 feet, provided better shelter but no luxuries. "The only fixtures or furniture is a double line of bunks, two tiers high, each four feet wide, and accommodating four men," said the surgeon. "All of the buildings of the post are irregular, being for the most part the remains of the old camp. There is no mess-room, the men eating their rations in quarters . . . The officers' quarters are miserable hovels . . . The guardhouse is . . . sufficiently lighted by the crevices between the posts forming the walls."

The bottomland location proved too unhealthy and in 1871 the post was moved a mile south to reduce the malarial influences. While the garrison diverted military talents to construction arts, Vincent Colyer met with 1,000 Yavapai at Camp

FORMER HEADQUARTERS of Fort Verde now is museum sponsored by Camp Verde Improvement Association. It is one of four original buildings left at post. Adobe building is 100 feet long, 20 wide and includes seven rooms which originally had no connecting doors. Adjutant quartermaster, commissary officer, school room, and post library were assigned to spaces in it. Building was given for museum by Mrs. Margaret Wingfield Hallett, owner of much of fort site. Rooms inside include scale model of fort and displays of military, pioneer, and Indian artifacts.

Verde. A reservation was established north of the post.

The arrival of Crook in Arizona was given by the Indians as an excuse for 500 to flee for the mountains. Occasionally some would return for rations, or send women or children to bargain for them. By 1872 only five were left at the reservation after another 800 left. Patrols chased them into their mountain hideouts. On one led by a captive squaw, the "soldiers, before starting out, wrapped their feet and knees with gunny sacks, so as to make as little noise as possible," Crook wrote.

This expedition took the Indians by surprise in a dawn attack. "Our people fired a volley into their camp and charged with a yell," said Crook. "So secure did they feel in this almost impregnable position that they lost all presence of mind, even running past their holes in the rocks. Some of them jumped off the precipice and were mashed into a shapeless mass. All of the men were killed; most of the women and children were taken prisoner."

The 1873 surrender was the immediate result of this patrol. A month after the council, the Indians heard rumors that the troops were going to massacre them. They "flew to the mountains like a flock of quail," Crook said "I sent word back at once to signal them by smoke to stop, and I at once proceeded to Verde. They all came back, looking as if they had been stealing sheep."

The reservation was almost a success. After an irrigation ditch was dug, the Apaches grew crops and sold them to the Army, as Crook had promised. But this cut into the profits of the Indian Ring in Tucson and, by edict from higher authority, the Verde reservation was abolished. The scene was set for another outbreak as the Apaches were forced to move to sterile San Carlos.

MILITARY DISPLAY in Verde Museum includes uniform coat and medical kit of Oscar Temple, enlisted medical steward who assisted at birth of Douglas MacArthur at Little Rock Ark. Temple later became Adjutant General of Arizona. Fireplace and whitewashed walls have been restored to original appearance in this room. Building was made of "pice"—mud poured in layers rather than in individual adobe bricks. "Shakes," hand hewn shingles, covered original on roof.

TO GET THERE: Town of Camp Verde is 36 miles directly east of Prescott and two miles east of turnoff from State 79. Post site covers north half of hamlet.

OFFICER'S QUARTERS was elaborate two-story building with wing that extended to rear. Although occupied at time of photography, future of building was doubtful, even though tarpaper sidings provided some protection for adobe. Until Apaches were subdued in Verde Valley, post was always alert to possible attack. "The ranchmen always take their rifles with them," visiting officer wrote in 1872, "and it is a common occurrence for herders to be picked off, or men shot, while at work in the fields. The Apache-Mojaves roam through this region, and their country extends east to the mountains beyond the Verde river. At the post of that name several hundreds were being fed. Quite a large number were found at Beaver Creek and, although then en route to the post to get their five days allowance, showed great insolence to a small advanced guard."

FORT APACHE, ARIZONA

He seemed an obsure medicine man with an unpronounceable Apache name and a typical desire to be heard. But as Brevet Brigadier General Eugene A. Carr listened to his visitor at Fort Apache in 1881, something told him there was more to it than that.

Nock-ay-del-klinne was the medicine man's name. His message had to do with dances he had been holding at Cibicu creek, near the fort—dances designed to raise the spirits of dead warriors. So far, he admitted, no one had been resurrected, but he had received messages from the spirits.

A few days later, Carr's suspicions were confirmed when Private Charles Hurle, an interpreter, discovered what the spirits had told Nock-ay-del-klinne. A telegram to the department commander summarized the whole thing and marked the opening of a new chapter in the Apache Wars.

". . . Nock-ay-del-klinne is telling the Indians that the dead say they will not return because of the presence of the white people," Carr telegraphed; "that when the white people leave the dead will return, and that the whites will be out of the country when the corn gets ripe. Hurle thinks his next move may be to induce the Indians to hasten the departure of the whites, and that he may be working them up to a frame of mind suitable for the purpose."

A four-week exchange of telegrams followed. The Indian Agent urged drastic action, including arresting and exiling the medicine man "or have him killed without arresting." Later developments were to suggest that the Agent's concern was mainly to hide his grafting schemes that caused the Apache unrest.

Isolated in the mountain wilderness surrounding Fort Apache, Carr's contact with the outside twice was broken when the telegraph line was cut. Finally on August 28 he received his orders: "Capture or kill Nock-ay-del-klinne."

Simple enough on the face of it, but the orders posed a delicate question.

What was Carr to do with his company of 25 Indian scouts, without whom he would be hard-pressed to find the medicine man? The near-religious nature of the medicine man's efforts and the fact that many of the Scouts' families had been converted, had put their status in doubt. Their weapons had been taken from them and were issued only in order to be cleaned for the weekly inspections.

It was decided to take the Scouts on the patrol rather than leave them behind at a lightly defended post made more vulnerable by the presence of families. In addition, the Scouts had proved loyal and effective in the past and the officer placed over them was confident this would continue.

Upwards of 100 men were in the patrol to arrest the one medicine man. Carr noted nothing untoward during the march from the fort, except for the frequent meetings with Apaches, all of whom seemed friendly, and armed. One chief insisted on shaking Carr's hand, then slowly moved down the column as if he were estimating its strength.

Late in the second day after leaving the fort, the patrol reached the Cibicu. The medicine man was at the entrance to his lodge and showed no signs of escaping when told of his arrest. Then the patrol moved upstream a few miles to a campsite.

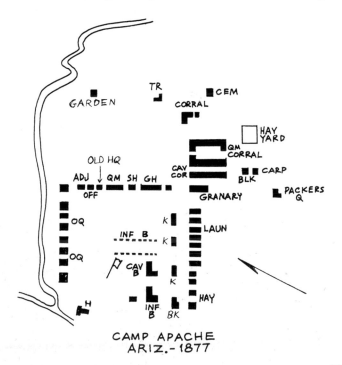

CAMP APACHE
ARIZ.-1877

BUILT IN 1870 and called Camp Ord, then Camp Mogollon, then Camp Thomas, by 1871 post was known as Camp Apache as token of friendship for tribe in its vicinity. At first, only building on post was that built by sutler. It also was best brewery in entire area. General George Crook stopped at post enroute to his first tour in charge of Arizona district. He talked with Indians in area "and finally got them to enlist as scouts and act in conjunction with our troops," he wrote in his *Autobiography.* His first company of Indian scouts was organized at Fort Apache at that time. Supposedly he occupied house at westernmost end of officers' row. Post was active until 1924, then became Indian Service school. (Redrawn from McDowell Report, 1877.)

FORT APACHE was comfortably located on plateau along banks of White River but was at mercy of high bluffs to north. This picture of 1870-era shows fort at its heyday. Hospital is at far left, barracks in foreground, officers' row in background, and administrative row of headquarters, storehouses, and guardhouse at right edge of parade ground. General O. O. Howard was here in 1872 on two occasions. On second trip he found Apaches unhappy over rations. His solution was to relieve the Indian Agent and replace him with post surgeon.

As Carr told another officer, "I was rather ashamed to come out with all this force to arrest one poor little Indian," he noticed the armed Apaches gathering around the camp.

"Here, those Indians must not come into camp!" he ordered.

A moment later his "faithful" scouts turned on the soldiers and opened fire. A captain was killed with a bullet in the heart. His orderly fell dead with eight bullets in his body. Eight of the mutinying Scouts and other tribesmen were killed and the medicine man was felled with three bullets in the head when he tried to escape.

One company of soldiers, still mounted, swept across the Apache flank. While an estimated 500 Indians poured fire on the troopers, a breastwork of boxes and logs was hastily erected. Carr cooly barked out orders for the defense, causing one officer to shout: "Well, if the old man isn't afraid, I guess the balance of us need not be!"

At nightfall, preparations were made for a silent withdrawal to the fort. A sergeant noticed Nock-ay-del-klinne crawling into the brush. Two blows with an axe killed him. The sergeant later explained that the unpleasant method was the only thing he could think of at the time when a shot in the dark might have done more harm than good.

Their dead were buried in a common grave. "I said over them as much of the service as I could remember, and had Taps sounded," Carr wrote

FORT APACHE today, taken from approximately same spot as old photograph, has few of large buildings left, but officers' row and some administrative and store buildings remain. After he relieved General Crook in 1886, General Miles visited Fort Apache where he found "over four hundred men, women and children, belonging to the Chiricahua and Warm Spring Indians, and a more turbulent, desperate, disreputable band of human beings I had ever seen before and hope never to see again," he wrote in his *Personal Recollections*. "The Apaches on this reservation were called prisoners of war, yet they had never been disarmed or dismounted. Some of them had a little land under cultivation on which they raised barley, out of which they manufactured 'tiswin,' a most intoxicating liquor, which has the peculiar characteristic of rousing all that is turbulent and vicious in the individual who had been imbibing; and the more barley they raised the more tiswin riots occurred. When I visited their camp they were having their drunken orgies every night, and it was a perfect pandemonium. It was dangerous to go near them, as they were constantly discharging pistols and rifles." At that time Miles decided that the Apaches would have to be moved from Arizona.

later. "This served for 'good night' to them and also to indicate to the Indians that we were going to sleep."

Everything to be left behind was destroyed, the wounded were lifted into saddles, and the command moved into the night.

Carr's approach was signalled to the fort late the next day. Upon arrival, he found the place in a state of siege. Several soldiers had been killed nearby shortly before his return. Four civilians had been shot down by Apaches less than a dozen miles from the fort.

Rumors that he had been massacred preceded him and already had gone to the outside world. The New York *Times* carried three columns of details that read strangely like the Custer massacre five years before. Carr was granted the edge over Custer because, the article commented, he "was always prudent in the conduct of his campaigns."

The district commander had telegraphed headquarters, "A few of Gen. Carr's command escaped Cibicu Creek . . . and are fighting their way to Fort Apache, but their success is doubtful."

In San Francisco, General McDowell telegraphed orders for reinforcement of Apache by other Arizona forts and asked Washington for other troops to be put "in readiness to reinforce me if necessary, as all may be needed."

Back at Fort Apache, Carr and his 60 troopers still faced a dangerous situation. In his absence, the post went on a full-scale alert. The rear guard set a continual vigil, especially when natives were seen packing their belongings as if to leave. The telegraph was cut. A courier was killed 15 minutes after he rode from the post. Open spots around the fort's perimeter were barricaded by boxes, logs, and wagons, and loopholes were cut into the walls of buildings.

The morning after Carr returned, the Indians ambushed a patrol outside the post and then drove in the work detail and guard at the sawmill. Heavy fire started from the northeast, then the south. A

BARRACKS, only one remaining of original four, provided considerable improvement over tents used by first contingents at Apache. "It was altogether a picturesque and pretty post," wrote Martha Summerhayes in *Vanishing Arizona* of her 1874 life at Fort Apache. "The officers' quarters at Camp Apache were log cabins, built near the edge of the deep cañon . . . There were enormous stables and government buildings, and a sutler's store." Because her husband was a second lieutenant, Mrs. Summerhayes found quarters choice was poor. "We were assigned a half of a log cabin, which gave us one room, a small square hall, and a bare shed, the latter detached from the house, to be used as a kitchen."

lieutenant was wounded in the leg. Carr's horse was shot from under him. Soon the outlying buildings were seen to be blazing.

Carr dispatched a detail of soldiers and civilians to attack a party of Indians who were advancing on the sawmill, 400 yards away. Firing continued until dark. After a night at their guns, the garrison noted few Apaches in sight the next day.

Although it reduced his defense force to 60 men, Carr sent a company to Fort Thomas to ask for reinforcements and to report the details of the battle.

On September 4, this information went out on the telegraph lines.

McDowell could state: "I am rejoiced to report that the massacre of Carr's command is not true." The New York *Times* had to admit editorially that its accounts of the "massacre, as it is called . . . appear to have been much exaggerated."

Reinforcements began to appear. "We arrived at the edge of the high bluffs overlooking Fort Apache," wrote one of them, Anton Mazzanovich, in *Trailing Geronimo*. "A veil of white smoke hung over the little valley below. Several fires were burning, and we could hear dogs barking, although but faintly. I was standing at the bluffs among some

GUARDHOUSE "was evidently built with one single object in view, security," reported surgeon in 1890. "Ventilation is defective, small airholes and windows. The capacity is entirely inadequate . . . The windows are too small and two few in number . . . The cells are relics of the subterranean dungeons of the Middle Ages; the fact that the purifying rays of the sun can never penetrate them is sufficient to condemn them. Fortunately they are rarely used." When General Carr was assigned to Fort Apache in 1881, he considered it "banishment to the most uncomfortable and out of the way Post possible."

CEMETERY at Fort Apache no longer has soldier dead, but still is in use by Indian Agency and town. After Battle of Cibicu, squad of men started to dig grave for private who died at post. "They were fired upon," according to Anton Mazzanovich in *Trailing Geronimo.* "They had to run for cover. They tried to continue their uncompleted task during the afternoon without succeeding in their accomplishment. The next day, two colored troopers, who were in the guard-house for desertion, volunteered to dig the grave. Colonel Carr promised to give them their freedom if they would try to do this, under the protection of a firing squad. He also agreed to give each an Indian pony and $150. In the afternoon, they managed to finish their lamentable task . . . On the following day Colonel Carr kept his promise and the two colored troopers were given their justly deserved free-dom." Not long after burial, Mazzanovich returned to graveyard and "found that some of the headboards that served for tombstones were torn down . . . We replaced the headboards where we thought they belonged."

HEADQUARTERS of Fort Apache, now post office for town and Indian Agency, was scene of one half of unusual reporting system when Apaches were exiled in 1886. Telegrapher at fort was asked by his counterpart at Wilcox Station, 12 miles from Fort Bowie, "Let me know fully what is going on." Telegrapher reported that troops had dispersed after usual Sunday morning inspection and had taken up "certain positions that commanded the positions of the Indians." Then he "saw the troops suddenly take position surrounding the large body of Indians . . . some commotion among the Indians . . . All of the warriors took a standing position ready for immediate action." The post commander passed among them, telling them to sit down. "Realizing the folly of resistance in the presence of this strong body of troops," they did. Fort Apache telegrapher did not know that his description was being heard by General Miles, who was standing next to Wilcox Station operator. Upon hearing that Indians had been rounded up and were ready to go to Florida, Miles felt that Army "had that entire camp—which was the arsenal, the breeding place, the recruiting depot, the hospital, the asylum of the hostiles, and had been so for years,—entirely under his control, and that we had seen the last of hostile Indians coming to and going from that camp."

of the Indian Scouts and overheard one of them remark in Spanish to Cook, the chief packer: 'All burned: Fort Apache—no more.' "

The aftermath of the Battle of Cibicu had a few highlights. Carr was sent to the battle site three weeks later and found the bodies dug up and mutilated. The renewal of Apache unrest gener-ated considerable activity in the district, but head-quarters' failure to act rapidly permitted many to escape.

Carr had one more close brush with the Apaches in mid-October. After reports that some hostile leaders had returned to a friendly band, Carr was ordered to move in and arrest them. "It was a very delicate situation," Carr commented, "they could only be taken unexpectedly and simultaneously."

He took an innocent-looking wagon train to the Indian village. On signal, two companies of infan-try appeared from behind the canvas covers and the hostiles were rounded up. Fort Apache's period of gravest Indian danger was ended.

TO GET THERE: From Globe, Arizona, take U.S. 60 northeast 66 miles to right turn on State 73. This comes to town of Fort Apache in 27 miles. Site of fort includes many fort buildings used by Indian Agency next to town.

GENERAL CROOK'S headquarters, or so the sign in front claims, is log cabin at western end of officers' row. Crook was at Apache in 1871 for first time; soon after leaving he heard that Vincent Colyer and General O. O. Howard had been sent to Arizona "to interfere with my operations . . . to make peace with the Apaches by the grace of God." In 1872, he returned and organized garrison and scouts into two independent commands "with a pack train for each, so they could act independently of each other." Then he told commanding officer "to obey no orders, even from the President of the United States, until I first saw it." He planned to take sweeping offensive action once his forces were organized at all posts, and wanted no outside orders to interfere. He was back at Apache in 1883 when he started his second Arizona tour and after visit reported, "There are insufficient barracks and officers' quarters."

FORT THOMAS, ARIZONA

Although Fort Thomas was established in order to remove the garrison from Fort Goodwin's unhealthy area, it was soon found that the seven-mile move accomplished nothing. At least at Goodwin the men had buildings in which to live; at Thomas they had nothing but tents.

What buildings they did get were what they could build themselves. After extravagant expenditures at Goodwin, the Army was determined not to repeat the mistake at Thomas. No money was authorized, so to speak, and for its first few years the post was built on a familiar theme: at no expense to the government with the labor of the troops.

The post was started in 1876 a half mile south of the Gila river and near the bottom of a 10,487-acre reservation. Three years later it consisted of only two adobe barracks, a two-room shanty for the commanding officer, a guardhouse, and an adjutant's office.

When troops were rushed to the post during the 1881 Apache outbreak at Fort Apache, Fort Thomas could provide the arrivals with little more than a shelter tent and a plot of ground on which to pitch it. Anton Mazzanovich tells in *Trailing Geronimo* of waiting two weeks at Thomas with these accommodations.

Mazzanovich's unit did not go to Apache that time, and returned to Fort Grant, instead. Soon after, a messenger arrived at Fort Thomas with word of the Cibicu Fight. Mazzanovich's company made a forced march back to Thomas, arriving at midnight. The next morning they continued on to Apache, spent most of the day fording the flooded Gila, but got to the besieged fort in two days. They were its first reinforcements.

Back at Fort Thomas as the outbreak continued, Brevet General Orlando B. Willcox, the department commander, established his "Headquarters in the Field." From here he relayed the telegraphic reports of the Apache difficulties. However, unreliability of the telegraph line, a poor grasp of the actual problem with the Apaches, and a running feud with General Carr at Fort Apache minimized Willcox's effectiveness. When the outbreak was settled, it was almost as if it was settled despite instead of because of Willcox's efforts.

Lieutenant Britton Davis was at Thomas at the time. In his *The Truth About Geronimo*, he tells that four troops of the Third Cavalry rushed there from Wyoming. "Fort Thomas was accredited the worst post in the domains of Uncle Sam," he writes, "and merited its reputation during the few months I spent there."

One officer was accompanied by his wife and four children from Wyoming. The 110 degree temperature of the bottomlands of the Gila made the entire family ill and it was necessary to move them to a more temperate climate for recovery.

The troops moved on to Apache. Because of the Indian threat, they attempted a night march through the torturous Mogollon mountains. One night of falling, sliding, and losing their way advanced them only ten miles and so completely exhausted the horses and pack mules that they were delayed in getting to Apache.

Davis noted that the only engagement left for them in the campaign was at the tail end of the so-called "Battle of Dry Wash." The major engagement was over, but Davis' command was pinned down until they could charge a "nest" of rapid-firing Apaches. The "nest" turned out to be a 19-year old Indian girl firing several rifles in desperate defense of her baby and a 60-year old woman. All were taken care of and returned to the reservation.

FORT THOMAS
ARIZ. –1886

PARADE GROUND of Fort Thomas was 170 by 230 yards, included, according to surgeon's report, "a few mesquite bushes, unworthy of the name of trees, and several ungainly buildings used for a variety of purposes." All buildings were of adobe except granary "constructed of upright logs supporting a canvas and earthen roof." Guardhouse was "a cheerless structure . . . poorly lighted and badly ventilated. The lack of ventilation is a serious fault as the house is often crowded with prisoners." It had one 18- by 24-foot prison room and two 8- by 10-foot cells. Corrals included large 300- by 255-foot hay and straw corral, a quartermaster corral of 100 by 160 feet, two for cavalry horses 95 by 180 feet apiece, and a 60- by 180-foot corral for pack train. Barracks in center was largest, measuring 111 by 12 feet with room for 46 men. Those flanking it were about 85 feet long, had ceiling between nine and 11 feet high, and room for about 30 men. Bakery did not have brick oven and surgeon objected to the amount of dirt that fell into dough from adobe-lined oven. Most of these buildings were begun in 1876, but construction by soldier labor was slow. (Redrawn from plat in National Archives.)

The Apache outbreak had one major effect on Fort Thomas. Funds were granted for construction of a permanent fort to replace or, at least repair, the dilapidated and makeshift camp. The surgeon noted that the barracks were so ineffective that when the Third Cavalry was camped there in tents, their sickness statistics were no worse than of men living in barracks.

"This post is regarded as and is one of the most unhealthy in the Department of Arizona," wrote the surgeon in his official record of the post. "Dry, lifeless character of the atmosphere resembling very closely the air in a close room heated by a stove . . . Absence of trees and plants—excepting the mesquite and cottonwood and sagebrushes, etc.—causes a monotony unvarying to the eye and depressing to the nervous system."

He suggested that "the extreme heat and depressing influences" during the summer were responsible for the fact that usually a third of the garrison was sick. Details absent from the post during the summer suffered less than half that percentage. The surgeon's proposed solution was to set up a summer camp for the garrison between June 15 and October 1. This was tried in 1887 with a camp at Ash Creek, but proved a failure because of "flies and mosquitos."

"The hottest post in the republic and the most sickly, excepting none," is the description of Fort Thomas by a former commander, Anson Mills, in his *My Story*. "It was one of the most desolate posts in which we ever served. The valley was very low and hot. The mountains on each side of the river were some six or seven thousand feet higher than the valley and only about six or eight miles apart, so what little rain there was fell on these mountains . . . Here many of our soldiers died in an epidemic of a very malignant, burning fever."

The surgeon found that by closing several suspicious wells and cleaning the fungus from the water barrels, his sick count dropped. Typhoid all but disappeared by 1887. Seldom did the sick report again look like it did every month with between 40 to 60 cases that ran the gamut of ills.

For December, 1884, the surgeon listed 39 cases, a typical month with a typical catalog of ills that included diarrhoeas, fever, neuralgia, itch, acute rheumatism, contused wounds, catarrh, enlarged spleen, ingrowing toe nail, palpitation of the heart, syphilis, gonorrheas, sprains, myalgia, cavies of the teeth, gonorrhoeal orchitis, ulcers, and headache.

With a monthly run-down like that, obviously the soldiers had little need for Indian fighting to fill the hospital!

FORT THOMAS in 1880's presented trim appearance. This view is from behind hospital, the pair of buildings in left foreground. Building with high sloped roof was hospital proper and included six rooms each 15 feet square and 12 feet high. Ward was building on left with veranda around it. Ward was 25 feet wide, 50 feet long. Row of officers' quarters can be seen at left edge of picture; two officers' quarters are behind hospital buildings. Headquarters and library building behind tree at right center of picture apparently was being built at time of photography. Three barracks are at right edge. Storehouses are at far end of parade ground; pair of buildings actually has third one between them; but it was an underground cellar. Guardhouse can barely be seen to left of these storehouses.

TO GET THERE: Town of Fort Thomas is on U.S. 70 about 55 miles south of Globe, Arizona. Site of post is covered by plowed fields north of town beside highway.

FORT THOMAS today is preserved in name of tiny market town, but traces of fort have disappeared. Battered cemetery in foreground harkens back to fort days when it was used by Colonel Anson Mills. Mills wrote that Apaches went on warpath, "Geronimo and his wild followers devastating the settlements and killing many men, women, and children, whom we buried in the post cemetery." Some business for cemetery was provided by other sources. It was "only a few hundred yards from the village of Maxey," surgeon reported. "This village is provided with usual dance-house and saloons of a frontier hamlet—and is a source of temptation to the enlisted men, and indirectly the cause of most courtmartials at this post." *Arizona Place Names* adds, "Maxey earned a reputation as a spot where government supplies could be bought from Indian traders. In 1880 Maxey was thoroughly disreputable. It consisted for the most part of saloons and houses of prostitution." Lawlessness was not uncommon even late in era. In 1889, Army paymaster and 11-man escort from Fort Thomas was ambushed and robbed of more than $28,000. Eight of the 11 troopers were wounded in spirited fight. Seven of the robbers were later captured by pursuing patrol. They were freed in jury trial termed by judge as greatest miscarriage of justice he had ever seen. Garrison was reduced in 1886 and fort was abandoned in 1892 after being a sub post of Fort Grant.

POST AT OJO CALIENTE, N.M.

Strung out for at least 200 yards along the usually dry Alamosa river of New Mexico, the adobe Indian Agency and army camp of Ojo Caliente was an inviting target for Geronimo on a day in spring, 1877.

From the low, rolling hills overlooking the place, Geronimo knew that the sometimes fort was hard to defend at best. And his vantage point told him that there were only 20 Apache police at the post, far too small a number to do any good. There were no soldiers at the moment.

What was more, Geronimo and his 100 braves were old hands in the Ojo Caliente area. Geronimo liked the solitude of the area and its hot springs—the basis for the Spanish version of the name. It was a favorite place of his and he was aware that Agent John Clum knew this. (This was the same Clum who later buddied with Wyatt Earp and edited the *Epitaph* of Tombstone, Arizona.)

Geronimo was not surprised to receive word that Clum was below in the Army buildings, and that the agent wanted Geronimo to surrender. It took the wily chief only a few seconds to decide to give himself up—or, at least, to make it appear that was going to happen. With only 20 men with him, Clum could hardly do anything about it if Geronimo changed his mind, the chief reasoned.

Dawn found Geronimo and his braves slowly moving onto the informal parade ground of the post. Across the way, the 20 men were drawn up in a semicircle waiting for them. His 100 braves close behind, Geronimo rode up to the Indian Agent and stolidly listened to Clum's demands for surrender. Almost with contempt he eyed the outnumbered Apache police backing Clum.

Then he noticed movements all around him. He and his braves watched through narrowing eyes as 80 more police came from the buildings. Seeing that they were surrounded and, considering the superior

arms and ammunition of Clum's "soldiers," the braves had no doubt about who had the upper hand now!

A surrender was negotiated at Ojo Caliente that spring day. It lasted barely three weeks before Geronimo was on the loose again, escaping from the guardhouse cell at arid San Carlos. It was not until 1886 that the stocky fighter finally would be subdued.

For Ojo Caliente, however, the incident was its main claim to posterity. For several years it had been a site for Indian agency business and other business between the Army, the Apaches, and the civilians. As early as 1859 it had a military garrison of sorts, but it was manned only sporadically—and then usually as an outpost or temporary camp of some other fort.

After the Civil War Ojo Caliente became the agency headquarters of the White Springs Apache reservation. Shortly after the Geronimo surrender and subsequent escape focused attention on the area, Ojo Caliente was re-garrisoned by a troop of the 4th Cavalry.

The troop had several duties, ranging from patrolling and reporting Indian movements in the area to watching over the Agency and guarding the horse herd. The outbreak of Chief Victorio in the late 1870's, a war that swept West Texas for several years, ran the Ojo Caliente post from its usual 60 men to almost 200.

Victorio had returned to the United States from Mexico in February, 1878, and surrendered with his band at Ojo Caliente. They refused to be moved to the San Carlos reservation but, after a short flirtation with hiding in the mountains, turned themselves in at that reservation. Assured that they now were at their permanent homes, the band sent for their families which were still at Ojo Caliente.

But the coincidental arrival of some civil officials

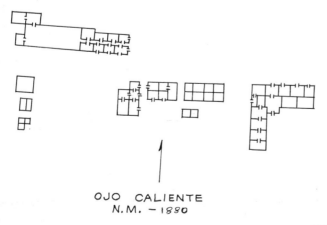

OJO CALIENTE
N.M. – 1880

RUINS AT Ojo Caliente cover more than 200 yards east-to-west with Alamosa river bed immediately to north. This is how adobe ruins were when visited; walls and doorways are indicated when it was possible to trace them on ground —otherwise they are left out. Possible Army uses can be only guesses because Indian Bureau used post throughout Army period and after soldiers had left. Guesses suggest that large building at north was barracks, cluster of smaller buildings in center, officers' quarters and headquarters building, and L-shaped building to east, storehouses. About 200 yards to west of this main post is a rectangular corral-style stone enclosure with suggestion of stockade leading from it to creekbed behind post. (Drawn from site inspection.)

NORTHERN building is in foreground in this picture. To right is cluster of several small buildings immediately south of supposedly haunted barracks. Westernmost wall of barracks apparently had two rooms jutting out, perhaps as guardhouses or adobe "blockhouses" from which sentries could observe area. Rolling country south and west of post made it possible for Indians to come close without being noticed. After Indian Bureau abandoned buildings, they became gathering place for ranchers who held square dances and picnics there at turn of century.

on a hunting party aroused the Indians' suspicions. Fearing that they were to be arrested and tried for the various crimes for which they felt guilty, the band left on a destructive raid that took them into Mexico and, ultimately, back to Ojo Caliente.

The cavalrymen at Ojo Caliente were routinely watching over the horseherd when Victorio and 60 warriors suddenly appeared. "They killed a small guard over public animals and drove off the stock," reported General Pope in his Annual Report for 1879-80. "News, more or less exaggerated, has been received from a settler in Grant County, near the line of Arizona, giving an account of the fight he had with the band, and that his stock was driven off and ten persons killed."

The garrison at Fort Bayard moved in pursuit of the hostiles while the detachment at Ojo Caliente totalled up their losses: eight men were killed or wounded and 56 horses driven off.

Although the Victorio force was estimated to be larger than the Army's, the future held little in store for the Indian. Within a year he was dead, killed by a sniper's bullet in Mexico. By 1882, the Post at Ojo Caliente was overtaken by the future, too, and it was abandoned.

HAUNTED BARRACKS of Ojo Caliente is favorite legend about later use of buildings by cowboys. According to story, cowboys spending night in ruined barracks heard horse arrive outside and rider enter building, walk down corridor dragging his saddle on floor behind him. When he did not appear, cowboys looked for him but could find no trace of rider, saddle, or horse. Modern-day Scout troops use buildings for camping trips and frequently hear the phantom rider—after a campfire session in which this story is told several times! This view is from eastern side of long northern building looking down corridor with entrances to small rooms noticeable at right.

TO GET THERE: From Socorro, N.M., go west on U.S. 60 through Magdalena to State 52, about 40 miles. Turn left (south) and go about 40 miles. Post is in box canyon to left as road crosses over bed of Alamosa river. Another approach is from south from Truth or Consequences and up State 142. Both ways are dusty and dry, but road is fairly good gravel and dirt.

WITHIN THE "L" of easternmost building, high ceilings predominated. Room in background is indicated in plat within elbow of the "L". It had only one door but all of its walls are interior; perhaps it was special storage or "vault" area because it was completely surrounded by other rooms. Drifted adobe gives misleading impression of height of doorways; those shown here are less than man-high, but obviously were higher when in actual use.

FORT BAYARD, NEW MEXICO

Fort Bayard was less than a year old in 1867 when it got a taste of Indian hospitality. As they rushed around in pre-dawn darkness clad only in their long drawers and blankets, the troopers at Bayard were unanimous in disapproving of the whole thing.

"Early in the morning, before guard mount," remembered Surgeon William T. Parker, "a considerable body of Apaches in war paint dashed into the post firing right and left at every one in sight, and even at the doors of the buildings as they passed, and then wheeling, yelling and firing, had ridden away.

"They were well mounted and although the gun squad had rushed to load the cannon, before the gun strings could be placed for firing, they were out of range, as their defiant yell died away in the distance."

About all the troopers could do was pull their blankets around them against the morning chill of autumn. At 6,200 feet altitude only a dozen miles from the Continental Divide, Bayard was one southwestern fort that could boast of having four seasons and a foot of snow in the winter.

Small protection against the elements was provided by "the usual collection of buildings typical of a so-called 'fort,' but no wall or stockade enclosed," Parker reported. "In the center was the usual parade ground with the staff for Old Glory, and a brass Napoleon 6 ft. gun, on each side of it, pointing towards the main approach."

Two years later the surgeon's official report had little new to say of the post. "The officers and men occupy temporary log huts, which are in bad condition," he commented. For emphasis, he repeated later that the officers' quarters were "in very bad condition."

Work had begun on a new post of adobe which would accommodate three companies around a parallelogram 650 by 400 feet. "Commodious and convenient" storehouses had been completed but the surgeon found fault with the new hospital. He said the site was poorly drained, the adobes badly made, the windows too small and too few, and the 25 degree slope of the rafters "contrary to all architectural principles."

By 1872, temporary quarters still remained for 300 men. Two were "built of logs, with mud roof, and one set of sawed lumber," an official report stated. "The log buildings are rapidly decaying and becoming unfit for occupation."

It was to be several more years before the permanent Fort Bayard construction would be finished. Repeated demands on the troops for military duties delayed their carpentry pursuits, something not surprising in view of the presence of almost 1,500 Indians in the vicinity.

From the first recorded instance of white settlement, there had been little love lost between settler and Indian. Ten miles to the northwest, in 1860 a group of miners located gold claims that quickly generated a rush to what the Indians called the "Pinos Altos" (tall trees). By the end of the year, 820 names were on the census report and equal that number scattered around the mountains at every likely gold source.

James H. Tevis—of Fort Buchanan and Camp Wallen discussions—was in the first rush to Pinos

FORT BAYARD
N. M. — 1877

WHEN IT was finally finished, Fort Bayard was a compact post surrounding a parade ground 800 by 500 feet, somewhat larger than original plans. Most buildings were of adobe. Officers' row could accommodate seven officers' families. By 1890 post was overcrowded with four companies of infantry and two cavalry troops. "The barracks are too small for the full strength of the companies and troops," reported surgeon. "The infantry barracks are only large enough for 40 men, and the cavalry 58 men." This was despite expansion of post by then, giving it official capacity for 19 officers and 400 men with two additional barracks. This large garrison was considered "well located for the work it is intended to perform, guarding the western and southern portions of New Mexico," Secretary of War reported in 1890. (Redrawn from McDowell Report, 1877.)

FORT BAYARD in 1855 was garrisoned for a short period by the headquarters and four troops of the 6th Cavalry, plus two companies of the 13th Infantry. Comment at the time described it: "Our 'fort' was the usual squatty quadrangle of adobes, sheds and corrals, and little was there to exhibit the dignity of a great nation, but the fluttering war flag on the parade, and the stout-hearted, spirited garrison." In this view, officers' row is at right, hospital in foreground in front of flagpole, warehouses across parade ground, barracks at left with corrals and out-buildings to their rear.

Altos. "I began building a rude house with a dirt roof," he wrote in his memoirs. "It was large enough to hold eight or ten men and was the first house to be erected in Pinos Altos . . . I took up the claim just in front of the cabin and . . . began placer mining for the first time in my life."

"After the town was begun, houses went up thick and fast. Saloons, dance halls, and a tenpin alley were in operation, with gamblers galore. Between them and the Mexican senoritas, the miners soon parted with their gold."

Apaches roamed the area. Both citizen posses and military patrols chased them with varying degrees of success. Tevis came across the results of a massacre that he blamed on Cochise. Three miners had been captured, "hung up to a juniper tree with their heads down, within a foot of the ground. Fires were built under them, and they were burned alive. Cochise cut some strips of flesh off the bodies, roasted it, and ate it to make him brave."

When the Civil War clouds withdrew all Federal protection from the area, the settlers and miners looked to the Confederacy for aid. After voting 339 to 0 in favor of the South, the Pinos Altoans subscribed to the newspaper editorial: "We hope that Congress in Montgomery will give us early hearing because, God knows, we have suffered long enough."

When 400 Apaches under Cochise attacked the settlement, the Confederacy did come to the rescue. Captain Thomas J. Mastin, Arizona Scouts, C.S.A., rallied his nine men, assumed command of the miners, and fought the Apaches for five hours. Two whites were killed and seven wounded; at least 15 Apaches died, including one who was attacked by a pet dog. Seven days later, Mastin died of blood poisoning.

This demonstration of Apache ferocity was enough to drive most of the population from the Pinos Altos. The California Column found 30 families "extremely poor and destitute . . . living on purslane and roots, and several had become insane from hunger.

"The Indians were represented as being extremely hostile and in the habit of committing depredations upon the settlers whenever they had anything to steal," reported Captain Edward D. Shirland. "All were extremely anxious to have the government extend to them sufficient protection and station at least one company in their neighborhood."

General Carleton directed that five beeves, 600 pounds of pemmican, 3,000 pounds of flour, and 1,500 pounds of Mexican sugar (panoche) be distributed "to the most needy." The matter of a military post was taken up in January, 1863, when a company of infantry was stationed at the spring which was to be the ultimate site of Fort Bayard. This temporary camp lasted for the first half of 1863 and engaged several Apache bands with the loss of one soldier. The establishment of neighboring Fort West permitted the temporary camp to be withdrawn.

The settlers felt secure as long as they kept close to their camps. They knew the penalty for wandering and in 1864 determined to settle the Apache question with the so-called "Bean Peace Council."

"A fine dinner of beans and other accessories of a square meal, was set for the Apaches, numbering 60, in a house since destroyed," wrote one settler 25 years later. "Everything being in readiness, and while the Indians were discussing the merits of the beans, the settlers fired on them, killing several, the rest escaping undoubtedly with the conviction that beans garnished with powder and lead, was a very unpalatable dish," he concluded.

This contributed little to the pacification of the Apaches. In 1866, troopers returned to the spring below Pinos Altos with orders "to protect the miners from the Warm Springs Apaches." Their problems were described in a report by a local judge in 1869:

"There are now present three companies of troops at Fort Bayard, but owing to the great number having been discharged lately on account of expiration of service I am informed by General Mason that there are hardly sufficient troops left to guard the post. In my opinion, if General Mason had a sufficient force to operate with, he would chastise these Indians as they deserve. As it is, he is powerless."

The Apache toll included: one woman killed, January, 1870; mules stolen from two ranches, April, 1870; two men dead of thirst after unsuccessfully chasing Apache rustlers, May, 1870; mules stolen, February, 1871, but posse ran down the thieves, killing 14, losing one; six whites killed while bringing supplies to Fort Bayard, March, 1871; one man killed, stripped, and mutilated outside of the fort, April, 1871, followed shortly by the killing of a teamster, a soldier, and a sheepherder.

The garrison brought a measure of peace to the area at the time of the Apache Campaign of the 1870's. Hostiles were pursued relentlessly with little

HOG RANCH for Fort Bayard was Central or Central City, New Mexico, formerly Santa Clara, at reservation's edge. It was county seat in 1867, prompting recommendation that fort be expanded to provide additional protection for it. Chief product of Pinos Altos area has been copper since eighteenth century—the Santa Rita mines, one of world's largest—is in area—but Central had even better income source. So-called "Butterfield Trail" from fort to Central was nickname for well trod path that led troopers to forbidden pleasures of town. Even in hospital days it was in use—in World War II it became "Burma Trail"—despite World War I order: "Any officer or soldier on duty at, or a patient in, this hospital, is forbidden to enter . . . any saloon or store where intoxicating liquors are sold." Other hog ranch entertainments were similarly prohibited. Central today is study in contrasts with this run-down, almost abandoned main street; modern houses and apartments are being built within one block of this reminder of yesteryear. Central theater building included justice of peace court. One hearing was broken up by defendant who took offense at witness' testimony and filled his breeches with buckshot.

FORT BAYARD today has little left of Army days. Former parade ground is flanked by modern hospital buildings. Occasional overgrown basement foundations and sidewalks that go nowhere are only reminders of military construction. Fort became tuberculosis hospital in 1899, was extensively remodeled when Veterans Administration took charge in 1922. Adobes of early fort had been replaced by 100 permanent buildings before hospital was closed in summer of 1965.

hesitation about crossing the Mexican border when necessary. When Apaches under Victorio attacked the Post at Ojo Caliente in 1879, the department commander reported to Washington: "Major Morrow, of the Ninth Cavalry, is now in pursuit of these Indians, and has subject to his orders about 450 men . . . The whole garrison of Fort Bayard, which is near to these scenes of difficulty, is out after these Indians . . . I consider the force at Bayard quite sufficient to deal with this party of Indians."

Bayard's role in General Crook's second Apache Campaign opened on this note. When the major activity shifted to Pinos Altos area in 1885, Crook moved his headquarters to Bayard for several weeks.

Three years previously, the area was witness to an Apache massacre that attracted national attention, and provided its share of impatience with the Crook management of the campaign. In 1883, Judge and Mrs. McComas were killed on the road 25 miles southwest of the fort, and their six-year-old son, Charlie, kidnapped.

When Crook pushed his troops across the border into Mexico's Sierra Madre mountain two months later, supposedly little Charlie was killed by a squaw during Crook's attack on the camp. Other stories said he was killed shortly after his kidnapping, but the most intriguing came out in 1938.

An archaeological expedition found a lost band of Apaches in Mexico, supposedly remnants of the Geronimo band. They were led by a red-haired, blue-eyed, 60-year-old white man. The white chief knew nothing of the past or of life outside his band, or that Charlie McComas had been red-haired and blue-eyed and, in 1938, would have been 62.

TO GET THERE: From Silver City, N.M., go east on U.S. 260 nine miles to Central. Turn left, follow signs one mile to Fort Bayard Hospital.

FORT WHIPPLE, ARIZONA

The telegraph was still clattering when "Boots and Saddles" precipitated the organized rush of men to the stables and mounts to the parade ground at Whipple Barracks in July, 1882. Hurried orders were barked and four troops of cavalry formed a column-of-twos on the road to the east.

Within four days, Captain Adna Chaffee's Troop I, 6th Cavalry, was to be involved in an Apache ambush and to win it. This was to be their answer to a mid-1882 Apache outbreak and would go down in the records as "The Fight at Chevelon's Fork" or "The Battle of the Big Dry Wash."

The Whipple column split three days after leaving the post, Chaffee taking his troops and eight scouts under Chief Scout Al Sieber in hot pursuit of a band of ranch-burning hostiles. In all there were 14 troops of cavalry from various Arizona forts

on the march, but Chaffee's was to draw the first blood.

As Chaffee moved into the Tonto Basin of eastern Arizona, he knew he was close on the heels of the Apache. So did the Apache. They had counted the number of men on the white horses that comprised his troop, and decided to ambush his numerically inferior command.

What they did not know was that late in the march Chaffee had been reinforced with Troop I, 3rd Cavalry, also a white horse troop. Nor did they know that three more troops were close behind Chaffee.

"The trap was ingeniously laid," described Lieutenant Britton Davis in *The Truth About Geronimo*. "The trail led down into a canyon, a volcanic crack in the earth over a thousand feet deep with almost perpendicular sides. From top to top it was about 700 yards across, with a stream of crystal clear water at the bottom. . . . The hostiles, with their

WHIPPLE WENT by many names, several of them simultaneously, the quartermaster command sometimes termed "Whipple Depot," the troop command "Whipple" or "Prescott Barracks," and the entire installation "Fort" or "Camp Whipple." Visited by Inspector Brevet Brigadier Whittier in January, 1866, in company with touring General McDowell, Whittier's report commented, "The quarters of the men afford comfortable shelter but are not sufficiently commodious or light." He said that at the first opportunity "the men shall commence work upon new quarters. These, like the present one, will be constructed without any expenditure from logs and entirely by the labor of the troops." He said that garrison had been "much engaged with patrols and escort duties" and area around post had been covered with snow until previous week. Although men did not make a good appearance when reviewed, Whittier added, "Taking these facts into consideration, the appearance of the post was as good as to be expected." Stockade itself was about 200 feet square along exterior walls, "of strong undressed pine logs, the crevices being filled in with mud, and the roofs of all the buildings shingled," said surgeon in 1870 report. (Redrawn from Circular No. 4, 1870.)

"AS AT THAT time the Apaches were bad, and the rebels threatening Northern Arizona, it was built as a regular palisade, loopholed block-houses, with salients, etc., to complete," is how Inspector Rusling described Fort Whipple after 1867 visit. "The offices, warehouses, quarters, barracks . . . are continuous, and the post as a whole presents just such a cramped up, confined and huddled appearance, as such a non-descript block-house fort must . . . There are wide cracks in the walls, the chinking having fallen out . . . No board floors except in two or three of the best rooms . . . The quartermaster's office was so penetrated by both wind and rain that I found it impracticable to do business there part of the time when at Whipple. And the quartermaster usually has the best, at any post; if he hasn't, it is his own fault." He found prices high, commented flagstaff was reputed to have cost $10,000 while post's only good building, built for commanding general, cost $100,000 for hewn log construction chinked with mortar. He added that general "humanely declined to occupy it," turning it into hospital until sick could be otherwise cared for.

(W. E. WELLS, "THE ARGONAUTS.")

CAMP WHIPPLE
ARIZ. - 1869

SITE OF ORIGINAL stockade is next to Granite Creek behind fence, marked today by rusted gate from early twentieth century Fort Whipple. Officer's wife in 1871 wrote of post at this site, "It is far from being a handsome post either on the outside or inside, but you know one's content is measured in a great degree by comparison with others that surround you, so we are more than contented with a log house, when we remember that Fort Whipple is one of the few posts in this territory where they have any quarters at all, almost all being quartered in tents, men, women and children. We have fixed up very comfortably, have the carpet on the parlor and gunny sacks on the dining room and bedroom."

plunder from the ranches they had raided and the horses they had stolen, had crossed the canyon, ascended the opposite side to near the top, and . . . building skillfully concealed parapets of loose rocks, they waited for what they supposed was only Chaffee's troop to get down into the canyon, where they would probably have been wiped out to a man."

But Chaffee's scouts had detected the ambush. While the 3d Cavalry white horse troop advanced in a skirmish line as if to go into the canyon, Chaffee took his command and another from the 6th Cavalry on a mile-wide arc around the Indian position. The remaining two troops left on a flanking movement in the other direction.

Two hours passed before the flanking units had negotiated the canyon and worked their respective ways along the opposite side. An Indian party obviously trying to do the same thing was encountered and the exchange of fire alerted—but confused—the Indian main line.

By dark, the battle was over. The bodies of 21 Indians were found. Later it was learned that 54 were in the fight, all of whom were wounded, five fatally.

It was on this note that General Crook arrived in Arizona for his second tour against the Apaches. Taking command of the District of Arizona on September 4, 1882, he spent enough time at district headquarters at Whipple to insure that the paperwork was under control, and then went on a tour of his district. As far as he was concerned, mail and telegraph reports were merely supplements to his personal knowledge of the territory. He moved his field headquarters in order to be at the scene of activity, but his district office remained at Whipple.

This seems to have been the case for most of Whipple's days. Centrally located in Arizona, it had a major influence on every Indian-fighting and

Indian-taming event, whether occuring within shadow of the flagpole or hundreds of miles away.

In December, 1863, John N. Goodwin arrived in Arizona during a snowstorm, went to a spot he was certain was in Arizona—Navajo Springs—and was sworn in as territorial governor. One of his first actions was to proclaim that the capitol would be near the new post the Army was to build, Fort Whipple.

Named for the Army officer who explored the southwest in the 1850's, the new post was started at Del Rio Springs, about 18 miles northeast of modern Prescott.

Governor Goodwin reported that the location was "too far from the mines to afford protection and for pursuit in case of an Indian raid." He recommended that the post be moved in order to stop the increasing abandonment of the mining areas under Indian pressure. "I am disposed to convene the Legislature at a point in the new mines if a post can be established sufficiently near to afford adequate protection."

Goodwin had two threats in mind: Indians and Confederates. Each he felt was sufficient reason that the territorial government should be located next to an Army post. The Army and the capitol moved in May, 1864, to a site which afforded "abundant timber for quarters for the men . . . sufficient grazing for the stock" and which was more convenient to the so-called Whipple Route between the Rio Grande and California.

In October the first session of the legislature was to meet when Goodwin wrote General Carleton, "Our people are becoming quite alarmed at the condition of the Indian affairs and great apprehension is felt that they intend to make a combined raid on us."

Captain A. L. Anderson of the fort sent Carleton two coded letters that warned of the Confederate threat. "I think the rebels will attempt to take this

FORT WHIPPLE IN 1880's can be identified from plat. Main post is at far left, commanding general's new quarters in foreground, department offices the long low building in center. Staff officers' quarters were along hillside at right. In main post, adjutant's office is at left in front of flagpole, old headquarters building next to it, then two storehouses. Officers' row is at right corner of parade ground, barracks on far side of parade.

WHEN POST was rebuilt after being condemned in 1869, it spread along hillside above Granite Creek. Whipple Depot in this plat is on approximate site of original stockade, and old commanding general's quarters were those built in 1866. "The quarters for the officers and their families were poor and unattractive," wrote Colonel James Biddle's wife in 1876. "The staff officers' quarters were better (because newer) than those of the garrison . . . They were all built alike . . . low, broad houses with hall in the center, and two rooms about 16 feet square on each side; pantry and kitchen back, also an attic above. I often looked through the cracks in my house to the light outside." Muslin was tacked on interior walls and wall paper pasted to it in order to reduce open-air condition. Most post buildings were of logs or frame used when still green and subject to warping, splitting, and shrinkage while drying. (Redrawn from McDowell report, 1877.)

POST
TR
DEPOT
ST
LAUN
H
H
ADJ
HQ
NCO
GH
DEPT CG Q
SH
B
OQ
OFF
QM
CH
OQ
COQ
OQ
OMH
OQ

FORT WHIPPLE
ARIZ. – 1877

NEW POST was built in 1904 with designs of architect Stanford White, served as prototype for buildings at many posts. This is along staff officers' quarters row, buildings now used as residences by staff of Veterans Administration Center. Structure is far cry from early days. As late as 1890 surgeon complained of requiring guardhouse prisoners to sleep on floor. In 1868, scurvy hit command, concentrating on cavalrymen as it hospitalized 31 of 183 men in garrison.

country unless they are overawed by a strong force," he said, adding that his garrison was so weak he could not spare a sentinel for the guardhouse. In fact, it was necessary for him to "make prisoners sleep on the sentinel's posts . . . In case of trouble our ammunition would last but a short time."

In December, 1864, a Whipple patrol ambushed two Indian camps, killing 11 of 15 in one, three of seven in the other. In attacking the first camp, the soldiers left their boots behind in order to creep silently as close as possible. The nature of the opposition is hinted by the official report: "The Indians were not alarmed until the very moment when the attack commenced, when they showed fight, but it was of very short duration, whereas they were shot down as fast as powder and lead would admit." One private "slightly wounded in the knee with an arrow . . . was the only casualty sustained on our side."

Crook arrived for his first Apache campaign in 1871. Before leaving Whipple to inspect his other posts, Crook formulated his plans for the vigorous, three-pronged, continuous patrolling that ultimately wore out the foe.

His aide, John G. Bourke, was not impressed by Whipple, according to *On The Border With Crook.* "A ramshackle, tumble-down palisade of unbarked pine logs hewn from the adjacent slopes," he described it. "It was supposed to 'command' something, exactly what I do not remember, as it was so dilapidated that every time the wind rose we were afraid that the palisade was doomed."

TO GET THERE: Fort Whipple, now a Veterans Administration Center, is a mile east of modern Prescott, Arizona, on U.S. 89 and State 69.

FORT BOWIE, ARIZONA

The circle completed itself at Fort Bowie, Apache Pass, Arizona.

The Apache Wars that began with the "Bascom Incident" at Apache Pass in 1861 ended when a railroad car pulled out of Bowie Station in 1886. Geronimo and his band were aboard, the last of the Apaches to bring terror and bloodshed to the Southwest.

As early as 1851, the strategic value was recognized of Apache Pass. The Bartlett Boundary Commission endured a trying climb through the pass to come upon "a beautiful amphitheatre among the mountains," Bartlett wrote. They "discovered a spring and fine pool of water . . . We gladly pitched our tents near a beautiful grove of oaks . . . the most eligible camping ground we had yet met with."

This was the future site of Camp Bowie. In the dawning days of westward emigration, the spring played a vital role in providing the water necessary for a shortcut between two longer routes. The drawback was the pass' reputation as the most likely location for Indian attacks. Bleached animal bones and clumps of human graves along the route supported this reputation.

A stage station began operating in the pass in 1857. A 45- by 55-foot stone corral provided protection from Indians. Portholes were in each stall for shooting purposes against attackers from the outside.

Cochise and upwards of 1,200 Indians camped in the area. Although raids on the stages were frequent, relations with Cochise usually were amicable. The Indians found that by staying friendly and providing firewood for the post, they would receive money in return. And money meant trading for a bottle of the favorite liquor: Castor oil.

The shaky peace ended with the 1861 attempt by a new lieutenant to arrest Cochise. This was the "Bascom Incident" described in the pages regarding Fort Buchanan. It opened a period of unrestrained raiding against stage and wagon train travel that increased when the Army left at the start of the Civil War. Cochise took the soldiers' departure to mean that he had won.

The arrival of 140 men of the California Column in 1862 was welcomed by Cochise by promising Lieutenant Colonel Edward E. Eyre "that neither my men nor animals should be molested," Eyre reported. He asked for tobacco and something to eat" and it was agreed that there would be another meeting at sundown.

There was no second meeting because shortly the bodies of three soldiers were found, "stripped of all their clothing and two of them were scalped." Unsuccessfull pursuit of the Indians followed. The three men were buried at the camp side, "the entire command being present."

Three weeks later, 126 men under Captain Thomas L. Roberts arrived at the pass. They found the three graves of the Eyre party after fighting their way through an Apache ambush. The Californians gave the Indians "a warm reception, my men killing four of them," Roberts reported. He was supported by two prairie howitzers which blasted the Indian positions among the rocks.

After fighting his way through to the spring, Roberts found he had to fight to stay there. "The Indians seemed very loath to let me have water," he commented, "and fought determinedly, but they found

FORT BOWIE
ARIZ. - 1889

AFTER FINAL surrender of Geronimo, Fort Bowie continued to be active until 1894, mainly devoting time to hunting small gangs of renegade Indians, especially notorious Apache Kid. He roamed almost at will through southern Arizona for six years with the cavalry hot on his trail, but there is no definite evidence that he was ever caught or killed, despite tales to the contrary. He was once an Apache scout and his knowledge of Army training helped him elude the Army. This is the ground plan of Fort Bowie during the time Apache Kid was a major nemesis. Most buildings were of adobe, many of them covered by wooden siding. Parade ground measured 450 by 350 feet on a straight line—somewhat more if the slopes were taken into count. (Redrawn from National Park Service plat.)

FORT BOWIE, September 8, 1886, the day that Geronimo and his band left the Southwest permanently, saw Fourth Cavalry band drawn up next to flagpole to play "Auld Lang Syne." This is how post looked that day. Tents were for reinforcements used for final Geronimo pursuit and also for cordon of guards Miles threw around reservation to prevent angry settlers from invoking "lynch law" on Apache prisoners. This photograph was taken from hillside north of post looking from northwest to southeast corners. Commanding Officer's double-story frame quarters is at far corner; Crook occupied these during second Apache campaign. Cavalry barracks are along far side of parade to left of flagpole, officers' quarters are right of flagpole. Infantry barracks are at far right edge of picture headquarters building is to its left; building at near corner is storehouse and old hospital with telegraph office tucked into its right rear. Guardhouse is building in foreground with windows set high in wall.

FORT BOWIE TODAY includes these elaborate ruins, somewhat dwarfed by camera lens, however. This view approximates that of 1886. Bakery is in foreground, although guardhouse which originally next to it has disappeared. Large ruins at right edge probably were post trader's. When Miles arrived for Apache campaign, he established heliograph station atop Bowie Peak with which to communicate by flashing mirror to 26 other stations, 13 of them in Arizona and 13 in New Mexico. Total of 802 messages were transmitted for Fort Bowie in addition to 1,644 relayed by the station to other stations.

us too much for them; but they kept us from the water until after 4 p.m." In order to clear the rocks above the spring, Roberts had to send flanking patrols up "on either side of the canyon, shelling the high points ahead of them."

Victory still was not his. A six-man patrol was sent back to bring the wagon train to the springs, but encountered an ambush by 40 Apaches. The running fight ended only after a lucky shot wounded Chief Mangas Colorado and the Indians lost interest.

The next morning, with the whole command finally together at the springs, Roberts found he had to fight again to stay there. The Indians had reoccupied the rocky heights and it took another artillery bombardment to drive them out.

In this two-day affair that cost two soldiers killed and two wounded, Roberts estimated he had killed nine Indians. This "Battle of Apache Pass" was far more costly to the Apaches than Roberts' estimate, however. Later, an Indian participant said that 63 warriors had been killed, 60 of them by the artillery. "We would have done well enough if you had not fired wagons at us," he complained.

The lesson learned by the California Column was that if Apache Pass and its springs were to be of use, "a force sufficient to hold the water and pass should be stationed there, otherwise every command will have to fight for water, and . . . are almost certain to lose some lives," Roberts advised. General Carleton agreed while inspecting the site personally and on the spot he issued orders for two companies of the Fifth California Volunteers to build a fort there. "Cause the Apache Indians to be attacked whenever and wherever he may find them near his post," the new commanding officer was ordered.

With only 40 men available, and 21 of them needed for the guard, Major Theodore A. Coult set to work on a hill that dominated the springs. Within three weeks, Coult had an elaborate cantonment about 100 by 80 feet square surrounded by rock breastworks four-and-a-half feet high, between two and three feet thick.

"The total length of wall around the post is 412 feet," Coult reported. "The works are not of any regular forms, my only object being to build defenses which could speedily be completed, and at the same time possess the requisites of sheltering their defenders, commanding every approach to the hill, and protecting each other by flank fires along their faces."

Tents and a 14-foot square stone guardhouse provided shelter for the garrison inside the enclosure. The guardhouse was a "last stand" redoubt that was loopholed on two sides.

A year later, it was reported that the temporary cantonment was little improved. "The quarters, if it is not an abuse of language to call them such, have been constructed without system, regard to health, defense, or convenience. Those occupied by the men are mere hovels, mostly excavations in the side hill, damp, illy ventilated, and covered with decomposed granite taken from the excavation, through which the rain passes very much as it would through a sieve. By the removal of a few tents, the place would present more the appearance of a California digger rancheria than a military post."

The Bowie garrison was changed regularly because of its primitive and dangerous situation. In two years it had six different commanding officers. None of this contributed to an improvement in the post nor to effective patrolling against the Apaches, although dozens of actions took place.

In 1868, the post was moved to a plateau southeast of the camp. Construction began on an adobe fort that would include three dozen structures before abandonment in 1894.

General Crook visited the post in 1871 at the start of his first Apache campaign, but action was suspended while Colyer and General O. O. Howard tried to negotiate with Cochise. In 1872, Howard and Tom Jefford—former mail supervisor of the Bowie-to-Tucson route and a friend of Cochise—met with the Chief and were able to reach an agreement that Cochise kept until his death in 1876. Bowie's troopers were deployed elsewhere during the first Apache campaign.

Political in-fighting over the Indian Agent's job disturbed the peace of Cochise after his death. By 1876, ten troops of cavalry and two companies of Indian scouts concentrated at Bowie. Geronimo and other chiefs broke out but returned in 1879.

When they left again in 1882, Crook came to settle the Apache issue once and for all. His field headquarters were at Bowie.

The surrender of a Geronimo warrior was the key. He agreed to lead Crook from Bowie into the Sierra Madre mountains of Mexico, Geronimo's stronghold. By this time, the United States and Mexico had signed a treaty that permitted pursuit of hostile Indians across the border. Crook took advantage of this at the head of a column that included Captain Adna Chaffee's I troop, 6th Cavalry, and 193 Apache scouts.

In a month and a half, Crook's expedition surprised one camp, killed nine warriors, and met with Geronimo and the other chiefs. After several days of verbal sparring, Crook bluntly told the Indians that either they accompany him back to the reservations, or await certain slaughter by Mexican troops that were nearing their camp.

That did the trick and the expedition returned to the states with 325 Apaches. Some stragglers took almost a year and several Bowie patrols before they, too, returned to the reservation.

The final outbreak came in the spring of 1885 at the height of the bickering between the Interior and War Departments as to who had final authority on the reservations. Written agreements that discipline rested with the Army commander were challenged by several Agents. The dissension provided the Apaches with the excuse they needed. A tizwin drunk on May 15, 1885, signalled the outbreak of Geronimo, 42 warriors, and 92 women and children.

Crook set up his headquarters again at Bowie on June 11, 1885. A second Sierra Madre campaign seemed to do nothing more than drive the Apaches back into the United States. Bloody raiding took place in a region protected by 83 companies of troops and General Sheridan himself came to Fort Bowie.

He could offer no solution to the problem because Crook actually had things under control. It was just a matter of time before the elusive Apache would be run down. This took place in 1886 about ten miles south of the border. Crook met with Geronimo after several false starts, and obtained the chief's promise to surrender.

Mescal peddled by a whiteman got to Geronimo the night before he was to return with Crook. Thirty-

WATER SYSTEM at Fort Bowie is still prominent. Water was pumped from Bear Spring into several reservoirs on post. This concrete-lined excavation is the remains of large reservoir behind commanding officer's house. In his 1869 report, surgeon predicted that Bear Spring, three-quarters of a mile from post, would be better source of water than Apache Pass spring. A report in 1872 said post "is supplied with water of excellent quality from a spring about 500 yards distant," but ultimately Bear Spring plan won.

five men, women, and children broke out for the Sierra Madre. The remaining 60 accompanied the troops to Fort Bowie.

In the aftermath, Crook and Sheridan exchanged a series of telegrams that were variously sarcastic, angry, and explanatory. One issue was Washington's failure to approve Crook's reasonable peace terms. Finally Crook said that if he could not be backed up, he should be relieved. Sheridan acted immediately, replacing Crook with Nelson A. Miles.

Miles reached Bowie Station, north of the post, on April 12, 1886, and found a battalion of the 2d Cavalry in camp "in a very unsatisfactory condition," he commented in his *Personal Recollections.* "They appeared to be not only discouraged but thoroughly disheartened. They had been in the field a long time doing most disagreeable and hazardous duty . . . The citizens and settlers . . . were the most terror-stricken people I had ever seen . . ."

Miles' solution was to strengthen the outpost system and organize an expedition into Mexico.

The expedition was headed by Captain Henry W. Lawton and included Captain Leonard Wood as surgeon, plus a company of infantry, 35 cavalrymen, and 20 Indian scouts. Except for flushing out the hostiles once, the expedition did not make contact with Geronimo. Its 1,400-mile close pursuit was effective in wearing down the tiny band. After several councils with Lieutenant Charles B. Gatewood, whom they respected and who had been led to them by former warrior, they agreed to surrender if they could talk with Miles.

Miles met Geronimo in Skeleton Canyon, 65 miles southeast of Fort Bowie. After their discussions culminated in Geronimo's surrender, Miles left for Fort Bowie.

"This is the fourth time I have surrendered," Geronimo commented to Miles on the way.

"And I think it is the last time you will ever have occasion to surrender," Miles answered. He was right. On September 8, 1886, Geronimo and his band left for the train and temporary imprisonment in Florida and for all intents and purposes the Indian Wars of the Southwest were over.

TO GET THERE: Bowie, Arizona, is on State 86 about 25 miles east of Willcox. In Bowie, at marker on north side of highway, turn south on gravel road. Go 12 miles to fork with sign "Chiricahua National Monument." Go left. In two miles, take right fork into canyon. Signs indicate "Old Fort Bowie." At head of canyon, follow trail on foot up hillside to fort site, one-half mile further. Signs indicate this is private property of L. C. Knapp and Earl Neel who ask that visitors treat the fort site with respect.

CAVALRY BARRACKS 120 feet long, is in rear in this view along eastern side of parade ground. Corner in immediate foreground is cavalry barracks that were on northern side of parade ground. In distant background, right of center is chimney that marks site of commanding officer's quarters. Tom Jefford, famed Indian agent, was familiar sight around Bowie before he became agent. After Civil War, he was superintendent of mail line between Tucson and Bowie for 18 months until he quit in disgust over Army failure to prevent Indian raids that killed 14 mail riders in that period.

This listing of 545 forts and fort-type places of the Far West is a complete revision of data that appeared in previous volumes of the *Forts of the Old West* series. This has been made possible by the cooperation of readers who provided information and sources not previously available.

All forts at which the military were stationed are eligible for this directory, and, it is hoped, most of them are included. The term "fort" has been used loosely in order to include everything from temporary camps to permanent installations. The mere notation of a camp name in an official report to higher headquarters frequently is the reason that a site is included that was considerably less than permanent.

Many of the non-Army places are included because they were used by militia or semi-military civil forces. Others provided protection to settlers or traders. In appearance many of them came closer to the common image of a "fort" than did official ones. For the sake of completeness, these non-Army forts are mentioned, although no claim is made that all are included. An asterisk identifies these.

The various sources in the Bibliography were drawn upon for this list. When names, locations, or dates were hazy or missing, a studied guess has been made to supply the missing data. When even this failed in locating a site, the description from the records is given with the hope that it will aid someone more familiar with local terms. The task was further complicated by the shifts of state and territorial boundaries during the period of military activity in the southwest. This caused a site to be in a different state than the one by which it is noted in the records.

The most common name is that by which a fort is listed. Its other names are listed below it. The abbreviations are those explained on the endsheet maps with one exception. The letters "PNB" mean "probably never built"—for forts noted on old maps and in old records, but which do not seem to have been officially established or occupied. The locations often are in reference to modern towns that did not exist at the same time as did the forts.

ARIZONA

Apache, Ft.	Near Fort Apache	1870-1922
(Cp. Ord, Cp. Mogollon, Cp. Thomas)		
Badger, Ft.	Junction Verde & Salado R.	c. 1866
Barrett, Ft.	Maricopa vicinity	1862
Beale's Spring, Cp.	40 mi. NE Ft. Mojave	1871-74
Bear Springs, Cp. at	Near Williams	1863-64
Blue Water Stn., Cp.	13 mi. E. Casa Grande	1864
Bowie, Ft.	S Bowie	1862-94
Buchanan, Ft.	Near Sonoita	1856-61
(Cp. Moore)		
Cameron, Cp.	#1 at Calabasas	1866-67
	#2 15 mi. NE Tubac	
Canada del Oro, Ft.	13 mi. N Tucson	1862
Canby, Ft.	28 mi. SW Ft. Defiance	1863-64
Canon de Chelly, Ft.	2 mi. NW mouth of canyon	1849
Casa Blanco, Cp.	Vic. Cp. Crittenden	1863
Cienega de Sauz, Cp.	11 mi. SE San Simon	1862
Clovedale, Cp. near	On border, SW Arizona	1822-86
Colorado, Cp.	40 mi. N LaPaz on river	1868-71
Colorado Chiquito, Cp.	Vic. Canyon Diablo town	1863
Crawford, Cp.	Chiracahua Mts., Cochise Co.	1886
Crittenden, Cp.	Near Ft. Buchanan site	1868-73
Date Creek, Cp. #1	3 mi. NE Date Creek	1867
Date Creek, Cp. #2	Date Creek	1867-73
(Cp. McPherson)		
Defiance, Ft.	Fort Defiance	1851-61
Ehrenberg, Det. at	Ehrenberg	c. 1875
El Reventon, Cp.	7 mi. NE Tubac	1862-64
(Cp. Reventon)		
Florilla, Cp.	Near Ft. Canby	1864
Galen, Cp.	60 mi. from Yuma (Confederate)	1862
Gaston, Old Ft.	Colorado R. above Gila R.	c. 1867

Goodwin, Cp.	N Geronimo	1864
Goodwin, Ft.	W Geronimo	1864-71
Grant, Ft. #1	Mouth San Pedro R., then 10 mi. NW Mammoth	1860-61; 62; 65-72
(Ft. Arivaypa, Ft. Breckenridge, Ft. Stanford)		
Grant, Ft. #2	Near Mt. Graham	1872-1907
(New Cp. Grant)		
Grassy Camp, Cp.	3 mi. E Grinnell's	1862
Grinnell's Stn., Det.	Vic. Aztec, 85 mi. E Yuma	1862
Huachuca, Ft.	Fort Huachuca	1877-1947; 50-53; 54-
Hualpai, Cp.	40 mi. NW Prescott	1869-73; 81
(Cp. Devin, Cp. Toll Gate)		
Ilges, Cp.	3 mi. S Ft. McDowell	1867
Jacob's Well, Cp. at	Vic. Sanders	1863
John A. Rucker, Cp.	SE Corner of state	1878
(Cp. Supply, Cp. Powers)		
John A. Rucker, Cp.	6 mi. White River	1878-80
Lake Carleton, Cp.	Vic. Mormon Lake	PNB
La Paz, Cp.	N Ehrenberg	1864; 74-75
Lemon Ranch, Cp.		1864
Lewis, Cp.	26 mi. E Cp. Verde	c. 1865-70
Lincoln, Cp.	Near La Paz	1864
Lowell, New Ft.	7 mi. E Tucson	1873-91
Lowell, Old Ft.	Tucson	1860-61; 62; 62-64; 65-73
(Pt. of Tucson, Cp. Tucson)		
Mansfield, Cp.	7 mi. S Ft. Defiance	1863
Maricopa Wells, Pt.	Maricopa vicinity	1865-67
Mason, Ft.	E. Ruby	1865-66
(Ft. McKeen, Pt. at Calabasas)		
McCleave, Cp.	24 mi. NW Ft. Goodwin	1864
*McDonald, Ft.	E Payson	1882
McDowell, Ft.	N Phoenix	1865-90
(Campo Verde)		
*Milligan, Ft.	1 mi. E. Eagar	n.d.
Mission Camp, Det.	35 mi. E Yuma, vic. Welton	1862
Mojave, Ft.	15 mi. N Needles, Calif.	
(Cp. Colorado, Ft. "Navajo")		
*Moroni, Cp.	6 mi. N Flagstaff	1882
(Ft. Rickerson, Ft. Valley)		
Nogales, Cp. near	Nogales	1887-88
O'Connell, Cp.	Tonto Valley	1808
Ojo de les Lemilas, Pt.	100 mi. NW Ft. Defiance	c. 1860
Patagonia, Cp. at	Patagonia	1862
(Cp. at Mowry's Silver Mines)		
Picket Post, Cp.	25 mi. W Superior	1871
Pinal, Cp.	2 mi. W Superior	1870-71
(Infantry Camp, Pinal Mts.)		
Price, Cp.	5 mi. W Paradise	1881-83
Rawlins, Cp.	27 mi. NW Prescott	1870-71
Reno, Cp.	S Tonto Basin town	1867-70
Rigg, Cp.	N Safford	c. 1864-70
Rio Gila, Cp. on	Sacaton	1866
Rio San Francisco, Cp.	Verde river	1863
Rio San Pedro, Cp.	Vic. Redington	1859
Robinson's Ranch, Cp. at	Rillito	1864
Rock Spring, Ft.	7 mi. NW Valentine	PNB
San Bernardino Springs, Cp.	On border, 18 mi. E Douglas	1883
San Carlos, Pt. at	San Carlos Reservation	1871-1900
San Pedro Presidio, Cp.	Near Cp. Wallen	c. 1878
(Picket Post on the San Pedro)		
San Pedro River, Cp	Old Cp. Grant site	1865-66
San Simon, Cp.	San Simon	1862
Skull Valley, Cp.	25 mi. N Date Creek #1	1867
(New Cp. Date Creek)		
Smith, Cp.	2.5 mi. N Ft. Goodwin	1864
Solomonsville, Cp. at	Solomon	1867
Sunset, Cp.	6 mi. E Winslow	c. 1858-c. 1882
Supply, Cp.	2 mi. E Holbrook	1863

Thomas, Ft.	N Fort Thomas	1876-92
(New Post on the Gila)		
Tonto, Cp.		1864
Tubac, Cp.	Tubac	1862-65; 65; 67-68
Tucson, Cp. near	Tucson	1859
Turkey Creek, Cp. at	17 mi. SW Ft. Apache	1882
Verde, Ft. #1	1 mi. N Camp Verde	1864-71
(Cp. Lincoln)		
Verde, Ft. #2	Camp Verde	1871-90
(New Cp. Verde)		
Wallen, Cp.	SE Elgin	1866-69
(New Pt. at Babocomari Ranch, New Post on Upper San Pedro)		
Whipple, Ft. #1	24 mi. NE Prescott	1863-64
(Cp. Pomeroy, Cp. Clark)		
Whipple, Ft. #2	E Prescott	1864-98; 1902-13
(Prescott Bks , Whipple Bks., Whipple Depot)		
Wickenburg, Pt. at	Wickenburg	c. 1866
Willow Grove, Cp.	Near Wikieup	1867-69
Wright, Cp.	On site Ft. Grant #1	1865
Yuma, Pt. at	Yuma	1885; 1911-13; 15-22
Yuma Depot	Yuma	1864-85

CALIFORNIA

Adobe Meadows, Cp. at	Vic. Benton	1862
Alcatraz, Cp. at	Alcatraz Island	1859-95
Alcatraz Prison Pt.	Alcatraz Island	1895-1934
Alert, Cp.	San Francisco	1861-62
Anderson, Ft.	NE Arcata	1862-66
Antelope Cr., Det. at	12 mi NE Sacramento	1865
Armstrong, Cp.	Vic. Leggett	1861
Babbitt, Cp.	Visalia	1862-66
Baker, Ft.	N side SF Bay entrance	1897-
(Fortification at Lime Pt.)		
Baker, Ft.	NE Bridgeville	1862-63; 64-66
Banning, Cp.	San Bernardino	1859
Banks, Cp.	Detroit	n.d.
Bear Valley, Cp. in	Mariposa	1864
Benicia, Posts at	Benicia	1851-1964
(Bks., Quartermaster Depot, Arsenal, Subsistence Depot)		
Bidwell, Cp.	Chico	1863-65
(Cp. Chico, Det. at Chico)		
Bidwell, Ft.	Fort Bidwell	1865-93
(Det. at Surprise Valley)		
Bishop Cr., Cp. at	Bishop	1863
Bitter Springs, Cp.	20 mi. WNW Baker	1859-60
Blunt Pt., Det. at	Angel Island, S.F. Bay	1863-65
Boynton's Prairie, Cp. at	E Eureka	1864
Bragg, Ft.	Fort Bragg	1857-64
Burnt Ranch, Cp. at	30 mi. N Hoopa	1864
Burton, Cp.	Near San Diego	1855
Butte Cr., Cp. near		1856
Cady, Cp.	Harvard Stn., Mojave desert c. 1856; 59-60; 63-64; 65-66; 66-71	
(Depot on the Mojave)		
Cajon, Cp.	15 mi. from Cajon Pass	1857-58
Calhoun, Ft.	Near Yuma	c. 1849
Calicienga Rancheria, Cp. at		
Callahan's Ranche, Cp. at	20 mi. S Ft. Jones	1855
Canoe Cr., Cp. on		1855
Cap-Ell, Ft.	15 mi. SSE Ft. Terwaw	1856
Carleton, New Cp.	10 mi. E Los Angeles	1862
(Cp. at El Monte)		
Carleton, Old Cp.	Near San Bernardino	1861
Cass, Cp.	Near Red Bluffs	1858-59
Chouchille, Cp. on	Vic. Chowchilla?	1856
Colusa, Det. at	Colusa	1865
Cook, Cp.		n.d.
Coster, Cp.	Near Cp. Independence	c. 1867
Crane, Cp.	Sierra Nevada Mts.	1852
Crescent City, Cp.	Crescent City	1856
Crook, Ft.	1.5 mi. from Glenburn	1857-69
(Cp. Hollenbush)		

Cucamonga Ranch, Cp. at Cp. Coco Mungo)	Cucamonga	c. 1850; 64
Curtis, Cp.	N Arcata	1862-65
Dalsy's Ferry, Det.	N Ft. Humboldt	1863
*Defiance, Ft.	4 mi. S Ft. Yuma	c. 1850
Downey, Cp.	Oakland	1861
*Dick, Ft.	Fort Dick	PNB
Dragoon Bridge, Cp.	Honey Lake Valley	1860-63
Drum Bks.	Wilmington	1862-71
(Cp. Drum, Wilmington Depot, Cp. Near San Pedro, Cp. New San Pedro)		
El Chino, Cp.	Chino	1862
Elk Camp, Cp. at	15 mi. NW Ft. Anderson	1862
Far West, Ct.	E Wheatland	1849-52
Fitzgerald, Cp.	Near Los Angeles	1861
Fitzgerald, Cp.	20 mi. SSW Ft. Yuma	1855
Fork of Salmon R., Cp. at	Forks of Salmon	1864
Frederica, Cp.	"150 mi. E. Monterey"	1850
Friday's Stn., Det. at	Near Lake Tahoe	1864
Gaston, Ft.	Hoopa	1858-92
Giftaler Ranch, Cp.	13.5 mi. SE Temecula	1863
Gilmore, Cp.	4 mi. N Trinidad	1863-64
Gold Bluffs, Dets.	Between Klamath & Orick	1863-64
Goose Lake, Cp. at	Goose Lake	1866
Grant, Cp.	Near Scotia	1863-65
Guejarros, Ft.	N side San Diego Bay	c. 1779-1849?
(Ft. Castillo Guijarros, Ft. Pio Pico)		
Halleck, Cp.	Stockton	1862-63
Hay Fork, Cp. at	Hayfork	1864
Hill, Ft.	Monterey	c. 1849
Hooker, Cp.	Near Stockton	1862
Hornitos, Cp. near	18 mi. NE Merced	1865
Hot Creek Stn., Cp.	35 mi. SW Ft. Crook	1862
Humboldt, Ft.	Eureka	1853-66
Iaqua, Cp.	Vic. Kneeland	1863-66
(Cp. Jaqua)		
Independence, Cp.	S Ft. Yuma	1850-51
Independence, Cp.	2 mi. S Independence	1862-77
Ione City, Cp. near	Near Ione City	1864-65
(Cp. Jackson)		
Johns, Cp.	Near Susanville	1864
Jones, Ft.	Fort Jones	1852-58; 64
Jurupa, Ft.	Riverside	1852-54
(Ft. Rancho de Jurupa, Ft. Fremont)		
J. W. Anderson, Ft.	4 mi. S Sacramento	1849
Kellogg, Cp.	Near Ft. Latham	1862
Kline's Ranch, Det.	Vic. Los Angeles	1862
Laguna Grande, Cp.	Elsinore.	1862
Latham, Cp.	Los Angeles & Santa Monica	1862
Lava Beds, Cp. in	SW shore Tule Lake	1873
(Gen. Gillam's Camp)		
Leonard, Cp.	15 mi. NE Keysville	1863
Lighthouse Pt., Det.	Humboldt Bay	1865
Lincoln, New Cp.	6 mi. N Crescent City	1862-69
(Lincoln's Ft., Ft. Lincoln, Cp. Long, Long's Ft.)		
Lincoln, Old Cp.	Near Crescent City	1862
Lippitt, Ft.	Near Ft. Humboldt	1862
Liscombe's Hill, Cp.	Blue Lake	c. 1865
Lone Pine, Det. at	Lone Pine	1862
Los Angeles, Pt. at	Los Angeles	1847-49; 61-65
Low, Cp.	10 mi. S Watsonville	c. 1865
(Det. at San Juan)		
Lyon, Ft.	20 mi. SE Arcata	1862
Mare Is. Navy Yd., Det. at	San Francisco Bay	1861-62
Marl Springs, Cp.	Mojave desert S Baker	1866-67
Mason, Ft.	San Francisco	1863-
(Ft. Point San Jose, Black Point)		
Mattole, Cp.	24 mi. W Weott	1864
McClear, Ft.	"Ferguo R."	c. 1851
McClellan, Cp.	Near Placerville	1861
McDougal, Cp.	Near Stockton	c. 1863
McDowell, Cp.	?	1864
Merchant, Cp.	Oakland	c. 1863
Miller, Cp.	Presidio, San Francisco	1898

Miller, Ft.	Millerton	1851-58; 63-64
(Cp. Barbour)		
Monterey Posts:	Monterey	
(Ft. Mervine, Pt. of Monterey, Ord Bks., Ft. Savannah, Ft. Cape of Pines, Ft. Stockton)		
Presidio		c. 1770
Monterey Redoubt		1847-52
Ordnance Depot		1852-56
Bks		1865-66
Montgomery, Ft.	San Francisco	1846-47
Moore, Ft.	Los Angeles	1847-63
Morris, Cp.	San Bernardino	1863
Mulgrave, Ft.		c. 1848
Newkirk's Mill, Det.	Near Ft. Gaston	1864
New Supply Cp.	Near Newell	1873
(Boyle's Camp)		
Nome Lackee, Cp.	16 mi. W Corning	1855-58
Old Supply Cp.	5.5 mi. S Newell	1873
Olney, Cp.	3 mi. SE Van Duzen	1862
Onion Valley, Cp. in	N Downieville	1860
Orleans Bar, Det. at	Orleans	1864
Pardee's Ranche, Cp	On "Old Trinity Trail"	1858
Pierson's Ranche, Cp. at	Colusa County	1865
Piute, Ft.	20 mi. SW Searchlight, Nev.	1860; 66-68
(Ft. Beale, Ft. Piute Hill)		
Point, Ft.	San Francisco	1853-1906
(Ft. Blanco, Castillo de San Joaquin, Old Ft. Scott)		
*Pool's Fort	20 mi. SE Fresno	n.d.
Prentiss, Cp.	Near San Bernardino	1859
Rancho del Chino	Chino	1850-52
Reading, Ft.	10 mi. SE Redding	1852-67
Redwood, Cp.	10 mi. SW Ft. Cap-Ell	1862
Reed's Ranch, Det.	SE Ft. Humboldt	1862
Resting Spring, Cp.	5 mi. E Tecopa	1859-60
Reynolds, Cp.	Angel Island, San Francisco	
(Ft. McDowell, Pt. of Angel Island)		1863-1946
Riley, Cp.	S San Diego	1849
Rock Springs, Cp.	Mojave Desert	1859-60; 63; 67-68
*Ross, Ft.	30 mi. N Bodega Bay	1812-41
San Bernardino, Cp.	San Bernardino	1855; 61
San Bernardino, Pt.	Dead Man's Is., Wilmington	1858
San Diego Posts:	San Diego	
(Ft. Stockton, Presidio of San Diego, Ft. San Diego, Garrison at San Diego)		
San Diego, Pt. at	Old San Diego	1849-52
Pt. Mission San Diego	Mission San Diego	1852-58
New San Diego Bks.	Downtown San Diego	1858-66; 69-1903
Rosecrans, Ft.	Ballast Point	1899-1950
San Felipe, Cp. at	15 mi. SE Watsonville	1855
San Francisco, Presidio of	San Francisco	1776 (Spanish); 1847-51; 51-
San Jose, Cp.	San Jose	1848; 63
San Luis Obispo, Det. at	San Luis Obispo	1864
San Luis Rey, New Cp.	Mission San Luis Rey	1850-52
San Luis Rey, Old Cp.	5 mi. S Mission San Luis Rey	1847-49
San Miguel, Cp.	Tulare Valley	1849
San Pedro, Cp. near	San Pedro	1892
Santa Barbara, Cp.	Santa Barbara	1847-48; 64
Santa Catalina Is., Cp.	Santa Catalina Island	1864
Santa Isabel, Cp.	Near Lake Henshaw	1851
Sequoia National Park, Cp. (Cp. at Mineral King)	Sequoia Park	1886-1916
Seward, Ft.	Fort Seward	1862-63
(Camp on Eel River)		
Sigel, Cp.	Near Auburn	1861-62
Soda, Ft.	Soda Lake, S Baker	1860; 66-68
(Hancock Redoubt, Cp. Soda Lake)		
Soldier's Grove, Cp.	18 mi. from Hyampon	1864
Sonoma, Cp.	Sonoma	1847-48; 48; 50-51; 51
Stanford, Cp.	Stockton	1863
Stanislaus, Cp.	20 mi. from Stockton	c. 1848
Steele, Cp.	Merced R.	1852
Sugar Loaf, Cp.	On Mojave R.	1858
Sumner, Cp.	Near Presidio, San Francisco	1861
Sutter's Fort, Cp. at	Sacramento	1847; 49-50
(Redoubts at Sacramento)		
Swasey, Cp.	Hydesville	1862
Taylor, Cp.	8 mi. SE Ft. Crook	1859
Tejon, Ft.	N Lebec	1854-61; 63-64
Temecula, Cp. near	Temecula	1862
Terwaw, Ft.	Klamath Glen	1857-62
Tulare, Cp.	Tulare Indian Reservation	1871
Union, Cp. #1	Across R. from Sacramento	1861
Union, Cp. #2	Near Suttersville	1861-66
Waite, Cp.	SE Red Bluff	c. 1863-65
Weller, Ft.	7 mi. N Calpella	1859-60
Whitney Mt. Stn.	Mt. Whitney	1883
Whistler, Cp.		1858
Wool, Ft.	140 mi. above mo. Klamath R.	1855
(Cp. Strowbridge)		
Worth, Cp.	5 mi. from Lighthouse Pt.	c. 1863
Wright, Cp.	Covelo	1861-75; 87
Wright, Cp.	Near San Francisco	1861
Wright, Cp. #1	Warner's Ranch	1861
Wright, Cp. #2	Oak Grove, 12 mi. W #1	1861-66
Yager Creek Crossing, Cp. at	Vic. Hydesville	1862
Yerba Buena Is., Cp.	San Francisco Bay	1868-c. 1880
Yosemite National Park, Det. at (Ft. Yosemite)	Yosemite Park	1886-1916
Yuma, Ft.	Across from Yuma, Ariz.	1849-51; 52-85

COLORADO

Bent's Old Fort	7 mi. E La Junta	1832-52
(Ft. Brent)		
Cedar Point, Ft.	Vic. Limon	1867-68
Chambers, Ft.	Boulder Valley	c. 1864
Collins, Cp.	Near LaPorte	1863-64
Collins, Ft.	Fort Collins	1864-67
(New Cp. Collins)		
Crawford, Ft.	8 mi. S Montrose	1880-90
(Ct. on the Uncompahgre)		
*Defiance, Ft.	Garfield county	c. 1879
Denver Depot & Arsenal	Denver	1859-65
*El Puebla, Ft.	Bent county	c. 1839
*El Pueblo, Ft.	Pueblo	1842-54
Evans, Cp.	2.5 mi. NE Denver	c. 1864
Fillmore, Cp.	2 mi. W Boone	c. 1864-65
Flagler, Ft.	2 mi. N Durango	1879
*Francisco, Ft.	La Veta	1861
Garland, Ft.	Fort Garland	1858-83
Gilpin, Cp.	Central City	1861
Gray's Ranch Stn.	20 mi. NE Trinidad	1864
Las Pinos, Cp. near	Cathedral	1880
Latham, Ft.	6 mi. S Kersey	c. 1864
Lewis, Ft. #1	Pagosa Springs	1878-80
(Ct. Pagosa Springs)		
Lewis, Ft. #2	S Durango	1880-91
(Ct. on Rio de la Plata)		
Lincoln, Cp.	19 mi. S. Castle Rock	1864
Livingston, Cp.	Near Julesburg	c. 1835
Logan, Ft.	SE Denver	1889-1946
(Ft. Sheridan, Cp. near Denver, Pt. near Denver)		
Lupton, Ft.	N Fort Lupton	c. 1864
(Ft. Lancaster)		
Lyon, New Ft.	Fort Lyon	1867-89
Mackall, Cp.	Round Valley	1857-58
Massachusetts, Ft.	6 mi. N Ft. Garland	1852-58
Monument Dell, Cp.	Monument	1869-70
Morgan, Ft.	Fort Morgan	1864-68
(Cp. Tyler, Pt. of Junction Stn., Pt. of Junction, Ft. Wardwell)		

*Narraguinnep, Ft.	25 mi. NW Dolores	1885
*Old Stone Fort	Monument	1865-68
Pike's Peak, Stn. on	Pike's Peak	c. 1873
Pike's Stockade	Canon City	1807
Pueblo, Cp. at	Pueblo	1846-47
Pueblo, Pt. of	N Pueblo	1867
Reed's Springs, Pt.	8 mi. NNW Ramah	1867
Reynolds, Ft.	E Pueblo	1867-72
(Marcy's Camp)		
Rio Mancos, Ct. on	Vic. Ft. Lewis #2	1880
Sanborn, Cp.	Orchard	1864-65
(Cp. at Fremont's Orchard)		
Sedgwick, Ft.	Near Julesburg	1864-71
(Cp. Rankin, Pt. at Julesburg, Stn.)		
Soda Springs, Cp.	4 mi. W Leadville	1838
St. Felipe, Cp.		1855
*St. Vrain, Ft.	6 mi. NW Platteville	c. 1837-45
Stevens, Ft.	Vic. Spanish Peaks	1866
Union, Cp.		n.d.
Valley Stn., Pt. at	7 mi. SW Crook	1864-65
*Vasquez, Ft.	1.5 mi. S Platteville	c. 1860
Weld, Cp.	Denver	1861-65
(Cp. Elbert)		
Wheeler, Cp.	Denver's Lincoln Park	c. 1864
White River, Cp. on	Meeker	1879-83
Wise Ft.	20 mi. E Ft. Lyon	1860-67
(Old Ft. Lyon, Ft. Faunterloy, Bent's New Fort)		

NEVADA

Antelope Stn., Det.	20 mi. E Schell Stn.	1863-64
Aurora, Cp. nr.	20 mi. SW Hawthorne	1862
Austin, Cp.	Austin	1865
*Baker, Ft.	Las Vegas	c. 1864-67
(Mormon Fort, Det. at Las Vegas)		
Benton, Ft.	N Luning?	1849
Big Antelope Cr., Cp	40 mi. E Cp. McKee	1863
Black, Cp.	Paradise Valley	1865
Black, Cp.	25 mi. NW Cp. McGarry	1865
Callville, Det. at	40 mi. E Las Vegas	1867
(Ft. Call)		
Carson City, Cp. nr.	Carson City	1860
Churchill, Ft.	S Silver Springs	1860-69
(Pt. on Carson R., U.T., Churchill Bks.)		
Deep Hole, Cp.	12 mi. W Cp. McKee	1865
Desert Wells, Cp. at	15 mi. N Fallon	1864
Dun Glen, Cp.	20 mi. SW Winnemucca	1856-66
Eighty-two, Cp. No.	N Cp. McGarry	1864
Eldorado, Cp.	7 mi. E Nelson	1867
(Cp. El Dorado Canyon)		
Elko, Cp.	Elko	PNB
Fairbanks Stn., Det.	Humboldt county	1865
Fish Lake, Cp.	W Dyer	1866-67
(Fish Lake Valley Military Stn.)		
Fourteen, Cp. No.	Paradise Valley area	1865
*Genoa, Ft.	Genoa	1849-51; 51-61
(Mormon Stn.)		
Halleck, Ft.	S Halleck	1867-86
Haven, Ft.	2 mi. NW Nixon	1860
Hays, Cp.	20 mi. E Carson City	1860
Lyon, Cp.	20 mi. NE Battle Mt. town	n.d.
McDermit, Ft.	Near McDermit	1865-89
(Quinn R. Cp. No. 33, Queen's River Sta.)		
McGarry, Cp.	Summit Lake	1865-68
(Cp. Summit Lake)		
McKee, Cp.	10 mi. N Empire	1865-66
(Granite Cr. Stn., Det. at Granite Cr.)		
Nye, Cp.	5 mi. N Carson City	1862-65
Ormsby, Cp.	7 mi. SE Nixon	1860
Otter Cr., Cp. at	Vic. Ft. McDermit?	1865
Overend, Cp.	SE Winnemucca	1865
Pollock, Cp.	Near Cp. Smoke Creek	1864
*Redskin, "Ft."	E Paradise Valley	1865
*Riley, Ft.	Virginia City	1860

Ruby, Cp.	Ruby Valley	1860; 62-69
Sadler, Cp.	Near Carson City	c. 1862-65
Sage, Cp.	Vic. Flanagan	c. 1870
Schell Creek Stn.	45 mi. N Ely	1860-65
(Ft. Schellbourne, Ft. Schell)		
Silver City Fortifi-	Silver City	1860
cations		
Sixteen, Cp. No.	25 mi. from Cp. No. 14	1865
Smoke Creek, Cp.	30 mi. W Empire	1865-66
(Smoke Creek Depot)		
Soldiers Meadow,	20 mi. SW Cp. McGarry	c. 1862
Cp.		
*Storey, Ft.	8 mi. N Wadsworth	1860
Trinity, Ft.	7 mi. SW Ibapah, U.	1863-64
(Det. at Eight Mile Stn.)		
Virginia City Provost	Virginia City	1864-65
Guard		
Willow Point, Cp.	25 mi. N. Winnemucca	1865
Winfield Scott, Cp.	E Paradise Valley	1866-71
Winthrop, Cp.	Vic. Beowawe	n.d.

NEW MEXICO

Abiquiu, Stn. at	Abiquiu	1849; 50-51
Abo Pass, Stn. at	20 mi. E Socorro	c. 1861
Alamo Vejo, Cp.		1885
Albuquerque, Pt. at	Albuquerque	1847-67
(Presidio at Albuquerque)		
Anton Chico, Cp. at	Anton Chico	1863-64
Baird's Ranch, Cp.	Near Albuquerque	1866
*Barclay's Fort	Near Watrous	c. 1850
Bascom, Ft.	N Tucumcari	1863-70
Bayard, Ft.	Bayard	1866-1900
Bear Spring, Cp.	25 mi. NW Socorro	1858
Beck's Rancho, Stn.	2 mi. NE Santa Rosa	1859-60
Blake, Cp.	3 mi. N Ft. Thorn	1856
Burbank, Cp.		1855
Burgwin, Ct.	S Taos	1852-60
Burro Mts., Cp. at	Vic. Tyrone	1853; 59
Butler, Ft.	WNW Tucumcari	PNB
Canon Largo, Cp. in	20 mi. SE Ft. Union	c. 1860
Cariso, Cp. near	N Ft. Conrad	1858
Carizallillo Spring,	Near Hermanas	1885
Cp.		
Carson, Cp.	Between Ft. Craig and river	1862
Casa Colorado, Cp.	5 mi. SE Belen	1855
Ceboleta, Pt. at	10 mi. N Laguna	1850-51
Chusco Valley, Cp.	NW Tohatchi	1858
Cogswell, Cp.	20 mi. NW Ft. Stanton	1860
Comfort, Cp.	25 mi. SW Alamagordo	1858-59
Connelly, Cp.	10 mi. N Socorro	1862
Conrad, Ft.	10 mi. S Socorro	1851-54
Cottonwood, Cp.	S Ft. Fillmore	c. 1854; 63
Craig, Ft.	S Ft. Conrad	1854-84
Cubero, Pt. at	5 mi. SE Domingo	c. 1862
Cummings, Ft.	N Deming	1862-70; 82-85
(Cp. at Ft. Cummings)		
Datil, Cp.	Datil	1885
Dona Ana, Cp.	Dona Ana	1850-51; 55-56; 62
Eight, Cp. No.	On Rio Grande	1860
Eighty-three, Cp.	Near Ft. Craig	1860
Fillmore, Ft.	S La Mesilla	1851-61; 62
Galisteo, Pt. at	22 mi. S Santa Fe	1851-58
Gallina, Cp.	6 mi. SW Corona	1858
(Cp. Sierra)		
Gila Depot	S Ft. West on Gila R.	1855-57; 63
(Cp. on Rio Gila, Rio Gila Depot)		
Guadalupe Mts.,	SW Carlsbad	1855
Cp. near		
Hatch's Ranch,	25 mi. SE Las Vegas	1859-64
Cp. at		
Hubbel's Rancho,	"Navajo Country"	1861
Stn. at		
Johnson, Cp.	N El Paso, Texas	1862-65

Laguna, Pt.	Laguna	1851-52
La Joya, Cp.	20 mi. N Socorro	1862-64
(Cp. La Hoya)		
Le Mesilla, Pt. of	Mesilla	1862-65
(Mesilla Depot)		
Las Animas, Cp. at	Vic. Dona Ana	1854
Las Cruces, Stn. at	Las Cruces	1863-65
Las Lunas, Pt. of	Las Lunas	1852; 59-60; 62
Las Vegas, Pt.	Las Vegas	1848-51
Lazuma, Pt. at		1851
Lincoln, Cp.	Vic. Ft. Union?	1865-66
Loring, Cp.	Near Red River	1858
Los Pinos, Stn. at	18 mi. S Albuquerque	1862-66
(Cp. at Peralto)		
Los Poros, Cp.		1860
Los Valles, Cp. at	49 mi. from Santa Fe	1863
Lowell, Ft.	Near Park View	1866-69
(Cp. Plummer)		
Magoffin, Cp.	Near Alto	1864
Mangues Ranch,	Vic. Pinos Altos	1863
Cp. at		
Marcy, Ft.	Santa Fe	1846-62; 62-67; 75-94
(Pt. at Santa Fe)		
Mason, Ct.		1855
McLane, Ft.	10 mi. S Bayard	1860-61; 63
(Ft. McLean, Cp. Webster, Ft. Floyd, Cp. Wheeler)		
McRae, Ft.	E shore Elephant Butte Lake	1863-82
Mimbres, Cp.	20 mi. NW Deming	1863-66
(Cp. Miembres, Cp. on Rio Mimbres)		
Mischler, Cp.	1 mi. S. Ft. Craig	1862
Mule Spring, Cp.		1856
Navajo Springs, Cp.	5 mi. NE Canjilon	1864
Niggerhead Spring, Cp.		1855
Ocate Sr., Stn. at	20 mi. N Ft. Union	1851-54
Ojo Caliente, Pt. of	60 mi. SW Magdalena	1859; 74-82
Pinos Altos, Cp.	Near Pinos Altos	1863
Pleasant Springs, Cp.		1855
Pope, Cp.		c. 1868
Rabbit Ear Cr., Cp.	N Clayton	1864
Rayado, Pt.	40 mi. E Taos	1850-51; 54
Robbero, Cp.	Near Ft. Thorn	1857
Robledo, Presidio	Near Mt. Robledo	1771
Robledo, Cp.	Near Mt. Robledo	1853; 63
(Cp. Roblero)		
Saguna, Pt.	35 mi. W Albuquerque	1851
San Pedro, Cp. at	14 mi. SE Socorro	1863-64
San Simon, Cp.		1856
Santa Tomas de Iturbide, Pt.		1854-55
Schroeder, Cp.		n.d.
Selden, Ft.	N Las Cruces	1865-79; 80-92
Shoeneman, Cp.		c. 1867
Socorro, Pt. of	Socorro	1849-51; 63; 77-81
Stanton, Ft.	Fort Stanton	1855-61; 61; 62-96
(Cp. Garland)		
Stevens, Ft.		1866
Sumner, Ft.	S Fort Sumner	1862-69
Taos, Pt.	Taos	1847-52; 65
(Cp. at Fernanda de Taos)		
Tecolate, Cp.	10 mi. S Las Vegas	c. 1870
Thorn, Ft.	N Hatch	1853-59; 62-63
(Ct. Garland)		
Tulerosa, Ft.	S Reserve	1863; 62-74
(Cp. at Tule Rosa Valley)		
Tuni-Cha, Cp.	Vic. Newcomb	1858
Union, "Cp."	1 mi. from Gila Depot	1857
Union, Ft.	NE Watrous	1851-91
Valverde, Cp.	Near Ft. Craig	1864
Valverde, Pt.	25 mi. from Socorro	1851
Vigilance, Cp.	Near Albuquerque	1852; 53
Webster, Ft. #1	2 mi. N Santa Rita	1852
(Pt. at Gila Copper Mines)		
Webster, Ft. #2	12 mi. E Ft. #1	1852-53; 59-60

(Stn. at Copper Mines)		
West, Ft.	Near Gila	1863-64
(Cp. Vincent)		
Winfield Scott, Cp.	W Corona	1860
Wingate, Ft. #1	Grant	1860-68
(Ft. Faunterloy, Ft. Lyon)		
Wingate, Ft. #2	Near Fort Wingate	1868-1911; 1914

UTAH

Battle Creek Settlement, Cp.	Near Salt Lake City	1859
Bear River, Cp. on	Vic. Randolph	1859
Bingham Creek, Cp.	10 mi. E. Tooele	1864
Birch Creek, Cp. on		1859
*Buenaventura, Ft.	Ogden	1844
Cameron, Ft.	NE Beaver	1872-85
(Post of Beaver)		
Canon Stn., Det. at	NE Goshute	1863-64
Cedar Fort, Det. at	5 mi. N Fairfield	1863
Cedar Swamps, Cp.	NE edge Great Salt Lake	1863
Church Buttes, Cp.	Great Salt Lake	1865
Clara, Ft.	Vic. Santa Clara	n.d.
Clarks, Cp.	San Pete Valley	1859
*Cove Fort	Cove Fort	1866
Crittenden, Ft.	Fairfield	1857-61
(Cp. Floyd)		
Crossman, Ft.	6 mi. W Neflic	1858
*Davy Crockett, Ft.	E Bridgeport	1837
(Ft. Misery)		
Deep Creek, Cp. at	Vic. Ibapah	1863-64
*Deseret, Ft.	1.6 mi. W Deseret	1866
Douglas, Ft.	Salt Lake City	1862-1965
Duchesne, Ft.	Fort Duchesne	1886-1912
Eastman, Cp.	14 mi. S Neflic	1859
Echo Canyon, Cp. in	Vic. Echo	1859
*Ephraim, Ft.	Ephraim	1859
Farmington, Cp. at	10 mi. N Salt Lake City	1863
Fillmore, Cp. at	Fillmore City	1858
Fish Springs Stn.	S edge Salt Lake desert	1863
Government Springs, Cp. at		1863
*Gunnison, Ft.	Gunnison	1860
*Hamilton, Ft.	Hamilton Fort	n.d.
*Harmony, Ft.	4 mi. SE New Harmony	1852-53; 55-62
Haven, Ft.		1860
Herriman, Ft.	Salt Lake	n.d.
Johnson, Ft.	5 mi. N Cedar City	n.d.
*Kanab, Ft.	Kanab	1865-70
Lolos Creek, Cp. on		1860
Loveland's, Cp. at		1864
*Meeks, Ft.	N Kanab	1869-70
Murray Camp of Instruction	Murray	1885
Ogden Stn.	Ogden	1878
Paige, Cp.	65 mi. N Ft. Ephraim	1859
Parker, Cp.		n.d.
Porter, Cp.		1859
Rawlins, Ft.	2 mi. from Provo	1870-71
Relief, Cp.	Vic. Webster Junction	1864
*Rockport, Ft. at	4 mi. S Wanship	1865
(Rock Fort)		
*Robidoux, Ft.	Vic. Ouray	1837-38
Rush Valley, Cp.	23 mi. W Cp. Floyd	1859; 64; 66
(Government Reservation, Rush Valley)		
Sevier, Cp.	Sevier	1859
Shunk, Cp.	25 mi. SW Cp. Floyd	1858
Thornburgh, New Ft.	4 mi. NW Vernal	1881-84
Thornburgh, Old Ft.	Near Ouray	1881
Timpanagos, Cp.	8 mi. from Provo	1859
Tyler, Cp.		1859
*Uintah, Ft.	E. Tridell	1838-44
*Utah, Ft.	Provo	1849-58
*Wah-Wiep, Ft.	N Kanab	1869-70

BIBLIOGRAPHY

The story of America's Western forts is spread across an unbelievable number of sources. Even to tell a simple tale or two of a fort requires more than consulting a single source.

In order to conserve space in volume II of the *Forts of the Old West* series, and because of near-duplication, its bibliography was postponed for inclusion in this volume. What follows is a consolidated bibliography for *Old Forts of the Southwest* and *Far West*.

Certain abbreviations have been used because of space limitations. Only the last names and initials of authors are given. The most common publishing cities and sources have been abbreviated: NY New York; SF San Francisco; LA Los Angeles; SD San Diego; Chi Chicago; Stl Seattle; DC Washington, D.C.; Gdl Glendale, Calif.; Nm Norman, Oklahoma; NMM New Mexico Magazine, Santa Fe; Colo Colorado Magazine, Denver; TW or FT True West or Frontier Times Magazine, Austin, Tex.; FT-Band Frontier Times, Bandera, Tex.; SW Southwesterner, Columbus, N.M.; SFe Santa Fe; WTex West Texas Historical Association; TSHQ Texas State Historical Quarterly; HSSC Historical Society of Southern California; WW or TT Westways or Touring Topics Magazines, Auto Club of Southern California; NPS National Park Service; Hbg Harrisburg, Pa.

OFFICIAL UNITED STATES GOVERNMENT SOURCES

Adjutant-General. *List of Military Posts, Etc., Established in the United States from Its Earliest Settlement to the Present Time.* DC 1902.
——. Records of the War Department, *Outline Index of Military Forts and Stations.* Record group 94, National Archives. 27 vol.
Army, Headquarters, Department of. *The Army in Peacetime.* DA PAM 360-217. 1964.
Bureau of Prisons. *Alcatraz.* DC. n.d.
Crook, BGen G. *Resume of Operations Against Apache Indians from 1882-1886.* Omaha. 1886.
House of Representatives. *Permanent Fortifications, Sea Coast Defenses.* 37 Cong 2d sess, no. 86. DC. 1862.
Inspector-General. *Outline Descriptions of the Posts and Stations of Troops in the Geographical Divisions and Departments of the United States.* MGen R. B. Marcy, I-G. DC. 1872.
Military History, Office of the Chief of. *Fort card and correspondence files.* DC.
Missouri, Military Division of the. *Outline Descriptions of the Posts in the Military Division of the Missouri.* MGen P. H. Sheridan, commanding. Chi. 1876.
National Archives. *Preliminary Inventory of Records of Army Posts 1813-1942.* Record Group 98. DC. 1949.
National Park Service. *Historic Site Inventory Reports of Military Forts in the Western, Southwestern, and Midwestern Regions.* SF, Omaha, Santa Fe. 1958-64.
——. *Camp Pena Colorado.* Ft. Davis, Tex. 1964.
Navy Department. *War of the Rebellion: Official Records of the Union and Confederate Navies.* DC. 1894-1927. 2 series, 31 vols.
Pacific, Military Division of the. *Outline Descriptions of Pacific Military Posts.* MGen I. McDowell, commanding. SF. 1879.
Presidio Information Office. *The Presidio of San Francisco.* SF. 1962.
Quartermaster General. *Outline Description of Forts and Stations in the Year 1871.* QMG M. C. Meigs. DC. 1872.
——. *Revised Outline Description of the Posts and Stations of Troops in the Military Division of the Pacific.* LtCol R. O. Tyler (ed). DC. 1872.
——. *A Pictorial History of the Housing of the Army.* DC. 1927.
——. *Report of Inspections* by BvtBGen Rusling. National Archives. 1866-67. 2 vol.
——. *Affairs in Utah and the Territories,* from BvtBGen Rusling's Report. House Misc. Doc 153, 40th Cong, 2d sess. DC 1868.
Surgeon General. *Report on Barracks and Hospitals with Descriptions of Military Posts.* J. S. Billings (ed). Circ. no. 4. DC. 1870.
——. *Report on the Hygiene of the United States Army with Descriptions of Military Posts.* J. S. Billings (ed). Circ. no. 8. DC. 1875.
War, Department of. *Official records* in National Archives of various posts. These include "*letters sent,*" "*letters received,*" "*medical history,*" etc. In addition to many scanned, the records of the following were searched in detail: Ft. Reynolds, Colo.; Ft. Scott, Kans.; Ft. Zarah, Kans.; Ft. Chadhourne, Tex.; Cp. Cooper, Tex.; Ft. Lancaster, Tex.; Ft. Aubrey, Kans.; Ft. Elliott, Tex.; Ft. Gates, Tex.; Ft. Ewell, Tex.; Ft. McGarry, Nev.; Cp. Dun Glen, Nev.; Cp. Wallen, Ariz.; Cp. Calabasas, Ariz.; Ct. Far West, Calif.; Ft. Mojave, Ariz.; Cp. Cady, Calif.; Ft. Thomas, Ariz.; Ft. Merrill, Tex.; Cp. on White River, Colo.; Cp. Pena Colorado, Tex.
War, Secretary of. *Annual Report.* DC. 1850-1892.
——. *War of the Rebellion: Official Records of the Union and Confederate Armies.* DC. 1880-1897. 4 series. 128 vols.
Whittier, BvtBGen C. A. Selected *Inspection Reports* of 1866. National Archives. Record Group 159.

OTHER SOURCES

Anonymous. *El Paso, Texas.* SW. 1963.
——. *Fort Bissell.* Hastings, Nebr. 1963.
——. *Coryell County Centennial.* Gatesville, Tex. 1954.
——. *Fort Burgwin Research Center.* Santa Fe. n.d.
——. *Fort Inge, A Forgotten Military Outpost.* Uvalde, Tex. n.d.
——. *Fort Larned, 1859.* Larned, Kans. n.d.
——. *Fort Martin Scott, 1847-1852.* Fredericksburg, Tex. n.d.
——. *Fort Stanton Tuberculosis Hospital, 1958-59-60.* Fort Stanton, N.M. 1960.
——. *Fort Stockton Centennial 1859-1959.* Fort Stockton, Tex. 1959.
——. *Gatesville—110 Years of Progress.* Gatesville, Tex. 1964.
——. *Historic Old Forts of Kansas.* Kansas! Magazine. Topeka. 1959.
——. *History of Fort Worth.* Fort Worth. n.d.
——. *History of Fort Bayard.* Fort Bayard, N.M. 1958.
——. *Kanopolis, Kansas.* Salina. 1948.
——. *Midnight Alarm.* Phillips County Post, Kans. 1906.
——. *Mojave River Valley.* Barstow, Calif. n.d.
——. *Notes on Early Clark County, Kansas.* Ashland. 1940.
——. *Visit Old Fort Concho and the Museum.* San Angelo, Tex. n.d.
——. *Welcome Guide to Fort Sam Houston, Texas.* San Antonio. n.d.
Abarr, J. *Ojo Caliente Army Outpost.* NMM. 1959.
Adams, E. H. *To and Fro, Up and Down.* Cincinnati. 1888.
Ainsworth, E. N. *Beckoning Desert.* Englewood Cliffs, N.J. 1962.
Alexander, T. G., and Arrington, L. J. *The Utah Military Frontier 1872-1912.* Utah Historical Quarterly. 1964.
Allen, R. S. *Pinos Altos, N.M.* Albuquerque. 1948.
Anderson, L. G. *Indian Country Outpost.* NMM. 1956.
Andrews, Ralph. *Indians As the Westerners Saw Them.* Stl 1963.
——. *Picture Gallery Pioneers.* Stl. 1964.
Angel, M. *History of Nevada.* SF. 1881.
Armes, Capt. G. *Ups and Downs of An Army Officer.* DC. 1900.
Army Times. *History of the U.S. Signal Corps.* NY. 1961.
Ashbaugh, D. *Nevada's Turbulent Yesterday.* LA. 1963.
Athearn, R. G. *West of Appomattox.* Montana Magazine. 1962.
——. *William Tecumseh Sherman and the Settlement of the West.* Nm. 1956.
Averett, W. R. *Directory of Southern Nevada Place Names.* Las Vegas. 1962.
Baily, L. R. *The Long Walk.* LA. 1964.
—— (ed). *The Navajo Reconnaissance.* LA. 1964.
Bair, E. *Bloody Trail of the Espinosas.* TW. 1960.
Baker, G. R. *Letter from Ft. Massachusetts.* Colo. Hist. Soc. Notes. October, 1964.
Ball, E. *Big Mouth—Apache Scout.* FT. 1958.
Bancroft, H. H. *History of Arizona and New Mexico.* SF. 1889.
——. *History of Utah.* SF. 1889.
——. *History of California.* SF. 1886-88. 9 vols.
——. *History of the Pacific States: Washington, Idaho, Montana.* SF. 1890.
——. *History of Nevada, Colorado, and Wyoming.* SF. n.d.
Bandel, E. *Frontier Life in the Army 1854-61.* Gdl. 1932.
Barrett, A. *Western Frontier Forts of Texas.* WTex. 1931.
Barrick, N. and Taylor, M. *History of Old Mesilla.* SW. 1963.
Bartholomew, E. *Earps Hid Out at Silver City.* SW. 1963.
Bartlett, J. R. *Personal Narrative.* NY. 1854. 2 vols.
Beattie, W. *Heritage of the Valley.* San Pasqual, Calif. 1939.
Beebe, L. and Clegg, C. *The American West.* NY. 1955.
Beers, H. *Western Military Frontier.* Philadelphia. 1935.
Bell, Maj. H. *Reminiscences of a Ranger.* Santa Barbara. 1927.
——. *On the Old West Coast.* NY. 1930.
Benicia Arsenal Public Information Officer. *Benicia Arsenal.* Benicia, Calif. 1961.
Bender, A. B. *The March of Empire.* Lawrence, Kans. 1952.
Bennett, J. A. (Edited by Brooks, C. E., and Reeve, F. D.). *Forts and Forays.* Albuquerque. 1948.
Benton, J. R. *Camp Nichols Influences Traffic on Santa Fe Trail.* Boise City, Okla., News. 1957.
Biddle, E. M. *Reminiscences of a Soldier's Wife.* Philadelphia. 1907.

Bieber, R. P. (ed). *Marching With the Army of the West.* Gdl. 1936.
Bierschwale, M. *Mason County, Texas.* TSHQ. 1949.
Billington, R. A. *Westward Expansion, A History of the American Frontier.* NY. 1960.
Blackmar, F. W. *Kansas Cyclopedia.* Chi. 1912.
Blackton, J. *Forgotten Port Piute.* TW. 1957.
Boatner, LtCol. M. M. *The Civil War Dictionary.* NY. 1959.
Bonnell, G. W. *Topographical Description of Texas.* Austin. 1840.
Bourke, J. G. *On the Border With Crook.* Omaha. 1891.
———. *An Apache Campaign in the Sierra Madre.* NY. 1958.
Brady, C. T. *Indian Fights and Fighters.* NY. 1904.
Brandes, R. *Frontier Military Posts of Arizona.* Globe. 1960.
Branham, M. *Place of the Cottonwoods.* NMM. 1958.
Bristow, J. Q. *Tales of Old Fort Gibson.* NY. 1961.
Broadstreet, L. *History of Luna County.* SW. 1963.
Brown, D. A. *The Galvanized Yankees.* Urbana. 1963.
Brown, J. C. *Calabasas.* SF. 1892.
Brown, M. H. and Felton, W. R. *The Frontier Years.* NY. 1955.
———. *Before Barbed Wire.* NY. 1956.
Brown, W. E. *The Santa Fe Trail.* NPS-SFe. 1963 (draft).
———. *The Cattleman's Empire* (Supplemental Report). NPS-SFe. 1963 (draft).
Burdett, C. *The Life of Kit Carson.* NY. 1902.
Bryant, D. W. *Reception for the General.* WW. 1942.
Burton, Sir R. *City of the Saints.* NY. 1860 (reprint Reno 1960).

California Division of Beaches and Parks. *Fort Tejon State Historical Monument.* Sacramento. 1960.
———. *Angel Island.* SF. 1963.
California Interstate Telephone Company. *Romantic Heritage of Inyo-Mono.* n p. 1961.
———. *Romantic Heritage of Mojave River Valley.* n.p. 1961.
Calvin, R. *Lieutenant Emory Reports.* Albuquerque. 1951.
Camp Verde Improvement Association. *Fort Verde Museum.* Cottonwood, Ariz. n.d.
Carter, R. G. *The Old Sergeant's Story.* NY. 1926.
Casey, R. J. *The Texas Border.* Indianapolis. 1950.
Chittenden, BGen H. M. *The American Fur Trade of the Far West.* Stanford. 1954.
Colby, C. B. *Historic American Forts.* NY. 1963.
Colorado State Historical Society. *Forts and Camps in Colorado.* Denver. n.d.
———. *Fort card file in society Library.* Denver.
Colton, R. C. *The Civil War in the Western Territories.* Nm. 1959.
Conkling, R. P. and M. B. *The Butterfield Overland Mail.* Gdl. 1947. 3 vols.
Connell, C. T. *Vagaries of Frontier Justice.* TT. 1933.
Connor, A. B. *Of the West That Used to Be.* SW. 1963.
Coombes, Z. E. (Ledbetter, B. N., ed). *Diary of a Frontiersman 1858-59.* Newcastle, Tex., 1962.
Coues, E. *On the Trail of a Spanish Pioneer.* NY. 1942. 2 vols.
Cowell, J. W. *History of Benicia Arsenal.* Berkeley. c. 1963.
Cox, T. *The Indian Scare at Kirwin—1871.* Phillips County Post, Kansas. 1906.
Cragen, Mrs. D. *Camp Independence.* California Historian. 1961.
Crawford, C. H. *Scenes of Early Days.* Petaluma, Calif. 1898.
Cremony, J. C. *Life Among the Apaches.* SF. 1868.
Crimmins, Col. M. L. *The First Line of Army Posts Established in West Texas.* WTex. 1943.
———. *Experiences of an Army Surgeon at Fort Chadbourne.* WTex. 1939.
———. *Fort Elliott, Texas.* WTex. 1947.
———. *The California Column in the Civil War.* FT-Band. 1938.
———. *Fort Worth Was an Early Army Post.* FT-Band. 1939.
——— (ed). *W. G. Freeman's Report on the Eighth Military Department.* TSHQ. 1948-50.
———. (ed). *Colonel J. K. F. Mansfield's Report of the Inspection of the Department of Texas in 1856.* TSHQ. 1938-39.
Crouch, C. J. *A History of Young County, Texas.* Austin. 1956.
———. *A History of Fort Belknap.* Graham, Texas. n.d.
Cullimore, Clarence. *Old Adobes of Forgotten Fort Tejon.* Bakersfield. 1941.
Cullum, BvtMajGen G. W. *Biographical Register.* NY. 1879. 3 vols.
Custer, Gen. G. A. *My Life on the Plains.* NY. 1962 edition.
Custer, E. *Boots and Saddles.* NY. 1885.
———. *Following the Guidon.* NY. 1890.
———. *Tenting on the Plains.* NY. 1893.

Danker, D. F. (ed). *Man of the Plains: Recollections of Luther North.* Lincoln. 1961.
Davis, B. *The Truth About Geronimo.* New Haven. 1929.
Davis, W. W. H. *El Gringo.* NY. 1857.
Day, Capt. W. H. *Letterbrook.* Cantonment Far West, Calif. 1849-51.
De Trobriand, MajGen P. R. D. de K. *Army Life in Dakota.* Chi. 1941.
Deu Pree, D. *History of Pinos Altos.* SW. 1963.
Doctor, J. E. *Rebels of Old Visalia.* Los Tulares Magazine. 1961.
Dodge, Gen. R. I. *Our Wild Indians.* Hartford. 1882.
Donald, D. *Divided We Fought.* NY. 1952.
Downey, F. *Indian-Fighting Army.* NY. 1941.
———. *Indian Wars of the U. S. Army* (1776-1865). NY. 1963.
Drago, H. S. *Wild, Woolly, & Wicked.* NY. 1960.
Dunn, J. P., Jr. *Massacre of the Mountains.* NY. 1886.

Eastman, S. *A Seth Eastman Sketchbook 1848-49.* Austin. 1962.
Eichler, G. R. *New Era for Ft. Logan.* Denver Post. July 7, 1946.
Eldridge, W. H. *An Army Boy in Colorado.* Colo. 1955.

Elkins, Capt. J. M. and McCarthy, F. W. *Indian Fighting on the Texas Frontier.* Amarillo. 1929.
Emmett, C. *The Camel Experiment.* Austin. n.d.
———. *Fort Union and the Winning of the Southwest.* Nm. 1965.
Encyclopaedia Britannica. *World Atlas.* Chicago. 1959.
Evans, Wick. *Arizona Hell Hole!* FT. 1959.

Farish, T. E. *History of Arizona.* SF. 1915. 2 vols.
Federal Writers Project. *Arizona . . . Grand Canyon State.* NY. 1940.
———. *Colorado . . . Highest State.* NY. 1941.
———. *California . . . Golden State.* NY. 1939.
———. *Kansas . . . Sunflower State.* NY. 1939.
———. *Los Angeles . . .* NY. 1951.
———. *Nevada . . . Silver State.* Portland, Ore. 1940.
———. *New Mexico . . . Colorful State.* NY. 1940.
———. *Oklahoma . . . Sooner State.* Nm. 1941.
———. *Texas . . . Lone Star State.* NY. 1940.
———. *Utah . . .* NY. 1941.
Fields, F. T. *Texas Sketchbook.* Humble Oil Co., Houston. 1962.
Finerty, J. F. *Warpath and Bivouac.* Chi. 1890.
Fisher, O. *Sketches of Texas.* Springfield, Ill. 1841.
Florin, L. *Western Ghost Towns.* Stl. 1961.
———. *Ghost Town Album.* Stl. 1962.
———. *Ghost Town Trails.* Stl. 1963.
———. *Western Ghost Town Shadows.* Stl. 1964.
Fohn, N. *Old Fort Lincoln.* Junior Historian, Austin. 1960.
Foreman, C. *The Cross Timbers.* Nm. 1947.
Foreman, G. *Advancing the Frontier.* Nm. 1933.
———. *Marcy and the Gold Seekers.* Nm. 1939.
——— (ed). *A Pathfinder in the Southwest.* Nm. 1941.
Forrest, E. R., and Hill, E. B. *Lone War Trail of Apache Kid.* Pasadena. 1947.
Forrest, J. T. *Old Fort Garland.* Denver. n.d.
Forsyth, BvtBGen G. A. *The Story of the Soldier.* NY. 1900.
———. *Thrilling Days of Army Life.* NY. 1900.
Fort Bascom Cattle Raising Company. *Fort Bascom Cattle Raising Company.* New Haven. 1878.
Fort Belknap Society. *A History of Fort Belknap.* Fort Belknap, Tex. 1962.
Fort Clark Guest Ranch. *Fort Clark Guest Ranch.* Austin. n.d.
Fort Smith Museum Board. *History of the Old Fort Museum.* Fort Smith. 1956.
Fort Stockton Chamber of Commerce. *Historical Leaflet.* Fort Stockton, Tex. n.d.
Fox, T. (comp.) *Nevada Treasure Hunters Ghost Town Guide.* San Jose. 1961.
———. *Arizona Treasure Hunters Ghost Town Guide.* San Jose. 1964.
Frazer, R. W. (ed). *Mansfield on the Condition of the Western Forts 1853-54.* Nm. 1963.
Freeman, D. S. *R. E. Lee: A Biography.* NY. 1934. 2 vols.
Fremont, J. C. *Report of the Exploring Expedition to the Rocky Mountains and to Oregon and California.* DC. 1845.
Frost, L. A. *The Custer Album.* Stl. 1964.
Fry, Col. J. B. *Army Sacrifices or Briefs from Official Pigeon Holes.* NY. 1879.

Garfield, M. H. *The Military Post as a Factor in the Frontier Defense of Kansas 1865-69.* Topeka. 1932.
Giffen, H. S. *Fort Miller and Millerton.* HSSC. 1939.
———. *Camp Independence—An Owens Valley Outpost.* HSSC. 1942.
Gilbert, B. F. *San Francisco Harbor Defense During the Civil War.* SF. 1954.
Gilbert, H. G. *Apaches Ambush Writer's Father . . . East of Ft. Bowie.* SW. 1963.
Gilstrap, L. *Cherokee General.* TW. 1961.
Glazier, W. *Three Years in the Federal Cavalry.* NY. 1870.
Gleason, D. *The Islands and Ports of California.* NY. 1958.
Glisan, R. *A Journal of Army Life.* SF. 1874.
Goetzmann, W. H. *Army Exploration in the American West 1803-63.* New Haven. 1959.
Gontz, Y. D. *Letter on building Fort Ewell, Tex.* Yale University, New Haven.
Graham, Col. W. A. *The Custer Myth.* Hbg. 1953.
Grange, R. T. *Fort Robinson, Outpost of the Plains.* Lincoln. 1958.
Granger, B. H. *Will C. Barnes' Arizona Place Names.* Tucson. 1960.
Grant, U. S. *Personal Memoirs.* NY. 1885. 2 vols.
Gregory, J. N. *Fort Concho: Its Why and Wherefore.* San Angelo, Tex. 1957.
Grivas, T. *Military Governments in California 1846-50.* Gdl. 1963.
Guinn, J. M. *Coast Counties* (California). Chi. 1904.

Hafen, L. R. *The Overland Mail, 1849-69.* Cleveland. 1926.
———. *Lewis Ledyard Weld and Old Camp Weld.* Colo. 1942.
——— (ed). *Far West and the Rockies* Historical Series 1820-75. Gdl. 1954-62. 15 vols.
Haley, J. E. *Fort Concho and the Texas Frontier.* San Angelo, Tex. 1952.
Hamlin, Capt. P. H. (ed). *The Making of a Soldier; Letters of General R. S. Ewell.* Richmond. 1935.
Hammersly, T. H. S. (comp). *Complete Regular Army Register of the United States for One Hundred Years 1779-1879.* DC. 1880.
Hammond, J. N. *Quaint and Historic Forts of North America.* Philadelphia. 1915.
Hancock, W. S. *Reminiscences of W. S. Hancock.* NY. 1887.
Handy, M. O. *History of Fort Sam Houston.* San Antonio. 1951.

Hanna, P. T. *Dictionary of California Land Names*. LA. 1951.
Hardy, W. H. *A Sack of Poisoned Sugar*. TW. 1965.
Harmon, W. A. *Hell on the Border*. Fort Smith. 1898.
Hart, H. M. *Old Forts of the Northwest*. Stl. 1963.
———. *Old Forts of the Southwest*. Stl. 1964.
———. *Military Posts and Camps in Official Records of the War of the Rebellion, Operations on the Pacific Coast; A Partial Working Index*. n.p. 1964.
Hein, E. *Death Comes to Fort Mojave*. WW. 1942.
Hein, LtCol. O. L. *Memories of Long Ago by an Old Army Officer*. NY. 1925.
Heitman, F. H. (comp.). *Historical Register and Dictionary of the United State Army*. DC. 1905. 2 vols.
Herr, MajGen J. K. and Wallace, E. S. *The Story of the U. S. Cavalry*. Boston. 1953.
Hertzog, Peter. *Old Town Albuquerque*. SFe. 1964.
———. *Little Known Facts About Billy, the Kid*. SFe. 1964.
Heyman, M. L., Jr. *Prudent Soldier*. Gdl. 1959.
Historical Society of Brownsville, Tex. *Historic Sites In and Around Brownsville*. Brownsville. n.d.
Hitchcock, Gen. E. A. *Fifty Years in Camp and Field*. NY. 1909.
Hollister, O. J. *Boldly They Rode*. Lakewood, Colo. 1949.
Holmes, L. A. *Fort McPherson, Nebraska*. Lincoln. 1963.
Hood, LtGen. J. B. *Advance and Retreat*. New Orleans. 1880.
Hoover, M. B., and Rensch, H. E. and E. G. *Historic Spots in California*. Stanford. 1958.
Howard, O. O. *My Life and Experiences Among Our Hostile Indians*. Hartford. 1907.
Hunt, A. *The Army of the Pacific 1860-1866*. Gdl. 1951.
———. *James H. Carleton Frontier Dragoon*. Gdl. 1958.
———. *The Far West Volunteer*. Montana Magazine. 1962.
———. *California Volunteers*. HSSC. 1952.
———. *California Volunteers on Border Patrol*. HSSC. 1948.
Hunt, E. *History of Fort Leavenworth 1827-1927*. Fort Leavenworth. 1929.
Hunt, O. E. (ed). *The Photographic History of the Civil War*. NY. 1911. 10 vols.
Hunter, C. M. *Apache Fox*. TW. 1958.
Hunter, J. M. *Old Camp Verde, the Home of the Camels*. Bandera, Tex. 1948.
Hussey, J. A. *Fort McDowell, Angel Island*. NPS, SF. 1949.
Hutchinson, W. H. *The Great Dromedary Race*. WW. 1949.

Ickis, A. F. *Bloody Trails Along the Rio Grande*. Denver. 1958.
Ikin, A. *Texas*. London. 1841.
Irving, W. *A Tour of the Prairies*. Philadelphia. 1835.

James, T. *Three Years Among the Indians and Mexicans*. Philadelphia. 1962.
Jelinek, G. *The Ellsworth Story*. Ellsworth, Kans. 1957.
Johnson, BGen. R. W. *Memories of Maj. Gen. George H. Thomas*. Philadelphia. 1881.
Johnson, V. *The Unregimented General*. Boston. 1962.
Johnston, Philip. *Saga of Old Fort Tejon*. TT. 1933.
———. *Gibralter of the Old Frontier*. WW. 1934.
Johnson, William. *The Life of General Albert Sidney Johnston*. NY. 1878.
Jones, I. *Port-Captain Ridley*. WW. 1958.
Jones, N. V. *Journal* extracts. Utah Historical Quarterly. 1931.
Joseph, R. *The Forts of Dubious Distinction*. Elks Magazine. 1964.
Josephy, A. M. Jr. (ed). American Heritage *Book of Indians*. NY. 1961.

Keim, D. B. R. *Sheridan's Troopers on the Border*. NY. 1885.
Keleher, W. A. *Turmoil in New Mexico*. SFe. 1952.
Keyes, Elizabeth. *Across the Plains in a Prairie Schooner*. Colo. 1933.
Keyes, MajGen. E. D. *Fifty Years Observation of Man and Events*. NY. 1884.
Kimball, M. B. *A Soldier Doctor of Our Army*. Boston. 1917.
King, Capt. C. *Campaigning With Crook*. Nm. 1964.
King, J. T. *War Eagle; A Life of General Eugene A. Carr*. Lincoln. 1963.
Kingery, C. *Fort Bissell, 1872-1878*. Phillipsburg, Kans. 1961.
Knight, O. *Fort Worth on the Trinity*. Nm. 1953.
Kuller, F. L. *Piracy on the Colorado*. FT. 1965.

Lackey, V. *The Forts of Oklahoma*. Tulsa. 1963.
La Farge, O. *Pictorial History of the American Indian*. NY. 1956.
Lane, L. S. *I Married a Soldier*. Philadelphia. 1893.
Lattimore, R. B. *Fort Pulaski*. DC. 1954.
Laufe, A. (ed). *An Army Doctor's Wife on the Frontier*. Pittsburgh. 1962.
Lavender, D. *Bent's Fort*. Garden City. 1954.
Layne, J. G. *Western Wayfaring*. LA. 1954.
Leadabrand, R. (ed). *The California Deserts*, Westerners Brand Book 11. LA. 1964.
Ledbetter, B. N. *The Fort Belknap of Yesterday and Today 1851-1963*. Newcastle, Tex. 1963.
Lesley, L. B. (ed). *Uncle Sam's Camels*. Cambridge. 1929.
Lockwood, F. C. *Early Military Posts in Arizona*. Arizona Historical Review. 1930.
Lord, Walter. *A Time to Stand*. NY. 1961.
Lott, LCdr. A. S. *A Long Line of Ships*. Annapolis. 1954.
Love, F. *No Place for the Glory Boys*. FT. 1965.
Lowe, P. G. *Five Years a Dragoon*. Kansas City, Mo. 1906.

MacArthur, General of the Army D. A. *Reminiscences*. NY. 1964.

Mack, E. M. *Nevada*. Gld. 1936.
Marcy, BvtBGen. R. B. *Prairie Traveler*. Philadelphia. 1856.
———. *Thirty Years of Life on the Border*. NY. 1874.
Mattes, M. J. *Indians, Infants, and Infantry*. Denver. 1960.
Mattison, R. H. *The Army Post on the Northern Plains 1865-85*. Nebraska History Magazine, Lincoln. 1954.
———. *The Indian Frontier on the Upper Missouri to 1865*. Ibid. 1958.
———. *The Military Frontier on the Upper Missouri*. Ibid. 1956.
———. *Report on the Santa Fe Trail*. NPS, Omaha. 1958.
Mazzanovich, A. *Trailing Geronimo*. Hollywood, Calif. 1931.
McConnell, H. H. *Five Years a Cavalryman*. Jacksboro, Tex. 1889.
McCoy, R. *Victory at Fort Fillmore*. NMM. 1961.
McCracken, H. *Frederic Remington, Artist of the Old West*. Philadelphia. 1947.
McDowell, H. *Reminiscences of Many Years Ago*. Phillips County Post, Kansas. 1906.
McKee, Maj J. C. *Narrative of the Surrender of a Command of U. S. Forces at Fort Fillmore, N. M.* DC. 1886.
McMaster, R. K. *Musket, Saber, & Missile*. El Paso. 1962.
Mears, M. W. *Coryell County Scrapbook*. Waco, Tex. 1963.
Merington, M. *The Custer Story*. NY. 1950.
Miles, Gen. N. A. *Personal Recollections*. Chi. 1896.
———. *Serving the Republic*. N.Y. 1911.
Milhollen, H. D. and Johnson, J. R. *Best Photos of the Civil War*. NY. 1961.
Miller, N. H. (ed) *A Survey of Historic Sites and Structures in Kansas*. Topeka. 1957.
Miller, R. D. *Shady Ladies of the West*. LA. 1964.
Miller, W. C. *The Pyramid Lake Indian War of 1860*. Reno. 1957.
Mills, Anson. *My Story*. DC. 1918.
Moat, L. S. (ed) *Frank Leslie's Illustrated Famous Leaders and Battle Scenes of The Civil War*. NY. 1896.
Molen, D. H. *Decisions at Glorieta Pass*. Montana Magazine. 1962.
Monaghan, J. (ed). *The Book of the American West*. NY. 1963.
Montgomery, Mrs. F. C. *Military Redoubts in Clark County*. Ashland, Kans. n. d.
Morgan, D. L. (ed). *Rand McNally's Pioneer Atlas of the American West*. Chi. 1956.
Morgan, L. H. *The Indian Journals 1859-62*. Ann Arbor. 1959.
Morrison, W. B. *Military Posts and Camps in Oklahoma*. Oklahoma City. 1936.
Motz, L. *Old Fort Hays*. Hays, Kans. 1959.
Mulford, A. F. *Fighting Indians in the 7th U. S. Cavalry*. Corning. N.Y. 1879.
Mumey, N. *Old Forts and Trading Posts of the West*. Denver. 1956
———. *Saga of Auntie Stone and Her Cabin*. Boulder. 1964.
Murbarger, N. *Ghosts of the Glory Trail*. Palm Desert, Calif. 1956.
———. *Ghosts of the Adobe Walls*. LA. 1964.
Myers, J. M. *Deaths of the Bravos*. Boston. 1962.
Myers, L. *Pope's Well Experiment*. NMM. 1961.
———. *Pope's Wells*. N.M. Historical Review. 1963.

Nankivell, Maj. J. H. *Fort Garland, Colorado*. Colo. 1939.
———. *Fort Crawford, Colorado, 1880-1890*. Colo. 1934.
National Park Service. *Soldier & Brave*. NY. 1963.
Navajo Tribal Parks Commission. *Something About Window Rock*. Window Rock, Ariz. n.d.
———. *Something About Fort Defiance*. Ibid. 1961.
Nordyke, L. *Killer Champ*. FT. 1958.
Nye, Col. W. S. *Carbine & Lance*. Nm. 1937.

Ormsby, W. L. II. *Overland to San Francisco 1858*. Van Buren, Ark. 1958.
Orton, BGen. R. H. *California Men in the War of the Rebellion*. Sacramento. 1890.
Parker, Dr. W. T. *Annals of Old Fort Cummings*. Northampton, Mass. 1916.
Parkhill, F. *The Last of the Indian Wars*. NY. 1962.
Parrish, S. R. *The Epic of Larimer County*. Fort Collins, Colo. 1959.
Patch, MajGen. J. D. *Reminiscences of Fort Huachuca, Arizona*. n.p. n.d. Tucson 1964?
Patton, J. F. *The History of Fort Smith, Arkansas*. Fort Smith. 1959.
Paulin, C. O. *Atlas of the Historical Geography of the United States*. DC. 1932.
Pearman, R. *Old Fort Larned Unique Relic of Indian Wars*. Kansas City Times. 1963.
Peterson, H. L. *Forts in America*. NY. 1964.
Pfanner, R. *The Genesis of Fort Logan*. Colo. 1942.
———. *Highlights in the History of Fort Logan*. Colo. 1942.
Pierce, P. N. and Hough, F. O. *The Compact History of the United States Marine Corps*. N.Y. 1960.
Pierson, L. A *Short History of Camp Verde, Arizona, to 1890*. El Paso. 1957.
Pillsbury, D. L. *Outpost of the West*. WW. 1952.
Pope, C. S. *Fort Point or Old Fort Scott*. SF. 1958.
Price, G. F. *Across the Continent With the Fifth Cavalry*. NY. 1883.
Pride, Capt. W. F. *The History of Fort Riley*. Fort Riley, Kans. 1926.
Prucha, Rev. F. P., S.J. *Broadax and Bayonet*. Madison, Wis. 1953.
———. *Guide to the Military Posts of the United States*. Ibid. 1964.
——— (ed). *Army Life on the Western Frontier*. Nm. 1958.
Public Information Officer, Fort Leavenworth. *Fort Leavenworth from Frontier Post to Home of the United States Army Command and General Staff College*. Fort Leavenworth. 1959.

———. *A Tour of Fort Leavenworth.* Ibid. 1963.

Quiner, E. B. *Military History of Wisconsin.* Madison. 1866.

Rahill, Rev. P. J. *The Catholic Indian Missions and Grant's Peace Policy 1870-1884.* DC. 1953.

Raht, C. G. *The Romance of Davis Mountains and Big Bend Country.* Odessa, Tex. 1919.

Rand-McNally, Inc. *Road Maps of the United States.* Chi. 1962-65.

Rawlins, G. J. *Camelius Americana.* TW. 1956.

Recruiting News. *Histories of Army Posts.* Governor's Island, N.Y. 1924.

Reeder, Col. R. *The Mackenzie Raid* (fictionalized). New York. 1955.

Reeve, F. D. (ed.) *Puritan and Apache: A Diary.* Albuquerque. 1948-49.

Rhoades, C. H. *The Second United States Cavalry, 1855-1861.* El Paso. n.d.

Richards, R. *Headquarters House and the Forts of Fort Scott.* Fort Scott, Kans. 1954.

———. *Internationally Famous Fort Scott Army Headquarters Building.* Ibid. n.d.

———. *Fort Scott's Heritage.* Ibid. n.d.

Richardson, R. N. *The Frontier of Northwest Texas.* Gdl. 1963.

———. *The Comanche Barrier to South Plains Settlement.* Gdl. 1933.

Rickey, D., Jr. *Forty Miles a Day on Beans and Hay.* Nm. 1963.

Ringgold, J. P. *Frontier Days in the Southwest.* San Antonio. 1952.

Risch, E. *Quartermaster Support of the Army.* DC. 1962.

Rister, C. C. *Robert E. Lee in Texas.* Nm. 1946.

———. *Fort Griffin on the Texas Frontier.* Nm. 1956.

——. *The Southwestern Frontier, 1865-1881.* Cleveland 1928.

———. *Border Command; General Phil Sheridan in the West.* Nm. 1944.

R. L. Polk Company. *A Pictorial History of Great Bend.* Great Bend, Kans. 1961.

Robinson, W. W. *The Story of San Bernardino County.* San Bernardino, 1962.

Rodenbough, T. *The Army of the United States.* DC. 1896.

Roe, F. M. A. *Army Letters from An Officers Wife 1871-1888.* NY. 1909.

Rogers, Col. F. B. *Early Military Posts of Del Norte County.* California Historical Society Quarterly. 1947.

———. *Early Military Posts of Mendocino County.* Ibid. 1948.

———. *Fort Bidwell, Modoc County, California.* SF. 1959.

———. *Fort Point, California.* SF. 1959.

———. *Soldiers of the Overland.* SF. 1938.

Ronzio, R. A. *Fort Crawford on the Uncompahgre.* Denver Westerners. 1963.

Ruhlen, Col. G. *Fort Thorn—An Historical Vignette.* El Paso. 1960.

———. *Carleton's Empty Fort.* Nevada Historical Quarterly. 1959.

———. *Early Nevada Forts.* Ibid. 1964.

Rumble, J. *History of the Old Government Road, the Mojave Desert to the Colorado River.* San Bernardino. 1939.

Rusling, J. *Across America.* N.Y. 1874.

Ruth, K. *Great Day in the West.* Nm. 1963.

Salisbury, A. and J. *Here Rolled the Covered Wagons.* Stl. 1948.

———. *Two Captains West.* Stl. 1950.

Sanford, A. B. *Camp Weld, Colorado.* Colo. 1934.

———. (ed). *Life at Camp Weld and Fort Lyon in 1861-62.* Colo. 1942.

Scanlan, T. (ed). *Army Times Guide to Army Posts.* Hbg. 1963.

Schmitt, M. F. (ed). *General George Crook, His Autobiography.* Nm. 1960.

Schmitt, M. F. and Brown, D. *Fighting Indians of the West.* NY. 1948.

Schofield, J. M. *Forty-Six Years in the Army.* NY. 1897.

Scobee, B. *Old Fort Davis.* San Antonio. 1947.

———. *Fort Davis Texas.* Fort Davis. 1963.

Settle, R. W. and M. L. *Thunder on the Arickaree.* FT. 1959.

Seymour, F. *Eagle Pass, Maverick County, Texas.* Eagle Pass. 1961.

Shelton, W. *Two Kiowa Chiefs Were Tried at Jacksboro 84 Years Ago.* Wichita Daily Times. 1955.

Sheridan, Gen. P. H. *Personal Memoirs.* NY. 1888. 2 vols.

Sherman, Gen. W. T. *Memoirs.* NY. 1875. 2 vols.

Simmons, E. E. *It Took Blood, Bravery to Make Ft. Bayard History.* El Paso Times, Jan. 20, 1963.

Simpson, A. *The Fort That Won the West.* NMM. 1950.

Skelly, J. *Camp Nichols, Oklahoma.* Boise City, Oklahoma, News. 1957.

Smith, P. D., Jr. *The Sagebrush Soldiers.* Nevada Historical Quarterly. 1962.

Snell, C. W. *A Study of the San Francisco Presidio and Fort Point, California.* NPS, SF. 1962.

Spotts, D. L. and Brininstool, E. A. *Campaigning with Custer and the Nineteenth Kansas Volunteer Cavalry on the Washita Campaign, 1868-69.* LA. 1928.

Sprague, M. *Massacre; The Tragedy at White River.* Boston. 1957.

Stanley, Gen. D. S. *Personal Memoirs.* Cambridge. 1917.

Stanley, F. (Rev. Stanley F. L. Crocchiola). *The Duke City.* Pampa, Tex. 1963.

———. *Fort Bascom, Comanche-Kiowa Barrier.* Ibid. 1961.

———. *Fort Union.* Ibid. 1961.

———. *Fort Craig.* Ibid. 1962.

———. *The Fort Fillmore Story.* Pantex, Tex. 1961.

———. *Fort Conrad.* Ibid. 1962.

Steele, J. W. *Frontier Army Sketches.* NY. 1883.

Stern, P. Van D. *Robert E. Lee, the Man and the Soldier.* NY. 1963.

Stewart, E. I. (ed). *Life and Adventures of Frank Grouard.* Nm. 1958.

Sullivan, J. A. *The Story of Fort Mason.* SF. 1961 (rev. 1965).

Sullivan, C. J. *Army Posts and Towns.* Burlington, Vt. 1935.

Summerhayes, M. *Vanished Arizona.* Salem, Mass. 1911.

Sumner, LtCol. E. V. *Besieged by the Utes.* Century Magazine. 1891.

Sunset Magazine. *Gold Rush Country.* Menlo Park, Calif. 1947.

Taft, R. *Artists and Illustrators of the Old West.* NY. 1953.

Talllack, W. *The California Overland Express: The Longest Stage Ride in the World, 1865.* Van Buren, Ark. 1959.

Taylor, E. and O. *Yuma Territorial Prison.* Desert Magazine. n.d.

Taylor, F. *The West's Bloodiest Pass!* TW. 1960.

Taylor, R. C. *Colorado: South of the Border.* Denver. 1963.

Tebbel, J., and Jennison, K. *The American Indian Wars.* NY. 1960.

Tevis, J. H. *Arizona in the '50's.* Albuquerque. 1954.

Texas State Parks Board. *Fort Griffin State Park.* Austin. n.d.

———. *Data Concerning Texas Forts.* Austin. n.d.

Thomlinson, Col. M. H. *The Garrison at Fort Bliss, 1849-1916.* El Paso. 1945.

Tibbets, R. *The White River Massacre.* TW. 1961.

Tilden, F. *Following the Frontier.* NY. 1965.

Toulouse, J. H. and J. R. *Pioneer Posts of Texas.* San Antonio. 1936.

Trumbo, T. M. *Guardians of the Trail.* NMM. 1946.

———. *Bronco Girl of Old Fort Craig.* NMM. 1947.

Utley, R. M. *Historical Report on Fort Bowie, Arizona.* NPS, SFo. 1962.

———. *Fort Davis.* Ibid. 1960.

———. (ed). *Military and Indian Frontier.* Ibid. 1962 (draft).

———. *Custer and the Great Controversy.* LA. 1962.

———. *The Last Days of the Sioux Nation.* New Haven. 1963.

———. *Fort Union.* NPS, DC. 1962.

Vestal, Stanley (Walter Stanley Campbell). *Dodge City, Queen of Cowtowns.* NY. 1952.

Veterans Administration. *Fort Lyon, Colorado.* Fort Lyon. 1962.

Waitman, L. *The History of Camp Cady.* HSSC. 1954.

Walbridge, L. S. *Tale of an Old Wagon Trail.* WW. 1942.

Wallace, E. S. *The Great Reconnaissance.* Boston. 1955.

Warner, E. J. *Generals in Gray.* New Orleans. 1959.

———. *Generals in Blue.* Baton Rouge. 1964.

Watrous, A. *History of Larimer County, Colorado.* Ft. Collins, Colo. 1911.

Watson, M. G. *Silver Theatre.* Gdl. 1964.

Webb, G. W. *Chronological List of Engagements Between the Regular Army of the United States and Various Tribes of Hostile Indians, Which Occurred During the Years 1790 to 1898, inclusive.* St. Joseph, Mo. 1939.

Webb, W. P. *Buffalo Hunt.* TW. 1961.

—— (ed). *Handbook of Texas.* Austin. 1952. 2 vols.

Weight, H. O. *Mystery of Fort Benton.* WW. 1958.

———. *Outpost on the Carson.* WW. 1952.

Wellman, P. I. *The Indian Wars of the West.* Garden City. 1954.

Werstein, I. *Kearny the Magnificent.* NY. 1962.

Westerners Potomac Corral. *Great Western Indian Fights.* Garden City. 1960.

Wheeler, Col. H. *Buffalo Days.* Indianapolis. 1925.

White Mountain Recreation Enterprise. *Fort Apache Indian Reservation.* Whiteriver, Ariz. n.d.

Whitford, W. C. *Colorado Volunteers in the Civil War.* Denver. 1906.

Whiting, J. S. *Forts of the State of Washington.* Stl. 1951.

—— and R. J. *Forts of the State of California.* Stl. 1960.

Whitman, S. E. *The Troopers.* NY. 1962.

Wilcox, V. L. *Comprehensive Guide to Westerners Brand Books 1944-61.* Denver. 1962.

Wiley, B. I. and Milhollen, H. D. *They Who Fought Here.* NY. 1959.

Wilkes, H. *John Teel, Trooper.* FT. 1965.

Wilson, S. *Mystery of the Disappearing Gold.* TW. 1964.

Wilson, T. C. (Advertising Agency). *Pioneer Nevada.* Reno. 1951.

Wiltsey, N. B. *Hawks of the Desert.* TW. 1955-56.

Wolfe, G. D. *The Indians Called Him Bad Hand.* TW. 1961.

Woods, Betty. *Fort Bayard.* NMM. 1958.

———. *Fort Stanton.* NMM. 1955.

Woodward, A. *Noted Artist Died at Carralitos.* SW. 1964.

Woolford, S. *The Pretty Girls of Old Fort Union.* NMM. 1961.

Wright, A. S. *The Founding of Fort Collins,* United States Military Post. Colo. 1933.

Wright, M. H. *A History of Fort Cobb.* Chronicles of Oklahoma. 1956.

———. *The Butterfield Overland Mail One Hundred Years Ago.* Ibid. 1957.

Young, BGen. G. R. (ed). *The Army Almanac.* Hbg. 1959.

Young, O. E. *The First Military Escort on the Santa Fe Trail 1829.* Gdl. 1962.

ACKNOWLEDGMENTS

Digging out data on forts that covered more than a hundred years of activity and thousands of square miles of the Southwest took more than just the efforts of the author.

The National Park Service, as usual, was a major help. These historians included William Brown, Santa Fe; Ray Mattison and Don Rickey, Jr., Omaha; Charles Snell and John Hussey, San Francisco; Roger Rogers, Charles S. Marshall, and Elbert Cox, Richmond; Michael J. Becker and Erwin Thompson, Ft. Davis; Homer Hastings and Mr. and Mrs. Dale Geise, Ft. Union; Jack McDermott, Ft. Laramie; Aubrey L. Haines, Yellowstone; and, at the main headquarters in Washington, D.C., Roy E. Appleman, Charles W. Porter III, and Robert Utley (formerly of the Sante Fe office).

Thanks are due to these staff members of the institutions or libraries indicated: *National Archives:* John Porter Bloom; Milton K. Chamberlain, Mrs. Sara D. Jackson, E. O. Parker, and Victor Gondos, Jr. (Old Army Branch); Josephine Motelywski and May E. Fawcett (Visual Aids); Mrs. Charlotte Ashby, Pat McLaughlin, and A. P. Muntz (Cartographic); Jane F. Smith (Social and Economic Branch). *Smithsonian Institution:* Frank H. H. Roberts, Jr. (Bureau of American Ethnology) and George Howell (Military History). *Office of the Chief of Military History:* Charles F. Romanus. *Bureau of Indian Affairs:* Merrill Tozier. *Gilcrease Collection:* Paul Rossi, *Geological Survey:* W. B. Sears and T. R. Custidero.

College of William and Mary Library: James Services. *Marine Corps Education Center Library:* George Mahoney and Mrs. Evelyn Daniels. *Northwestern University Deering Library:* Florence Stewart. *West Point Museum:* Frederick P. Todd. *Virginia Beach, Va., Library:* Mrs. Frank Maestas, Mrs. Jeane Kaplan, Mrs. Margaret Capps; *Denver Public Library Western History Collection:* Alys Freeze. *Bancroft Library:* John Barr Tompkins. *Colorado State Historical Society:* Mrs. Enid M. Thompson, Mrs. Alice Wallace, Mrs. Kathleen Pierson, Mrs. Laura Allyn Ekstrom. *Arizona Pioneers Historical Society:* Sidney B. Brinckerhoff, Mrs. Yndia S. Moore, and Mrs. W. W. Alderson. *Historical Society of Southern California:* Mrs. Maragret J. Cassidy. *San Francisco College for Women, Library:* Mother K. Cassidy. *Church of Jesus Christ of Latter-Day Saints Archives:* Earl E. Olson. *Yale University Western Collection:* Archibald Hanna. *Museum of New Mexico:* Bruce T. Ellis and Mrs. J. K. Shishkin. *New Mexico Magazine:* George Fitzpatrick, editor, *Westways Magazine:* Patrice Manahan, editor. *Oklahoma State Library:* Mary O. Carnahan. *San Antonio Public Library:* Mrs. Mary Steel. *Austin, Tex., Library:* Mrs. Jane Rowley and Mrs. Carl Swanson.

The staffs of the Confederate Museum, Richmond; Library of Congress, Army War College, Newberry Library, Chicago Historical Society, San Bernardino County Library, University of Southern California Library, Virginia State Library, and Harvard University Medical School Library.

Advice and loan of materials came from many researchers in the Western Americana field: Barbara Neal Ledbeter, Newcastle, Tex.; Mrs. Frank Wedin, Marathon, Tex.; Judge Barry Scobee, Ft. Davis, Tex.; William Covington, Placerville, Calif.; Aurora Hunt, Pacific Palisades, Calif.; Nell Murbarger, Costa Mesa, Calif.; James D. Horan, Newark, N.J.; Mrs. Lillie Gerhardt Anderson, Tucumcari, N.M.; Arthur and Bonnie Ocheltree, Gila, N.M.; Mrs. Tom R. Mears and Captain and Mrs. Tom McClellan, U.S.N., Gatesville, Tex.; Francis P. Farquhar, Berkeley, Calif.; Harold Schutt, Lindsay, Calif.; L. Burr Belden, San Bernardino, Calif.; Fred M. Mazzulla, Denver, Colo.; and Albert Salisbury, Seattle.

Lee Myers, Carlsbad, N.M., and Marvin King, Arenas Valley, N.M., became so involved in the matter of fort research that they braved 110 degree temperatures, off-road exploring, and near-empty gas tanks to accompany the author.

Two retired Army colonels now living in California provided both the contents of their files and considerable encouragement. Experts in the field, as indicated by the Bibliography, they are George Ruhlen, San Diego, and Fred B. Rogers, San Francisco.

Thanks are inadequate for the many hours of darkroom trickery used by Red and Rosemarie Richardson of Imperial Beach, Calif., who processed all of the photography, and for the cleverness with which Paul Hartle deciphered illegible notes and rough sketches in making the ground plans. The author's wife, Teresa, and three children, Bridget, Erin, and Bret, accompanied and assisted on the 10,000 mile trip to photograph these sites. When a new baby curtailed typing assistance by the aforementioned Teresa, William Hoge helped.

By states, here are the folks who helped:

Arizona: K. J. O'Brien, Veterans Center Director, Whipple; Mrs. Glen Porter, Thatcher; Tribal Patrolman Reginald Eswonia, La Paz; Mrs. Ruth G. Elam, Tombstone; Jack Redmand, Tucson; Lt. Col. John H. Healy, Hereford; Frank A. Krupp, Sr., and W. J. Macgregor, Nogales; Tony Ehrman, Bayard; Mrs. C. B. Carrington, Sonoita; Mrs. Peter Bidegain and Frank Brophy, Elgin; Andy Chesley and Lee Wilson, Geronimo; Mrs. Lucille German, Mrs. Louella Stevens, and Malcolm Stenhouse, Camp Verde; Howard R. Phillips, Safford; James D. Sparks, Whiteriver; Steven Vukcevich, superintendent, Arizona State Industrial School.

California: Jerry MacMullen and Dr. Ray Brandes, Junipero Serra Museum; Dr. R. Coke Wood, Conference of California Historical Societies; Allan R. Ottley, State Library; James de T. Abajian, State Historical Society; Jack R. Dyson, John Beggio, and John Cenovich, California Beaches and Parks; Irene Simpson, Wells Fargo Bank Historical Collection; Mrs. Jessie O'Connor, Los Angeles Title Insurance and Trust Company; Sergeant First Class Charles S. Hawkins and L. E. Barber, Presidio of San Francisco; James A. Sullivan, Army Terminal Command; Edmond Jackson, Chairman, Quechan Tribal Council, Fort Yuma; Joseph Doctor, Exeter; Mrs. Dorothy Cragen, Ada Bell, and John Symmes, Independence; Dr. Curtis Howe Springer and John Rundstrom, ZZYZX Springs, Baker; R. Glen DeYoe and Gerald A. Smith, San Bernardino; George Owens, Cedarville; E. Clemens Horts, Wheatland; and the Chamber of Commerce, Blythe.

Colorado: Peter C. Moshisky and Mrs. Harold Flowers, Montrose; Mrs. Margaret Nieslanik, Meeker; Harry Smiley, Ft. Collins.

Nevada: Mrs. Clara Beatty, Historical Society; Rev. Albert Muller, O.P., Reno; Mrs. Nellie Basso, Lovelock; Janet Meyer, Robert L. Brown, and Barbara Drum, Las Vegas; Apache Jack Dillon, Searchlight; and Mrs. Ruth Russell and George Bender, McGill; and Fritz Buckingham, Paradise Valley.

New Mexico: Bill Slevin and Ben Bowen, Department of Development; Mr. and Mrs. J. Paul Taylor and William Taylor, Mesilla; H. S. Wiley, Highway Commission; P. W. Christiansen, School of Technology; R. A. Bieberman, Bureau of Mines; Mayor Alfred M. Ramirez and Fred R. Luna, Central; Mrs. Helen B. Stauder, Socorro; Mrs. Peggy Schmidt, Albuquerque; Herman Moncus, Howard Hampton, and John Otero, Tucumcari; Mr. and Mrs. George C. Harsh, Gila; Darlene Lewis, Steve Villarreal, and Dr. John C. Mitchell, Silver City; and Mr. and Mrs. Edward Sweet, V. J. Rogers, Mrs. W. W. Sullivan, and Rick Sullivan, Fort Sumner.

Texas: Carolyn Berg, Historical Society; Madge Grba, West Texas Historical Society; Tom H. Taylor, Highway Department; James M. Thomas, Park Board; Senator Ralph Yarborough; J. N. Gregory, San Angelo; Fred Skyles, Langtry; Mr. and Mrs. Blas Payne, Marathon; Thomas Lemmons, Fort Worth; Tom and Bob Coquet and Mrs. Baryl Ackerman, Cotulla; Alfred H. Hopkins, Gatesville; Neal Blanton, Hillsboro; Louis H. Clymer, Whitney; Rhylma Higginbotham and Mrs. L. C. Ross, Burnet; Opal Miller, George West; and Mary Hayes, Sinton.

Utah: John James, Historical Society; Kate B. Carter, President, Daughters of Utah Pioneers; Henry J. Reynolds, Fort Duchesne; Leon P. Christensen and Mrs. Vel Sorensen, Vernal; and Ward Roylance, Tourist and Publicity Council.

INDEX